Windows® 8

COURSE TECHNOLOGY
CENGAGE Learning™

Australia • Brazil • Japan • Korea • Mexico • Singapore • Spain • United Kingdom • United States

MARAN ILLUSTRATED™ Windows® 8

Distributed in the U.S. and Canada by Course Technology PTR, Cengage Learning. For enquiries about Maran Illustrated™ books outside the U.S. and Canada, please contact maranGraphics at international@maran.com.

For U.S. orders and customer service, please contact Course Technology PTR, Cengage Learning at 1-800-354-9706. For Canadian orders, please contact Course Technology PTR, Cengage Learning at 1-800-268-2222 or 416-752-9448.

ISBN-13: 978-1-133-94374-7
ISBN-10: 1-133-94374-8

Library of Congress Catalog Card Number: 2012942785

Printed in the United States of America

1 2 3 4 5 6 7 14 13 12

Trademarks

maranGraphics is a trademark of maranGraphics Inc. Maran Illustrated, the Maran Illustrated logos and any trade dress related to or associated with the contents or cover of this book are trademarks of maranGraphics Inc. and may not be used without written permission.

The Course Technology PTR, Cengage Learning logo is a trademark of Cengage Learning and may not be used without written permission.

Windows is a registered trademark of Microsoft Corporation in the United States and/or other countries.

All other trademarks are the property of their respective owners.

Important

maranGraphics and Course Technology PTR, Cengage Learning have attempted throughout this book to distinguish proprietary trademarks by following the capitalization style used by the source. However, we cannot attest to the accuracy of the style, and the use of a word or term in this book is not intended to affect the validity of any trademark.

Copies

Educational facilities, companies, and organizations located in the U.S. and Canada that are interested in multiple copies of this book should contact Course Technology PTR, Cengage Learning for quantity discount information. Training manuals, CD-ROMs, and portions of this book are also available individually or can be tailored for specific needs.

COURSE TECHNOLOGY
CENGAGE Learning™

Course Technology PTR, a part of Cengage Learning
20 Channel Street, Boston, MA 02210 www.courseptr.com

maranGraphics is a family-run business.

© maranGraphics Inc.

At maranGraphics, we believe in producing great books—one book at a time.

Each maranGraphics book uses the award-winning communication process that we have been developing over the past 30 years. Using this process, we organize screen shots, text, and illustrations in a way that makes it easy for you to learn new concepts and tasks.

We spend hours deciding the best way to perform each task, so you don't have to! Our clear, easy-to-follow screen shots and instructions walk you through each task from beginning to end.

We want to thank you for purchasing what we feel are the best books money can buy. We hope you enjoy using this book as much as we enjoyed creating it!

Sincerely,

The Maran Family

We would love to hear from you!
Send your comments and feedback about our books to family@maran.com.

To sign up for sneak peeks and news about our upcoming books, send an email to newbooks@maran.com.

Please visit us on the web at:

www.maran.com

CREDITS

Author:
Diane Koers with Ruth Maran

Project/Copy Editor:
Karen A. Gill

Technical Editor:
Elaine Marmel

Layout Design & Illustrations:
Jill Flores
Mike Tanamachi

Indexer:
Sharon Shock

Proofreader:
Tonya Cupp

Publisher and General Manager, Course Technology PTR, a part of Cengage Learning:
Stacy L. Hiquet

Associate Director of Marketing, Course Technology PTR, a part of Cengage Learning:
Sarah Panella

Manager of Editorial Services, Course Technology PTR, a part of Cengage Learning:
Heather Talbot

ACKNOWLEDGMENTS

This was a very interesting book to write. I would especially like to thank Heather Hurley for the opportunity to write it; Karen Davis for her unlimited patience in keeping me on track; Elaine Marmel for her dedication to making sure the book is accurate; Mike Tanamachi for his wonderful creative illustrations; and Jill Flores for her hard work in making it look so beautiful.

Finally, a huge thank-you goes to everyone else who worked behind the scenes making this book the creative work that it has become.

Diane Koers

TABLE OF CONTENTS

Chapter 1 WINDOWS 8 AND MODERN UI

© Microsoft® Corporation

Chapter 2 WINDOWS BASICS

© Microsoft® Corporation

Chapter 3

USEFUL WINDOWS PROGRAMS

Chapter 4

WORKING WITH FILES

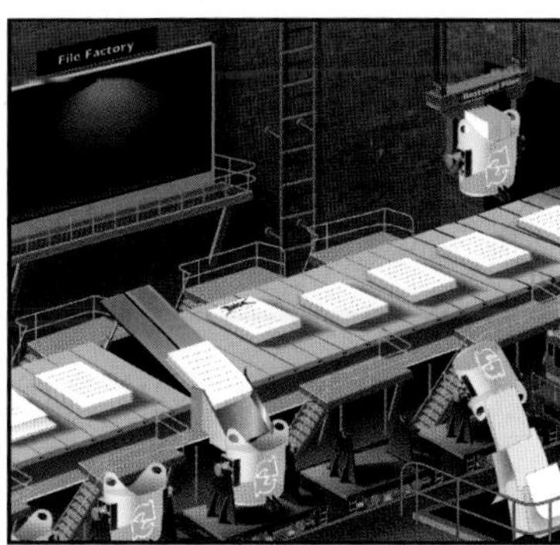

TABLE OF CONTENTS

Chapter 5 WORKING WITH PICTURES

© EpicStockMedia/Shutterstock.com

Chapter 6 WORK WITH MUSIC AND VIDEOS

© EpicStockMedia/Shutterstock.com

Chapter 7 CUSTOMIZE WINDOWS

© Microsoft® Corporation. © Cengage Learning®

Chapter 8

SHARE YOUR COMPUTER

Chapter 9

BROWSE THE WEB

© maranGraphics, Inc. © National Weather Service
© Smithsonian Institution © US Forest Service

Chapter 10 EXCHANGE EMAIL

Chapter 11 WORK ON A NETWORK

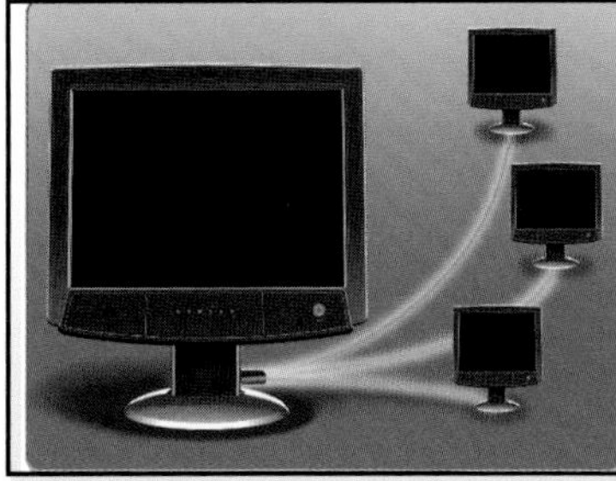

Chapter 12

OPTIMIZE COMPUTER PERFORMANCE

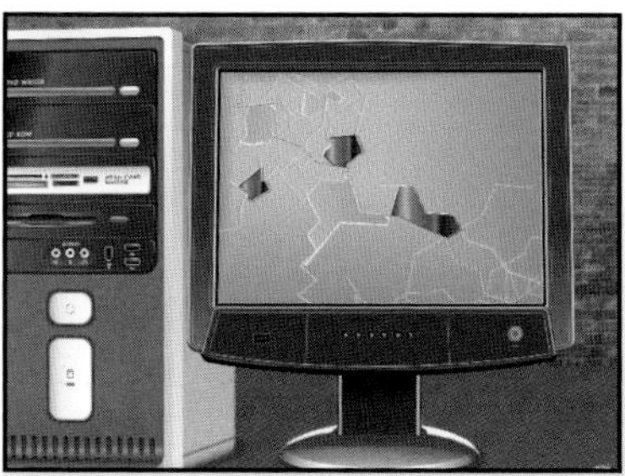

Start
DVD-WRITER
CD-ROM
MULTI-CARD READER
-AUDIO-

Windows 8 and Modern UI

SIGN IN

Windows 8 starts with the Lock screen. From here you need to enter your information to gain access to the rest of the Windows applications.

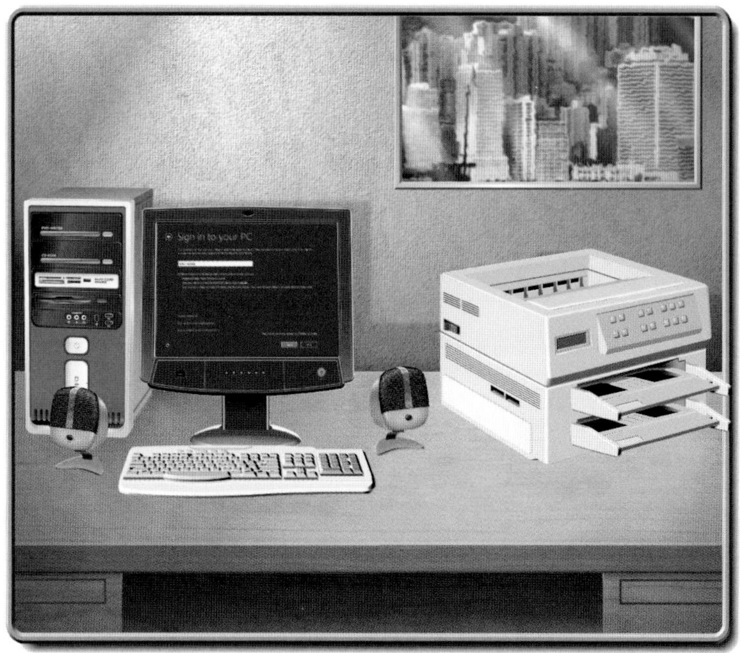

© Microsoft® Corporation

You can sign in using your Microsoft account, which is an email address and password that you use to sign in to all Microsoft sites and services. If you use Hotmail, SkyDrive, Xbox LIVE, or a Windows phone, you already have a Microsoft account. If you don't already have a Microsoft account, you can sign up for one.

SIGN IN

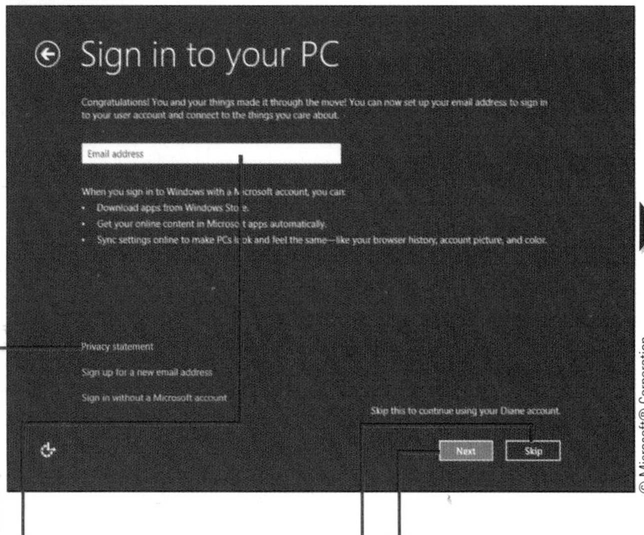

© Microsoft® Corporation

© Microsoft® Corporation

1 Enter your Microsoft account email address.

■ If you don't have a Microsoft account, click here to create a new one. You are prompted to enter an email name, password, and some identifying information.

2 Click **Next**.

■ If you don't want to sign in with a Microsoft account, click **Skip**. Windows then creates a Local account for you.

THE LOCK SCREEN

1 Click anywhere in the Lock screen.

Do I have to use a Microsoft account to use Windows 8?

No. If you don't want to use a Microsoft account, you can sign in without it, but if you don't use a Microsoft account, you can't access many of the new Modern UI apps that appear in Windows 8.

Originally, I didn't want to use a Microsoft account, but now I do. What should I do to change this?

You can switch to a Microsoft account by pressing ⊞ + C, which displays the Charm bar. Click **Settings**, and then click **Change PC settings**.

Click **Users**. Then click **Switch to a Microsoft account** and follow the instructions.

You can also use the same steps to switch from a Microsoft account to a local account.

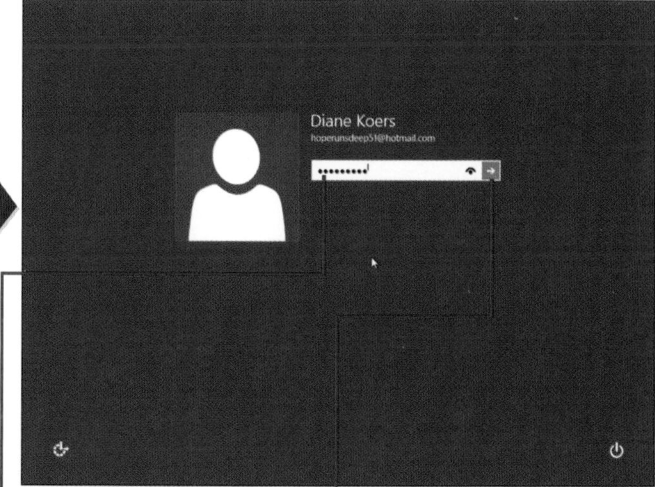

■ A screen appears prompting you for your password.

2 Enter your password.

Note: Remember that passwords are case sensitive. For example, ***Happyday1*** *is different from* ***HAPPYDAY1*** *and* ***happyday1***.

3 Click here.

■ The Windows 8 Start screen appears.

■ You are ready to begin your journey through Microsoft Windows 8.

THE START SCREEN

The first screen you see after you sign in is called the Start screen. The Start screen is a tile-based screen with blocks on it called Modern UI apps.

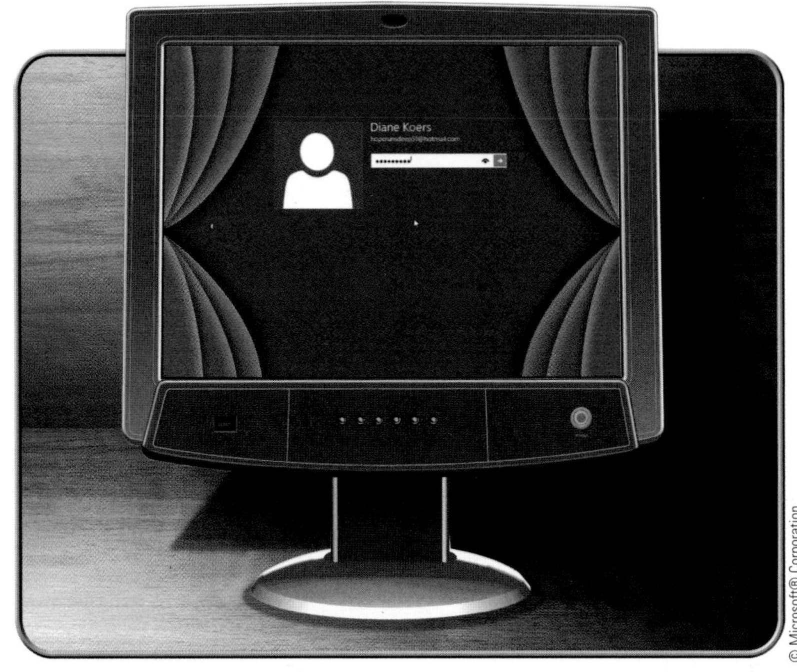

© Microsoft® Corporation

Modern UI apps are designed to have a single window that fills the entire screen by default, so there are no distractions.

Windows 8 provides several mouse pointing gestures you can use to access different areas of the Start screen, as well as keyboard shortcuts to many of them.

THE START SCREEN

© Microsoft® Corporation. © Cengage Learning®

© Microsoft® Corporation. © Cengage Learning®

1. Move your pointer to the top left of your screen.
2. Slowly drag your pointer downward, and you will see a preview of your open apps.

■ In this example, you see the Desktop, Weather, and Maps apps open.

3. Hover your pointer in the top or bottom right to reveal the Charm bar. (See "**Display Charms**" later in this chapter.)

THE WINDOWS KEY

If you've ever used a previous version of Windows, you know that most tasks began with a click of the Start button. In Windows 8, because the Modern UI apps have replaced the desktop as the home screen of Windows, you need a way to move around.

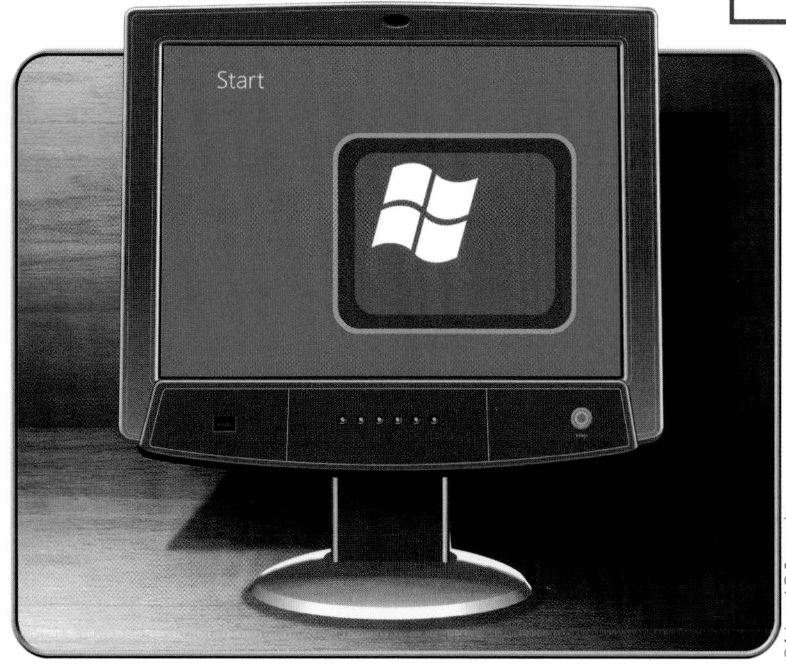

© Microsoft® Corporation

Windows 8 extensively uses the ⊞ key, called the Windows key, to accomplish tasks. Used by itself or in combination with other keys, the ⊞ key gets the job done. The ⊞ key is located on the bottom row of your keyboard, and it's the second key from the left, just next to the Ctrl key.

THE WINDOWS KEY

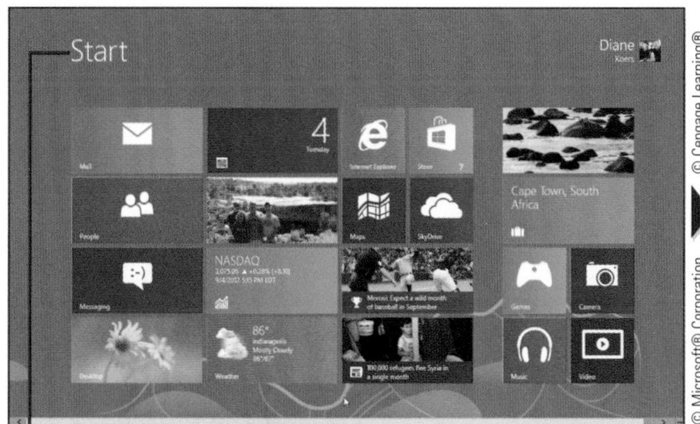

© Cengage Learning® © Microsoft® Corporation.

1 From the Start screen, press ⊞.

© Microsoft® Corporation

■ The Windows desktop appears.

2 From the Windows desktop, press ⊞.

CONTINUED

THE WINDOWS KEY

You can use in combination with many keys as shortcuts to perform Windows 8 tasks.

Some of these keyboard shortcuts only work while you are in non-Modern UI apps, such as when using Office or File Explorer.

You use the keyboard shortcuts by tapping and holding down on your keyboard while striking another character on the keyboard.

Press the Windows key ( ) with

Key	**Result**
A	Select all
C	Open charms
D	Show desktop
E	Open File Explorer
F	Go to Files in Search charm
H	Share charm
I	Settings charm
K	Devices charm
L	Switch users
M	Minimize all windows (desktop)
O	Lock screen orientation
P	Projection options
Q	Search charm
R	Run…
T	Set focus on taskbar and cycle through running desktop apps
U	Ease of Access Center
V	Cycle through notifications
W	Go to Settings in Search charm
X	Display System menu
Z	Open app bar
Esc	Exit Magnifier
Home	Minimize nonactive desktop windows
Left arrow	Snap active desktop window to the left
Left arrow	Snap active desktop window to the right
Up arrow	Maximize active desktop window
Down arrow	Restore/minimize active desktop window
F1	Windows Help and Support

ABOUT MODERN UI APPS

Windows 8 comes with 19 Modern UI apps, and many more are available for purchase or for free.

© Microsoft® Corporation

The Modern UI tile icons may remind you of signs commonly found at public transportation systems.

Many Modern UI apps also use animation such as transitions. Throughout this book, we will work with several of the Modern UI apps.

MAIL

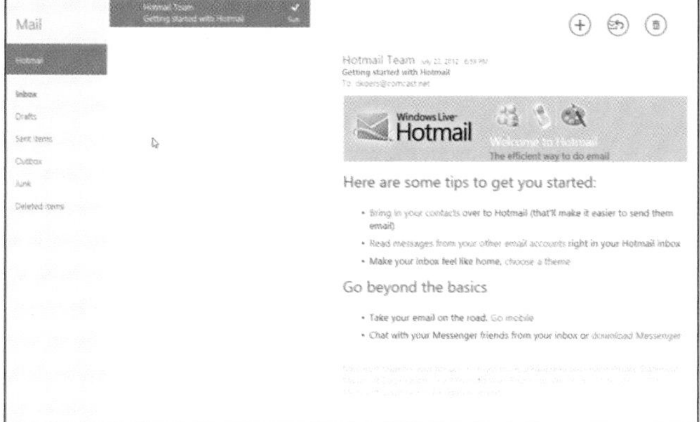

© Microsoft® Corporation

Send and receive email. The Mail app in Modern UI supports Hotmail, Microsoft Exchange, and Google Mail. (See **Chapter 10**.)

PEOPLE

© Microsoft® Corporation

The People app is your Windows 8 address book. Keep track of family, friends, and acquaintances by storing addresses and phone numbers in the People app.

CONTINUED

MESSAGING

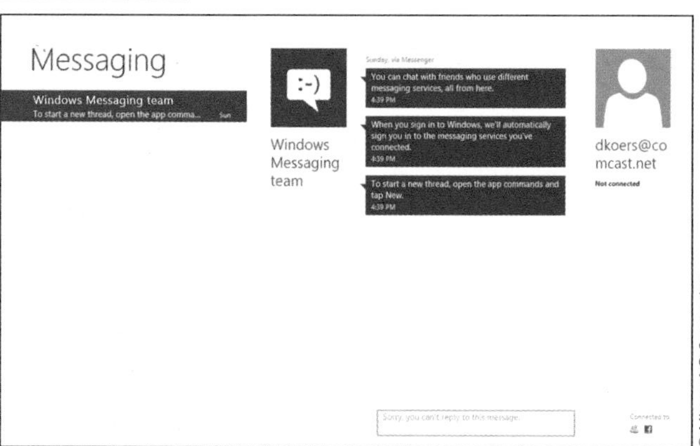

The Messaging app is where the instant messaging action happens. Instant messaging is the process of typing in real time to communicate with others, also in real time. (See **Chapter 11**.)

DESKTOP

The desktop is probably the app you will use most often. Through the desktop, you can access non-Modern UI applications such as Office, File Explorer, WordPad, Paint, and other programs. You can also customize many of your computer settings through the desktop. (See **Chapter 13**.)

CALENDAR

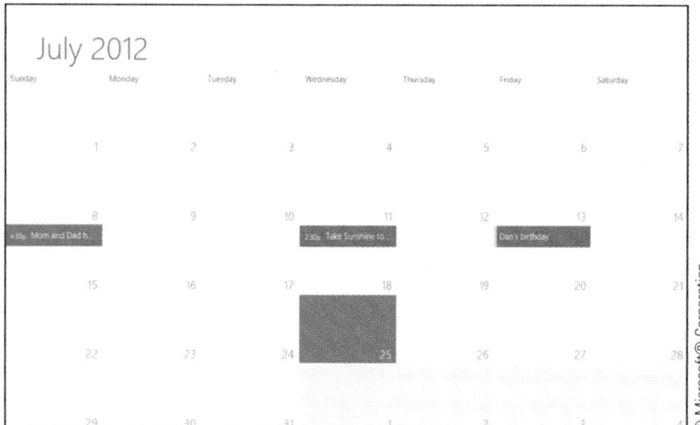

Keep track of your schedule by using the Calendar. Set reminders to alert you of upcoming events. (See **Chapter 3**.)

PHOTOS

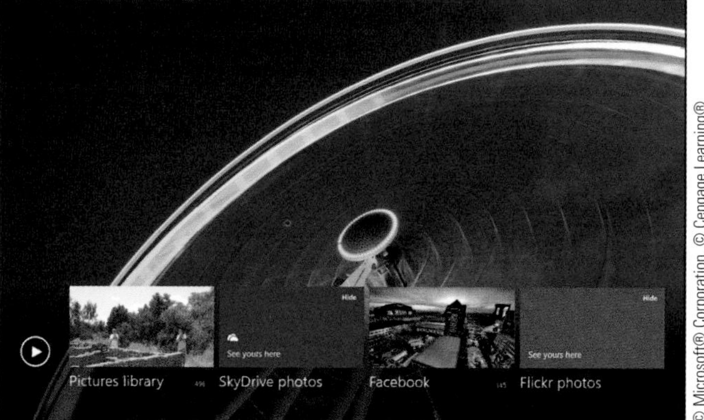

Browse photos stored not just on your computer, but on all your cloud accounts, including SkyDrive, Facebook, and Flickr. (See **Chapter 5**.) View your favorite images in a slide show format.

VIDEO

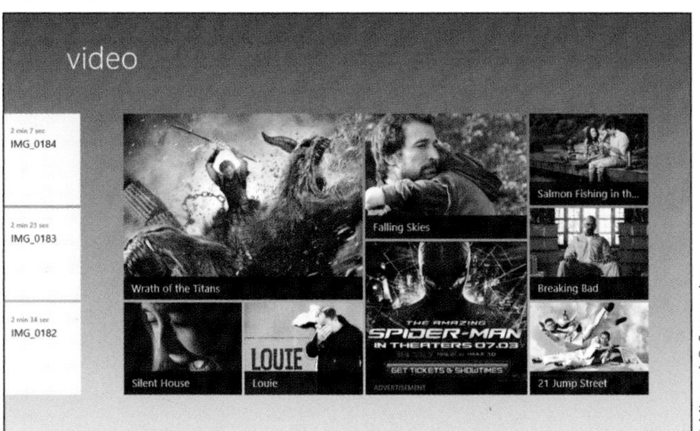

The Video app allows you to view many of the cute videos that friends send you through your email. You can also purchase, download, and watch movies and television shows.

WEATHER

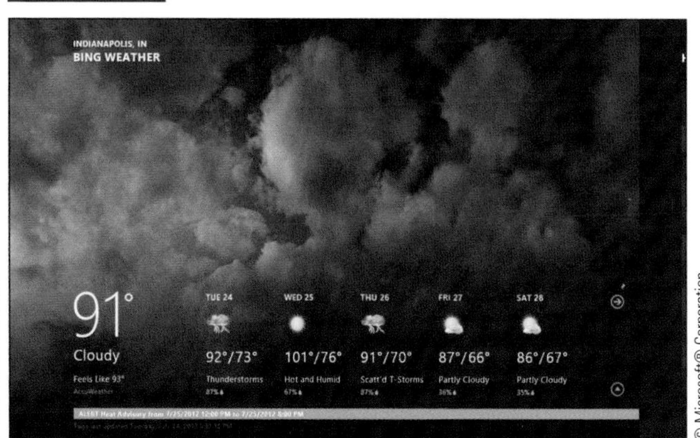

The Weather application's live tile shows you the current weather for your default location. You can view the weather for multiple locations around the world.

INTERNET EXPLORER

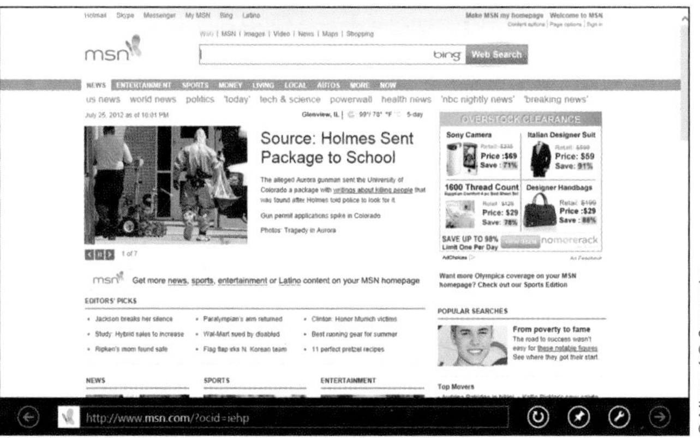

Browse the Internet and surf to your heart's delight. Modern UI Internet Explorer is similar to the Internet Explorer you may have used before. (See **Chapter 9**.)

STORE

This is where you'll add new Modern UI apps to your Windows 8 system. Many useful free apps are available, along with other apps that you can purchase. (See **"Get Modern UI Apps"** later in this chapter.)

CONTINUED

ABOUT MODERN UI APPS

MAPS

© Microsoft® Corporation

The Maps app is a Modern UI app version of the Bing Maps service provided by Microsoft. Use the Maps app to find any address or directions between two addresses.

SKYDRIVE

© Microsoft® Corporation

SkyDrive is Microsoft's online storage solution. Store your documents, photos, and other files where you can access them with any Internet-capable device or computer. (See **Chapter 4**.)

MUSIC

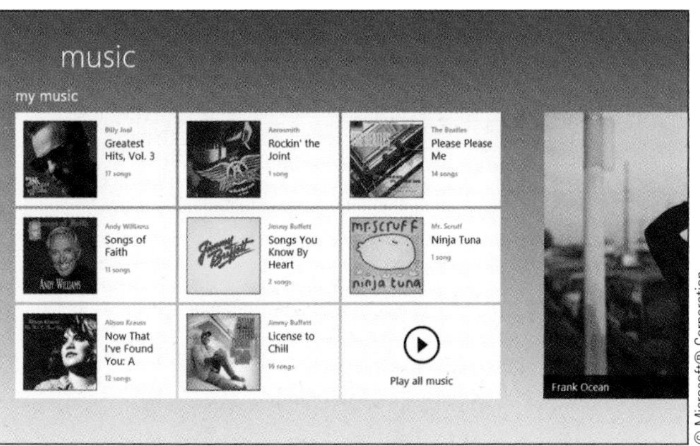

© Microsoft® Corporation

The Music app allows you to manage and listen to music you keep on your computer. You can also purchase, download, and listen to music from the Internet. (See **Chapter 6**.)

XBOX LIVE GAMES

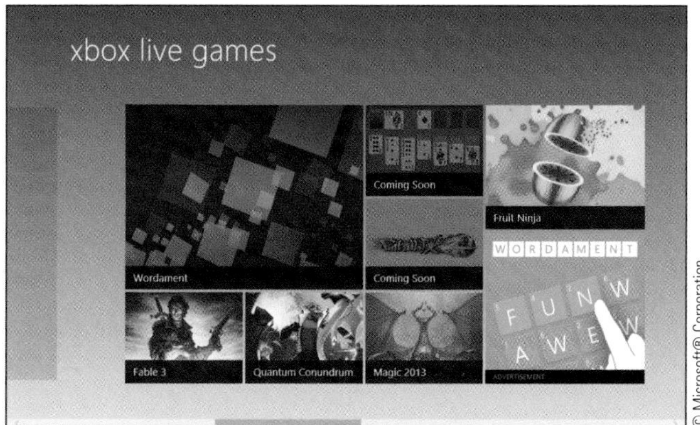

© Microsoft® Corporation

You can use the Xbox LIVE Games app to connect with others using an Xbox account. Purchase and play online games alone or with other Xbox users.

CAMERA

You can use this app when you have a webcam attached to your computer. Visit with family and friends without leaving your house.

NEWS

Read news from Bing Daily, which presents stories from the Associated Press and other news sources. You can select which news sources you want to use, such as CNN News, Fox News, *The New York Times*, and many others.

SPORTS

Catch up on your favorite sports news from Bing Sports. Select all sports or just the sports you enjoy.

TRAVEL

View beautiful photos of exotic places around the world. Plan a trip by booking a flight or hotel.

USE A MODERN UI APP

Opening a Modern UI app is a single mouse click away.

© Microsoft® Corporation

The first time you use some of the Modern UI apps, Windows may prompt you with a question.

USE A MODERN UI APP

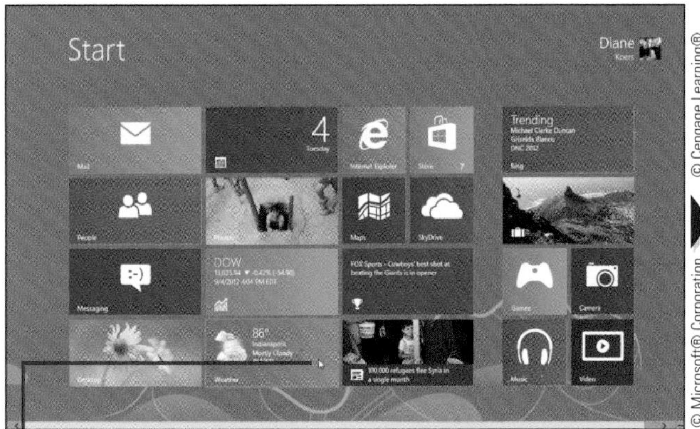

© Microsoft® Corporation. © Cengage Learning®

1 Click the Modern UI app you want to open. As an example, click **Weather**.

■ If prompted to use your current location, choose Allow.

© Microsoft® Corporation

■ You see the current weather for your city.

2 Press ⊞ to return to the Start screen.

Is there another way to locate an app?

Yes. From the Start screen, simply begin typing the first letters of the app you want. As you type, Windows 8 displays a list of apps with the letters you type. When you see the app you want to use, click the tile.

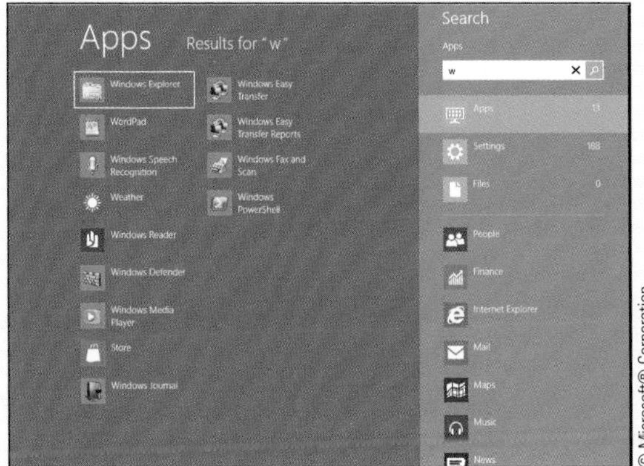

Can I have more than one app open at a time?

Yes, you can have as many apps open as you want. You can switch between the apps by holding down the Alt key and tapping the Tab key. Keep tapping the Tab key until you get to the app you want to use. Then release the Alt key.

CLOSE A MODERN UI APP

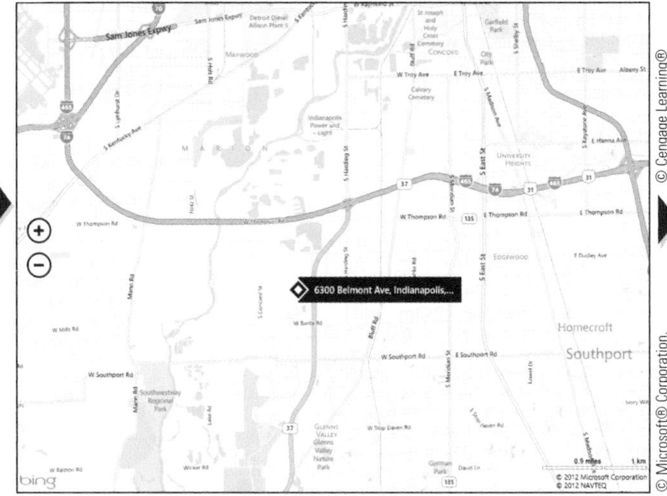

■ Modern UI apps don't have close buttons, and you don't *need* to close them because Modern UI apps are automatically suspended when you switch to something else.

■ Even though suspended apps use minimal system resources, you can close them if you want to.

1 Press Alt and F4.

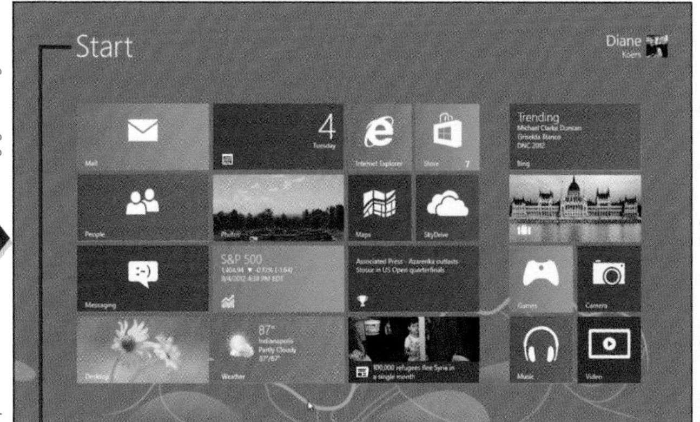

■ Windows shuts down the app and returns to the Start screen.

THE APP BAR

While in the Start screen or in any Modern UI screen, you can bring up the App bar.

© Microsoft® Corporation

The App bar displays some of the available options while you're in the app.

The choices you see vary, depending on which app you are using.

THE APP BAR

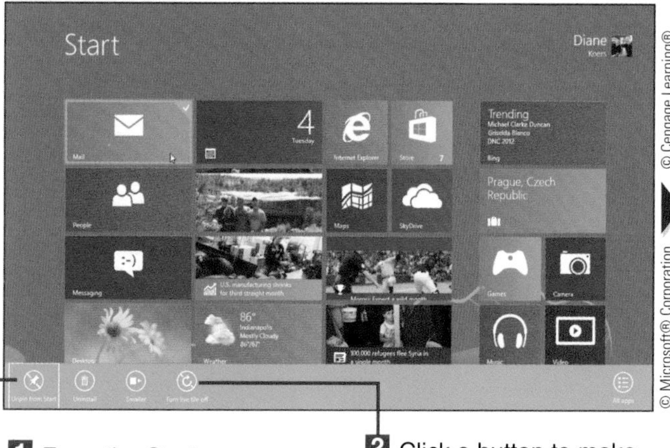

© Microsoft® Corporation. © Cengage Learning®

1 From the Start screen, right-click, press ☰, or press ⊞ + Z.

■ The App bar appears for the Start screen.

2 Click a button to make a choice, or press Esc to close the App bar without making a selection.

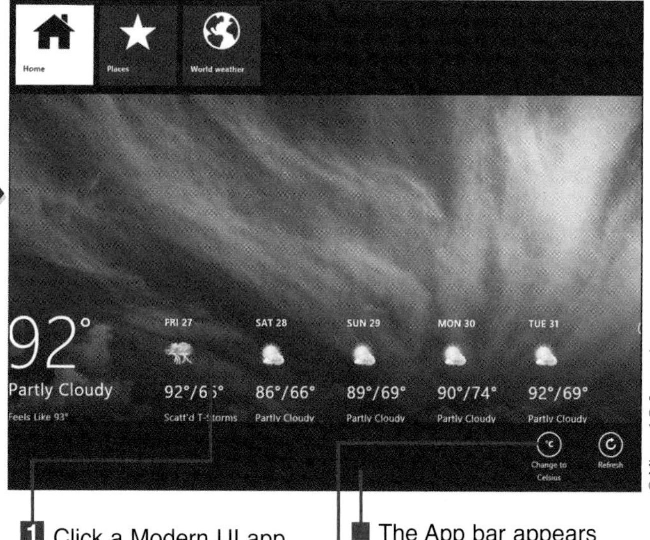

© Microsoft® Corporation

1 Click a Modern UI app. In this example, you see the Weather app.

2 Right-click, press ☰, or press ⊞ + Z.

■ The App bar appears with options for the Weather app.

3 Click a button to make a choice, or press Esc to close the App bar without making a selection.

SHOW ALL APPS

Besides the standard Modern UI apps you see on the Start screen, Windows 8 comes with many other tools and desktop apps such as WordPad, Paint, and StickyNotes.

Over time, you may add additional apps from the Windows Store or install non-Modern UI programs such as Microsoft Office or Peachtree Accounting.

SHOW ALL APPS

1 Right-click anywhere on the Start screen.

■ The App bar appears at the bottom of the screen.

2 Click **All apps**.

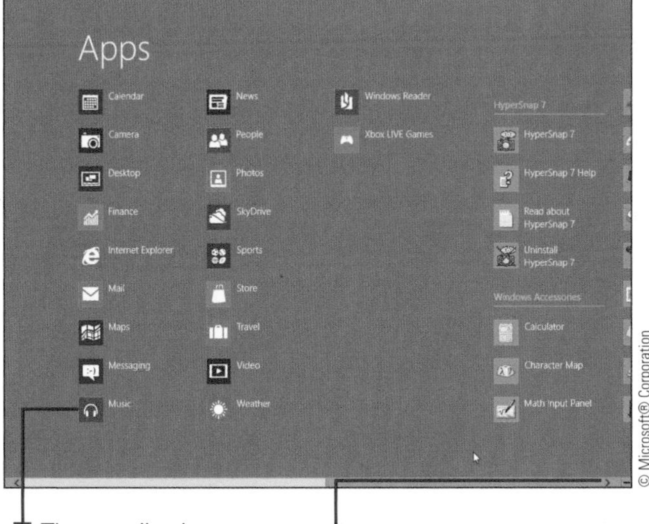

■ The app tiles become smaller, and you see more choices.

■ Scroll to the right to see additional selections.

3 Click on a tile to open the app or program.

MOVE TILES

While on the Start screen, you can reorganize the Modern UI app tiles.

© Microsoft® Corporation

Make your favorite apps more accessible by placing them next to each other.

MOVE TILES

© Microsoft® Corporation. © Cengage Learning®

© Microsoft® Corporation. © Cengage Learning®

1 Position the ⇖ over the tile you want to move.

2 Press and drag the ⇖ until the tile is in the location you want.

3 Release the mouse button.

■ The tile moves to the new location.

RESIZE TILES

On the Start screen, some tiles are larger than others.

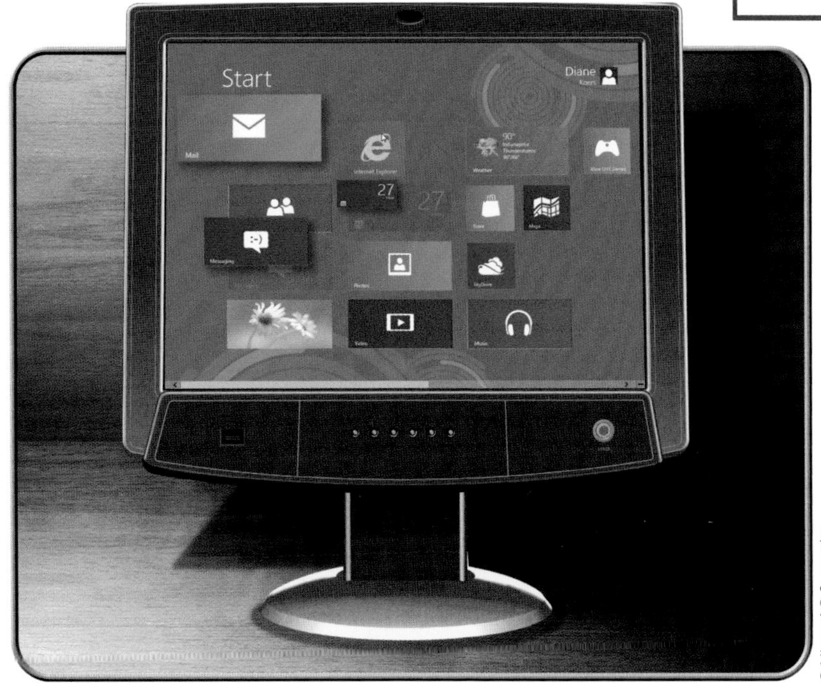

© Microsoft® Corporation

You can change the size of any tile to make it large or small.

RESIZE TILES

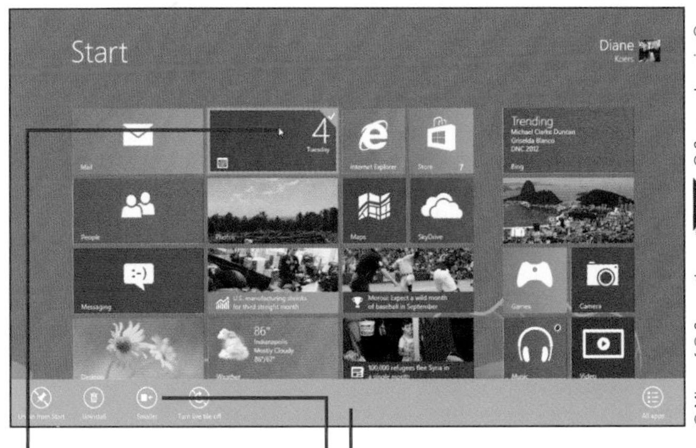

© Microsoft® Corporation. © Cengage Learning®

© Microsoft® Corporation. © Cengage Learning®

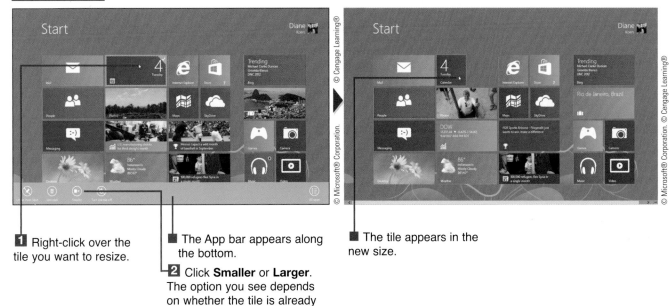

1 Right-click over the tile you want to resize.

■ The App bar appears along the bottom.

2 Click **Smaller** or **Larger**. The option you see depends on whether the tile is already large or small.

■ The tile appears in the new size.

PIN A TILE TO THE START SCREEN

If you have a program that you use frequently and would like easier access to it, you can pin it to the Start screen.

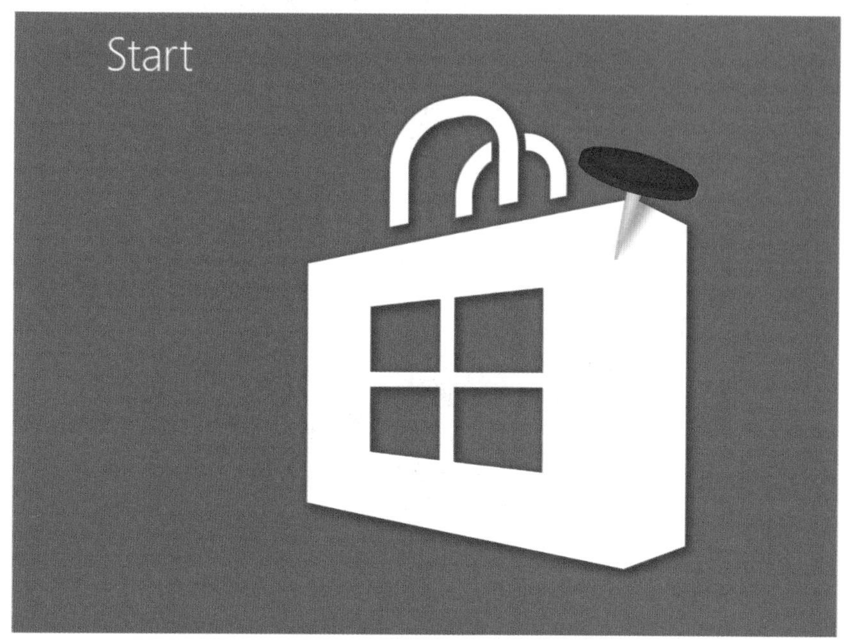

© Microsoft® Corporation

You can select from Modern UI apps or from programs that run on the desktop.

PIN A TILE TO THE START SCREEN

© Microsoft® Corporation

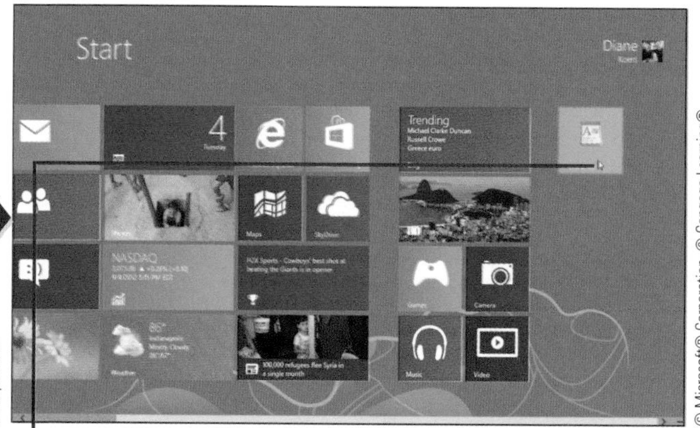

© Microsoft® Corporation. © Cengage Learning®

1 Right-click the Start screen to display the Apps bar.

2 Choose **All apps**.

3 From the All Apps screen, locate and right-click the program or app you want to display on the Start screen.

4 Choose **Pin to Start**.

5 Press ⊞.

■ A tile representing the program or app appears on the Start screen.

■ You can drag the tile to a convenient location. See "**Move Tiles**" earlier in the chapter.

Note: To remove a tile from the Start screen, right-click the tile and, from the Apps bar, click ***Unpin from Start****.*

SHOW THE DESKTOP

In Windows 8, the tiled Start screen is the first screen that appears, but the Windows desktop is available as its own application.

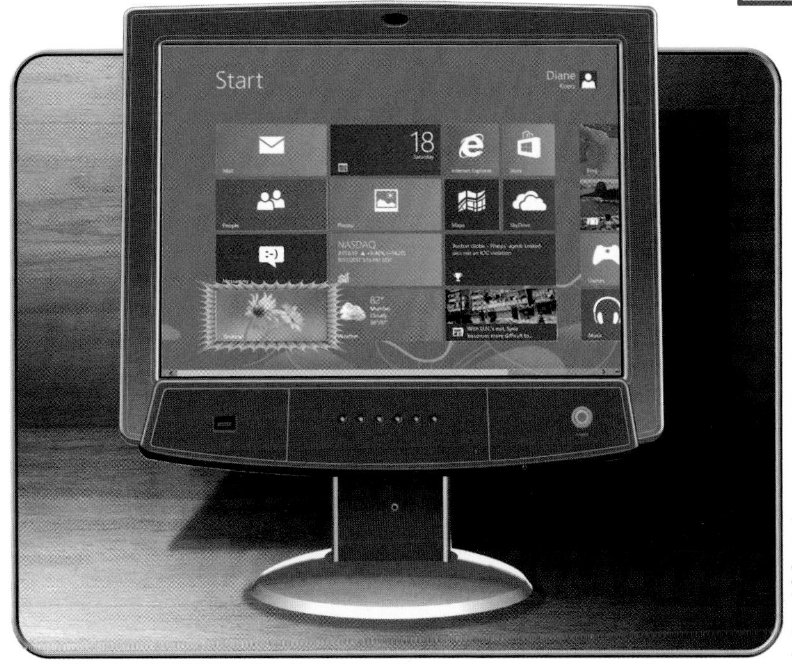

© Microsoft® Corporation

From the desktop, you work in non-Modern UI applications such as WordPad, Paint, and Calculator.

SHOW THE DESKTOP

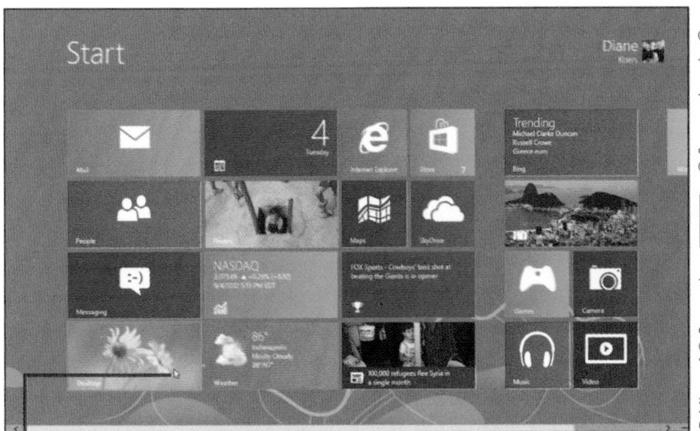

© Microsoft® Corporation. © Cengage Learning®

1 From the Start screen, click the desktop tile or simply press the ⊞ key.

© Microsoft® Corporation

■ The Windows desktop appears.

*Note: See **Chapter 7** to customize the Windows desktop appearance.*

DISPLAY CHARMS

The Charm bar is a specific set of icons and commands available to every app.

© Microsoft® Corporation

The Charm bar has five charms: Search, Share, Start, Devices, and Settings.

Charms provide quick access to key areas of Windows 8.

DISPLAY CHARMS

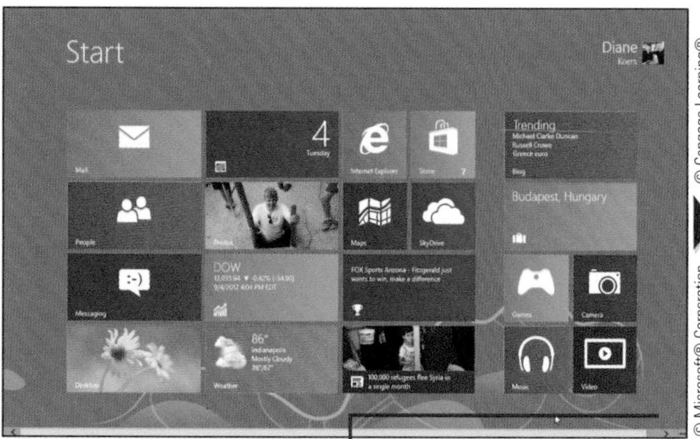

© Microsoft® Corporation. © Cengage Learning®

© Microsoft® Corporation. © Cengage Learning®

1 Press [Windows key] + C.

■ You can also display the Charm bar from the Start screen by moving your [pointer] to the lower-right corner of the screen.

■ The Charm bar appears with five different charms.

2 Click any charm to see the charm options.

Note: Click the Start charm to return to the Start screen.

SEARCH CHARM

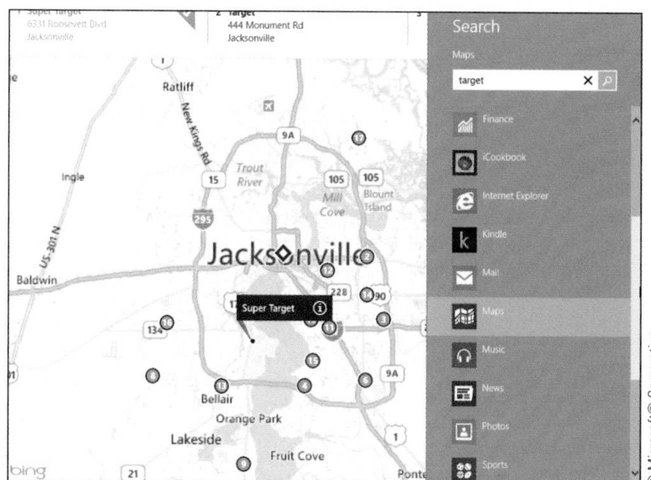

© Microsoft® Corporation

Using the Search charm is the same as just typing in an application or filename. However, the Search charm is context sensitive, so it will perform a search of whichever Modern UI app you're currently using.

For example, you can search the Maps app to find the closest Target store.

SHARE CHARM

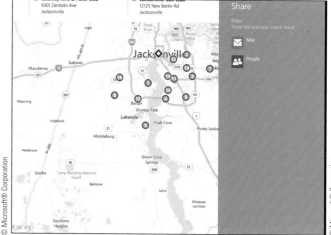

© Microsoft® Corporation

While viewing various Modern UI apps, you can share the current content with others via the People or Mail apps.

In this example, a business location found using the Maps can be shared.

DEVICES CHARM

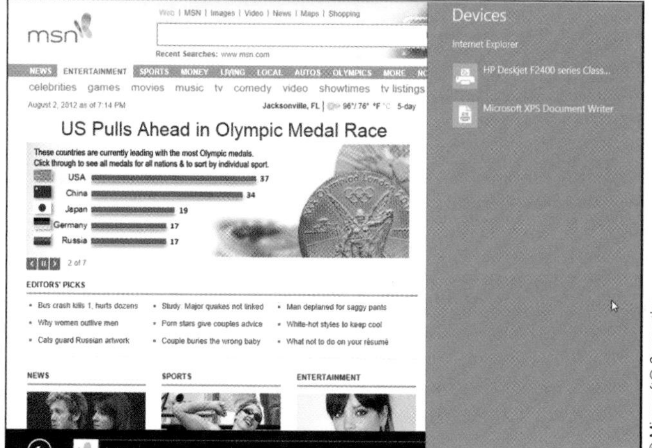

© Microsoft® Corporation

Here you'll find a list of all connected devices, such as a printer, a scanner, a second screen, or a projector.

Selecting one of the devices presents you with a different sidebar menu containing relevant options and actions for that device.

SETTINGS CHARM

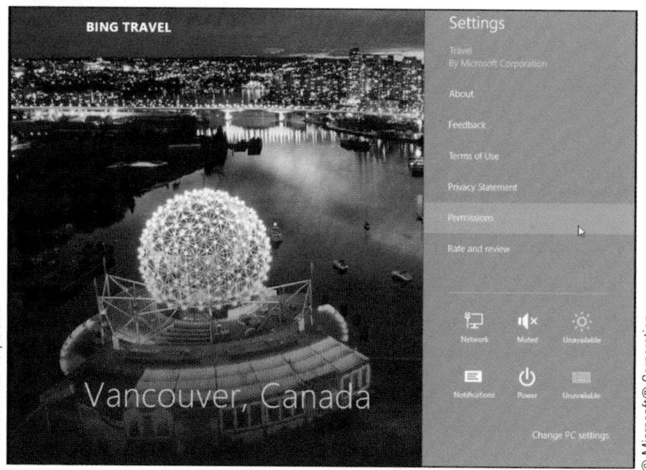

© Microsoft® Corporation

Use the Settings charm to adjust your app preferences.

The Settings charm is context sensitive, which means it will present the settings of whichever Modern UI app you're currently using. Some settings such as volume and brightness are static no matter which app you're in. You'll also always find a link to Change PC settings to get to the main Modern UI settings.

Here you see the settings for the Travel app.

GET MODERN UI APPS

Hundreds of additional apps are available. Some are free, and some are for purchase.

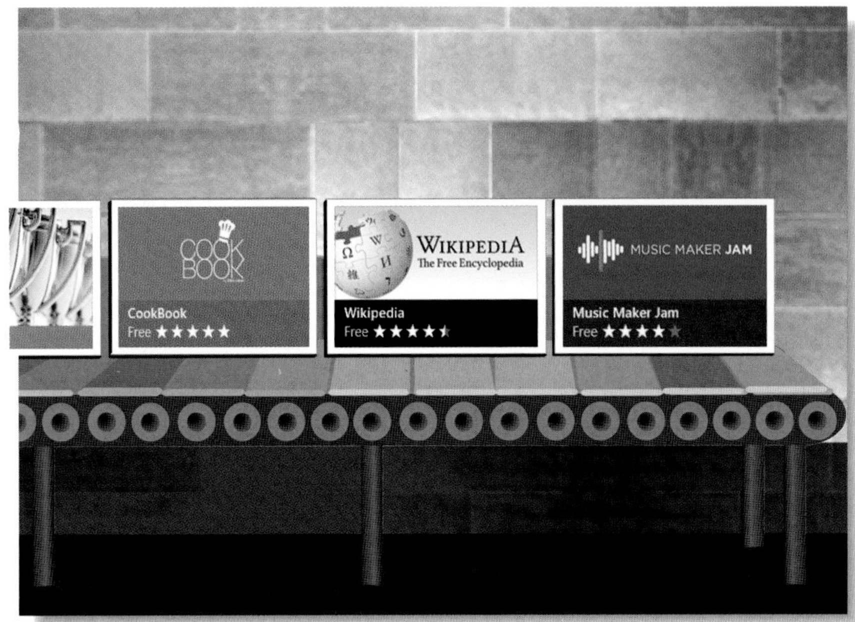

© Microsoft® Corporation

Apps fall into many categories, such as Shopping, Lifestyle, Entertainment, and Games.

Installing an app usually takes just a few seconds.

GET MODERN UI APPS

© Microsoft® Corporation. © Cengage Learning®

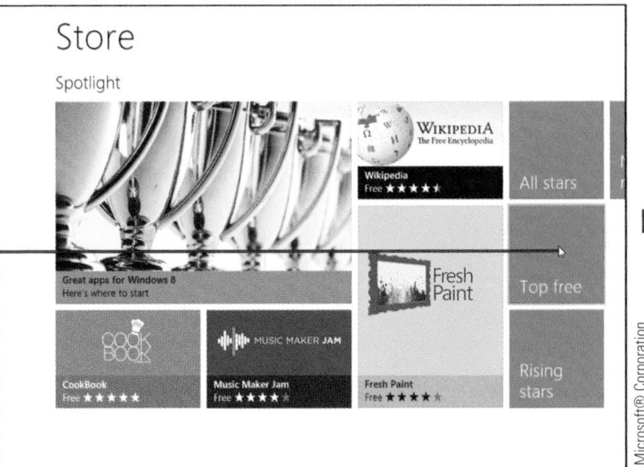

© Microsoft® Corporation

1 From the Start screen, click the Store app.

2 Locate and click a category for the app you want.

■ Scroll to the right to see more categories.

Can I install an app without a Windows Live ID?

No. To install an app, you must use your Windows Live ID.

If you are not signed into Windows 8 with a Live ID, you can either sign out of the local account and sign in with a Live ID account before you enter the Store, or you can enter your Live ID information before you install the app.

To sign out of your local account, use the Charm bar. Click the **Settings** charm, click **Change PC Settings**, click **Users**, and then click **Sign In with a Microsoft Account**. Follow the onscreen instructions.

How do I install a non-Modern UI app?

You install a non-Modern UI app from the desktop. Either download the program you want to install, or, if it's on a CD or DVD, insert the disc into the disc drive. Most programs launch an AutoPlay or a Setup screen, from which you can choose the options you want for the program you are installing.

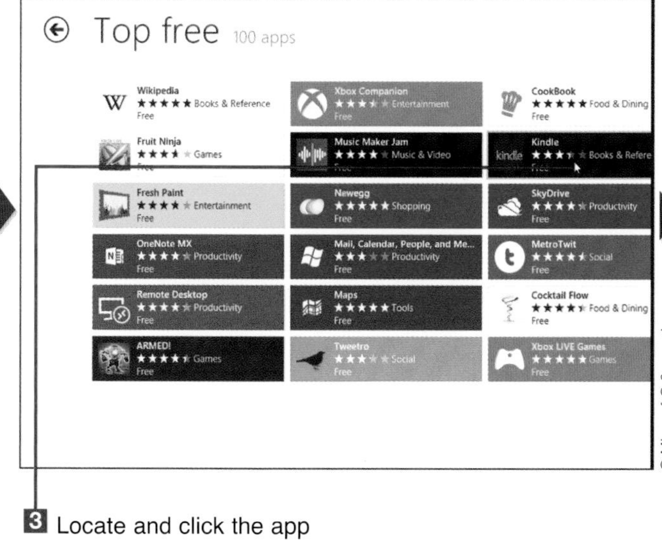

© Microsoft® Corporation

3 Locate and click the app you want.

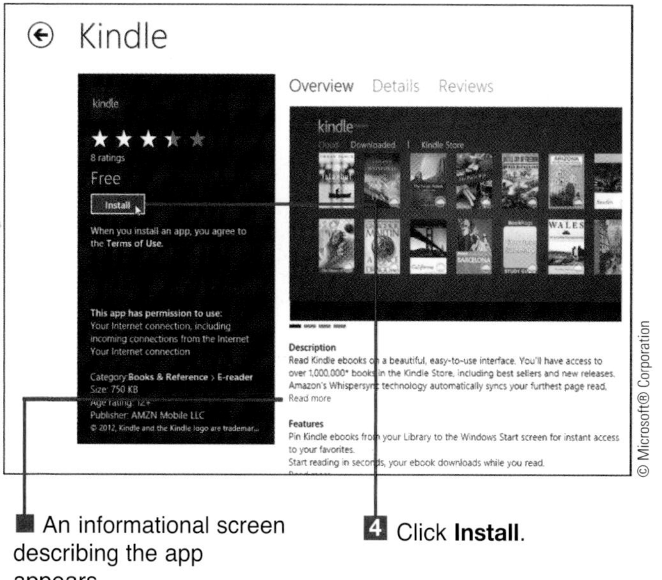

© Microsoft® Corporation

■ An informational screen describing the app appears.

4 Click **Install**.

CONTINUED

GET MODERN UI APPS (CONTINUED)

As you try new apps, use the Store to rate the app. Let others know what you think of the app.

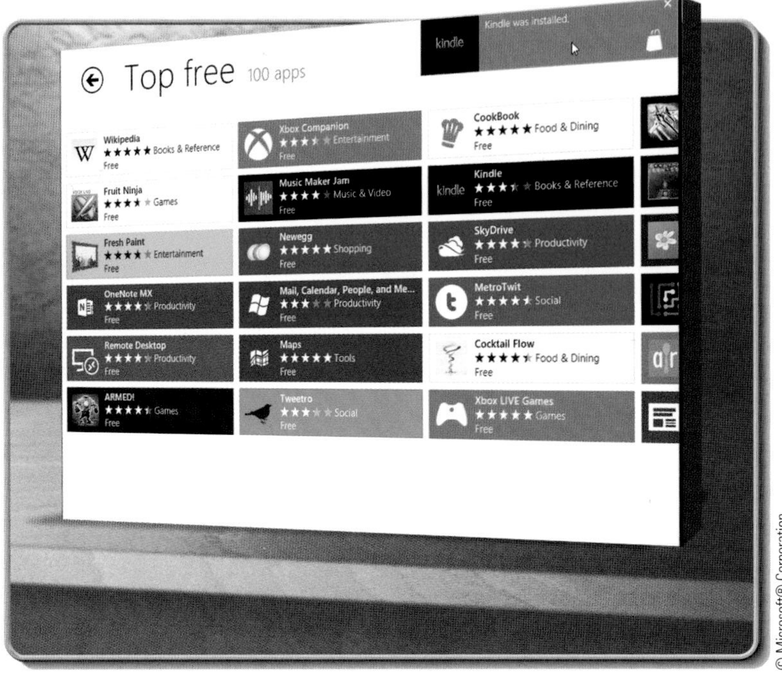

GET MODERN UI APPS (CONTINUED)

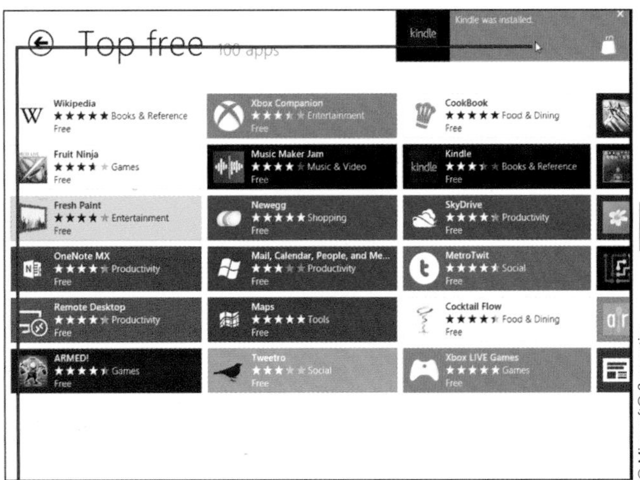

■ When the app is finished installing, a screen briefly appears showing you the app is installed. You are also notified with a short musical ding.

5 Choose another app to install or press ⊞ to return to the Start screen.

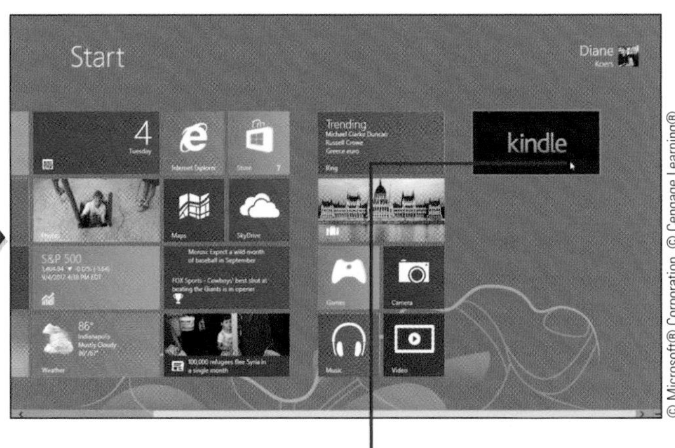

■ The app appears on your Start screen.

6 Click the app tile to launch the app.

Note: You can resize and move the app.

UNINSTALL MODERN UI APPS

If you decide you no longer want an app, you can uninstall it with only a couple of simple mouse clicks.

You can even uninstall the core applications discussed in this chapter and reinstall them later from the Store.

UNINSTALL MODERN UI APPS

1 From the Start screen, right-click the app you want to uninstall.

■ A check mark appears in the app.

■ The App bar appears at the bottom of the screen.

2 Click **Uninstall**.

■ A confirmation message bar appears.

3 Click **Uninstall**.

■ The app is removed from your system.

Start
Diane
Koers
18
Saturday
Internet Explorer
Store
Mail
Photos
Maps
SkyDrive
Boston Globe - Phelps' agent: Leaked pics not an IOC violation
People
NASDAQ
Messaging
82°
Mumbai
Cloudy
Weather
Desktop
Games
Music
Bing

CHAPTER 2

Windows Basics

OPEN A WINDOW

Even though the Windows 8 Modern UI apps don't open in a window, other applications that you run from the desktop, such as File Explorer or Microsoft Office, use the traditional window style.

OPEN A WINDOW

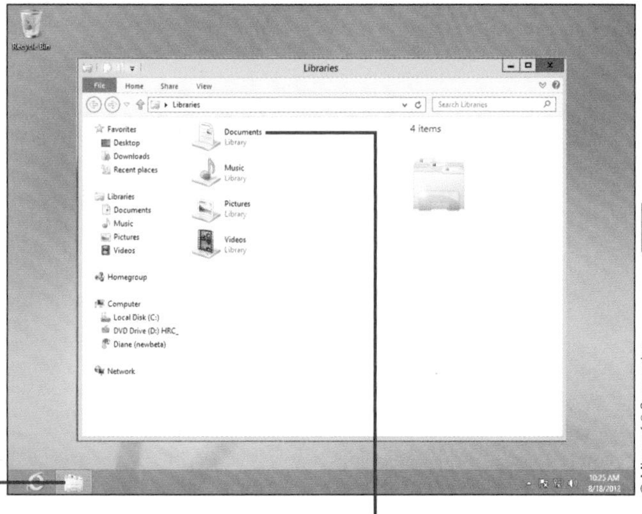

1 From the Start screen, click **Desktop**.

2 From the desktop, click File Explorer.

3 Double-click **Documents**.

■ A window appears with a list of files.

■ The window's title bar displays the current window name.

Note: The games that you see depend on the edition of Windows you are using.

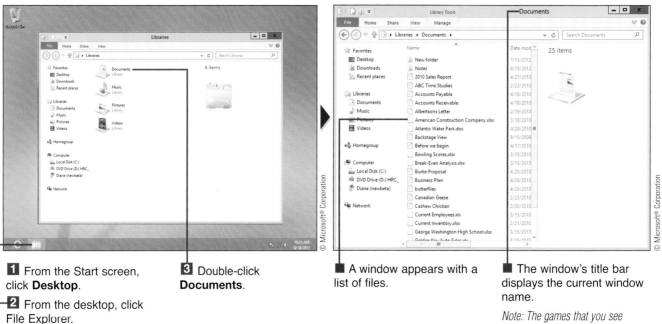

SCROLL THROUGH A WINDOW

You can use a scroll bar to browse through the information in a window. Scrolling is useful when a window is not large enough to display all the information it contains.

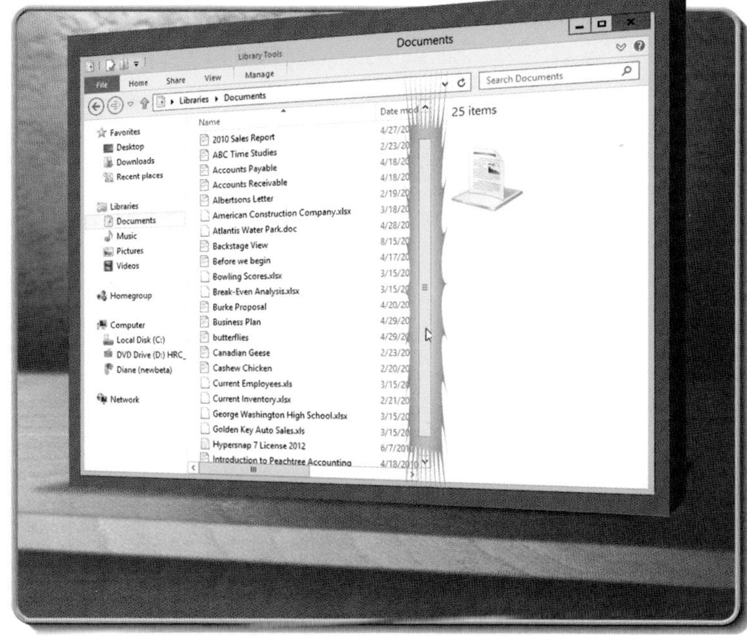

© Microsoft® Corporation

If your mouse has a wheel, you can use the wheel to scroll through a window. To scroll down, roll the wheel toward you. To scroll up, roll the wheel away from you.

SCROLL THROUGH A WINDOW

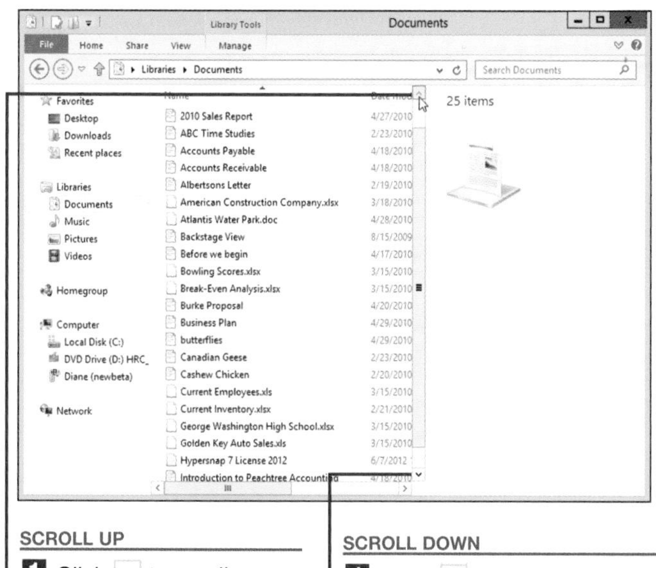

© Microsoft® Corporation

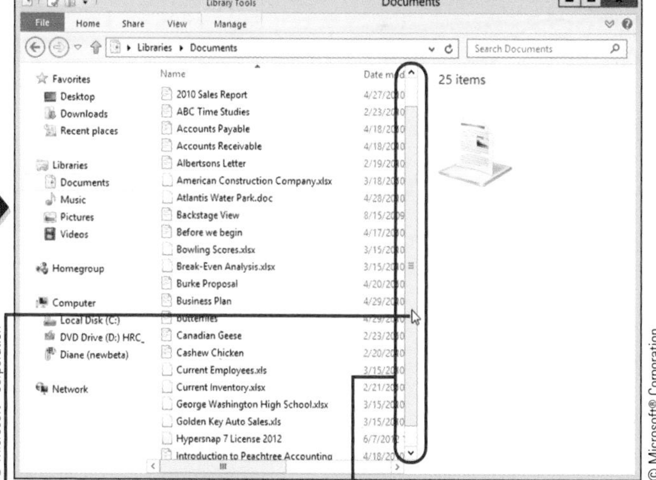

© Microsoft® Corporation

SCROLL UP

1 Click ^ to scroll up through the information in a window.

Note: If all the information in a window is displayed, a scroll bar does not usually appear in the window.

SCROLL DOWN

1 Click ˅ to scroll down through the information in a window.

SCROLL TO ANY POSITION

1 Position the ↖ over the scroll box.

2 Drag the scroll box along the scroll bar until the information that you want to view appears.

■ The location of the scroll box indicates which part of the window you are viewing. For example, when the scroll box is halfway down the scroll bar, you are viewing information from the middle of the window.

CLOSE A WINDOW

When you finish working with a window, you can close the window to remove it from your screen.

© Microsoft® Corporation

CLOSE A WINDOW

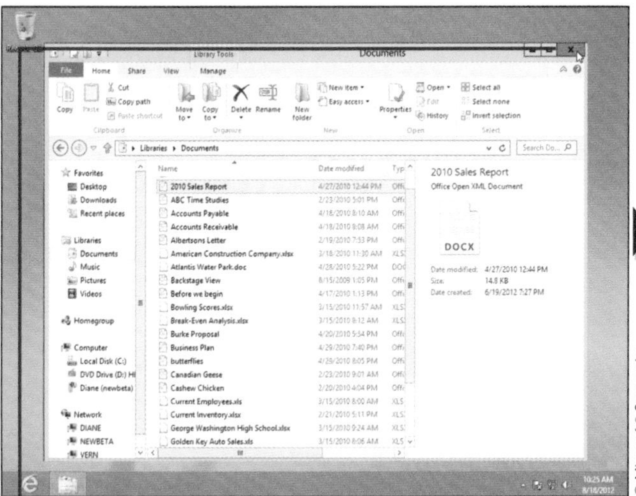

© Microsoft® Corporation

1 Click ✕ in the window you want to close.

© Microsoft® Corporation

■ The window disappears from your screen.

Note: If you close a document without saving your changes, a message will appear, allowing you to save your changes.

MOVE A WINDOW

If a window covers items on your screen, you can move the window to a different location.

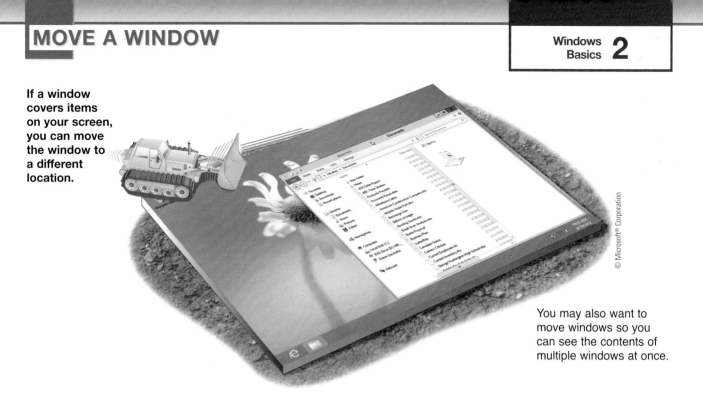

You may also want to move windows so you can see the contents of multiple windows at once.

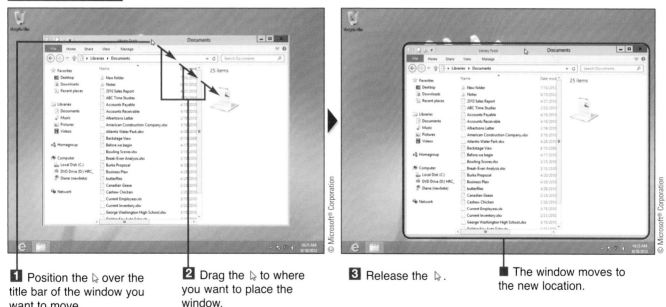

MOVE A WINDOW

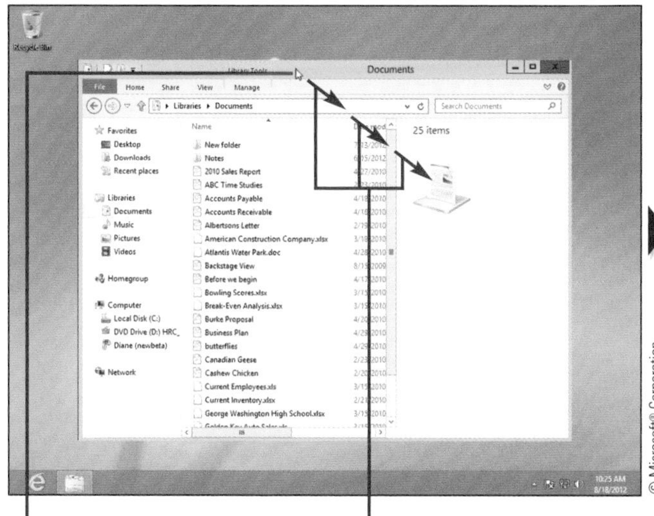

1 Position the ⇖ over the title bar of the window you want to move.

2 Drag the ⇖ to where you want to place the window.

3 Release the ⇖.

■ The window moves to the new location.

You can easily change the size of a window displayed on your screen.

© Microsoft® Corporation

Increasing the size of a window allows you to view more information in the window. Decreasing the size of a window allows you to view items covered by the window.

RESIZE A WINDOW

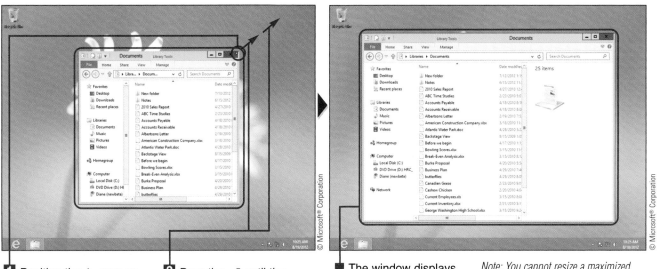

© Microsoft® Corporation

1 Position the ⇖ over an edge of the window you want to resize. ⇖ changes to ⤢, ⤡, ⇔, or ⇕.

2 Drag the ⤢ until the window is the size you want.

© Microsoft® Corporation

■ The window displays in its new size.

Note: You cannot resize a maximized window. For information on maximizing a window, see the next page.

MAXIMIZE A WINDOW

You can maximize a window to fill your entire screen. This allows you to view more of the window's contents.

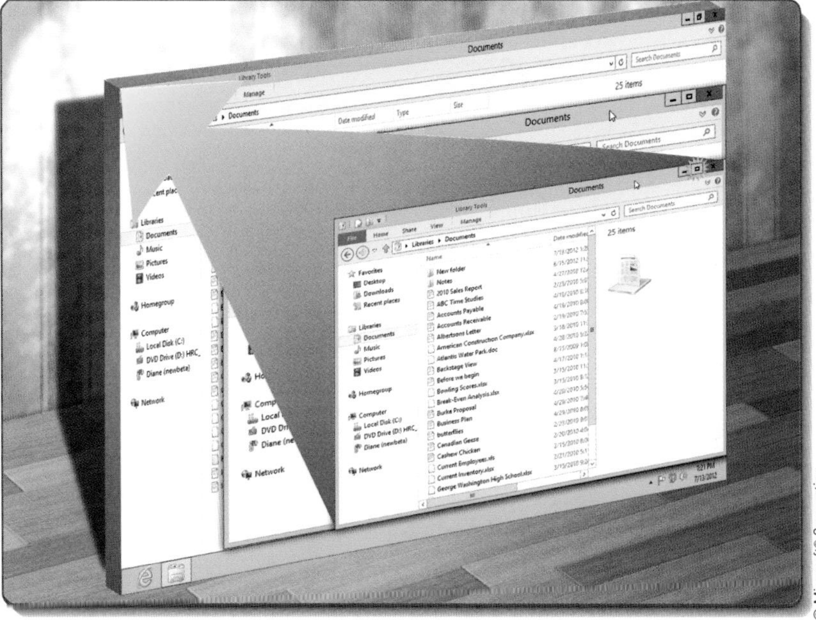

© Microsoft® Corporation

MAXIMIZE A WINDOW

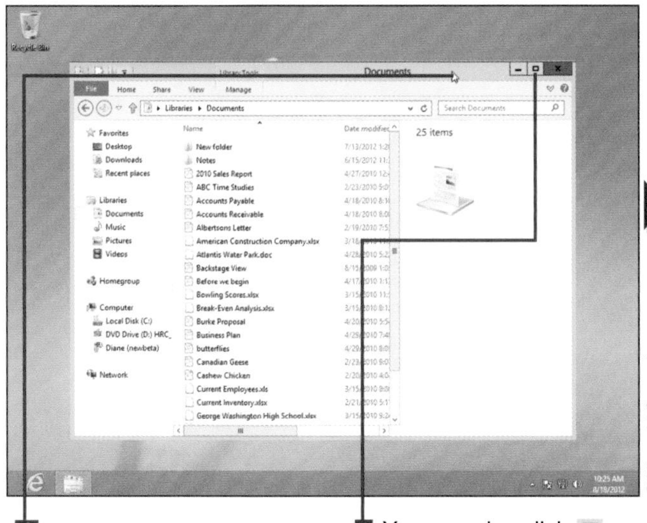

© Microsoft® Corporation

1 Double-click the title bar of the window you want to maximize.

■ You can also click ▭ in a window to maximize the window.

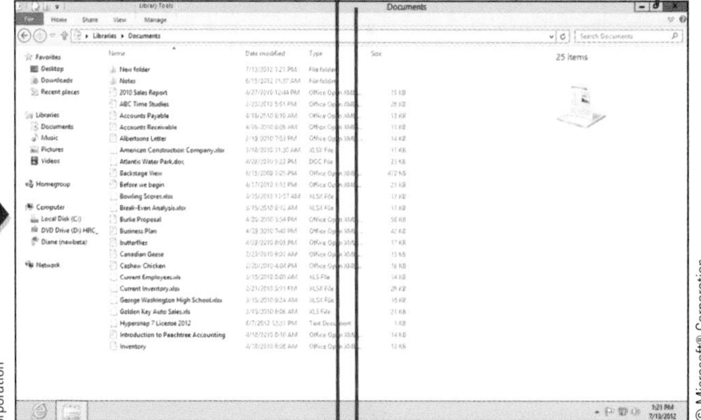

© Microsoft® Corporation

■ The window fills your entire screen.

■ To return the window to its previous size, double-click the window title bar.

■ You can also click ⧉ in a window to return the window to its previous size.

MINIMIZE A WINDOW

If you are not using a window, you can minimize it to temporarily collapse it to the taskbar. You can redisplay the window at any time.

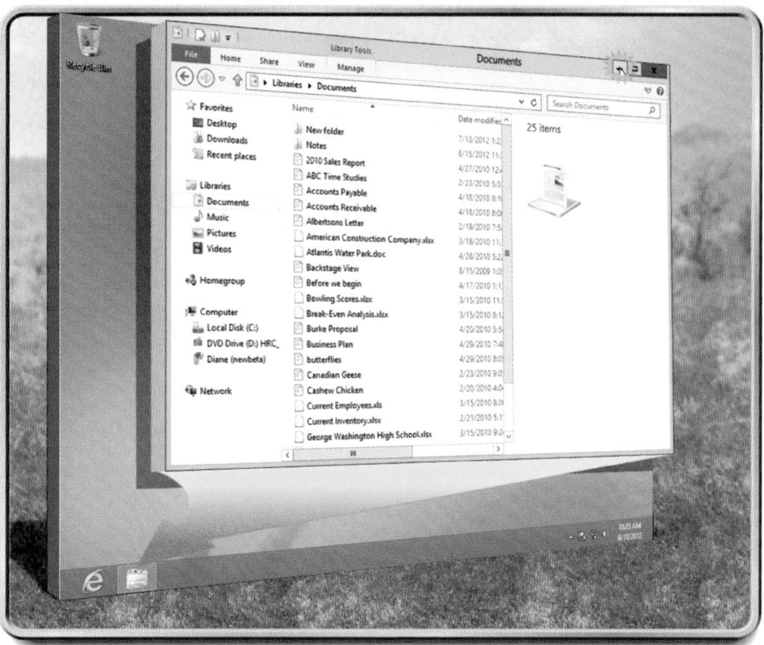

Minimizing a window allows you to temporarily put a window aside so you can work on other tasks.

© Microsoft® Corporation

MINIMIZE A WINDOW

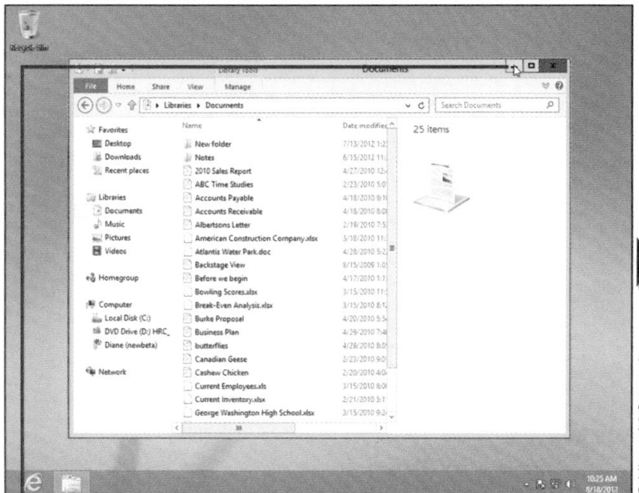

© Microsoft® Corporation

© Microsoft® Corporation

1 Click ▬ in the window you want to minimize.

■ The window hides from your screen.

■ To redisplay the window, click the icon for the window on the taskbar.

Note: If you have more than one window open in the same program, a preview of each open window will appear when you point your ↖ at the program in the taskbar. Click the preview of the window you want to redisplay. For more information, see ***"Switch Between Windows."***

MINIMIZE ALL BUT ONE WINDOW

If you have several windows open but only want to focus on one window, you can instantly minimize all the other open windows on your screen.

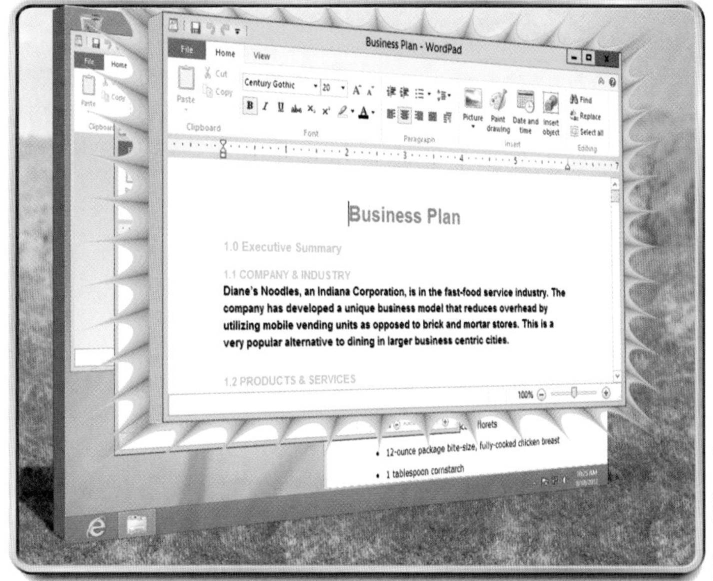

MINIMIZE ALL BUT ONE WINDOW

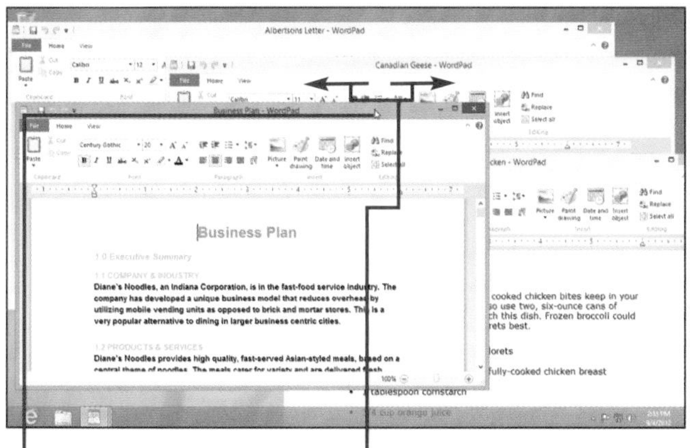

1 Position the ⇖ over the title bar of the window you want to focus on.

2 Press and hold down the mouse button and quickly move the ⇖ from side to side several times to shake the window on your screen. Then release the mouse button.

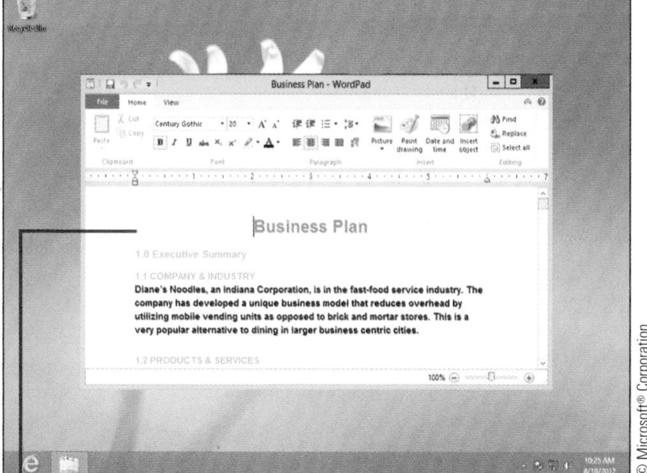

■ Windows instantly minimizes all the other open windows on your screen except the window on which you choose to focus.

■ To once again display all your open windows, repeat steps **1** and **2**.

SWITCH BETWEEN WINDOWS

If you have more than one window open on your screen, you can easily switch between the windows.

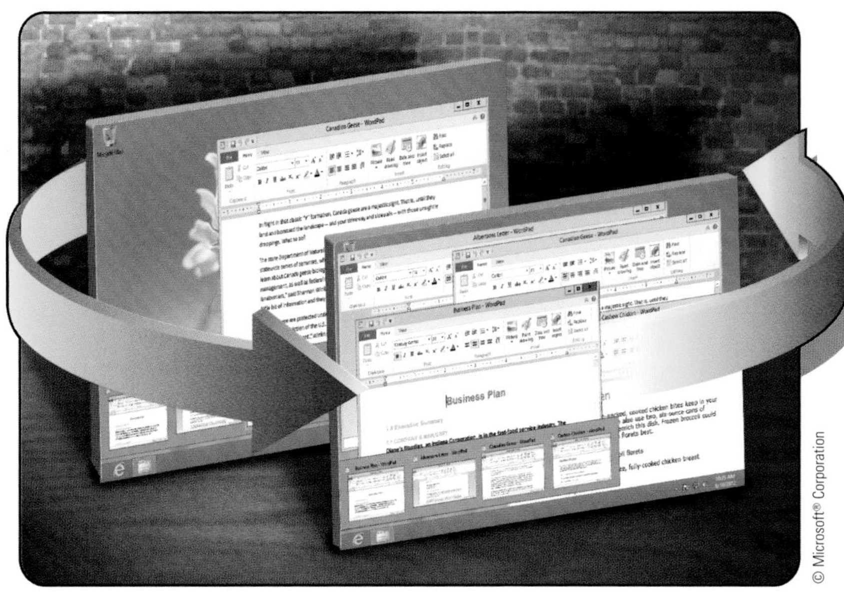

© Microsoft® Corporation

Each window is like a separate piece of paper. Switching between windows is like placing a different piece of paper at the top of the pile.

SWITCH BETWEEN WINDOWS

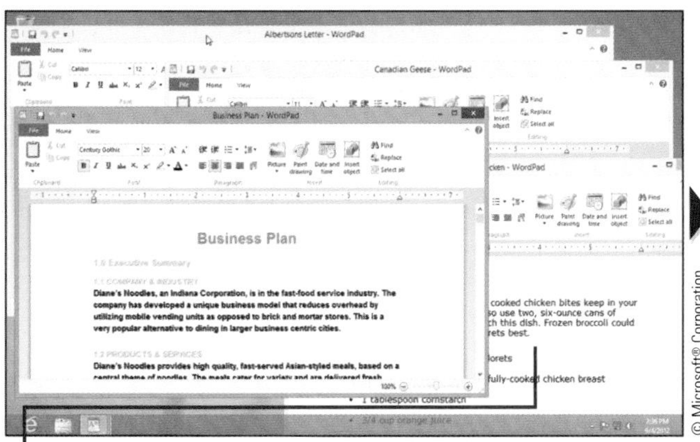

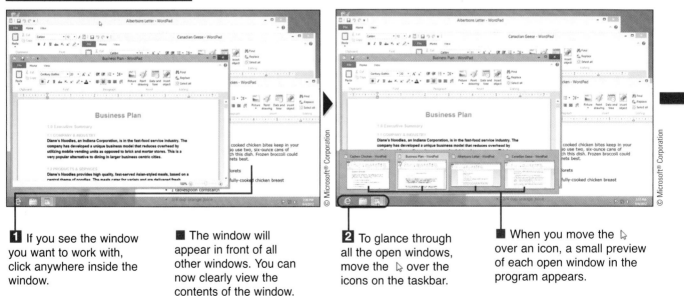

© Microsoft® Corporation

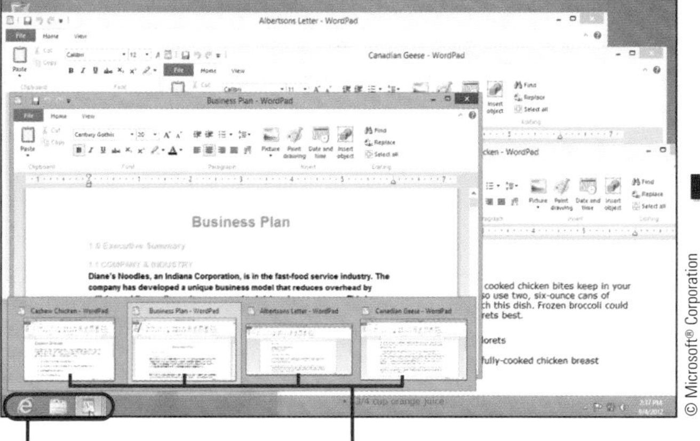

© Microsoft® Corporation

1 If you see the window you want to work with, click anywhere inside the window.

■ The window will appear in front of all other windows. You can now clearly view the contents of the window.

2 To glance through all the open windows, move the ⇖ over the icons on the taskbar.

■ When you move the ⇖ over an icon, a small preview of each open window in the program appears.

Does the taskbar offer any visual clues about my programs?

Yes. If a program has an open window, a border will appear around the program's icon on the taskbar. If a program has more than one window open, more than one line appears to the right of the program's icon on the taskbar.

© Microsoft® Corporation

Do some preview windows offer special features?

Yes. Some preview windows offer special features. For example, when playing a song in Windows Media Player, the preview window displays playback controls that you can click to play the previous song, play the next song, or pause the song.

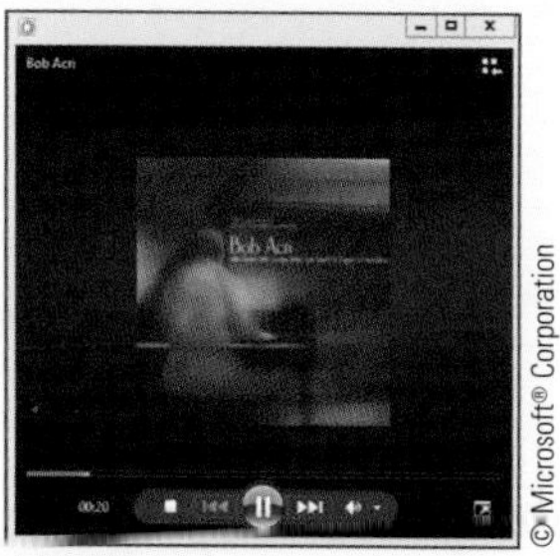

© Microsoft® Corporation

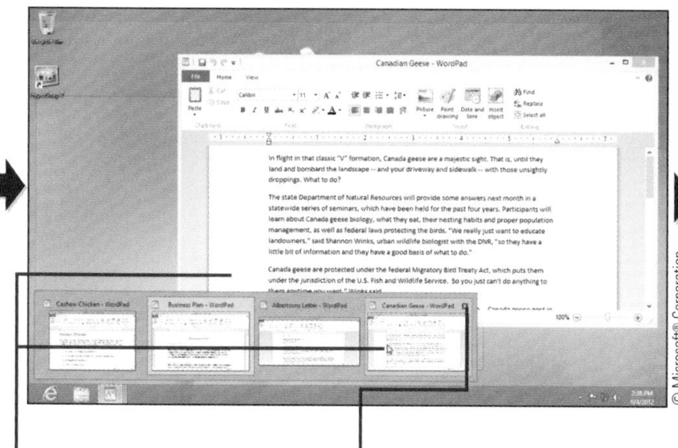

© Microsoft® Corporation

3 To view a larger preview of a window, move the pointer over the small preview of the window.

■ A larger preview of the windows appears. All other windows appear transparent.

■ If you want to close the window, click the close button in the small preview of the window.

4 When you see the window you want to use, click the small preview of the window.

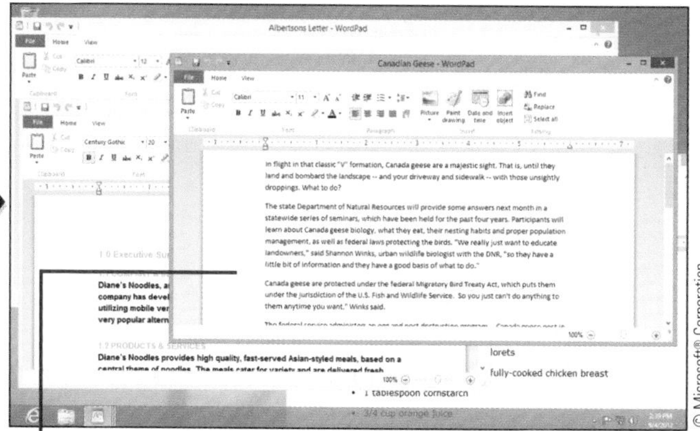

© Microsoft® Corporation

■ The window will appear in front of all other windows.

DISPLAY WINDOWS SIDE BY SIDE

You can display two or more windows side by side on your screen. This allows you to easily review the contents of several windows at the same time.

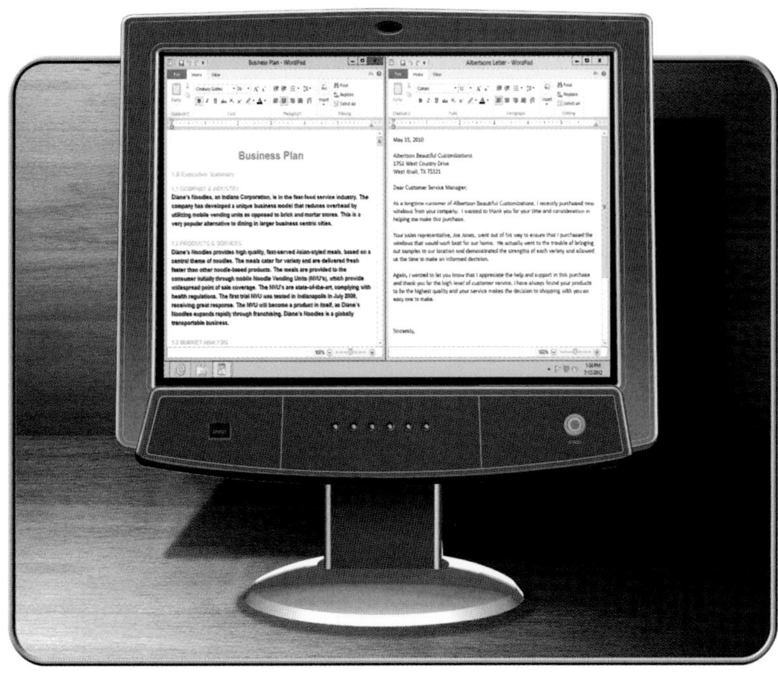

© Microsoft® Corporation

Displaying windows side by side also allows you to easily move and copy information between the windows.

DISPLAY WINDOWS SIDE BY SIDE

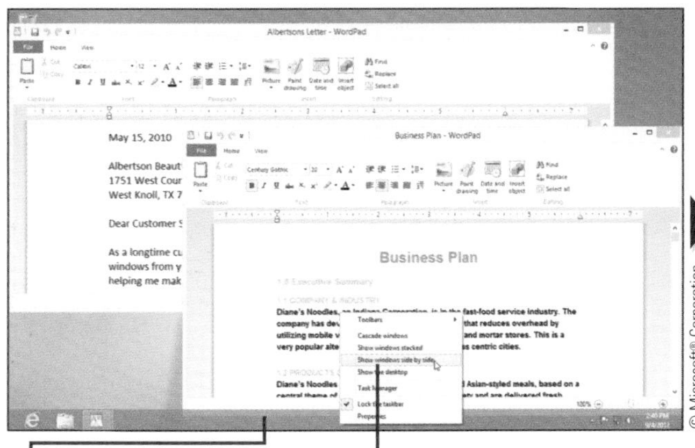

© Microsoft® Corporation

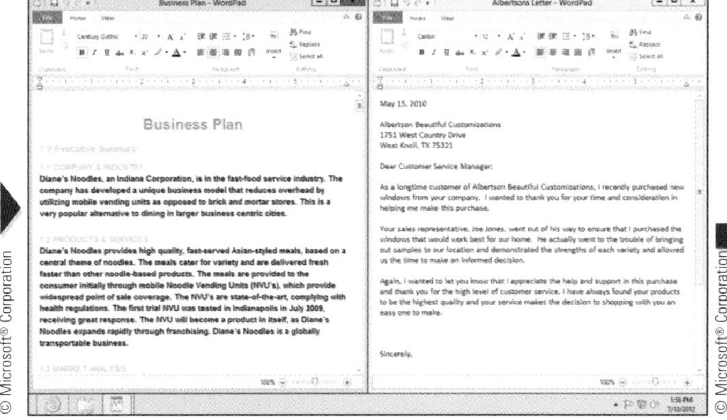

© Microsoft® Corporation

1 To display windows side by side on your screen, right-click the ↖ over a blank area of your taskbar.

■ A shortcut menu appears.

2 Click **Show windows side by side**.

■ All open windows snap into place and resize to fill your screen.

Tip: Is there another way to display two windows side by side?

Yes. Press ⊞ and ←. The window snaps into place and is resized to fill the left half the screen.

Repeat for the other window but press ⊞ and → to fill the right half of the screen.

Tip: Is there another way I can display windows on my screen?

Yes. You can cascade your open windows so the windows neatly overlap each other. To cascade your open windows, right-click a blank area of the taskbar and then click **Cascade windows** from the menu that appears.

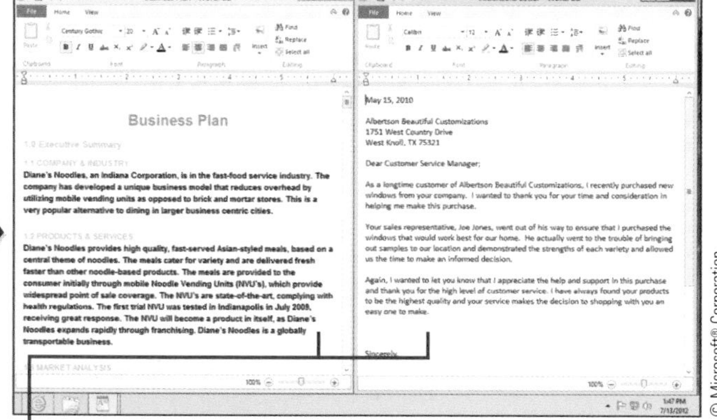

■ The windows now appear next to each other displaying the title bar of each open window.

UNDO SIDE BY SIDE

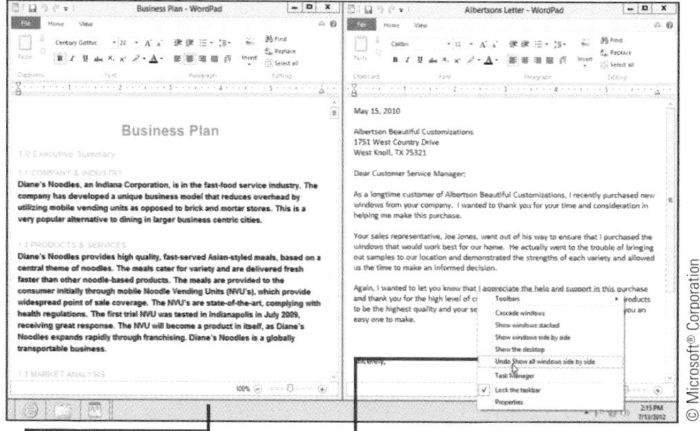

1 If you no longer want windows to appear side by side on your screen, right-click the ⇖ over a blank area of your taskbar.

■ A shortcut menu appears.

2 Click **Undo Show all windows side by side**.

■ The windows return to their original size.

SHUT DOWN WINDOWS

When you finish using your computer, you should shut down Windows, which then turns off the computer power. You should never just push the power button to turn off your computer.

© Microsoft® Corporation

You should shut down Windows and turn off the computer before installing new hardware inside your computer or before changing a laptop computer battery.

SHUT DOWN WINDOWS

© Microsoft® Corporation

© Microsoft® Corporation

■ Before shutting down Windows, you should save your work and close all the programs you have open.

1 From any screen, hold down the ⊞ key on your keyboard and tap the letter C.

■ The charms options appear.

2 Click **Settings**.

■ The Settings panel appears.

3 Click **Power** to display the power options.

4 Click **Shut down**. If Windows has available updates, you will see an additional option for Update and Restart.

■ Windows shuts down and then turns off your computer.

■ Press the power button on the computer to turn your computer back on.

Note: If Windows needs to install any updates, it does so before shutting down Windows.

RESTART YOUR COMPUTER

If your computer is not operating properly, you can restart your computer to try to fix the problem. Before restarting your computer, make sure you close all the open programs.

© Microsoft® Corporation

Some programs and updates also prompt you to restart your computer.

RESTART YOUR COMPUTER

© Microsoft® Corporation

© Microsoft® Corporation

1 Hold down the ⊞ key and tap the letter C to display the charms options. The Windows charms appear.

2 Click **Settings**. The Settings panel appears.

3 Click **Power** to display the power options.

4 Click **Restart**.

■ Windows shuts down and then restarts. If you assigned a Windows password, you are prompted to enter it.

Note: If Windows needs to install any updates, it does so before restarting Windows.

CHAPTER 3

Useful Windows Programs

CREATE STICKY NOTES

You can create electronic sticky notes that are similar to paper sticky notes.

© Microsoft® Corporation

Sticky notes are useful for storing small pieces of information, such as to-do lists, phone numbers, short notes, and reminders. You can create as many sticky notes as you need.

CREATE STICKY NOTES

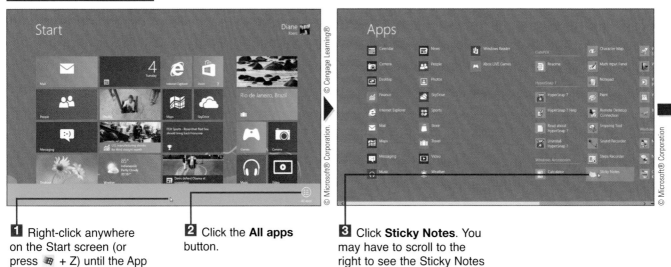

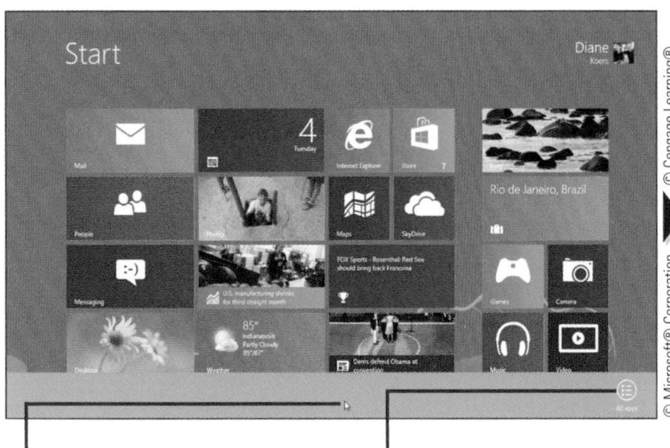

© Microsoft® Corporation. © Cengage Learning®

© Microsoft® Corporation

1 Right-click anywhere on the Start screen (or press ⊞ + Z) until the App bar appears.

2 Click the **All apps** button.

3 Click **Sticky Notes**. You may have to scroll to the right to see the Sticky Notes option.

Can I change the color of a sticky note?

Yes. To change the color of a sticky note, right-click the note you want to change. On the menu that appears, click the color you want to use for the sticky note: Blue, Green, Pink, Purple, White, or Yellow. The sticky note will appear in the new color.

How do I delete a sticky note?

To delete a sticky note you no longer need, position the ⇖ over the top of the sticky note and then click ×. In the confirmation dialog box that appears, click Yes to delete the sticky note.

© Microsoft® Corporation

■ A sticky note appears on the desktop.

4 Type the text you want to appear on the sticky note.

■ If you want to create another sticky note, move the ⇖ to the top of the sticky note and then click +.

© Microsoft® Corporation

MOVE A STICKY NOTE

1 To move a sticky note, position the ⇖ over the top of the sticky note.

2 Drag the sticky note to a new location on your desktop.

USE THE CALCULATOR

Windows provides a calculator that you can use to perform calculations.

You can use the Calculator to perform the same calculations you would perform on a handheld calculator.

USE THE CALCULATOR

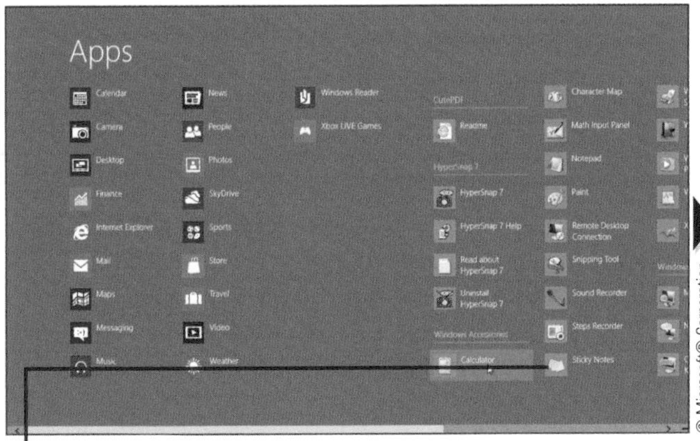

1 Right-click anywhere on the Start screen (or press ⊞ + Z) until the App bar appears.

2 Click the **All Apps** button.

3 Click **Calculator**.

■ The Calculator window appears on the desktop.

Note: If you don't see the Calculator, scroll to the right side of the screen to view more apps.

4 To enter information into the Calculator, click each button as you would press the buttons on a handheld calculator. You can also use the keys on your keyboard to enter information.

■ This area displays the numbers you enter and the result of each calculation.

Can I enter numbers using the keys on the right side of my keyboard?

Yes. To use the number keys on the right side of your keyboard to enter information into the Calculator, make sure the Num Lock feature is on. To activate the Num Lock feature, press the Num Lock key on your keyboard.

What else can the Calculator do?

■ You can use the Calculator to convert values from one unit of measurement to another, such as Celsius to Fahrenheit or pounds to ounces. To do so, click **View** in the Calculator and then click **Unit conversion** on the menu that appears. An area appears where you can perform unit conversions.

■ You can also use the Calculator to calculate mortgage payments, lease payments, and fuel economy. To do so, click **View** in the Calculator and then click **Worksheets** on the menu that appears. Click the worksheet you want to use, and an area appears for you to perform the calculation.

*Note: To return to the basic view of the Calculator, click **View** and then click **Basic**.*

5 To change to a different type of calculator, click **View**.

6 Click the type of calculator you want to use.

■ The calculator you selected appears.

*Note: To return to the Standard calculator, repeat steps **4** and **5**, selecting **Standard** in step **5**.*

7 When you finish using the Calculator, click to close the Calculator window.

WRITE WITH WORDPAD

You can use WordPad to create and edit documents, such as letters and memos.

If you need more advanced features than WordPad provides, you can obtain a more sophisticated word processing program, such as Microsoft Word.

WRITE WITH WORDPAD

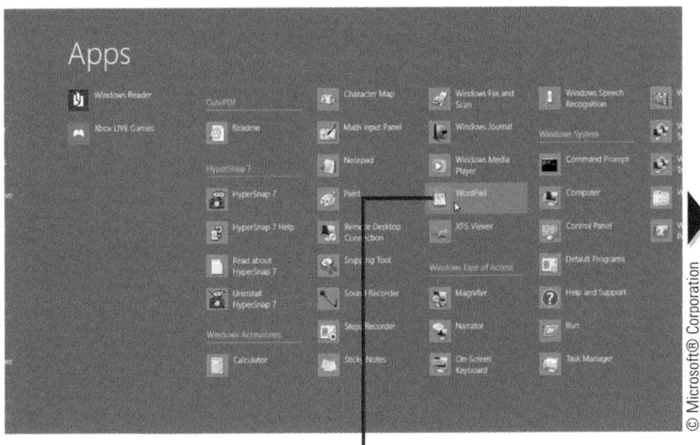

© Microsoft® Corporation

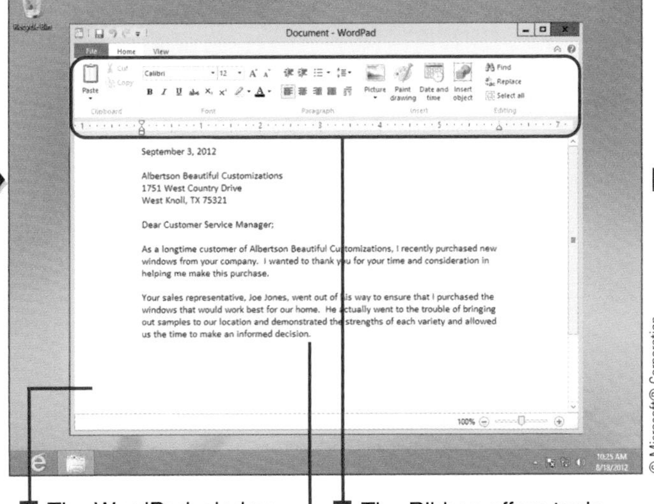

© Microsoft® Corporation

1 Right-click anywhere on the Start screen (or press ⊞ + Z) until the App bar appears.

2 Click the **All apps** button.

3 Click **WordPad**.

Note: If you don't see WordPad, scroll to the right side of the screen to see more apps.

■ The WordPad window appears on the desktop, displaying a blank document.

■ The Ribbon offers tools you can use to perform tasks in WordPad. The Ribbon is organized into groups: the Clipboard, Font, Paragraph, Insert, and Editing groups.

4 Type the text for your document.

How do I format text in a document?

To format text in a document, drag the I across the text to select the text you want to format. You can then use the following tools from the Ribbon to format the text:

Calibri Change the text font.

12 A A Make the text larger or smaller.

B I U **Bold**, *italicize*, or underline the text.

Highlight the text with a color.

A Change the text color.

How do I open a document I saved?

To open a document you saved, click the **File** tab. From the menu that appears, click the document you want to open from the Recent documents list. If the document you want does not appear in the Recent documents, click **Open**. In the Open dialog box, click the document you want to open and then click **Open**.

Note: If you are currently working with a document, make sure you save the document before opening another one.

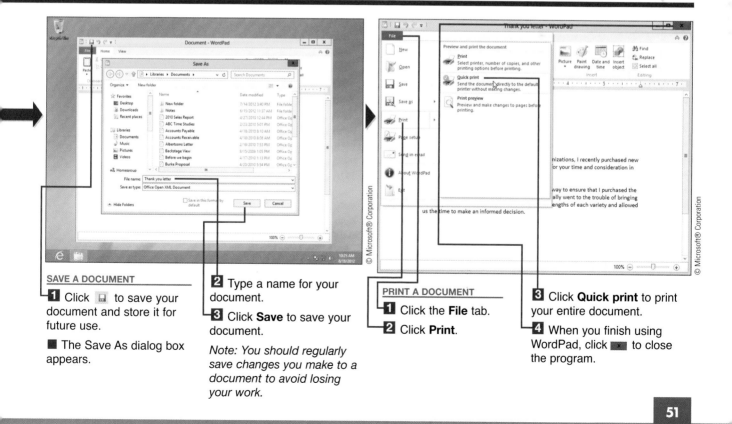

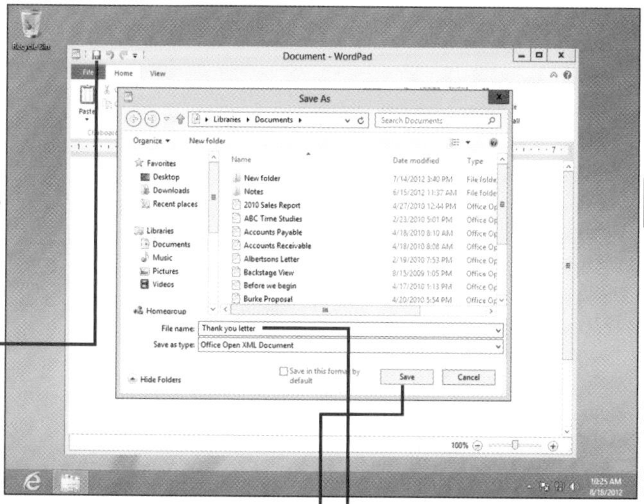

SAVE A DOCUMENT

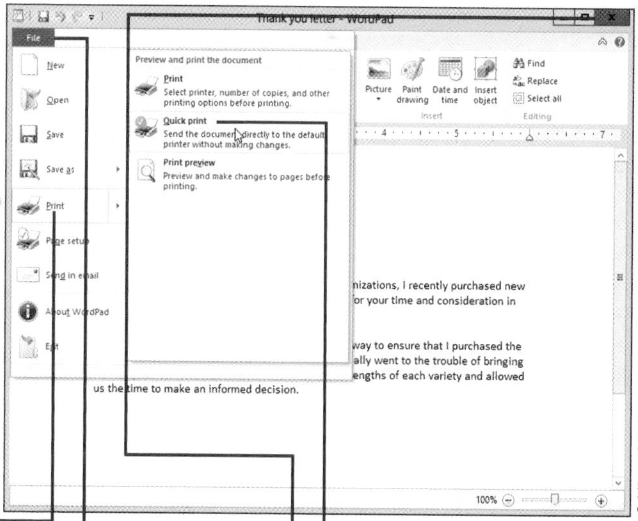

1 Click the Save icon to save your document and store it for future use.

■ The Save As dialog box appears.

2 Type a name for your document.

3 Click **Save** to save your document.

Note: You should regularly save changes you make to a document to avoid losing your work.

PRINT A DOCUMENT

1 Click the **File** tab.

2 Click **Print**.

3 Click **Quick print** to print your entire document.

4 When you finish using WordPad, click the Close button to close the program.

DRAW WITH PAINT

Paint is a simple program you can use to draw pictures on your computer. You can also use Paint to draw in existing pictures.

If you need more advanced features than Paint provides, you can obtain a more sophisticated drawing program, such as Corel PaintShop Pro.

DRAW WITH PAINT

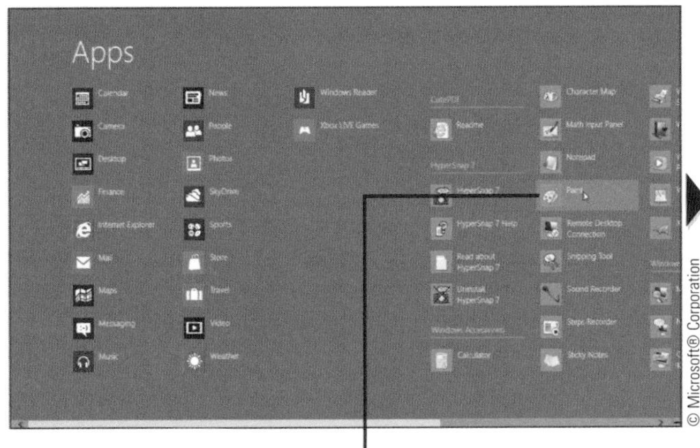

© Microsoft® Corporation

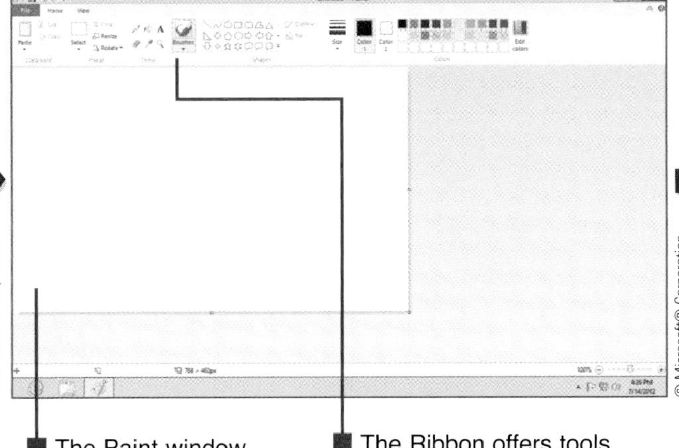

© Microsoft® Corporation

1 Right-click anywhere on the Start screen (or press ⊞ + Z) until the App bar appears.

2 Click the **All apps** button.

3 Click **Paint**.

Note: If you don't see Paint, scroll to the right side of the screen to see more apps.

■ The Paint window appears.

■ The Ribbon offers tools you can use to perform tasks in Paint. The Ribbon is organized into groups: the Clipboard, Image, Tools, Shapes, and Colors groups.

Can I fill an area with color?

Yes. You can fill a shape or your entire drawing with color. Click the tool and then click the color you want to use. Then click the inside the shape you want to fill with color. If you want to fill your entire drawing with color, click a blank area in your drawing.

Can I cancel a change I made?

Yes. Paint remembers the changes you make to a drawing until you close it. If you regret a change, you can click the Undo button at the top-left corner of the Paint window to cancel the last change you made. You can click the Undo button repeatedly to cancel previous changes you made.

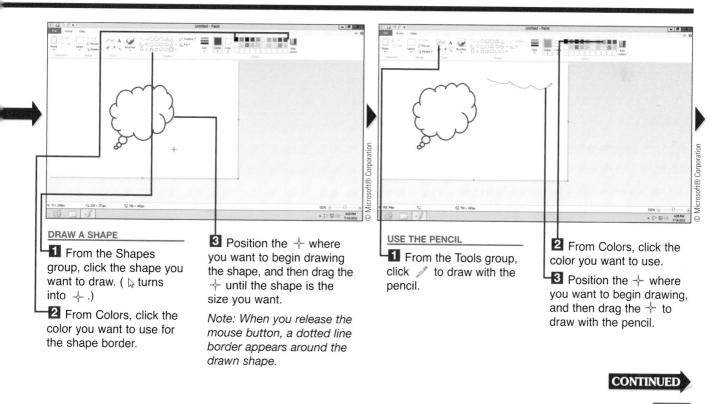

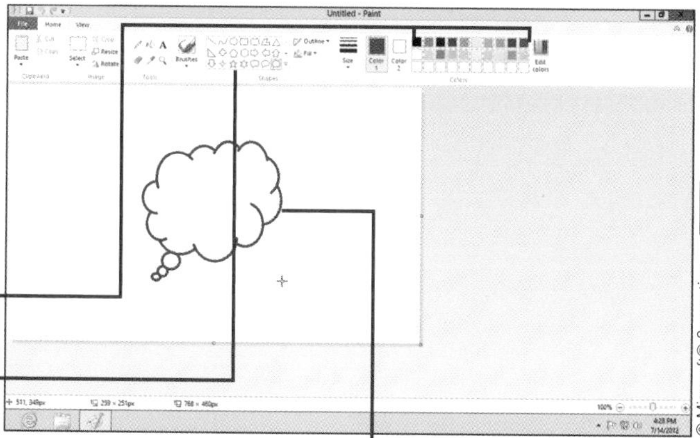

© Microsoft® Corporation

DRAW A SHAPE

1 From the Shapes group, click the shape you want to draw. (turns into .)

2 From Colors, click the color you want to use for the shape border.

3 Position the where you want to begin drawing the shape, and then drag the until the shape is the size you want.

Note: When you release the mouse button, a dotted line border appears around the drawn shape.

© Microsoft® Corporation

USE THE PENCIL

1 From the Tools group, click to draw with the pencil.

2 From Colors, click the color you want to use.

3 Position the where you want to begin drawing, and then drag the to draw with the pencil.

CONTINUED

DRAW WITH PAINT (CONTINUED)

Create the different looks you want for your drawing by using the various tools provided.

Tools included with Paint are the Pencil, Brush, Fill with Color, Text, and Eraser.

You also get seven different brush styles you can use, including a standard brush, a calligraphy brush, and a watercolor brush.

DRAW WITH PAINT (CONTINUED)

USE A BRUSH

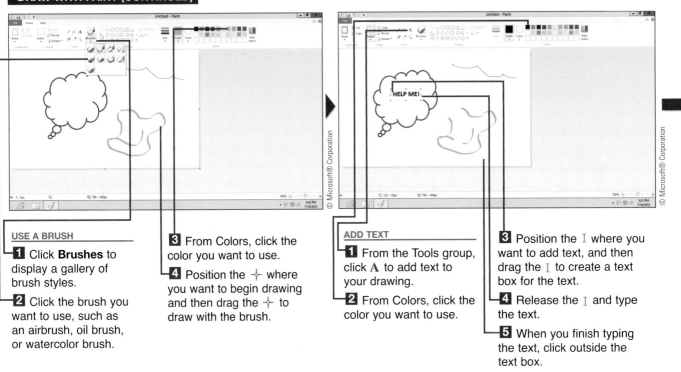

1 Click **Brushes** to display a gallery of brush styles.

2 Click the brush you want to use, such as an airbrush, oil brush, or watercolor brush.

3 From Colors, click the color you want to use.

4 Position the + where you want to begin drawing and then drag the + to draw with the brush.

ADD TEXT

1 From the Tools group, click **A** to add text to your drawing.

2 From Colors, click the color you want to use.

3 Position the I where you want to add text, and then drag the I to create a text box for the text.

4 Release the I and type the text.

5 When you finish typing the text, click outside the text box.

How do I print a drawing?

If you want to print your drawing, click the **File** tab, and then click **Print**. Click **Quick print**, and then from the Print dialog box that appears, click **Print** to print your drawing. Before you print your drawing, make sure your printer is turned on and contains paper.

How do I open a drawing I saved?

To open a drawing you saved, click the **File** tab. From the menu that appears, click the drawing you want to open from the Recent pictures list. If the drawing you want does not appear in the Recent pictures list, click **Open**. In the Open dialog box, click the drawing you want to open, and then click **Open**.

Note: If you are currently working with a drawing, make sure you save the drawing before opening another one.

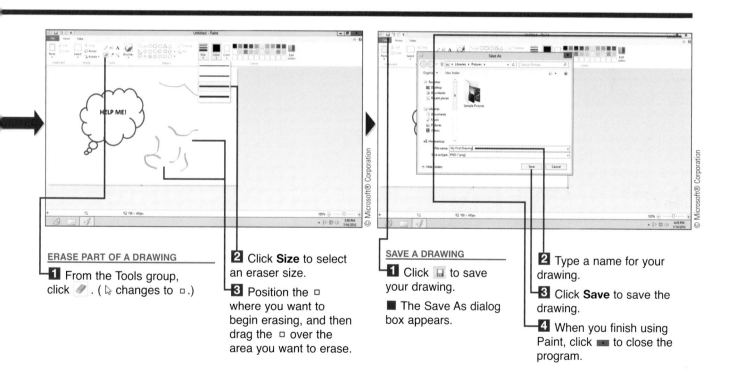

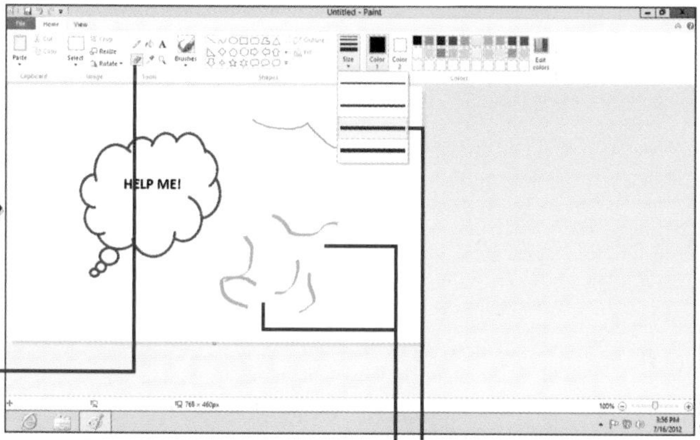

ERASE PART OF A DRAWING

1 From the Tools group, click . (changes to .)

2 Click **Size** to select an eraser size.

3 Position the where you want to begin erasing, and then drag the over the area you want to erase.

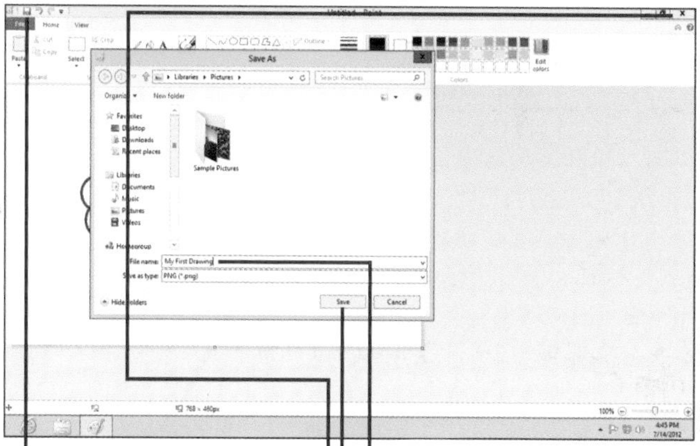

SAVE A DRAWING

1 Click to save your drawing.

■ The Save As dialog box appears.

2 Type a name for your drawing.

3 Click **Save** to save the drawing.

4 When you finish using Paint, click to close the program.

SCHEDULE WITH THE CALENDAR

Make your plans with the Windows Calendar. You can schedule appointments for a specific time, or you can create an all-day event.

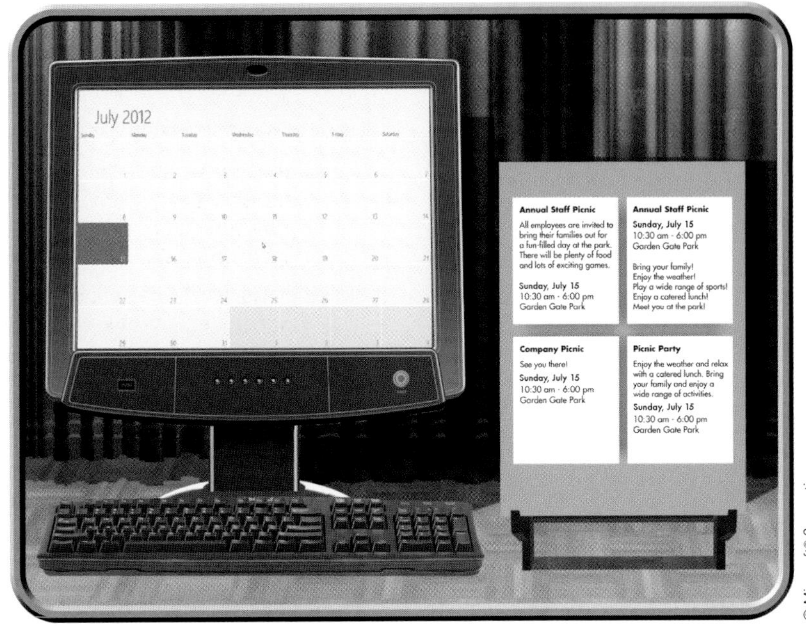

© Microsoft® Corporation

Upcoming appointments appear on the Start screen in the Calendar.

SCHEDULE WITH THE CALENDAR

© Cengage Learning® © Microsoft® Corporation.

© Microsoft® Corporation

1 From the Start screen, click Calendar.

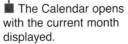

■ The Calendar opens with the current month displayed.

2 Click the date on which you want to create an appointment.

Instead of viewing the entire month, can I view the calendar in different increments?

Yes. You can view the calendar by the week or by two days at a time. Right-click anywhere on the Calendar screen, and from the bar that pops up at the bottom of the screen, choose Day, Week, or Month.

How do I view a different time period?

You can scroll to the previous or next month, week, or day. Click ‹ to see the previous dates, or click › to see the upcoming dates.

If you don't see ‹ or ›, click the ↖ anywhere along the top of the calendar.

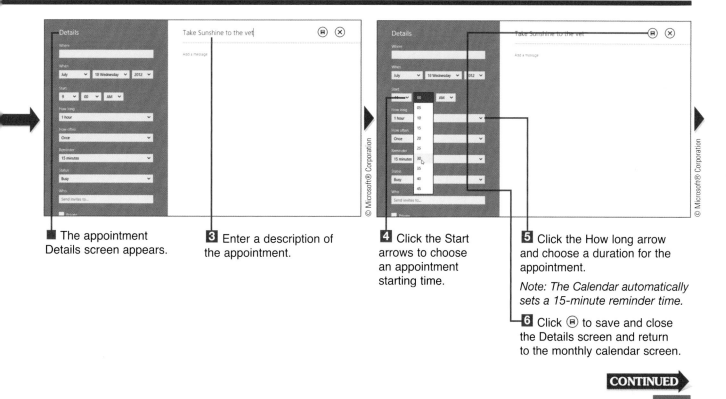

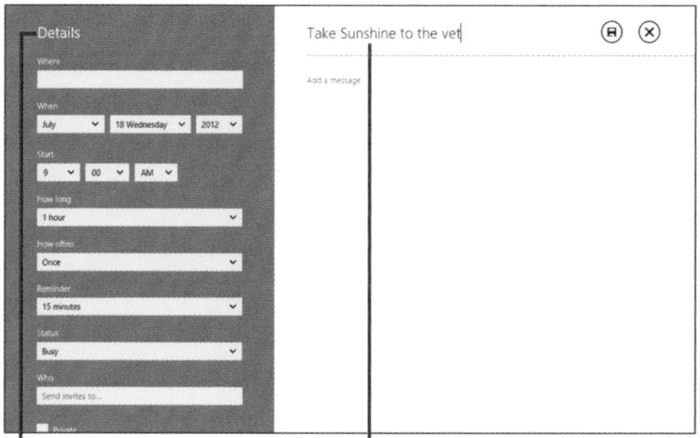

■ The appointment Details screen appears.

3 Enter a description of the appointment.

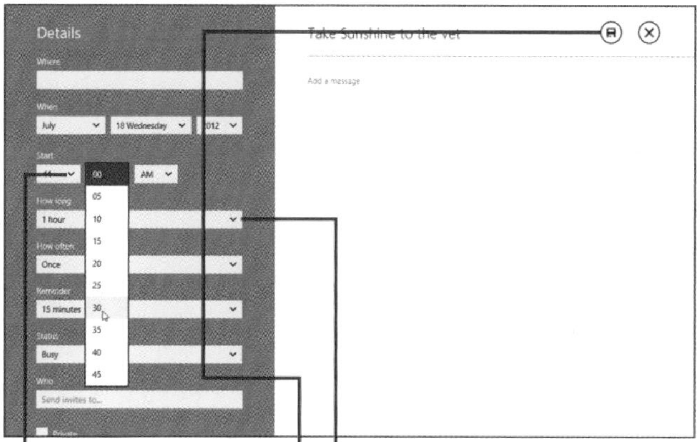

4 Click the Start arrows to choose an appointment starting time.

5 Click the How long arrow and choose a duration for the appointment.

Note: The Calendar automatically sets a 15-minute reminder time.

6 Click (🖫) to save and close the Details screen and return to the monthly calendar screen.

CONTINUED

If needed, you can easily change the appointment by revising the date, time, or location.

© Microsoft® Corporation

You can also delete unwanted appointments.

SCHEDULE WITH THE CALENDAR (CONTINUED)

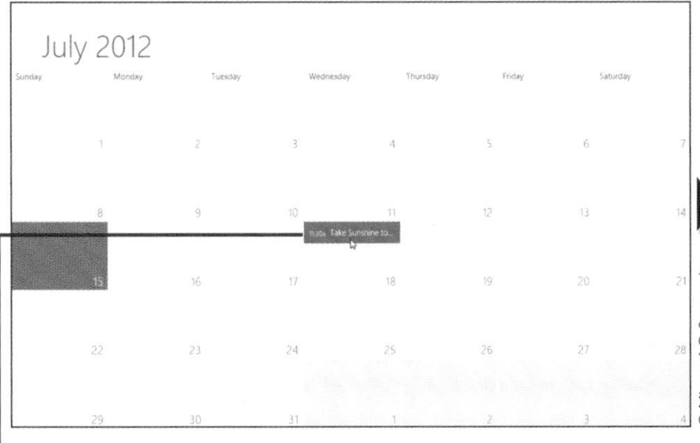

© Microsoft® Corporation

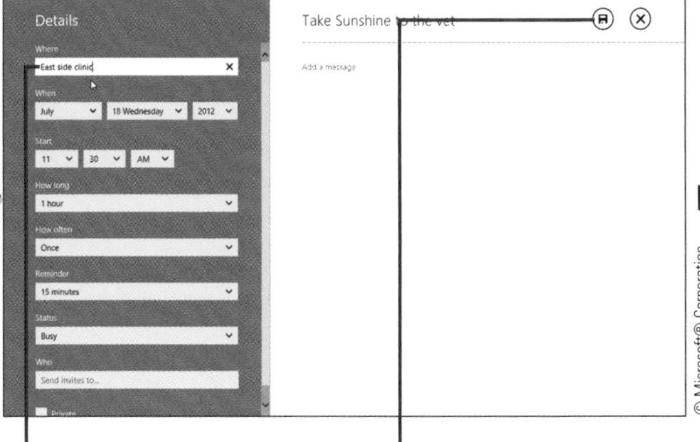

© Microsoft® Corporation

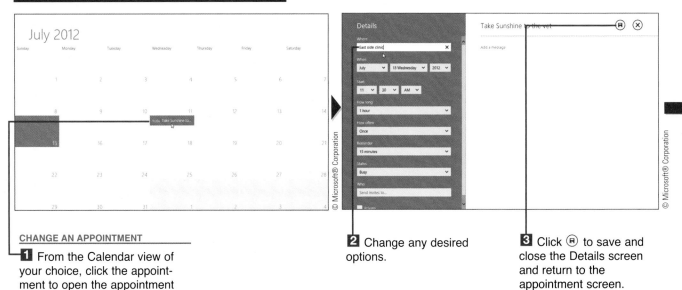

CHANGE AN APPOINTMENT

1 From the Calendar view of your choice, click the appointment to open the appointment Details screen.

2 Change any desired options.

3 Click (🖫) to save and close the Details screen and return to the appointment screen.

Can I set an appointment to last all day?

Yes. From the appointment Details screen, click the How long arrow and choose All Day. The Start time setting becomes unavailable.

© Microsoft® Corporation

Can I set an appointment to recur periodically?

Yes. From the appointment Details screen, click the How often arrow, which displays a menu of options. Choices include Once, Every day, Every weekday, Every week, Every month, and Every year.

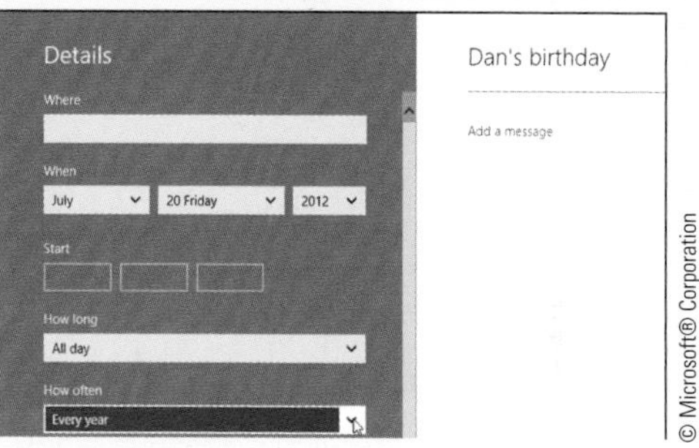

© Microsoft® Corporation

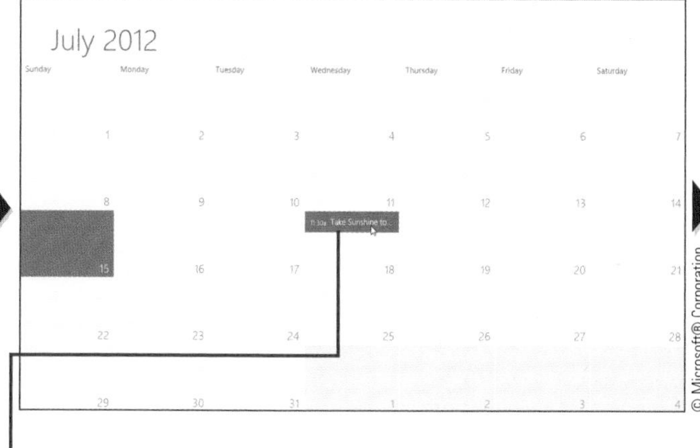

© Microsoft® Corporation

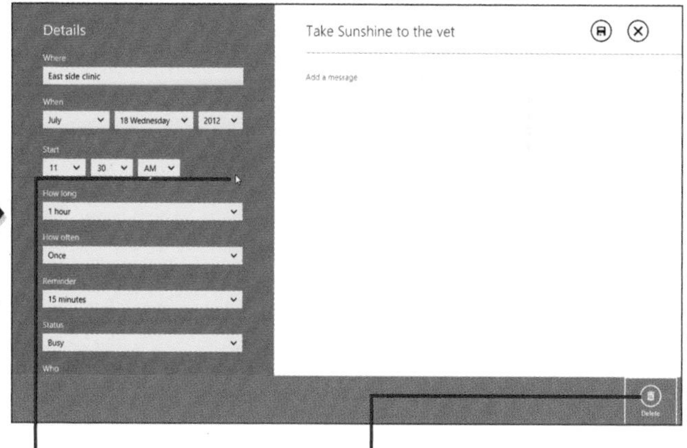

© Microsoft® Corporation

DELETE AN APPOINTMENT

1 From the Calendar view of your choice, click the appointment to open the appointment Details screen.

2 Right-click anywhere in the colored section on the left side of the screen.

3 From the bar that appears at the bottom of the screen, click **Delete**.

4 Click **Delete** again to confirm the deletion.

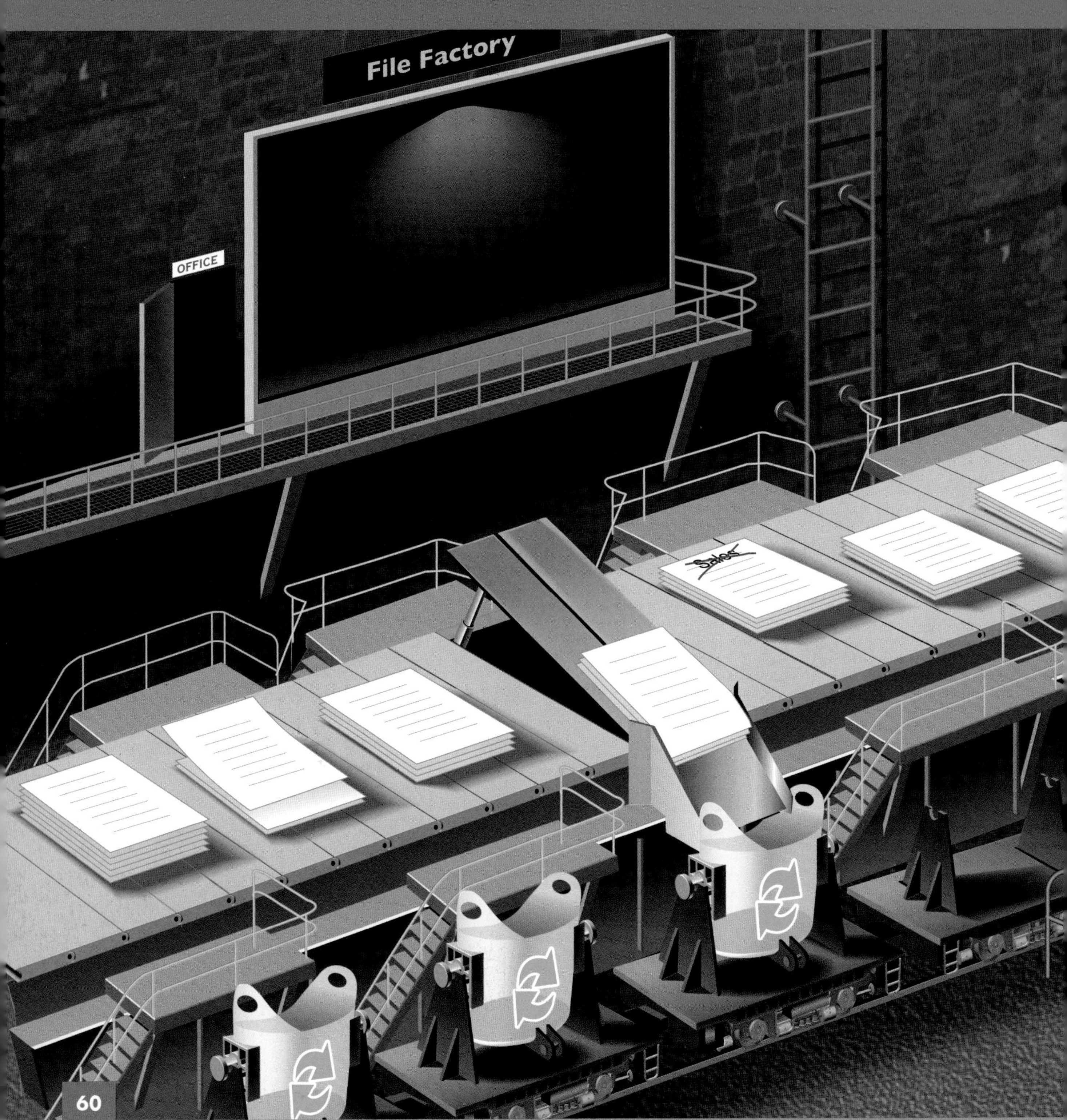
File Factory
OFFICE

Working with Files

VIEW YOUR FILES

Windows provides several default libraries that allow you to easily access and organize the files you use most often. You can view the contents of the libraries at any time.

PRINT PICTURES

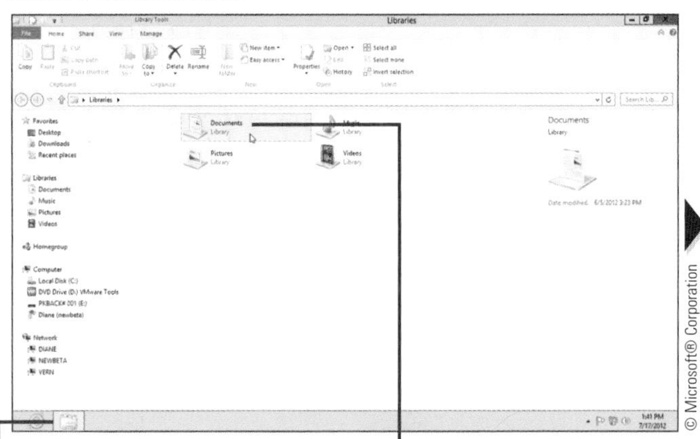

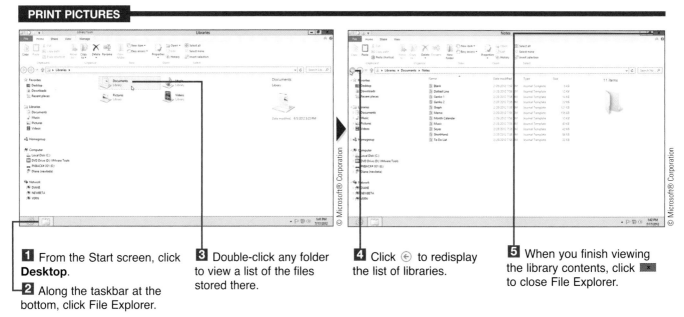

1 From the Start screen, click **Desktop**.

2 Along the taskbar at the bottom, click File Explorer.

Note: Libraries are shortcuts to folders stored on your computer hard drive.

3 Double-click any folder to view a list of the files stored there.

4 Click ⊖ to redisplay the list of libraries.

5 When you finish viewing the library contents, click ✕ to close File Explorer.

DEFAULT WINDOWS LIBRARIES

DOCUMENTS LIBRARY

The Documents library allows you to access your letters, reports, presentations, spreadsheets, and other types of documents. Many programs automatically save documents you create in the Documents library.

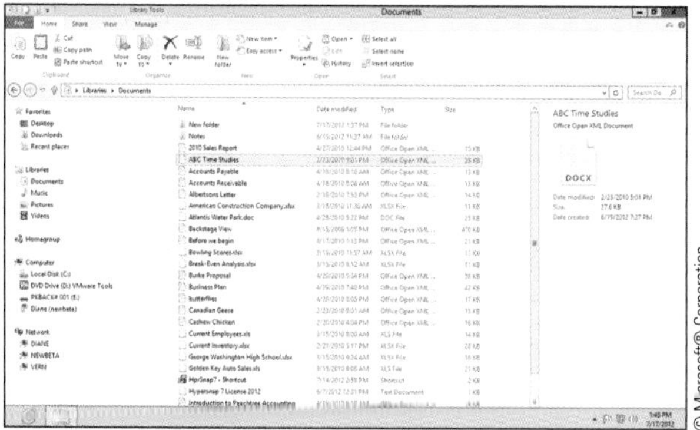

PICTURES LIBRARY

The Pictures library typically contains photographs, images, and graphics files. Many programs automatically save pictures you create or edit in this library. When you transfer pictures from a digital camera to your computer, the pictures appear in the Pictures library.

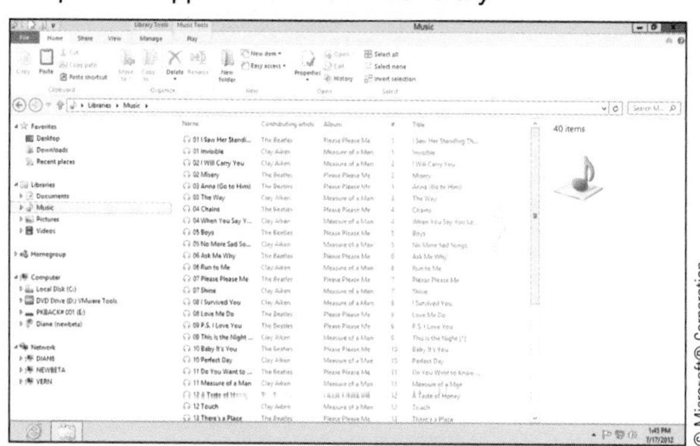

MUSIC LIBRARY

The Music library allows you to access music and other sound files. When you copy songs from a music CD to your computer or download music from the Internet, the music often appears in the Music library.

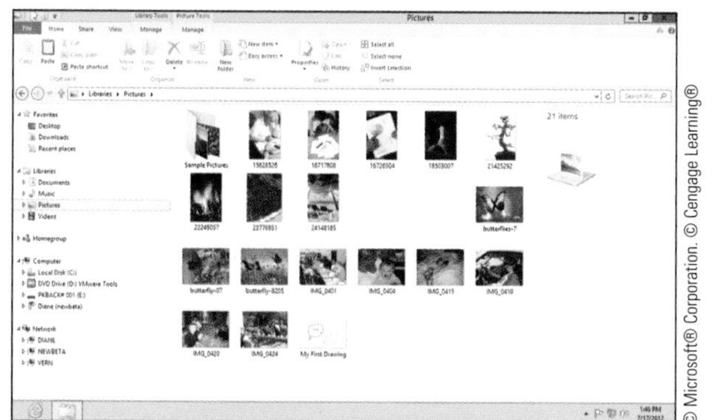

VIDEO LIBRARY

The Video library allows you to access videos. When you download videos from the Internet, the videos often appear in the Video library.

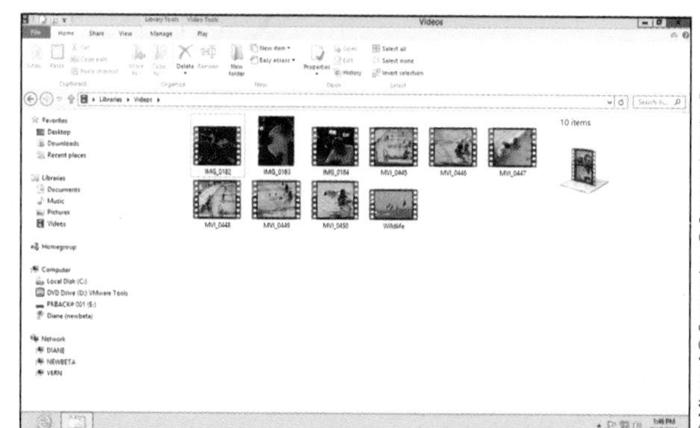

ACCESS DRIVES ON YOUR COMPUTER

You can easily access your hard drive, CD drive, DVD drive, and any other storage devices that are connected to your computer.

ACCESS DRIVES ON YOUR COMPUTER

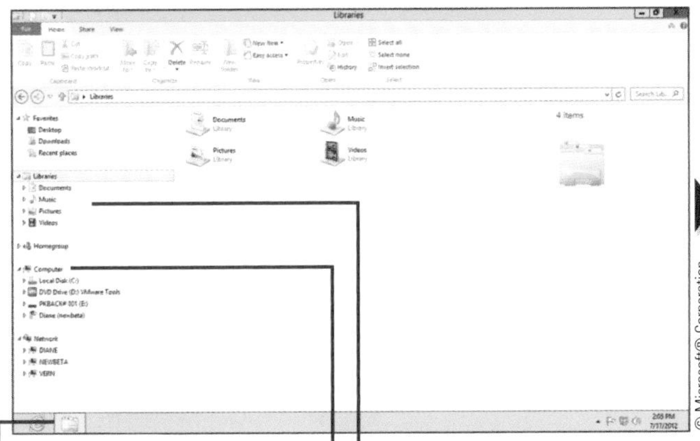

© Microsoft® Corporation

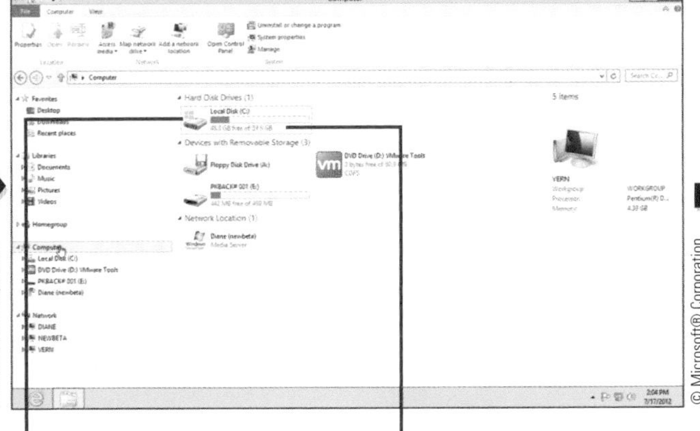

© Microsoft® Corporation

1 From the Start screen, click **Desktop**.

2 Along the taskbar at the bottom, click File Explorer, which opens the Libraries window.

■ This area is called the Navigation pane.

3 From the Navigation pane, click **Computer** to view the drives and other storage devices that are connected to your computer.

■ This area displays an icon for your hard drive, which is the primary storage location for programs and files on your computer.

Note: Some computers may display an icon for more than one hard drive.

■ Windows displays the amount of free space that is available on your hard drive.

Note: Checking the available free space on your hard drive allows you to ensure that your drive is not running out of space.

What is a USB flash drive?

A USB flash drive is a small, lightweight storage device that plugs into a USB port on your computer. You can use a USB flash drive to easily transfer information between computers. USB flash drives are also known as *memory keys*, *pen drives*, *thumb drives*, and *key drives*. See "**Copy Files to a USB Flash Drive**" later in this chapter.

What is a memory card reader?

Most new computers come with a memory card reader, which is a device that reads and records information on memory cards. Memory cards are most commonly used to transfer information between a computer and an external device, such as a digital camera or a video camera.

A memory card reader typically has several slots that enable you to insert memory cards of different sizes from different manufacturers and devices.

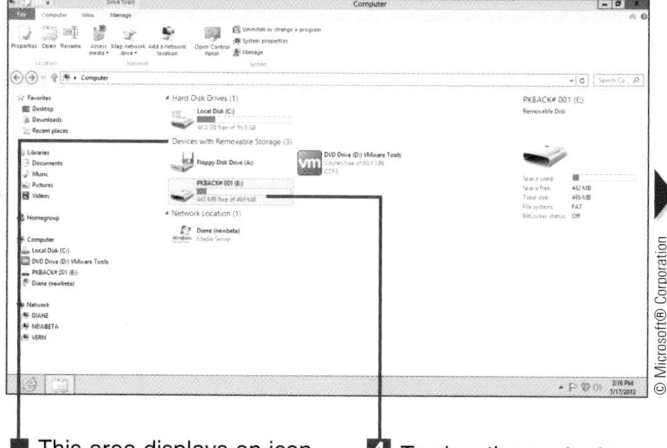

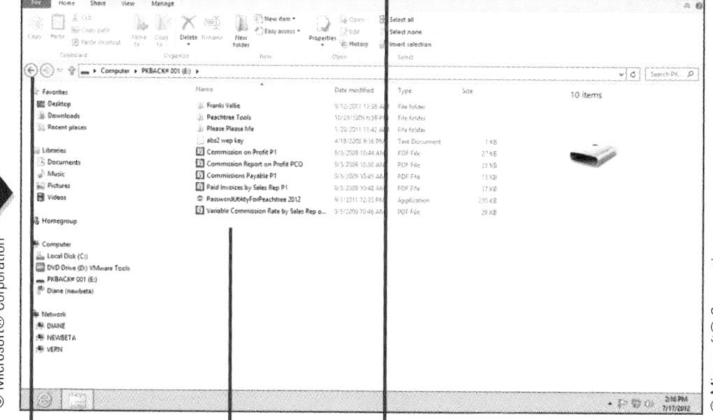

■ This area displays an icon for each storage device using removable storage media that is available on your computer, including CD drives, DVD drives, USB flash drives, and memory card readers.

4 To view the contents of a drive, double-click the drive.

■ The contents of the drive appear.

■ You can click ⊙ to redisplay the previous window.

5 When you finish viewing the drives and other storage devices that are connected to your computer, click ✕ to close the window.

CHANGE VIEW OF FILES

You can change the view of files and folders in a window. The view you select determines the way files and folders appear in the window.

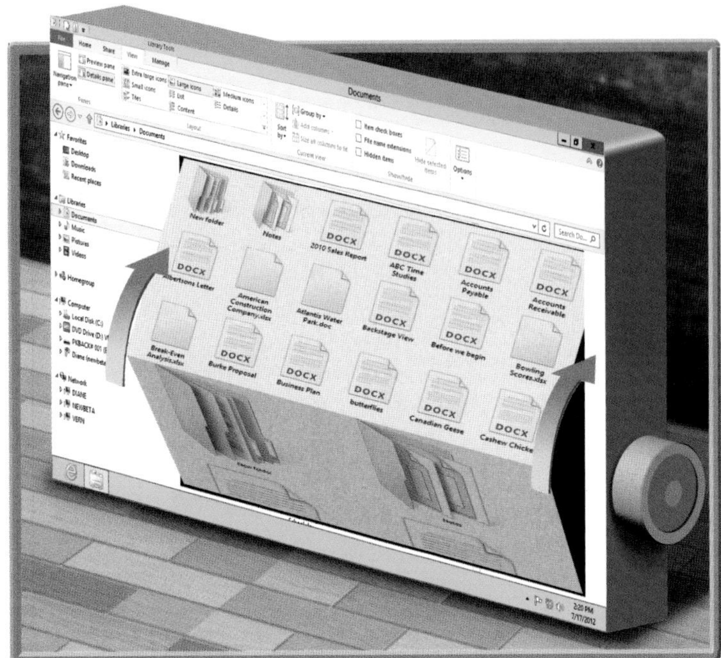

© Microsoft® Corporation

CHANGE VIEW OF FILES

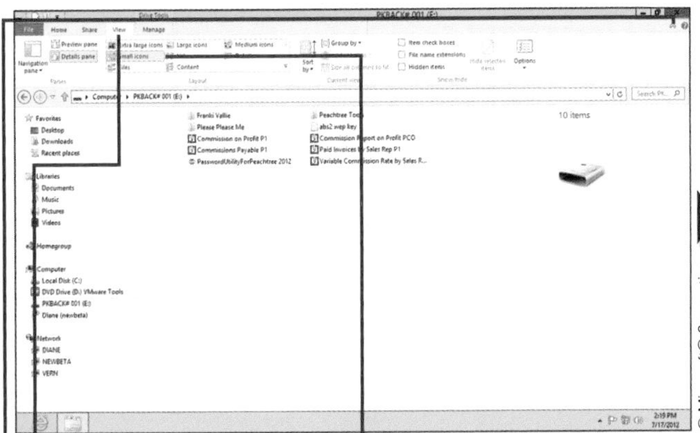

© Microsoft® Corporation

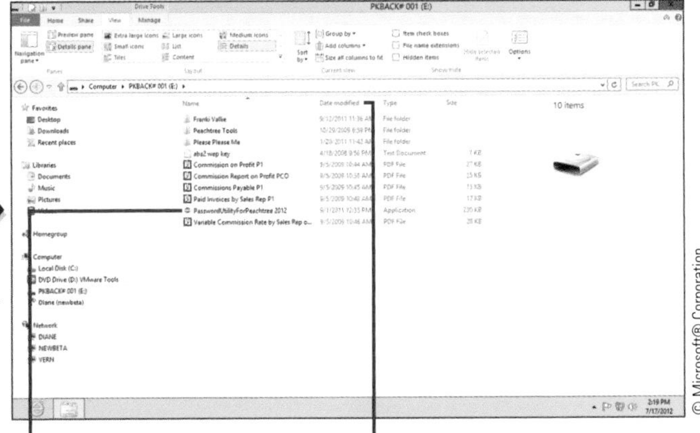

© Microsoft® Corporation

1 From an open folder in the File Explorer, click **View** to display the Ribbon and its options.

■ If you don't see the Ribbon, click ⌄ to display it.

Note: If you do not see eight layout choices, click ▢ to maximize your screen.

2 Click the way you want to view the files and folders in the window.

■ In this example, the files and folders appear in the Details view.

■ To sort the files and folders in the Details view, click the heading for the column you want to use to sort the files and folders. Click the column heading again to sort the files and folders in the reverse order.

THE VIEWS

EXTRA LARGE ICONS

The Extra Large Icons view displays files and folders as extra large icons.

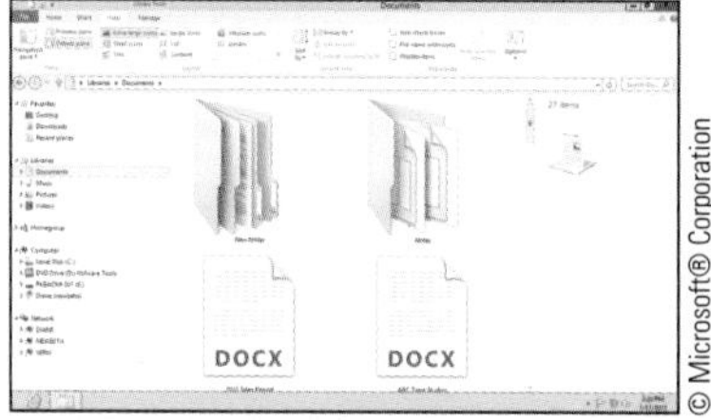

LARGE ICONS

The Large Icons view displays files and folders as large icons.

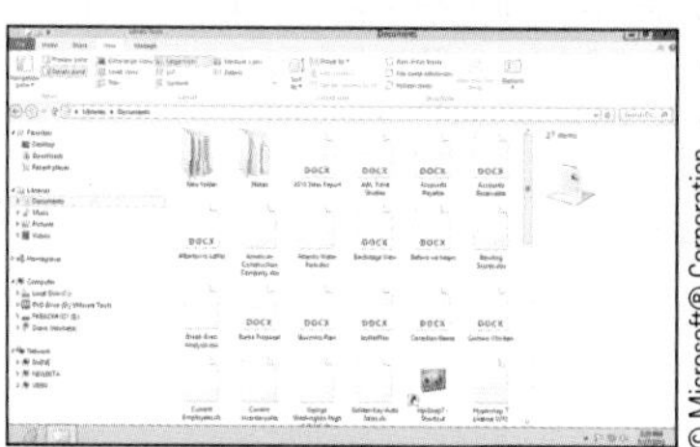

MEDIUM ICONS

The Medium Icons view displays files and folders as medium-sized icons.

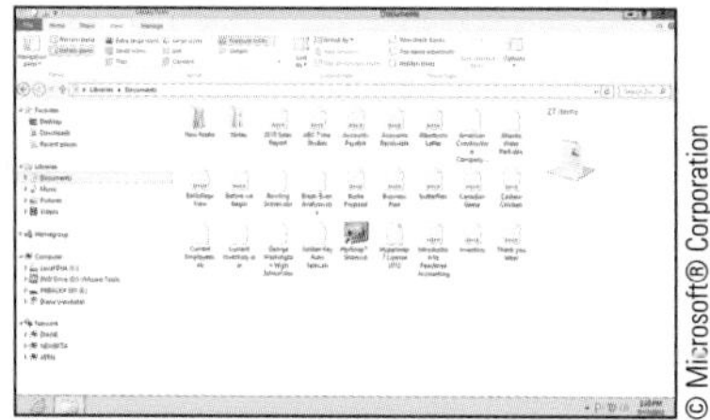

SMALL ICONS

The Small Icons view displays files and folders as small icons.

LIST

The List view displays files and folders as small icons arranged in a list.

DETAILS

The Details view displays files and folders as small icons and provides information about each file and folder.

TILES

The Tiles view displays files and folders as medium-sized icons and provides the file type and size of each file and folder.

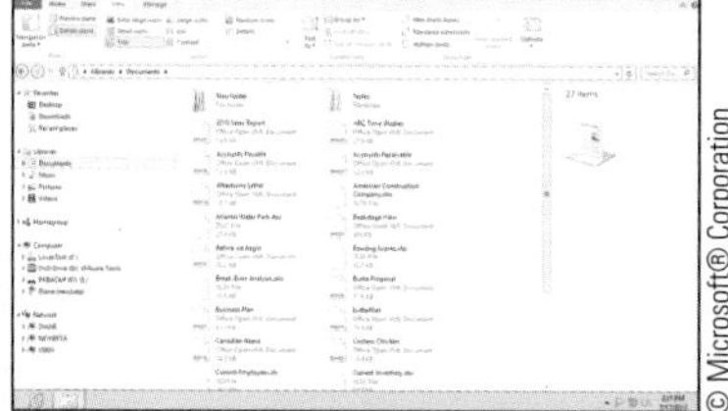

CONTENT

The Content view displays files and folders as medium-sized icons and shows some of the content of each file.

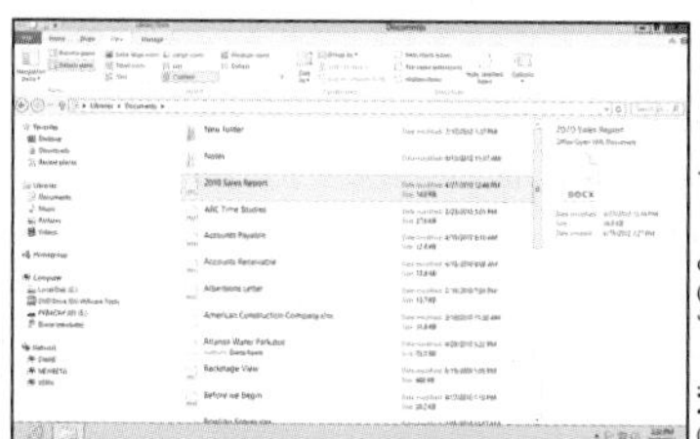

SELECT FILES

Before working with files, you often need to select them. Selected files appear highlighted on your screen.

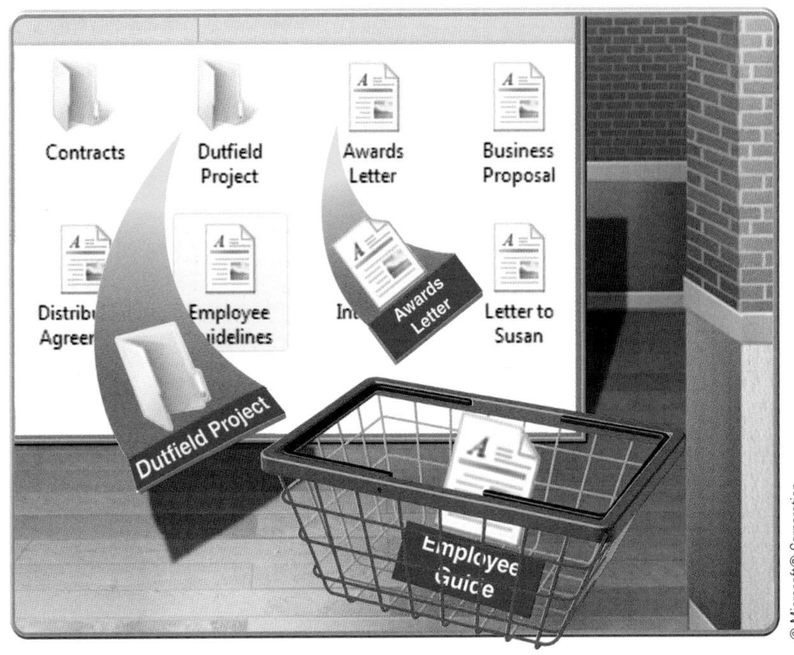

© Microsoft® Corporation

You can select folders the same way you select files. Selecting a folder selects all the files in the folder.

SELECT FILES

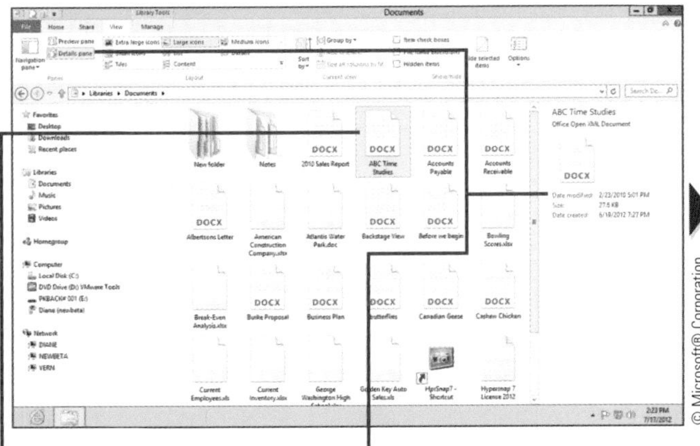
© Microsoft® Corporation

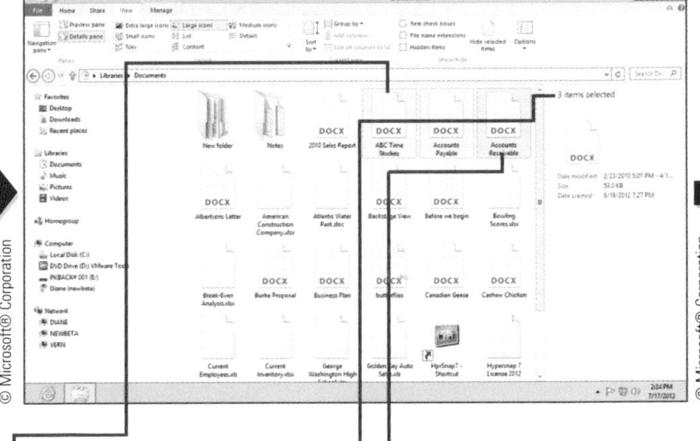
© Microsoft® Corporation

SELECT ONE FILE

1 In File Explorer, from an open folder, or from the desktop, click the file you want to select. The file is highlighted.

■ If you want to view information about the selected file, such as the date and time the file was last changed and the size of the file, click **View**. Then from the Panes group, click **Details pane**.

Note: The information displayed depends on the file type you selected.

SELECT A CONTIGUOUS GROUP OF FILES

1 Click the first file you want to select.

2 Press and hold down the Shift key as you click the last file you want to select.

■ The Details pane displays the number of files you selected.

How do I deselect files?

To deselect all the files in a window, click a blank area in the window.

To deselect one file from a group of selected files, press and hold down the Ctrl key as you click the file you want to deselect.

You can also click **Home** on the Ribbon and, from the Select group, click **Select none**.

Can I select a group of files without using the keyboard?

Yes. To select a group of files without using your keyboard, position the ⇖ slightly to the left of the first file you want to select. Then drag the ⇖ diagonally over the files. While you drag ⇖, Windows highlights the files that will be selected. Release the mouse button when you finish selecting the files.

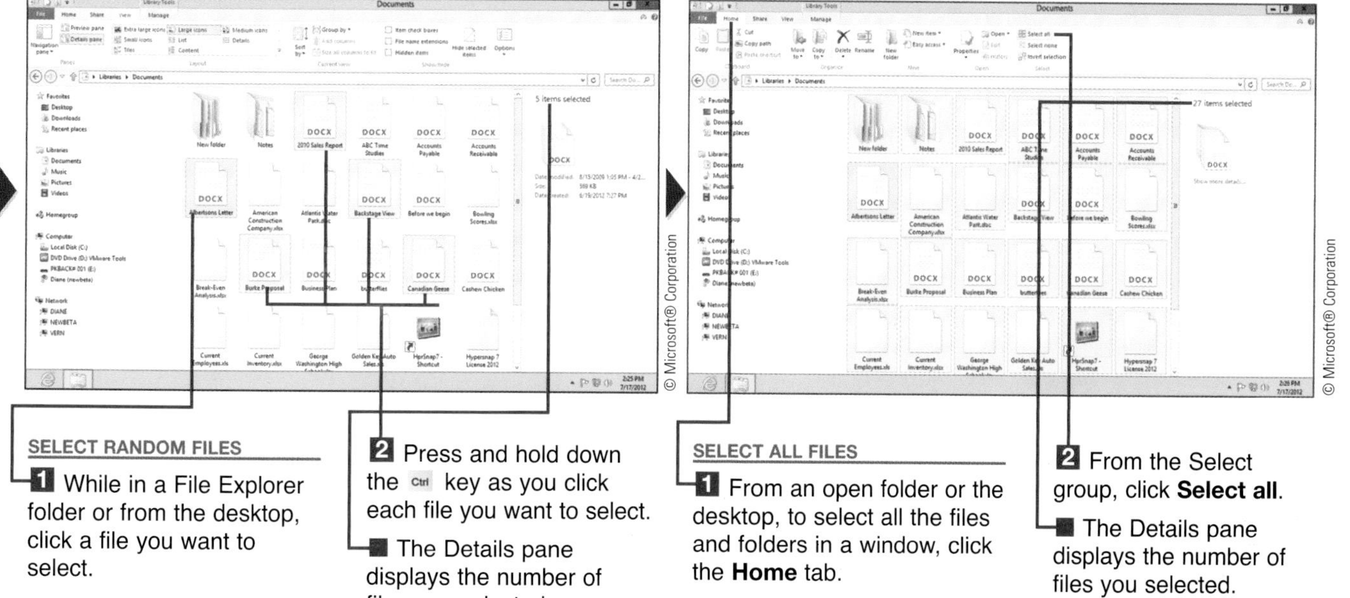

© Microsoft® Corporation

© Microsoft® Corporation

SELECT RANDOM FILES

1 While in a File Explorer folder or from the desktop, click a file you want to select.

2 Press and hold down the Ctrl key as you click each file you want to select.

■ The Details pane displays the number of files you selected.

SELECT ALL FILES

1 From an open folder or the desktop, to select all the files and folders in a window, click the **Home** tab.

2 From the Select group, click **Select all**.

■ The Details pane displays the number of files you selected.

RENAME A FILE

You can rename a file to better describe the contents of the file. Renaming a file can help you more quickly locate the file in the future.

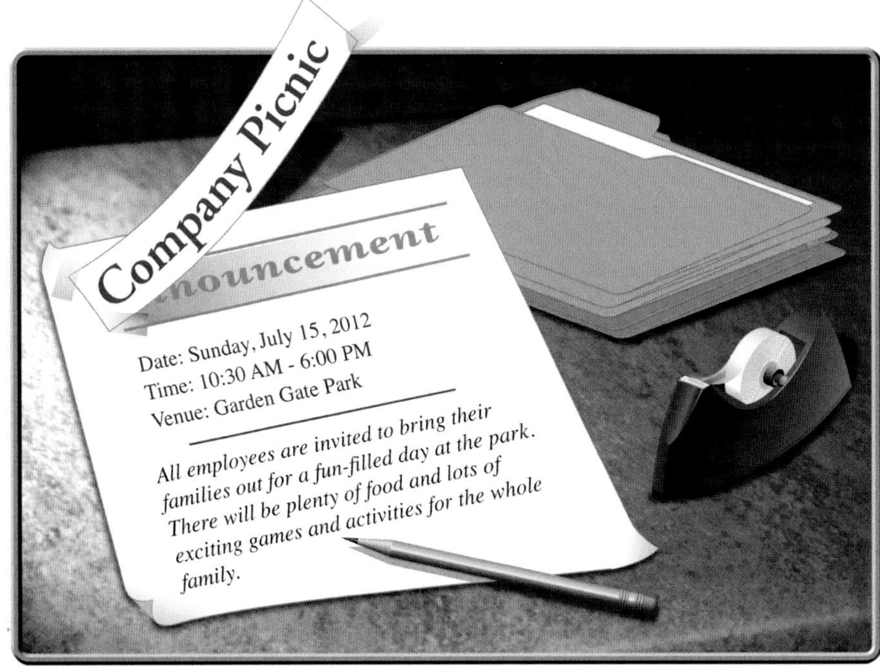

You can rename folders the same way you rename files.

RENAME A FILE

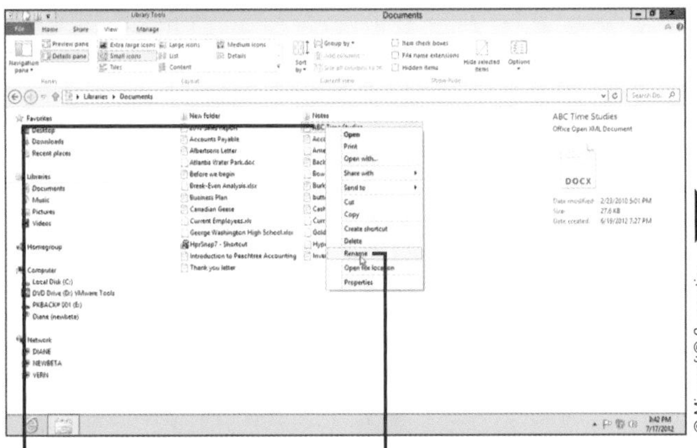

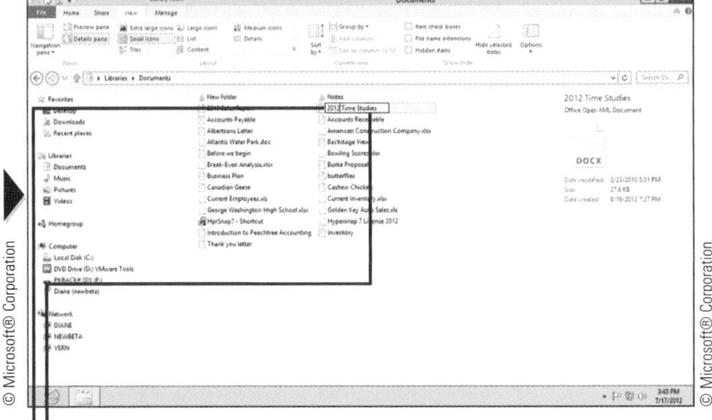

1 While in a File Explorer folder or from the desktop, right-click the file you want to rename. A menu appears.

2 Click **Rename**.

Note: You can also rename a file by clicking the file and then pressing the F2 *key.*

■ A box appears around the filename, and the current filename appears highlighted.

3 Type a new name for the file, and then press Enter.

*Note: A filename cannot contain the \ / : * ? " < > or | characters.*

■ If you change your mind while typing a new filename, you can press Esc to return to the original filename.

OPEN A FILE

You can open a file to display its contents on your screen. Opening a file allows you to review and make changes to the file.

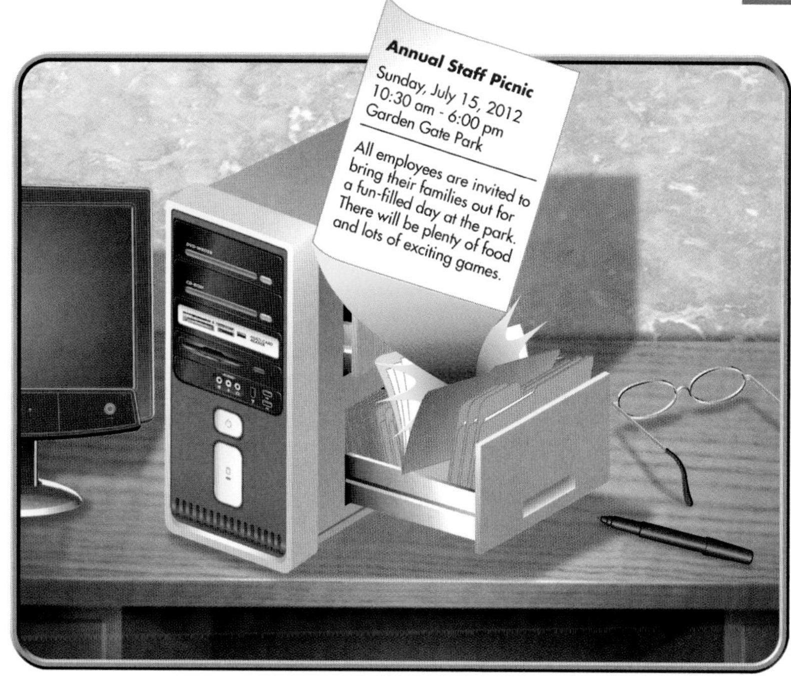

You can open folders the same way you open files.

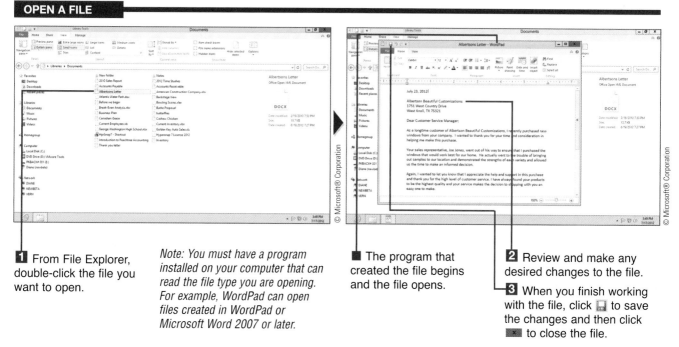

OPEN A FILE

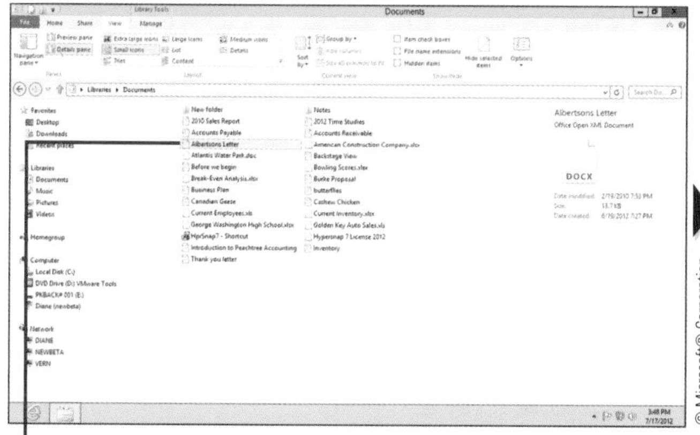

© Microsoft® Corporation

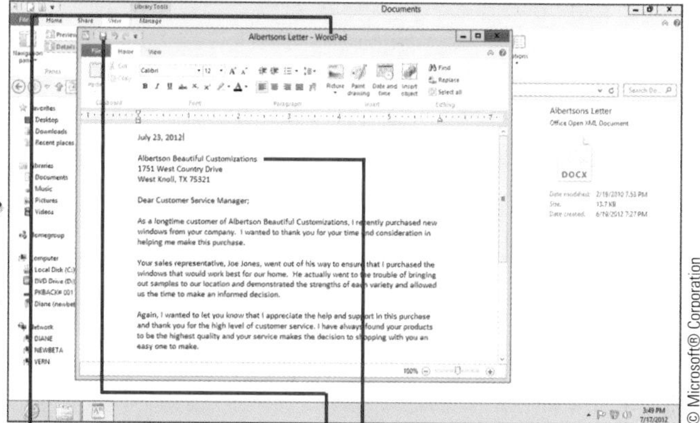

© Microsoft® Corporation

1 From File Explorer, double-click the file you want to open.

Note: You must have a program installed on your computer that can read the file type you are opening. For example, WordPad can open files created in WordPad or Microsoft Word 2007 or later.

■ The program that created the file begins and the file opens.

2 Review and make any desired changes to the file.

3 When you finish working with the file, click the Save icon to save the changes and then click the Close icon to close the file.

CREATE A NEW FILE

You can instantly create, name, and store a new file in the location you want without starting any programs.

Creating a new file without starting any programs allows you to focus on the organization of your files rather than the programs you need to accomplish your tasks.

CREATE A NEW FILE

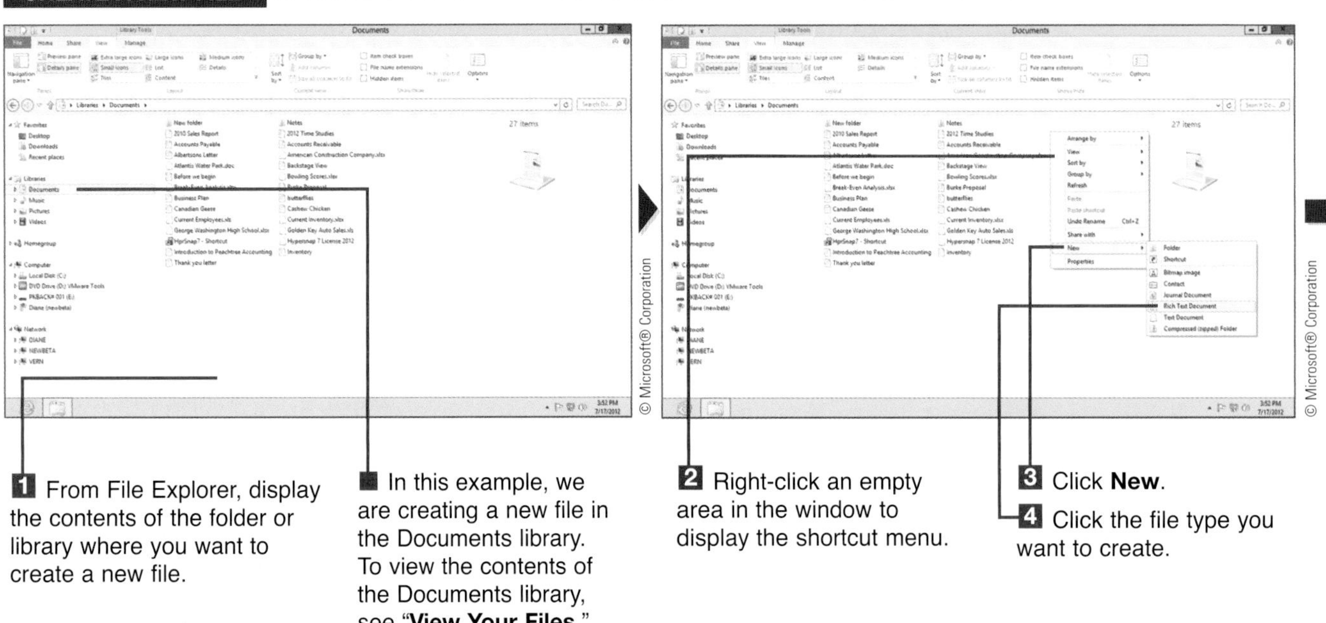

1 From File Explorer, display the contents of the folder or library where you want to create a new file.

■ In this example, we are creating a new file in the Documents library. To view the contents of the Documents library, see "**View Your Files**," earlier in this chapter.

2 Right-click an empty area in the window to display the shortcut menu.

3 Click **New**.

4 Click the file type you want to create.

What types of files can I create?

The types of files you can create depend on the programs installed on your computer. By default, programs installed with Windows enable you to create the following types of files.

File Type	Description
Bitmap image	Creates an image file.
Contact	Creates a contact, which allows you to store a collection of information about a person, such as a person's email address, phone number, and street address.
Journal document	Creates a note you can record in your own handwriting.
Rich text document	Creates a document that can contain formatting, such as bold text and colors. The file opens in Windows WordPad.
Text document	Creates a document that cannot contain formatting. The file opens in Windows Notepad.
Compressed (zipped) folder	Creates a folder that reduces the size of the files it contains to save storage space.

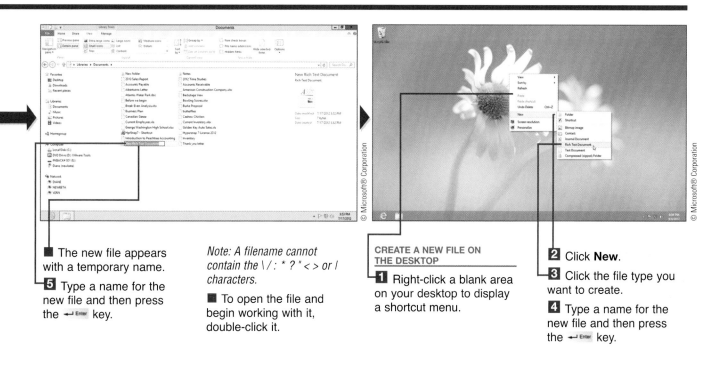

CREATE A NEW FILE ON THE DESKTOP

1 Right-click a blank area on your desktop to display a shortcut menu.

2 Click **New**.

3 Click the file type you want to create.

4 Type a name for the new file and then press the Enter key.

■ The new file appears with a temporary name.

5 Type a name for the new file and then press the Enter key.

*Note: A filename cannot contain the \ / : * ? " < > or | characters.*

■ To open the file and begin working with it, double-click it.

CREATE A NEW FOLDER

You can create a new folder to help you organize the files stored on your computer.

Creating a new folder is useful when you want to keep related files together, such as the files for a particular project.

Creating a new folder is like placing a new folder in a filing cabinet.

CREATE A NEW FOLDER

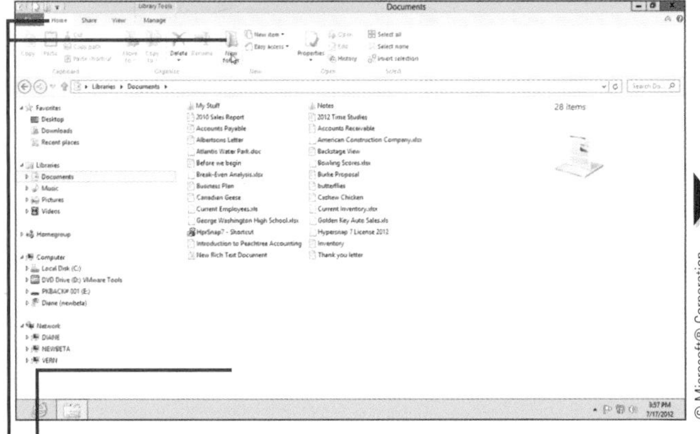

1 From File Explorer, click the folder where you want to place a new folder.

2 From the Home tab, click **New folder**.

*Note: To create a new folder on your desktop, right-click an empty area on the desktop. On the menu that appears, click **New** and then click **Folder**.*

■ The new folder appears displaying a temporary name.

3 Type a name for the new folder, and then press the Enter key.

*Note: Like a filename, a folder name cannot contain the \ / : * ? " < > or | characters.*

DELETE A FILE

You can delete a file you no longer need. The Recycle Bin stores all the files you delete until you empty it.

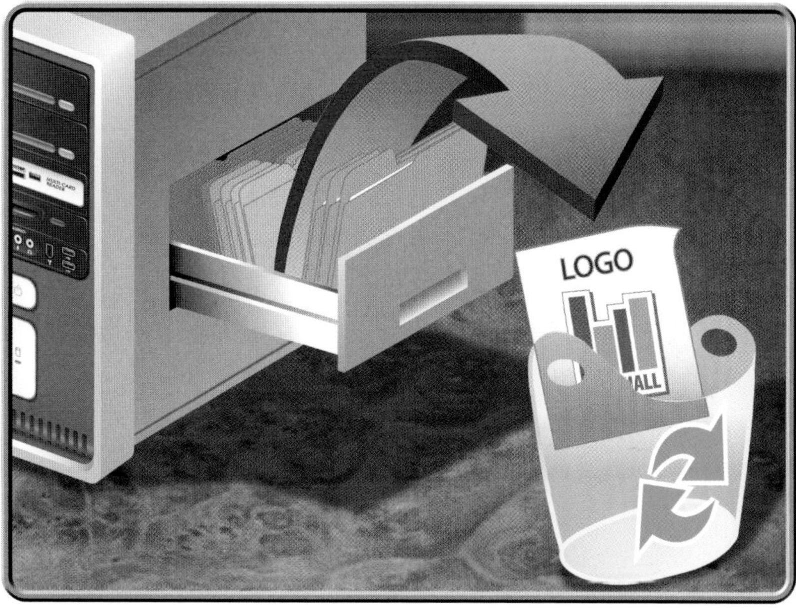

Before you delete a file, make sure you will no longer need it.

You can delete a folder the same way you delete a file. When you delete a folder, all the files in the folder are also deleted.

DELETE A FILE

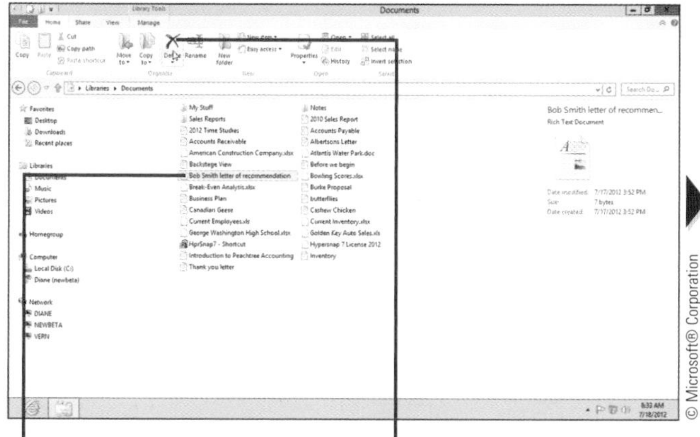

© Microsoft® Corporation

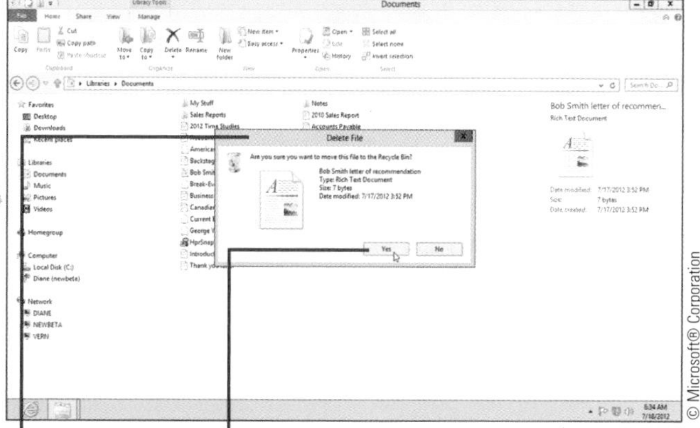

© Microsoft® Corporation

1 From File Explorer, click the file you want to delete.

■ To delete more than one file, select all the files you want to delete and then right-click one of the files. To select multiple files, see "**Select Files**" earlier in this chapter.

2 From the Home tab, in the Organize group, click **Delete**.

Note: You can also delete a file by clicking the file and then pressing the Delete *key.*

■ The Delete File dialog box appears.

3 Click **Yes** to delete the file.

■ The file disappears.

■ Windows places the file in the Recycle Bin in case you later want to restore the file.

Note: To restore a file from the Recycle Bin, see ***"Restore a Deleted File."***

RESTORE A DELETED FILE

Located on the Windows desktop, the Recycle Bin stores all the files you have deleted. You can easily restore any file in the Recycle Bin to its original location on your computer.

© Microsoft® Corporation

You can restore folders the same way you restore files. When you restore a folder, Windows restores all the files in the folder.

You can empty the Recycle Bin to create more free space on your computer. When you empty the Recycle Bin, the files are removed and cannot be restored.

RESTORE A DELETED FILE

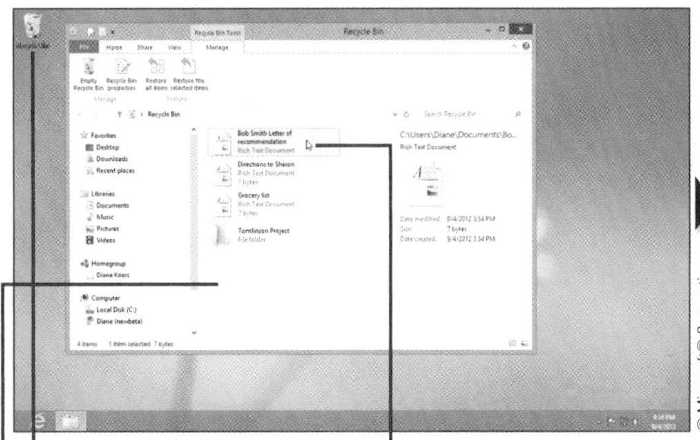

© Microsoft® Corporation

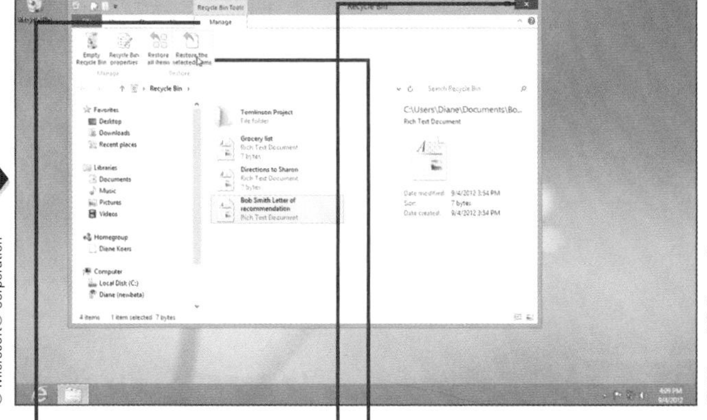

© Microsoft® Corporation

1 From the Windows desktop, double-click **Recycle Bin**.

■ The Recycle Bin window opens, displaying all the files you have deleted.

2 Select the file you want to restore.

■ To restore more than one file, select all the files you want to restore. To select multiple files, see "**Select Files**" earlier in the chapter.

3 Click **Manage** to display the Recycle Bin Tools' Manage tab.

4 From the Restore group, click **Restore the selected items**.

■ The file disappears from the Recycle Bin window and returns to its original location on your computer.

5 Click ✕ to close the Recycle Bin window.

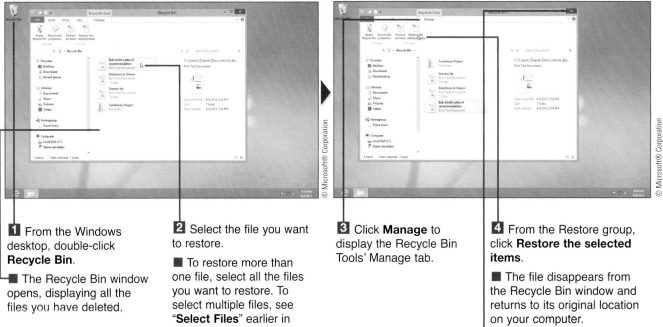

Why is the file I want to restore not in the Recycle Bin?

The Recycle Bin may not store files you delete from a location outside your computer, such as a file you delete from a network folder or a USB flash drive. Files deleted from these locations may be permanently deleted rather than placed in the Recycle Bin. Also, a file can be too big to store in the Recycle Bin; in this case, Windows warns you before deleting the file.

Can I permanently remove a file from the Recycle Bin?

You may want to permanently remove a file from the Recycle Bin, such as a file that contains confidential information. To permanently remove a file from the Recycle Bin, click the file you want to permanently remove in the Recycle Bin window and then press the Delete key. In the confirmation dialog box that appears, click **Yes** to permanently remove the file.

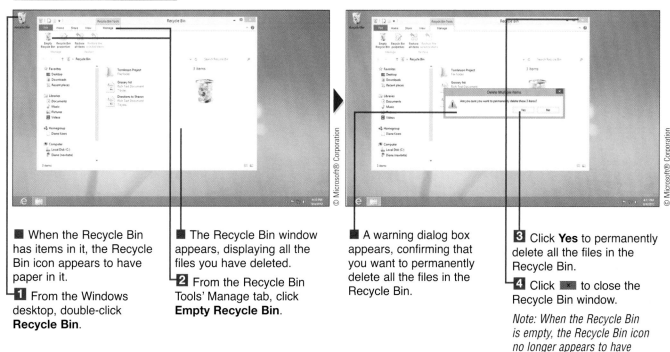

EMPTY THE RECYCLE BIN

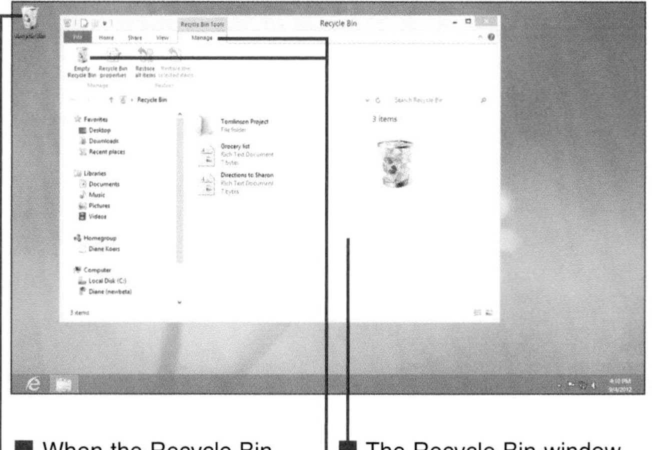

■ When the Recycle Bin has items in it, the Recycle Bin icon appears to have paper in it.

1 From the Windows desktop, double-click **Recycle Bin**.

■ The Recycle Bin window appears, displaying all the files you have deleted.

2 From the Recycle Bin Tools' Manage tab, click **Empty Recycle Bin**.

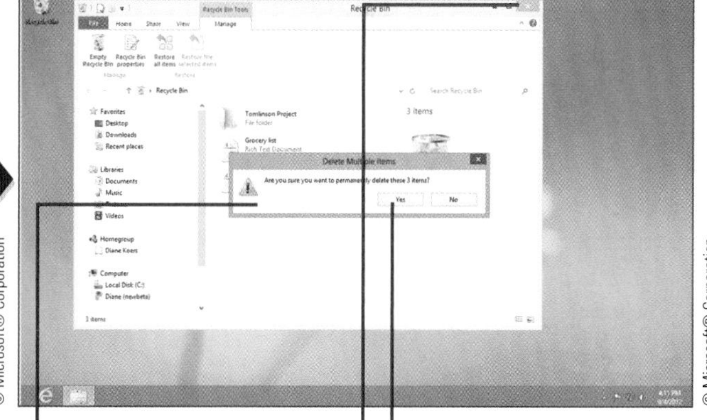

■ A warning dialog box appears, confirming that you want to permanently delete all the files in the Recycle Bin.

3 Click **Yes** to permanently delete all the files in the Recycle Bin.

4 Click ✕ to close the Recycle Bin window.

Note: When the Recycle Bin is empty, the Recycle Bin icon no longer appears to have paper in it.

MOVE OR COPY A FILE

You can move or copy a file to a new location on your computer.

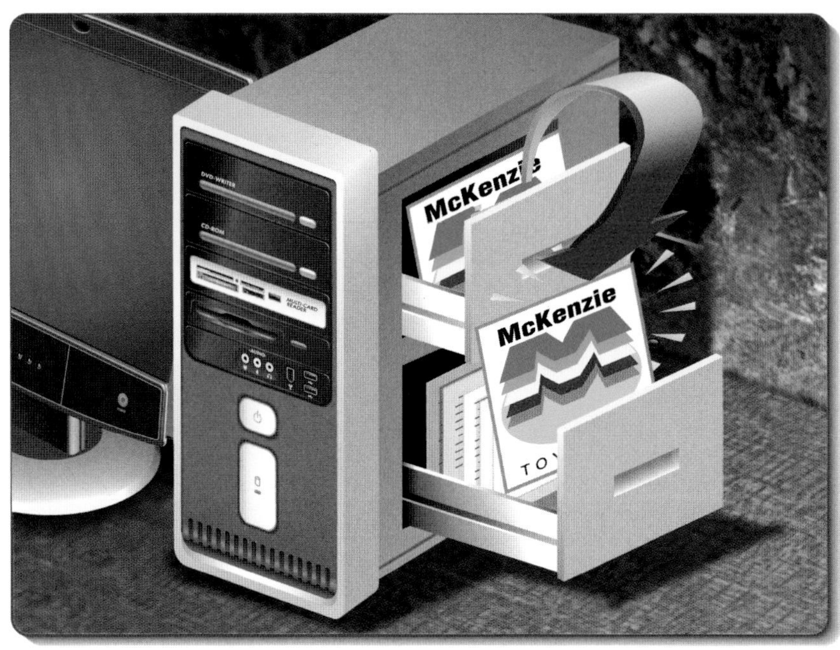

When you move a file, the file disappears from its original location and appears in the new location.

When you copy a file, the file appears in both the original and the new locations.

You can move or copy a folder the same way you move or copy a file. When you move or copy a folder, all the files in the folder are also moved or copied.

MOVE A FILE

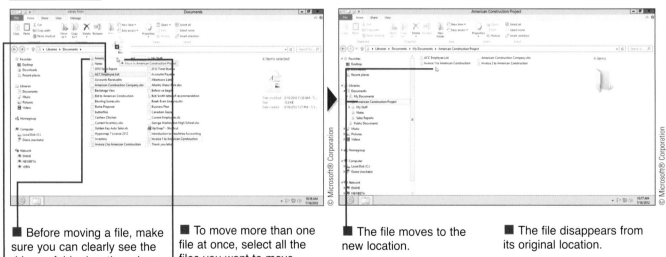

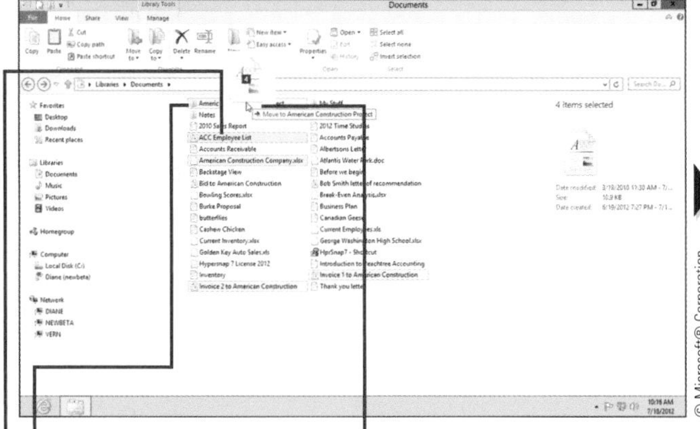

© Microsoft® Corporation

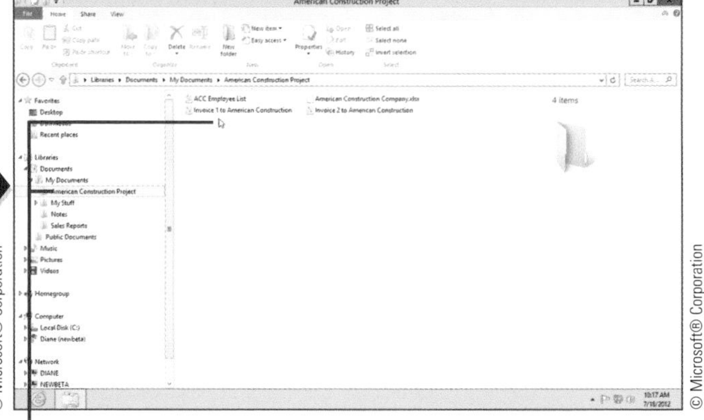

© Microsoft® Corporation

■ Before moving a file, make sure you can clearly see the drive or folder location where you want to move the file.

1 While in File Explorer, position the ⇖ over the file you want to move.

■ To move more than one file at once, select all the files you want to move. Then position the ⇖ over one of the files. To select multiple files, see **"Select Files"** earlier in this chapter.

2 Drag the file to a new location.

■ The file moves to the new location.

■ The file disappears from its original location.

Why would I want to move or copy a file?

You may want to move a file to a different folder to keep related files in one location. For example, you can move all the files for a particular project to the same folder. You may want to copy a file before you make major changes to it. This will give you two copies of the file: the original file and a file that you can change.

How can I make it easier to move or copy a file?

Before you move or copy a file from one window to another, you may want to display the two windows side by side on your screen. This allows you to clearly see the contents of both windows at the same time so you can more easily move or copy a file between the windows. To display two windows side by side, see **Chapter 2.**

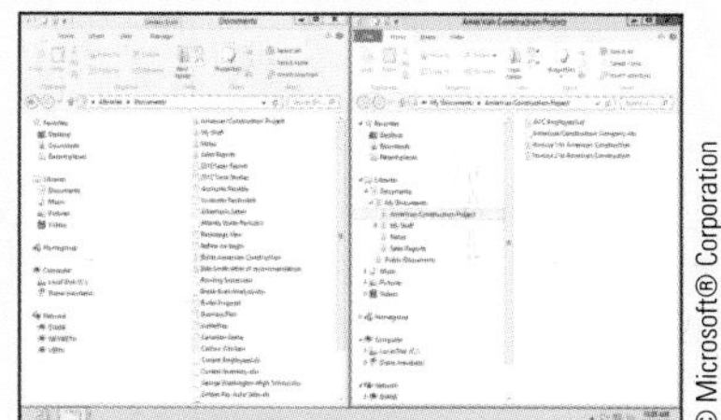

COPY A FILE

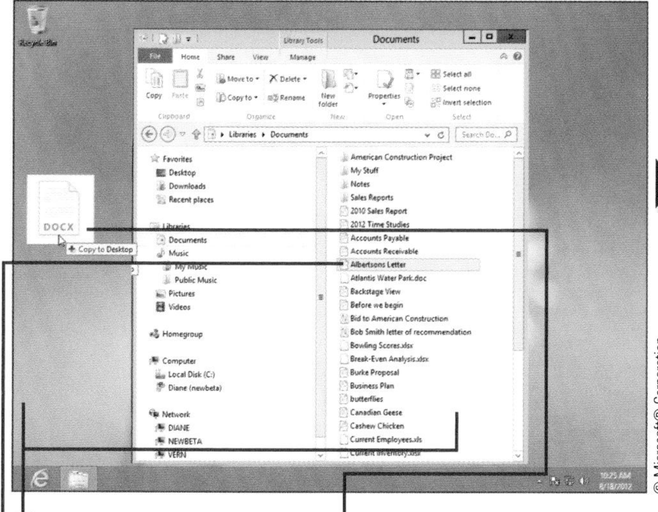

■ Before copying a file, make sure you can clearly see both the file you want to copy and the location where you want to copy the file. You might want to display two windows side by side.

1 Position the ↖ over the file you want to copy.

■ Select all the files you want to copy. Then position the ↖ over one of the files. To select multiple files, see **"Select Files"** earlier in this chapter.

2 Press and hold down the Ctrl key as you drag the file to a new location.

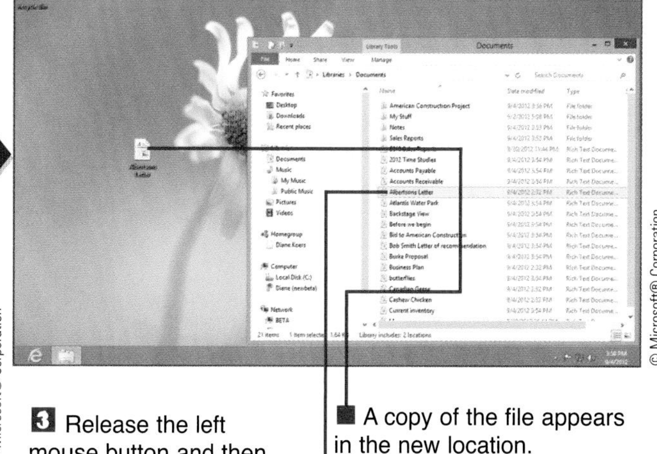

3 Release the left mouse button and then the Ctrl key.

■ A copy of the file appears in the new location.

■ The original file remains in the original location.

SEARCH FOR FILES

If you do not remember where you stored a file on your computer, you can have Windows search for it.

As you create files on your computer, Windows updates an index to keep track of your files. The index is similar to one you would find at the back of a book.

When you want to find a file on your computer, Windows scans the index instead of searching your entire computer. This allows Windows to perform very fast searches.

SEARCH FOR FILES

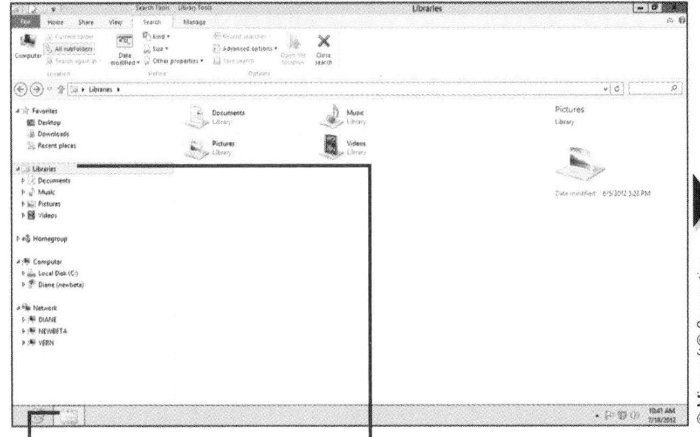

© Microsoft® Corporation

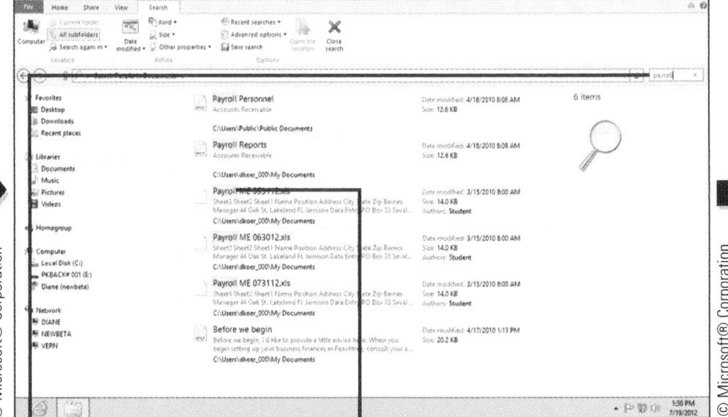

© Microsoft® Corporation

1 From the Windows desktop, click File Explorer to open a File Explorer window.

2 Click **Libraries** if you want to search all libraries, click the name of the individual library or folder in which you want to search, or click **Computer** to search your entire computer.

3 In the Search text box, type the word or phrase for which you want to search.

- You can type all or part of a filename, or a word or phrase contained a file.
- As you type, the names of any matching files appear.

What types of files can Windows search for?

Windows searches your personal files, including the files in your Documents, Pictures, and Music libraries, as well as the files on your desktop. Windows also searches your email messages, your list of favorite web pages, and the programs available on your computer. Because Windows searches the programs on your computer, typing a program name into the search box provides a quick way to find a program.

Is there another way to search for files?

Yes. From the Windows desktop, press F3, which displays the Search panel. In the Search text box, type all or part of a file-name, or a word or phrase contained in a file. Click 🔍. A list of files that match your request appears on the left side. The Apps, Settings, and Files icons display the number of search matches. Click the Apps or Settings icons to view the items in those areas that match your search.

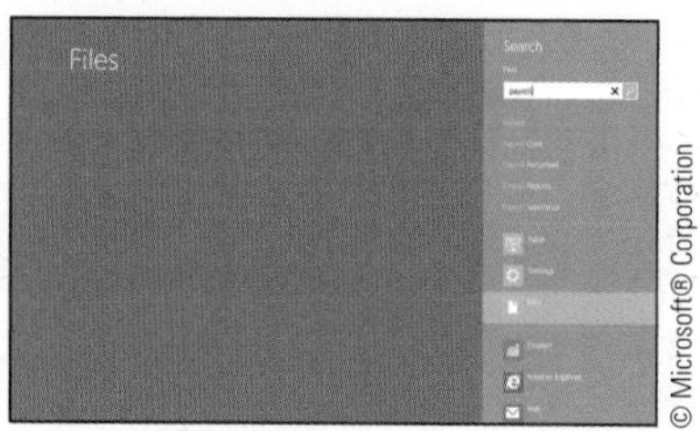

© Microsoft® Corporation

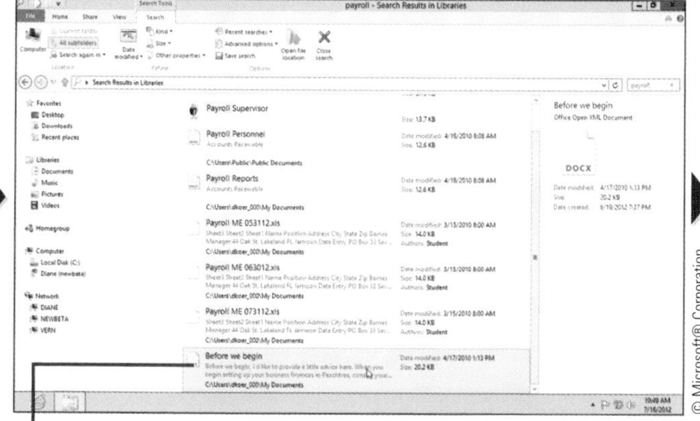

© Microsoft® Corporation

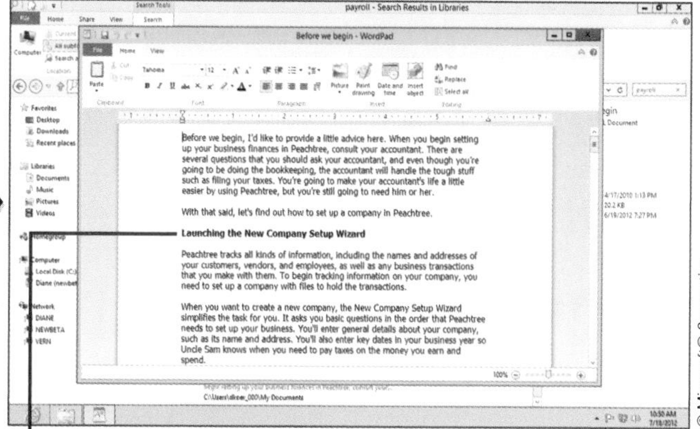

© Microsoft® Corporation

4 If Windows found the file you want to work with, double-click the file to open it.

Note: If you do not want to open a file, click ✕ to close the window.

■ The file you double-clicked opens in the originating program.

ADD A SHORTCUT TO THE DESKTOP

You can add a shortcut to your desktop to provide a quick way of opening a file you regularly use.

© Microsoft® Corporation

A *shortcut* is an icon, usually displayed on your desktop, that leads directly to a program, file, or web page. During installation, many programs offer to place icons on the desktop for you.

ADD A SHORTCUT TO THE DESKTOP

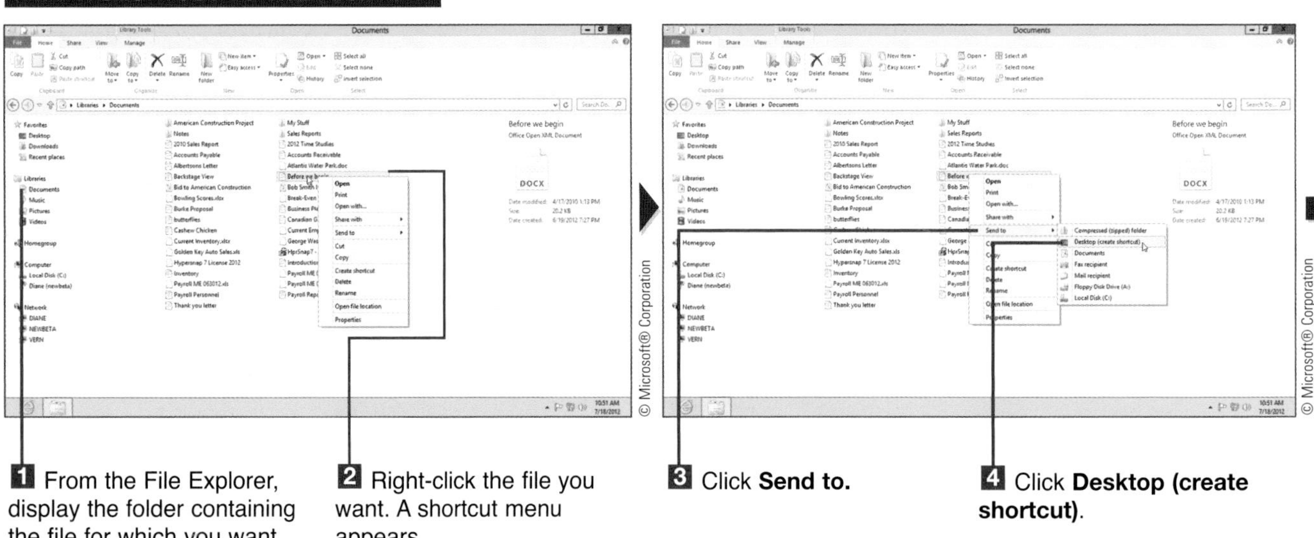

© Microsoft® Corporation

© Microsoft® Corporation

1 From the File Explorer, display the folder containing the file for which you want to create a shortcut.

2 Right-click the file you want. A shortcut menu appears.

3 Click **Send to.**

4 Click **Desktop (create shortcut)**.

How do I rename or delete a shortcut?

You can rename or delete a shortcut the same way you would rename or delete a file. Renaming or deleting a shortcut does not affect the original file.

■ To rename a shortcut, click the shortcut and then press the F2 key. Type a new name for the shortcut and then press the Enter key.

■ To delete a shortcut, click the shortcut and then press the Delete key. In the dialog box that appears, click **Yes** to delete the shortcut.

Can I move a shortcut?

Yes. If you do not want a shortcut to appear on your desktop, you can move the shortcut to a different location on your computer. You can move a shortcut the same way you would move a file. To move a shortcut, position the pointer over the shortcut and then drag it to a new location.

© Microsoft® Corporation

■ The shortcut appears on your desktop.

■ You can tell the difference between the shortcut and the original file because the shortcut icon displays an arrow.

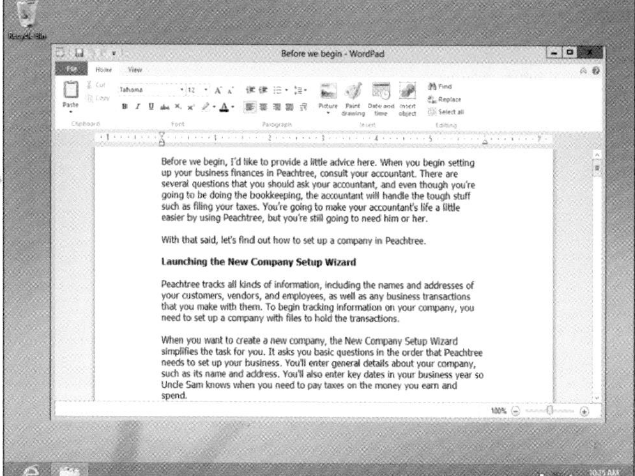

© Microsoft® Corporation

■ You can double-click the shortcut to open the file at any time.

Note: You can create a shortcut to a folder the same way you create a shortcut to a file. Creating a shortcut to a folder gives you quick access to all the files in the folder.

COPY FILES TO A USB FLASH DRIVE

You can copy files stored on your computer to a USB flash drive.

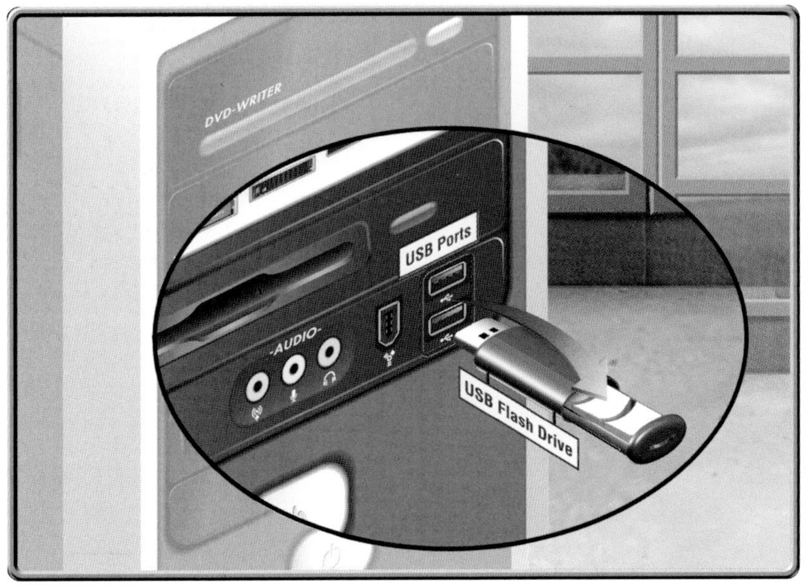

Copying files to a USB flash drive is useful when you want to transfer files between computers. For example, you may want to transfer files between your home and work computers or give a copy of a file to a friend, family member, or colleague.

COPY FILES TO A USB FLASH DRIVE

© Microsoft® Corporation. © Cengage Learning®

© Microsoft® Corporation. © Cengage Learning®

1 Insert a USB flash drive into your computer's USB port.

■ A message box briefly appears displaying the name and drive letter assigned to the USB flash drive.

2 Click the box to see available options.

Note: On some computers, you may not see the message box, and a window automatically opens to display the files. If so, skip steps 2 and 3.

3 Click **Open folder to view files**.

The message box disappeared before I could click it. How can I open the folder to view the files?

From the Windows desktop, click File Explorer.

In the Navigation pane on the left side, under the section titled Computer, you will see your USB flash drive. The letter assigned to your USB flash drive varies. Click the letter that represents your flash drive. From there you will see the window displaying the drive contents.

How do I copy files stored on a USB flash drive to my computer?

If you want to copy files stored on a USB flash drive to your computer, perform the steps, except drag the files from the USB flash drive to your computer. Windows places copies of the files on your computer.

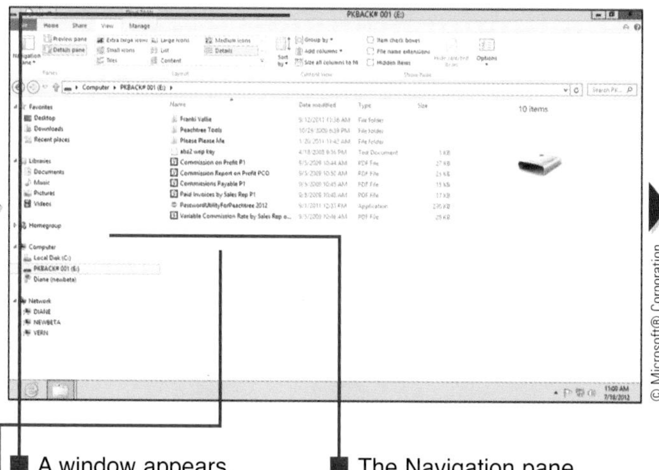

© Microsoft® Corporation

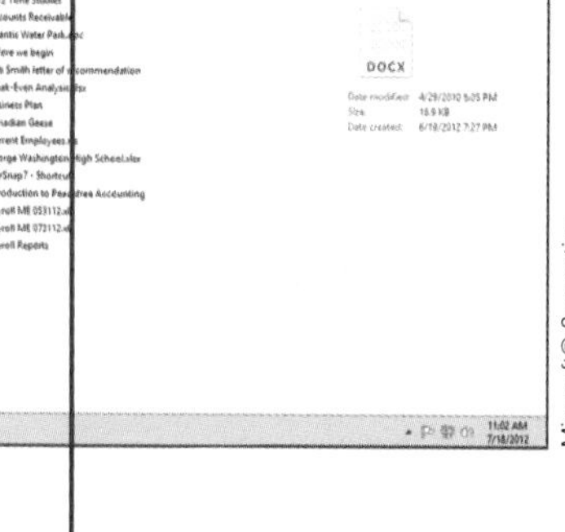

Microsoft® Corporation

■ A window appears, displaying the contents of the USB flash drive.

■ This area displays the folders and files stored on the USB flash drive.

■ The Navigation pane displays the different folders and drives on your computer.

4 Locate and position the ⇖ over the file on your computer that you want to copy to the USB flash drive. To select multiple files, see **"Select Files"** earlier in the chapter.

5 Drag the file to the drive letter representing the USB flash drive.

■ Windows places a copy of the file on the USB flash drive.

6 Click ✕ to close File Explorer.

Note: You can now use the USB flash drive to transfer the file to another computer.

COPY FILES TO SKYDRIVE

SkyDrive is an online file storage solution Microsoft offers. The SkyDrive Modern UI application allows you to browse and manage the files you have stored online as well as download and upload files.

© Microsoft® Corporation

By using SkyDrive to store your files, you have access to your files wherever you are—at your desk or on the road. You can access your files from most smartphones, tablet PCs, or any computer with Internet access.

To use SkyDrive, you must be logged into Windows using your Microsoft account.

COPY FILES TO SKYDRIVE

© Microsoft® Corporation. © Cengage Learning®

© Microsoft® Corporation

1 From the Start screen, click **SkyDrive**.

■ The SkyDrive screen appears displaying any documents you have already saved in your SkyDrive.

2 Right-click anywhere in a blank area of the SkyDrive screen.

■ A list of SkyDrive options appears at the bottom of the window.

3 Click **Add**.

What types of files can I store on my SkyDrive?

You can store any file type or size on your SkyDrive, including documents, spreadsheets, pictures, presentations, and music.

Does SkyDrive cost anything?

You get 7 GB of free storage with SkyDrive, which is enough for more than 7,000 photos or 20,000 Office documents.

If you need more than that, you can also purchase additional storage space.

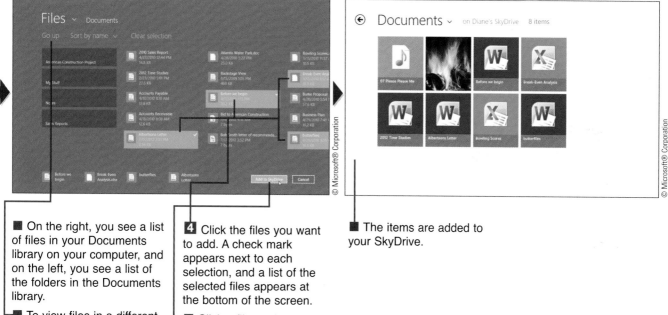

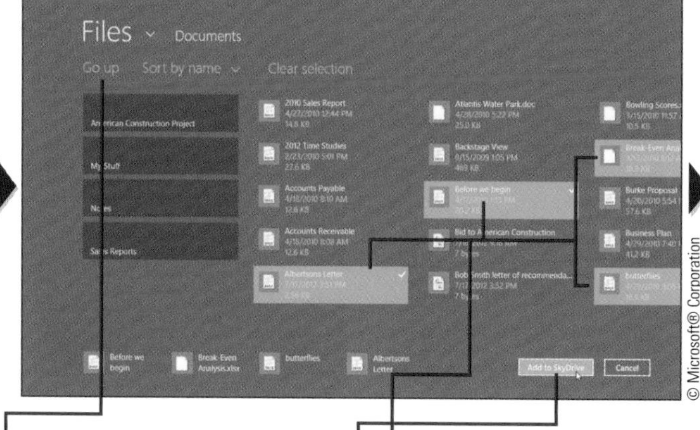

© Microsoft® Corporation

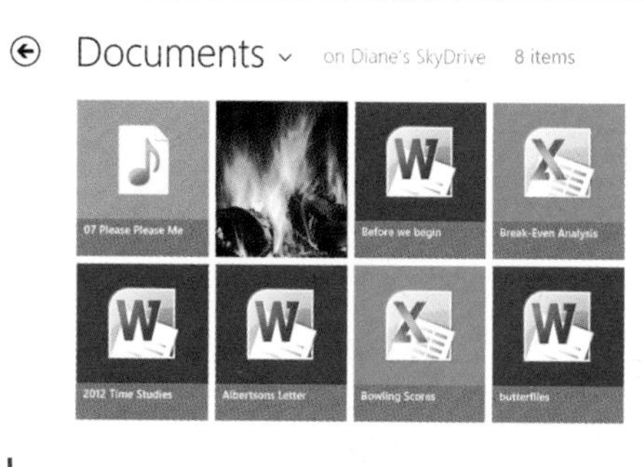

© Microsoft® Corporation

■ On the right, you see a list of files in your Documents library on your computer, and on the left, you see a list of the folders in the Documents library.

■ To view files in a different library, click **Go up** and locate the folder you want to use. To view files in a folder inside the Documents library, click that folder.

4 Click the files you want to add. A check mark appears next to each selection, and a list of the selected files appears at the bottom of the screen.

■ Click a file again to remove it from the selections.

5 Click **Add to SkyDrive**.

■ The items are added to your SkyDrive.

ACCESS SKYDRIVE REMOTELY

If you are at another location and want to access your SkyDrive files, you need your Windows Live password (see Chapter 1) and Internet access.

ACCESS SKYDRIVE REMOTELY

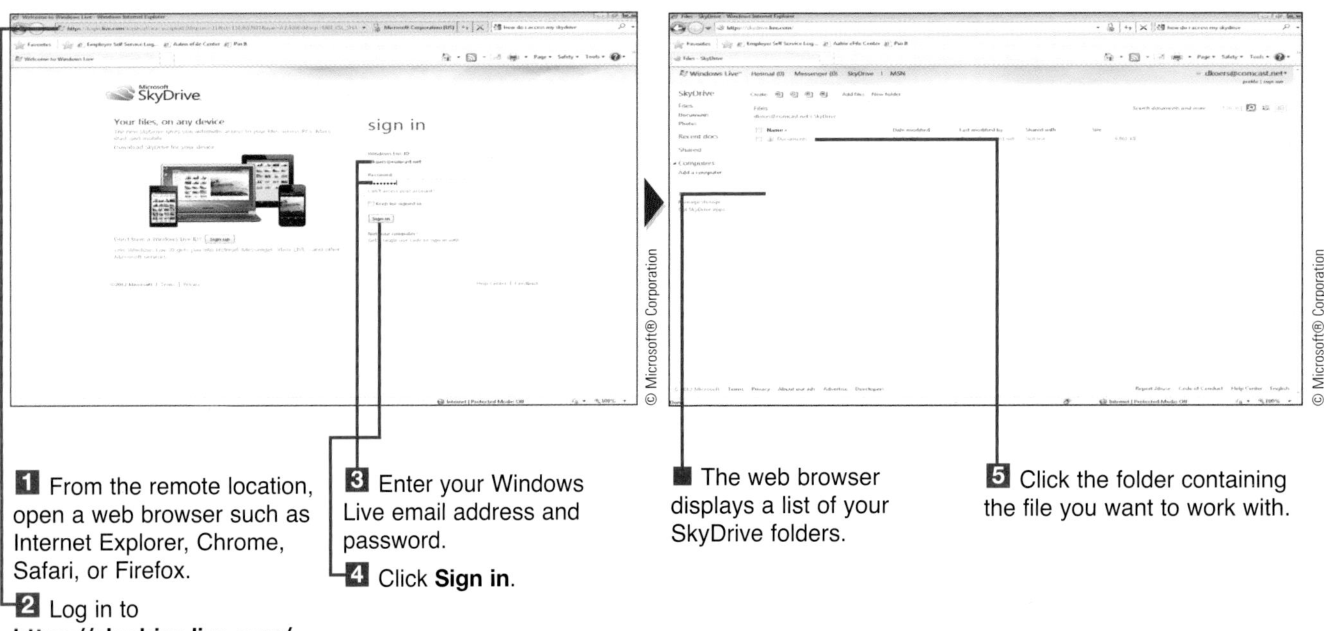

1 From the remote location, open a web browser such as Internet Explorer, Chrome, Safari, or Firefox.

2 Log in to **https://skydrive.live.com/**.

3 Enter your Windows Live email address and password.

4 Click **Sign in**.

■ The web browser displays a list of your SkyDrive folders.

5 Click the folder containing the file you want to work with.

DELETE FILES FROM SKYDRIVE

If you no longer want a file stored on SkyDrive, you can delete it.

© Microsoft® Corporation

Deleting a file from SkyDrive does not delete it from your computer.

DELETE FILES FROM SKYDRIVE

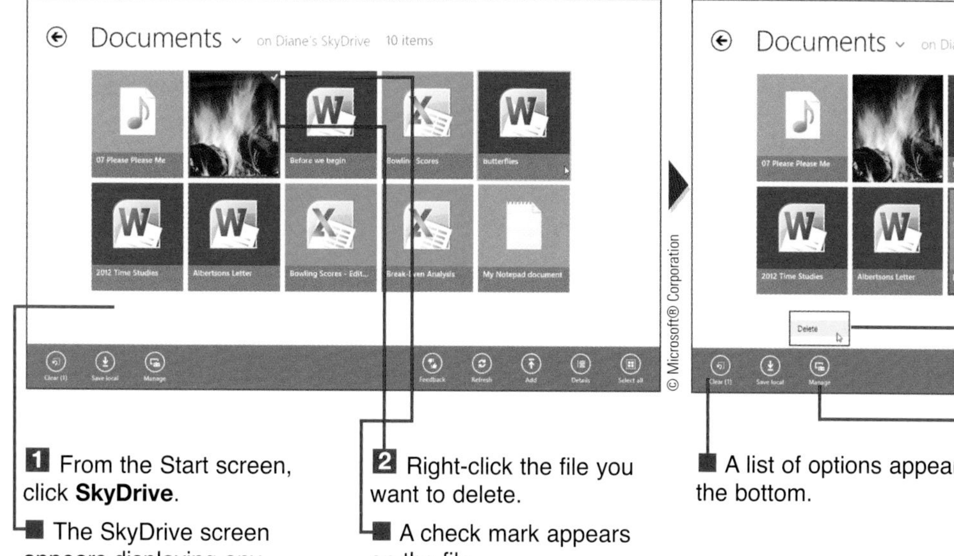

© Microsoft® Corporation

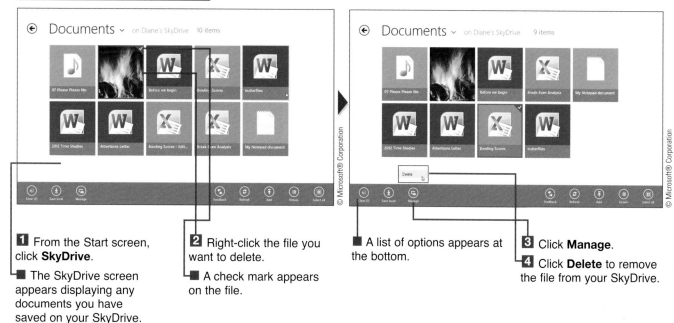

© Microsoft® Corporation

1 From the Start screen, click **SkyDrive**.

■ The SkyDrive screen appears displaying any documents you have saved on your SkyDrive.

2 Right-click the file you want to delete.

■ A check mark appears on the file.

■ A list of options appears at the bottom.

3 Click **Manage**.

4 Click **Delete** to remove the file from your SkyDrive.

Printing Picture...
MULTI-CARD READER

CHAPTER 5

Working with Pictures

COPY PICTURES FROM A DIGITAL CAMERA

You can copy pictures stored on a digital camera to your computer.

You can copy pictures to your computer by using a USB cable or, if your camera has a memory card that is compatible with your computer's memory card reader, you can transfer the pictures to your computer directly from your memory card.

After copying pictures to your computer, you can work with them as you would any pictures on your computer. For example, you can print or email them.

COPY PICTURES FROM A DIGITAL CAMERA

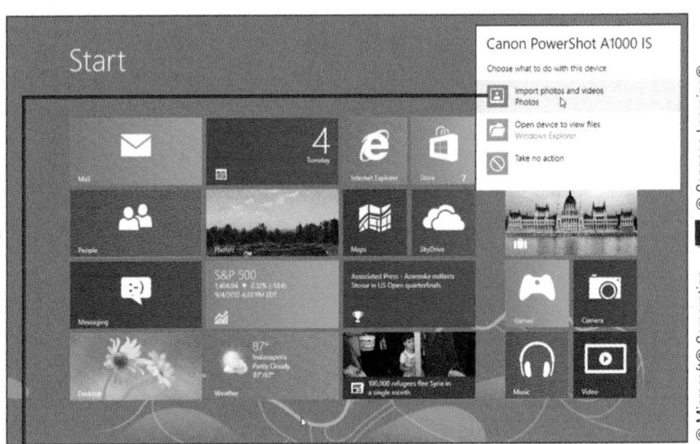

1 With the camera turned off, connect the USB cable that came with your camera to the camera, and plug the other end into a USB port on your computer.

2 Turn on your camera.

■ From either the Start screen or the Windows desktop, a message box appears, identifying your camera.

3 Click the message box.

4 Click **Import photos and videos**.

How do I copy the photos from the camera memory card by using the memory card reader on my computer?

Remove the memory card from your digital camera and insert the memory card into your computer's memory card reader.

When the message box appears, choose **Import pictures and videos**.

Follow steps **5** through **7** in this section.

Where does Windows place the pictures I copied from my digital camera?

When you copy pictures from your digital camera to your computer, Windows creates a new folder to store the pictures and places the folder in your Pictures library. By default, Windows names the folder using the date you copied the pictures, but you can change the folder name before you download the photos or even after, using File Explorer. To rename the folder using File Explorer, see **Chapter 4**. To display the Pictures library, see **"View the Pictures Library"** coming up next.

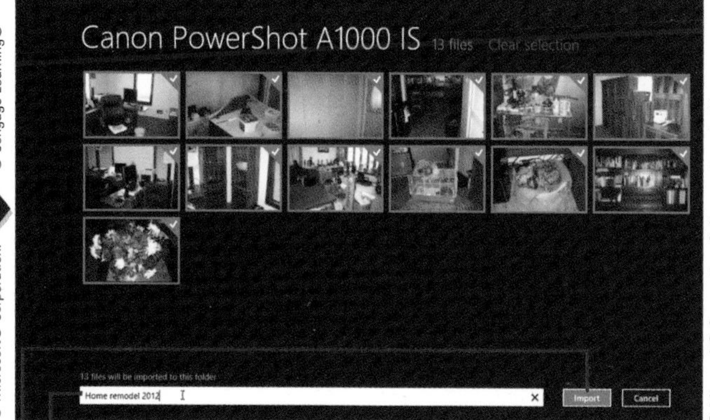

■ A screen appears displaying thumbnail images of the photos on your camera or memory card.

■ All images have a check mark next to them, marking them as ready to import.

5 Remove the check mark from any image you do not want to import.

6 Optionally, type a different folder name to identify the images.

7 Click **Import** to copy the pictures.

■ When the import process is complete, a box appears telling you the process is finished.

8 Click **Done**.

■ You can now view the photos through the Pictures library or through the Photos Modern UI app. See "**View the Pictures Library**" or "**See Photos Modern UI Style**."

VIEW THE PICTURES LIBRARY

Similar to the Documents library, where you store the documents you create, the Pictures library contains links to a collection of folders on your computer where you can store your pictures.

The Pictures library provides a convenient place where you can create new folders, rename, delete, copy, move, and organize your photos.

VIEW PICTURES LIBRARY

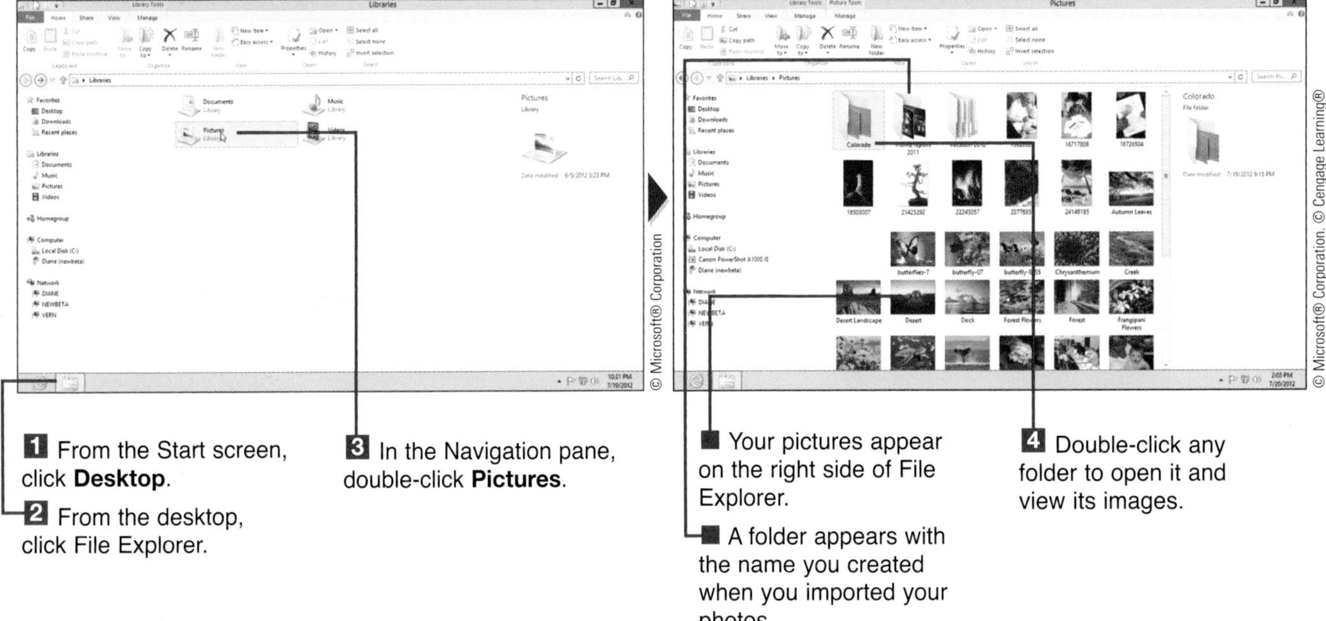

1 From the Start screen, click **Desktop**.

2 From the desktop, click File Explorer.

3 In the Navigation pane, double-click **Pictures**.

■ Your pictures appear on the right side of File Explorer.

■ A folder appears with the name you created when you imported your photos.

4 Double-click any folder to open it and view its images.

SEE PHOTOS MODERN UI STYLE

The Photos Modern UI app is a handy place to view not only the photos you have stored in your Pictures library, but also those that you have in online locations such as SkyDrive, Facebook, and Flickr.

© Microsoft® Corporation

By connecting your Microsoft account to those social networks, you can link all your photos within Windows.

SEE PHOTOS MODERN UI STYLE

© Microsoft® Corporation. © Cengage Learning®

1 From the Start screen, click **Photos**.

© Microsoft® Corporation

- The Photos app launches.
- Boxes appear for your Pictures library, SkyDrive, Facebook photos, and Flickr photos.
- The number here indicates how many images are stored in each area.

Note: Scroll to the right for a box you can click to see the images on your camera or other device.

2 Click **Pictures library** or **SkyDrive**.

- If you click Facebook or Flickr, you are asked to log in to your Facebook or Flickr account.

CONTINUED

The Modern UI app displays your images in a seamless arrangement of thumbnail views, or you can view a larger perspective of an image in its own screen space.

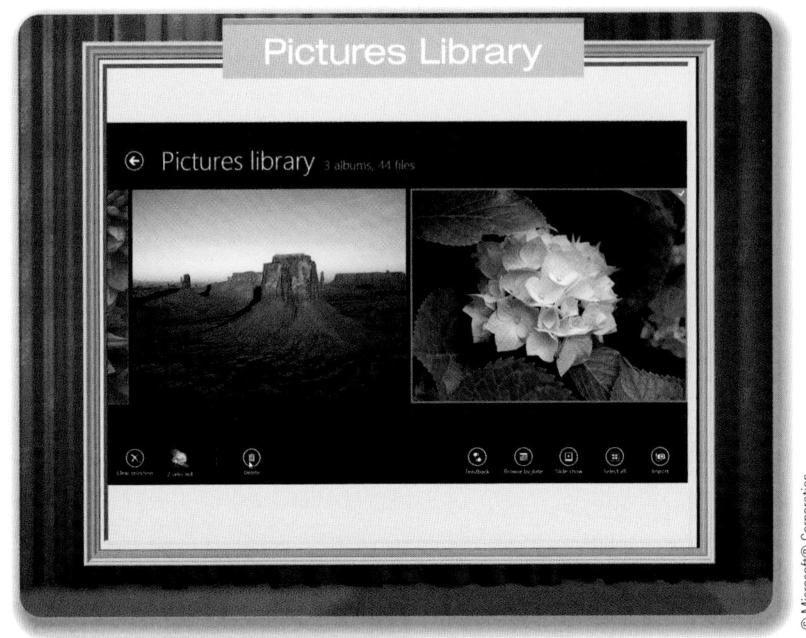

SEE PHOTOS MODERN UI STYLE (CONTINUED)

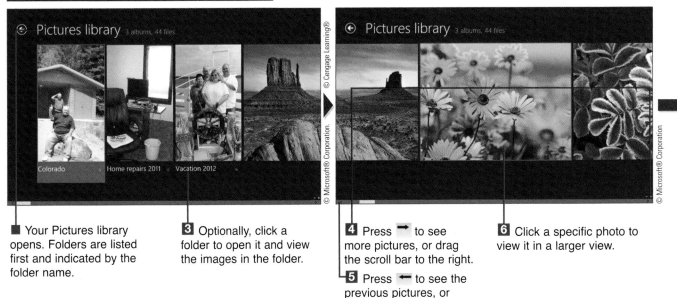

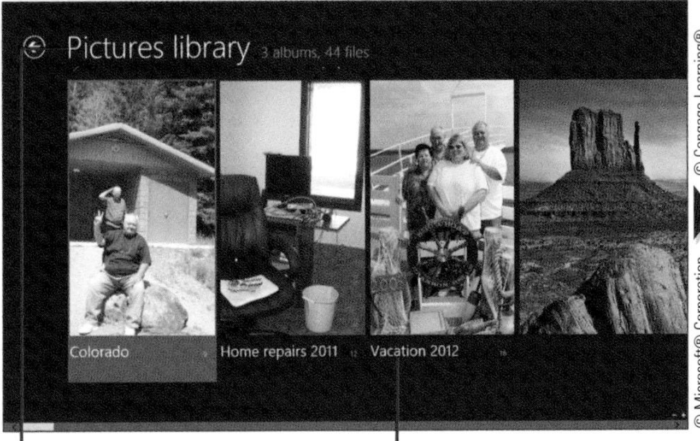

■ Your Pictures library opens. Folders are listed first and indicated by the folder name.

3 Optionally, click a folder to open it and view the images in the folder.

4 Press → to see more pictures, or drag the scroll bar to the right.

5 Press ← to see the previous pictures, or drag the scroll bar to the left.

6 Click a specific photo to view it in a larger view.

What happens when I delete an image from the Pictures library?

If you delete an image from the Pictures library, the image goes to the Recycle Bin. If you deleted the image in error, you can restore it from the Recycle Bin. See **"Restore a Deleted File"** in Chapter 4.

What happens when I delete an image from SkyDrive?

When you delete an image from SkyDrive, you are only deleting it from the SkyDrive and not from your computer.

© Microsoft® Corporation

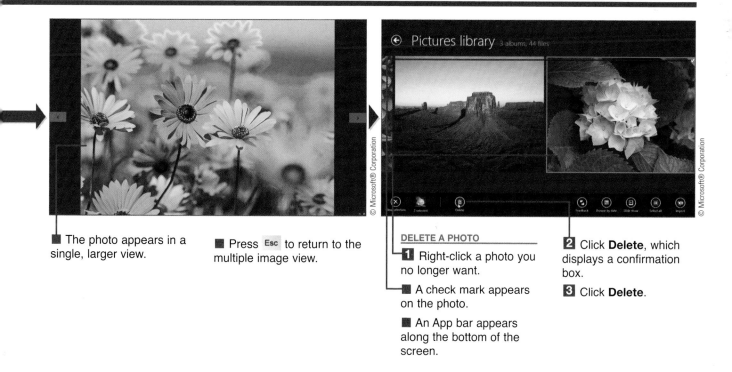

- The photo appears in a single, larger view.
- Press Esc to return to the multiple image view.

© Microsoft® Corporation

DELETE A PHOTO

1. Right-click a photo you no longer want.
- A check mark appears on the photo.
- An App bar appears along the bottom of the screen.
2. Click **Delete**, which displays a confirmation box.
3. Click **Delete**.

VIEW A SLIDE SHOW

Windows provides a slide show format to view your photos. In a slide show, you see each image in a full screen, with no distractions such as buttons, arrows, or Ribbons.

You can view a slide show from the Libraries window or from the Photos app.

Viewing the slide show from the Libraries window gives you more control over the slide show.

VIEW A SLIDE SHOW

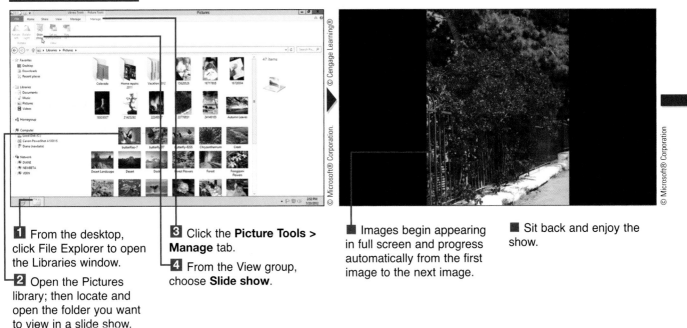

1 From the desktop, click File Explorer to open the Libraries window.

2 Open the Pictures library; then locate and open the folder you want to view in a slide show.

3 Click the **Picture Tools > Manage** tab.

4 From the View group, choose **Slide show**.

■ Images begin appearing in full screen and progress automatically from the first image to the next image.

■ Sit back and enjoy the show.

Can I select only some pictures to display in the slide show?

Yes. Before you start the slide show, click the first image you want to see, and then hold down the Ctrl key and select any additional images you want for the slide slow.

How do I view a slide show from the Photos app?

First, from the Photos app, display the folder containing the images you want to view. Next, right-click anywhere on the Photos screen.

From the Options gallery that appears, click **Slide show**. The show automatically launches. Press Esc to cancel the slide show.

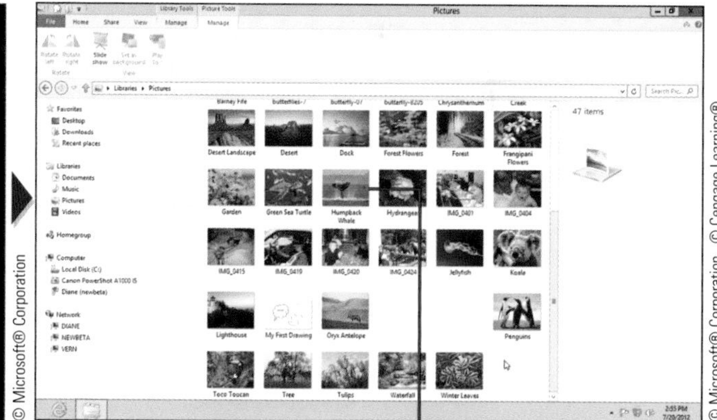

■ Right-click an image to view the slide show settings.

■ From here you can also control the speed at which the images change.

5 Press Esc to cancel the slide show.

■ You return to the Pictures library in File Explorer.

A photo is more than a picture. You can also view the properties of image files. Image properties typically include the image size, the date the photo was taken, the camera used, and the cameras settings.

© Microsoft® Corporation

When you use the Search feature, you can enter any portion of the image property to search for images containing that property.

Some images do not show all the information.

DRAW WITH PAINT (CONTINUED)

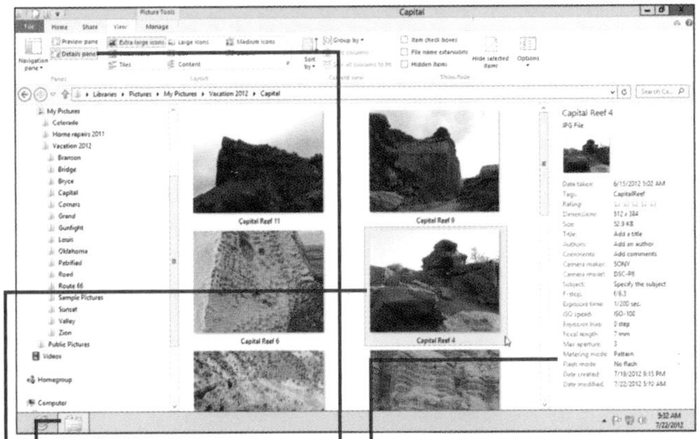

© Microsoft® Corporation

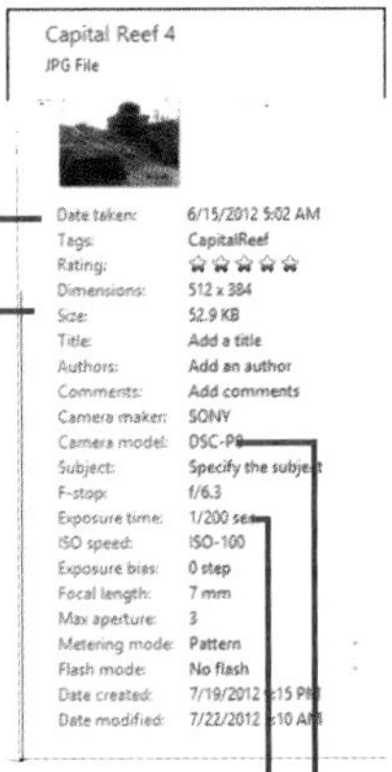

Capital Reef 4
JPG File

Date taken: 6/15/2012 5:02 AM
Tags: CapitalReef
Rating:
Dimensions: 512 x 384
Size: 52.9 KB
Title: Add a title
Authors: Add an author
Comments: Add comments
Camera maker: SONY
Camera model: DSC-P8
Subject: Specify the subject
F-stop: f/6.3
Exposure time: 1/200 sec.
ISO speed: ISO-100
Exposure bias: 0 step
Focal length: 7 mm
Max aperture: 3
Metering mode: Pattern
Flash mode: No flash
Date created: 7/19/2012 9:15 PM
Date modified: 7/22/2012 5:10 AM

© Microsoft® Corporation. © Cengage Learning®

1 From the desktop, click File Explorer to open the Libraries window.

2 Open the Pictures library; then locate and select the image you want to view.

- The Details pane, on the right side of the screen, displays details about the photo.
- If you don't see the image information, click the **View** tab, and from the Panes group, click **Details pane**.

- Date the photo was taken.
- The image size.

- The camera make and model.
- Exposure settings.

Can I change any of the image information?

Yes. You can manually edit most of the image information fields; however, the image dimensions and size as well as some of the camera settings are not changeable.

What is the Rating option used for?

Based on a scale of 1 to 5, with 5 being your favorite photos, you can assign a rating. Then, if you have your images displayed using the Details view, you can sort the images by their ratings.

Click the **Ratings** column heading to sort the images by their rating.

Click the arrow next to the Ratings column heading and select a rating. Windows only displays the images matching the selected rating.

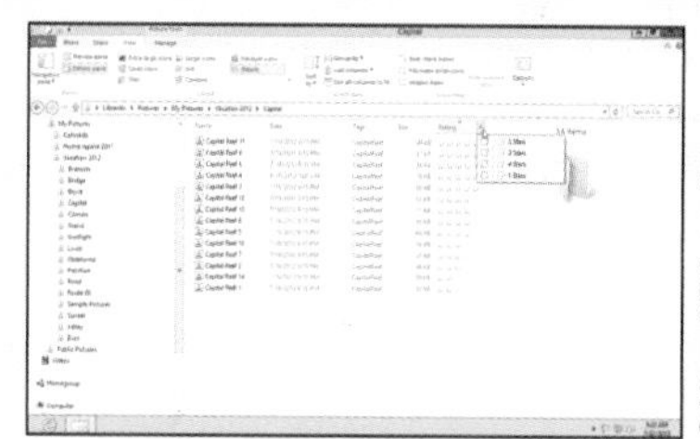

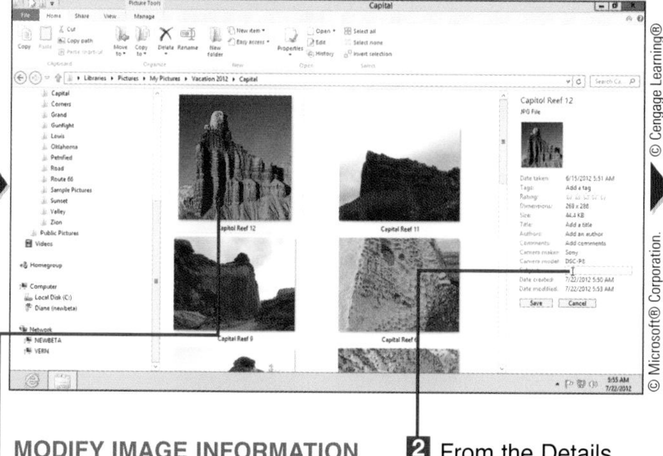

MODIFY IMAGE INFORMATION

1 Select the image for which you want to modify information.

2 From the Details pane, click the field you want to edit.

3 Enter the information you want to record.

4 Click **Save**. The information you entered is saved with the image.

ADD TAGS TO PHOTOS

Another image property is a tag. You can add tags to your photos to make your photos easier to find and organize.

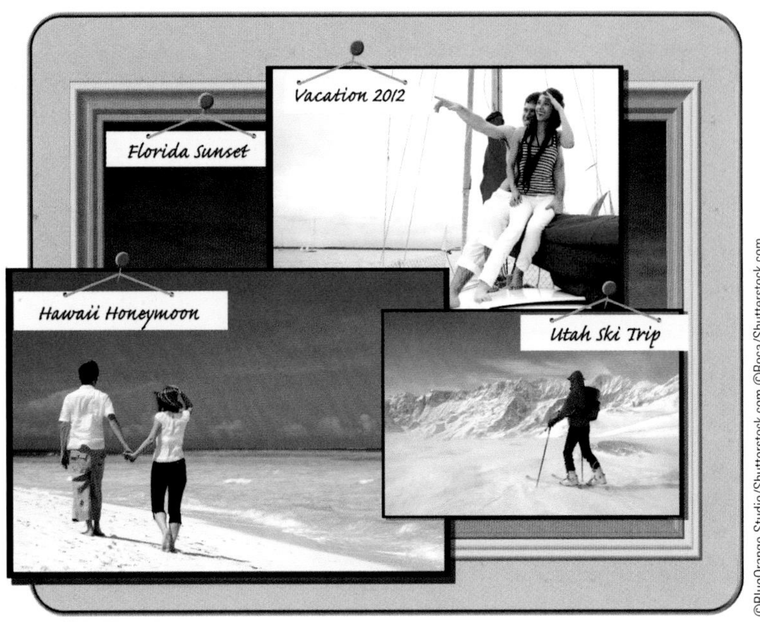

A *tag* is a meaningful word that you can add to your photos. You can create people tags to identify the people in your photos, or you can create descriptive tags to describe the locations and events in your photos. Photos can have multiple tags.

When you use the Search feature, you can enter any portion of the image property to search for images containing that property.

You can add tags to the photos at any time.

ADD TAGS TO PHOTOS

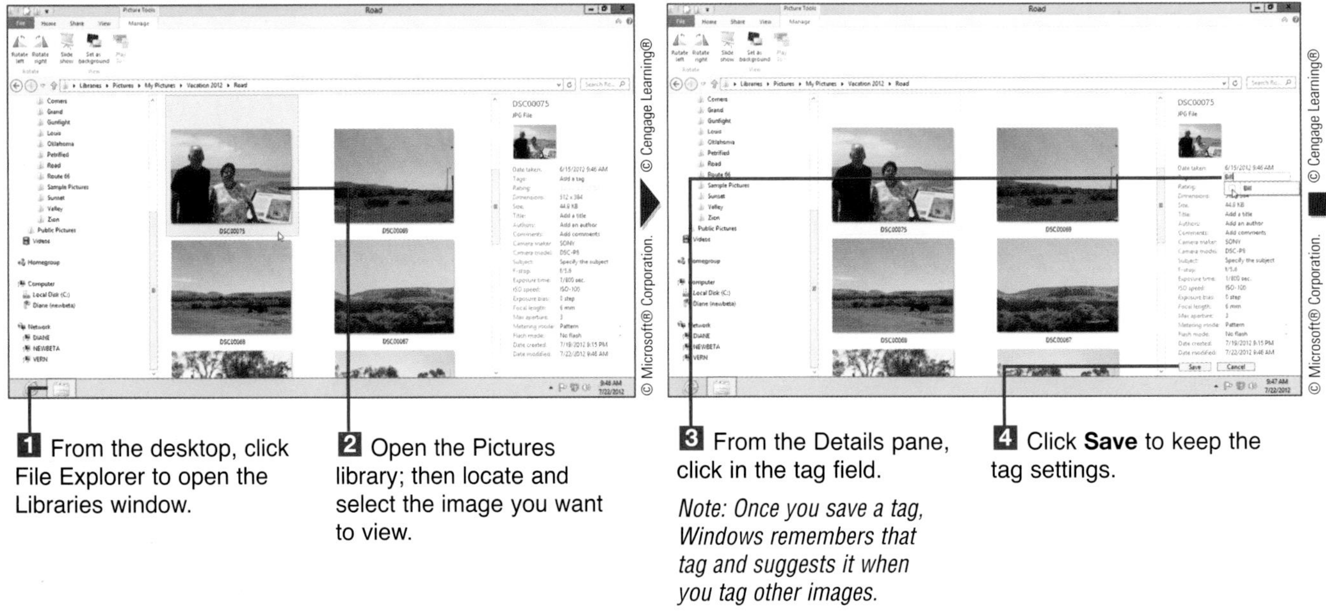

1 From the desktop, click File Explorer to open the Libraries window.

2 Open the Pictures library; then locate and select the image you want to view.

3 From the Details pane, click in the tag field.

Note: Once you save a tag, Windows remembers that tag and suggests it when you tag other images.

4 Click **Save** to keep the tag settings.

Is there a way to add tags to multiple photos at the same time?

Yes. You can instantly add the same tag to many photos at once. For example, you can add a "graduation" tag to 20 photos of a graduation ceremony. In the Pictures library, press and hold down Ctrl as you click each photo you want to add a tag to.

In the Details pane, type or select the tag you want to assign; then click the **Save** button.

Can I remove a tag I added to a photo?

Yes. If you want to remove a tag from a photo, click the photo in the Pictures library. In the Information pane, click the tag line and drag the pointer over the tag you want to remove from the photo. Then press the Delete When the tag is removed, click the **Save** button.

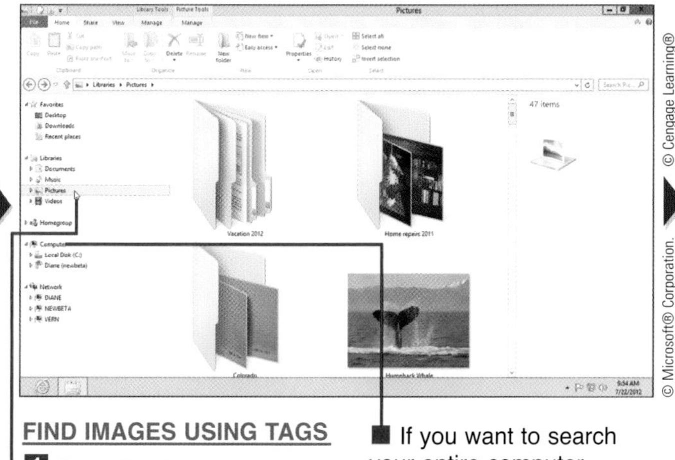

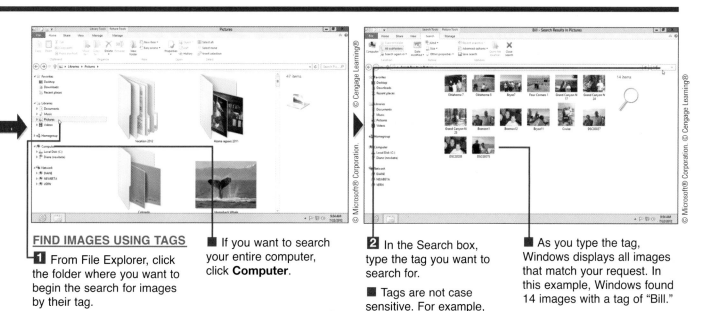

FIND IMAGES USING TAGS

1 From File Explorer, click the folder where you want to begin the search for images by their tag.

■ If you want to search your entire computer, click **Computer**.

2 In the Search box, type the tag you want to search for.

■ Tags are not case sensitive. For example, Bill, bill, and BILL are all the same tag.

■ As you type the tag, Windows displays all images that match your request. In this example, Windows found 14 images with a tag of "Bill."

■ To clear a search, delete any words from the Search box.

You can print the pictures stored on your computer.

©Rich Carey/Shutterstock.com ©James Laurie/Shutterstock.com ©Nastya Pirieva/Shutterstock.com

Printing pictures is especially useful when you want to print photos you transferred from a digital camera to your computer.

PRINT PICTURES

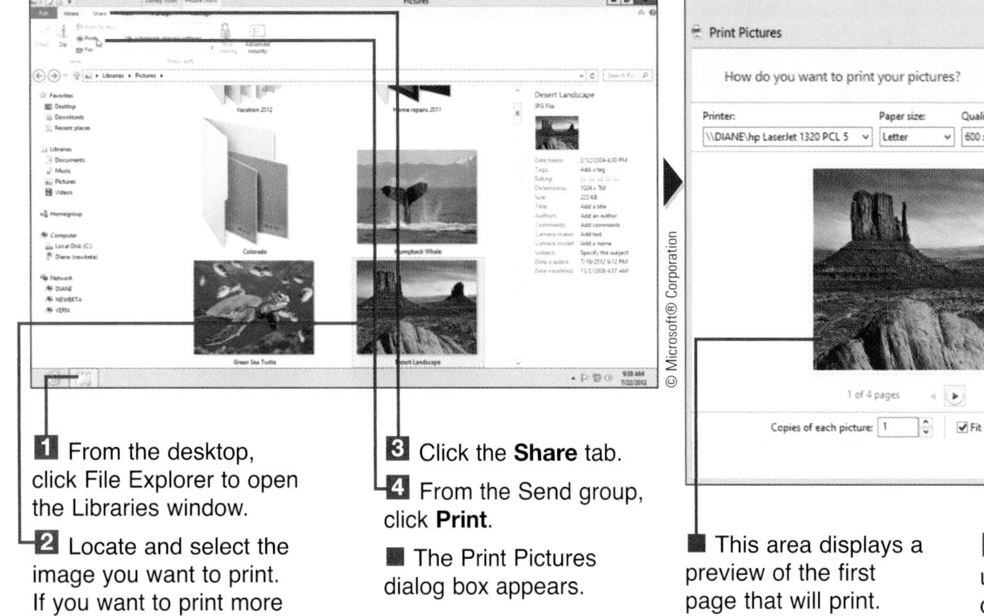

© Microsoft® Corporation

1 From the desktop, click File Explorer to open the Libraries window.

2 Locate and select the image you want to print. If you want to print more than one picture, select all the pictures you want to print. See **Chapter 4**.

3 Click the **Share** tab.

4 From the Send group, click **Print**.

■ The Print Pictures dialog box appears.

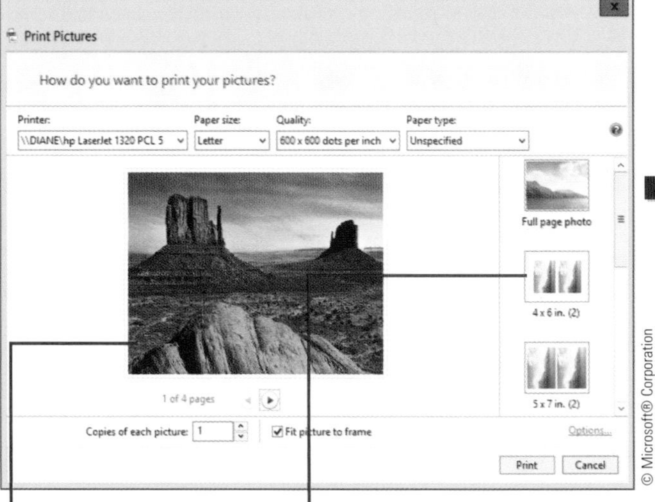

© Microsoft® Corporation

■ This area displays a preview of the first page that will print.

5 Click the layout you want to use to print your pictures. You can choose to print one or many pictures on each page.

Note: You can use the scroll bar to browse through the available layout options.

How can I get the best results when printing pictures?

The type of paper you use to print your pictures can significantly affect the quality of the pictures you print. For the best results when printing pictures, use a premium glossy or matte photo paper that is specifically designed for use with your printer. In the Print Pictures dialog box, you can click the area below Paper type and select the type of paper you are using.

Why do my printed pictures look blurry?

If your original pictures are clear but your printed pictures look blurry, you are most likely printing the pictures too large. Try printing your pictures at a smaller size. For the best results when printing pictures, make sure you use the appropriate megapixel setting on your digital camera for the print size you want to use. For example, 8 × 10 prints require a 7-megapixel setting, 5 × 7 prints require a 3-megapixel setting and 4 × 6 prints require a 2-megapixel setting.

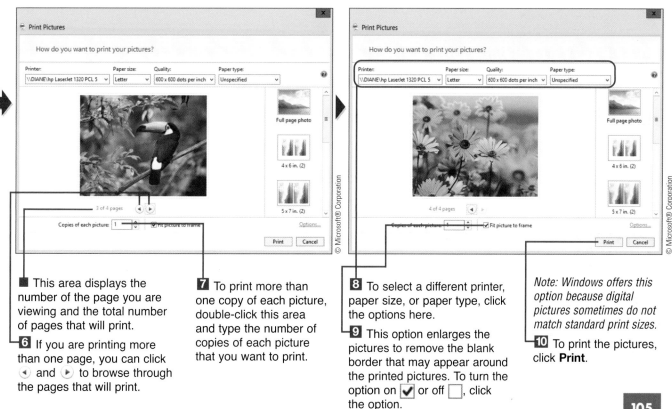

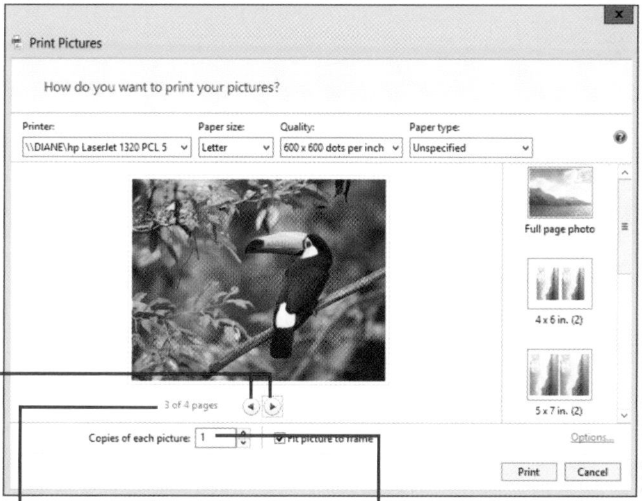

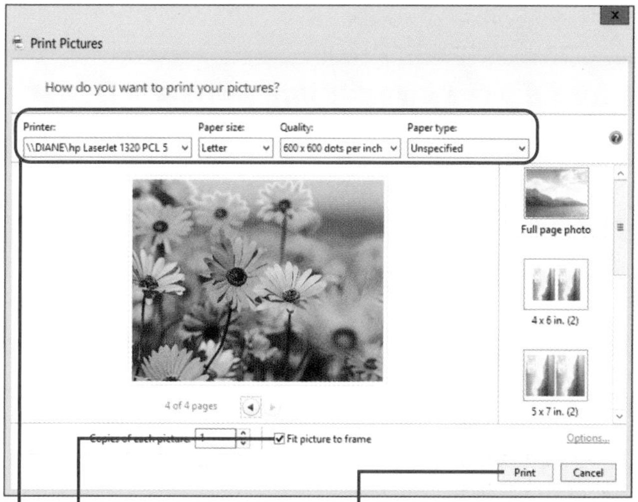

■ This area displays the number of the page you are viewing and the total number of pages that will print.

6 If you are printing more than one page, you can click ◀ and ▶ to browse through the pages that will print.

7 To print more than one copy of each picture, double-click this area and type the number of copies of each picture that you want to print.

8 To select a different printer, paper size, or paper type, click the options here.

9 This option enlarges the pictures to remove the blank border that may appear around the printed pictures. To turn the option on ☑ or off ☐, click the option.

Note: Windows offers this option because digital pictures sometimes do not match standard print sizes.

10 To print the pictures, click **Print**.

COPY PICTURES TO A DVD

You will probably want to place a copy of your photos on a DVD in case something happens to your computer. This is called making a *backup*.

Backing up photos to a DVD leaves the original photos on your computer and puts a copy on the DVD.

COPY PICTURES TO A DVD

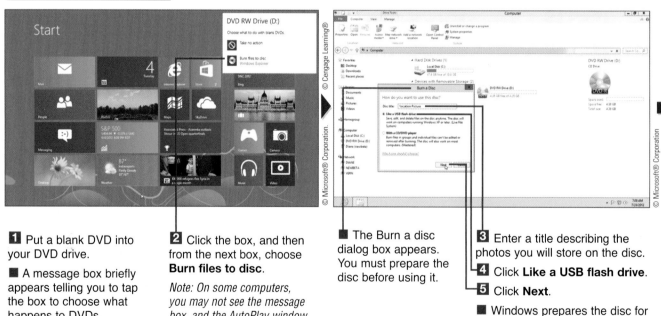

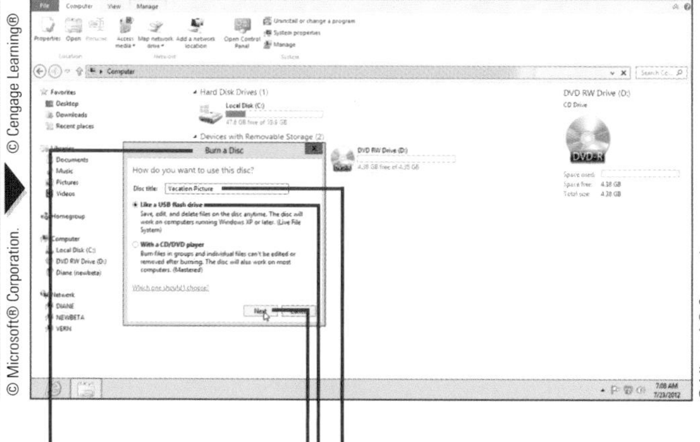

1 Put a blank DVD into your DVD drive.

■ A message box briefly appears telling you to tap the box to choose what happens to DVDs.

2 Click the box, and then from the next box, choose **Burn files to disc**.

Note: On some computers, you may not see the message box, and the AutoPlay window automatically opens. If so, skip step 2.

■ The Burn a disc dialog box appears. You must prepare the disc before using it.

3 Enter a title describing the photos you will store on the disc.

4 Click **Like a USB flash drive**.

5 Click **Next**.

■ Windows prepares the disc for use and displays the blank DVD window in File Explorer.

Can I add more than one picture at a time?

Yes. When you select the images you want to copy, hold down Ctrl as you click each picture you want to add. If you want to add all the pictures in a folder, from the Home tab's Select group, choose **Select all**.

Can I remove a picture that I added in error to the DVD?

Yes, if you choose to remove it before you close the session. From the DVD window, select the image you do not want, and then press Delete. From the confirmation message that appears, choose **Yes**. Windows deletes the image from the DVD but does not delete it from your computer.

6 From the DVD window, open another window by clicking the **File** tab.

7 Select **Open new window.**

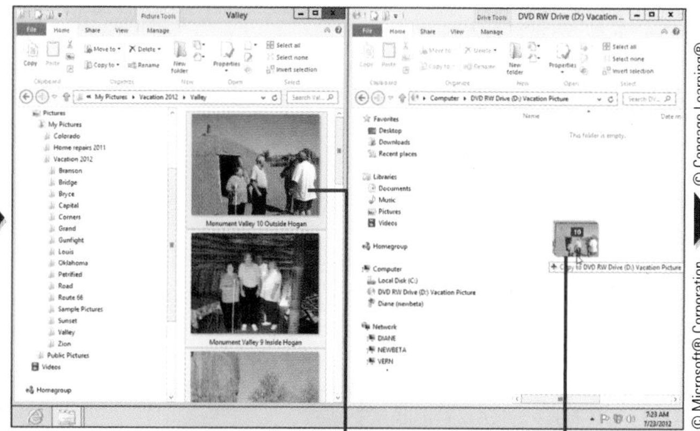

8 Display the DVD windows side by side with the window containing the photos you want to copy by right-clicking the taskbar and choosing **Show windows side-by-side**.

9 In the new window, locate and select the photos you want to copy.

10 Drag the photo icons from the new window to the DVD window.

■ Windows copies the photos to the DVD.

CONTINUED

COPY PICTURES TO A DVD (CONTINUED)

You can also give a copy of the DVD to friends and family so they can enjoy your photos.

Additionally, you can take the DVD and view the images as a slide show on your TV through your DVD or Blu-Ray player.

COPY PICTURES TO A DVD (CONTINUED)

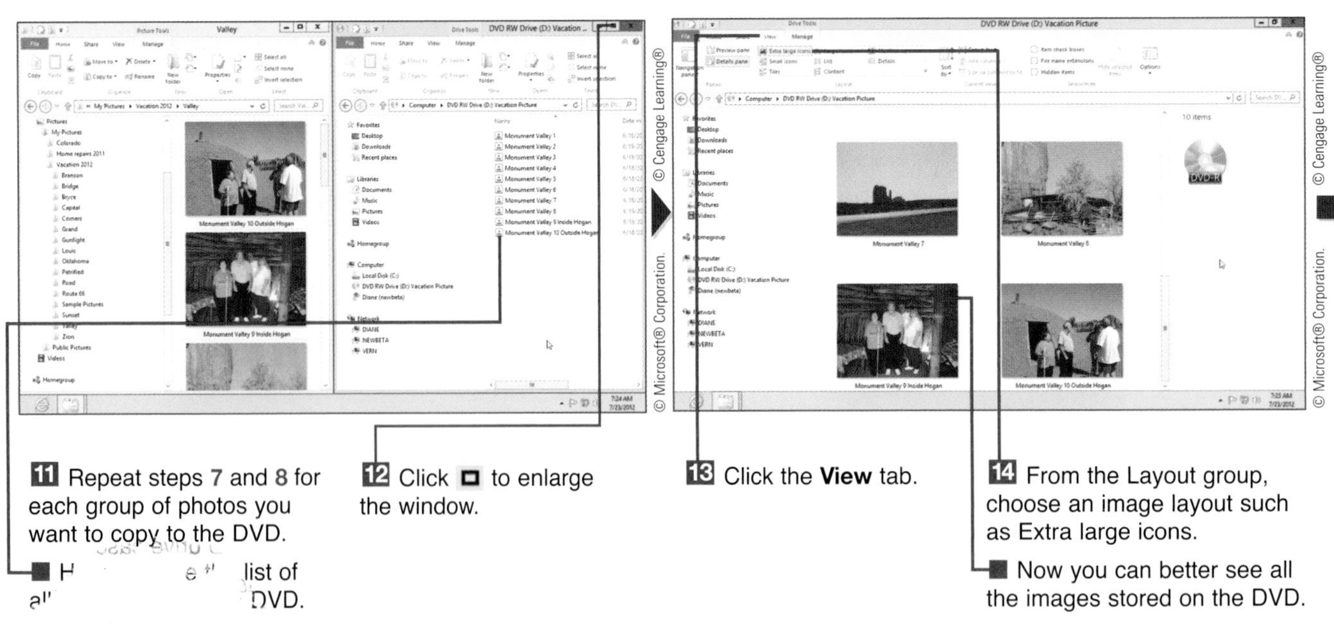

11 Repeat steps 7 and 8 for each group of photos you want to copy to the DVD.

■ H[illegible] list of al[illegible] DVD.

12 Click ◘ to enlarge the window.

13 Click the **View** tab.

14 From the Layout group, choose an image layout such as Extra large icons.

■ Now you can better see all the images stored on the DVD.

How many images can I fit on a DVD?

It depends on how large your photo files are. A typical DVD holds about 4.7 gigabytes of data, including images. So, for example, if your photos are about 1 megabyte each, you can fit between 4,000 and 6,000 files on the DVD.

If your images are very high resolution, they will be larger, and the DVD can hold fewer images than if the images are at a lower resolution.

How do I copy my images to a CD instead of a DVD?

To copy images to a CD, you follow the same steps as copying to a DVD. However, a CD stores about 650 megabytes of data, so you can fit between 600 and 700 photos on the CD if the images are about 1 megabyte each.

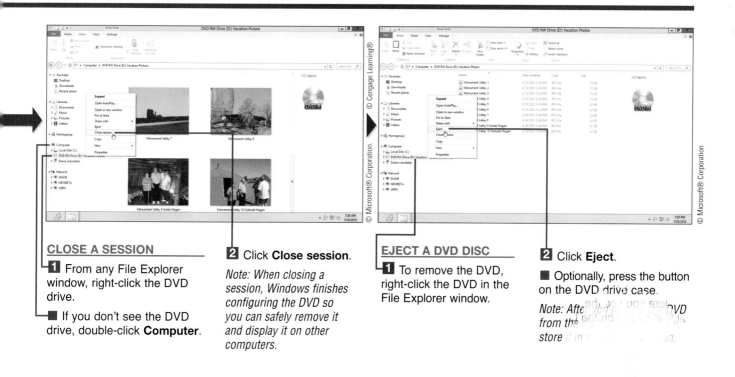

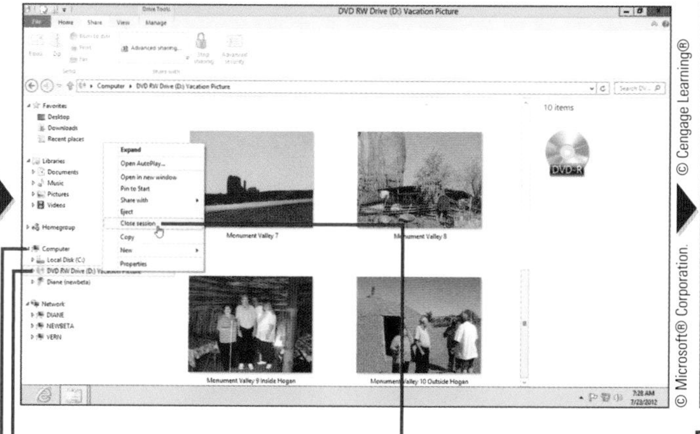

CLOSE A SESSION

1. From any File Explorer window, right-click the DVD drive.

- If you don't see the DVD drive, double-click **Computer**.

2. Click **Close session**.

Note: When closing a session, Windows finishes configuring the DVD so you can safely remove it and display it on other computers.

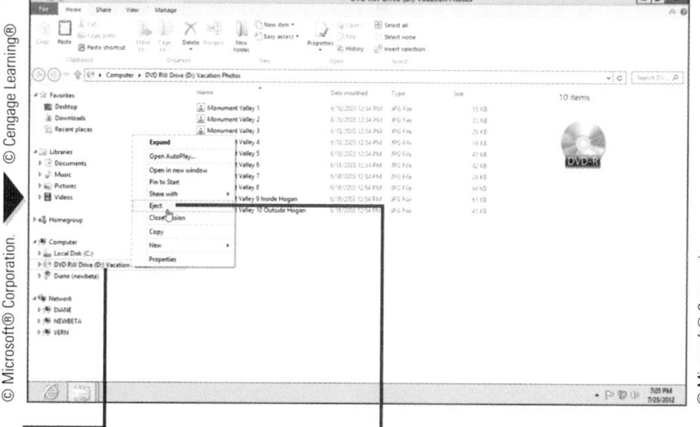

EJECT A DVD DISC

1. To remove the DVD, right-click the DVD in the File Explorer window.

2. Click **Eject**.

- Optionally, press the button on the DVD drive case.

Note: Afte[illegible] DVD from th[illegible] store [illegible]n.

Jazz
Selected Hits From
•Charlie Parker
•Count Basie
•Duke Ellington
•Cole Porter
MOVIE MUSIC
Theme music from
Hollywoods biggest films

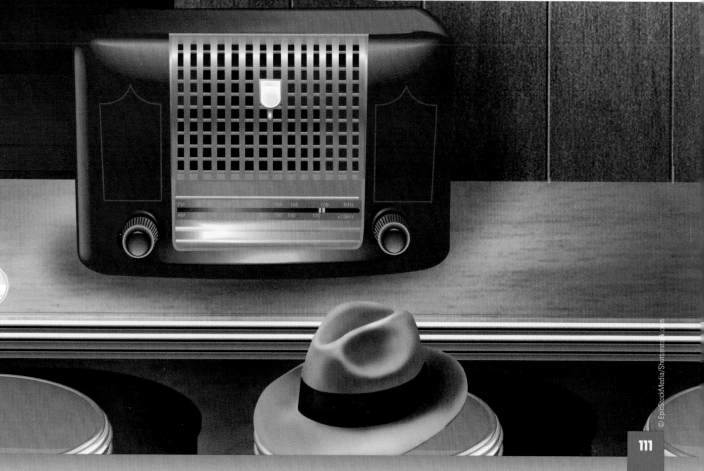

CHAPTER 6

Work with Music and Videos

PLAY A VIDEO OR SOUND

You can use Windows Media Player to play videos and sounds on your computer.

You can obtain videos and sounds on the Internet or in email messages you receive from friends, family members, or colleagues.

You can also obtain videos by transferring video from a video camera to your computer or obtain sounds by copying songs from music CDs to your computer.

PLAY A VIDEO OR SOUND

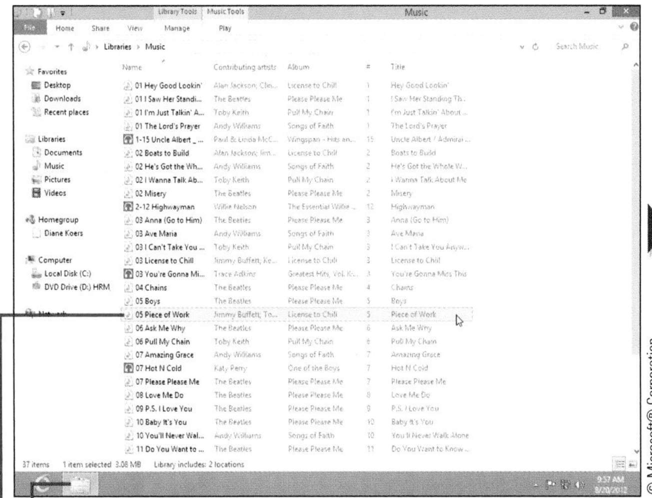

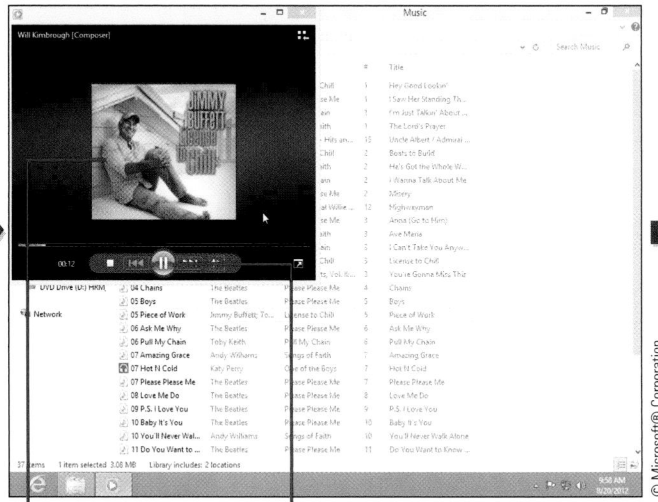

1 From the Windows desktop, click File Explorer.

2 Locate and double-click the video or sound you want to play.

■ If you get a message concerning how to open this type of file, choose **Windows Media Player**.

Note: You can find videos in your Videos library and sounds in your Music library. To view the files in your libraries, see ***Chapter 4****.*

■ The Windows Media Player window appears, and the video or sound begins to play.

3 To display controls you can use to adjust the playback of the video or sound, move the ⇖ over the window.

■ The playback controls appear.

Note: To hide the playback controls, move the ⇖ away from the window.

Why does the Welcome to Windows Media Player window appear when I try to play a video or sound?

The first time Windows Media Player starts, the Welcome to Windows Media Player window appears, asking you to choose your settings for the player. In the window, click **Recommended settings**, and then click **Finish**. These settings make Windows Media Player your default program for playing sound and video files and allow the program to automatically retrieve information for your media files online.

Can I use the entire screen to view a video?

Yes. You can use your entire screen to view a video. While watching a video, position the ▷ over the Windows Media Player window, and then click ⧉ at the bottom-right corner of the window. The video will continue playing using your entire screen. To once again view the video in a window, click ⧉ at the bottom-right corner of your screen.

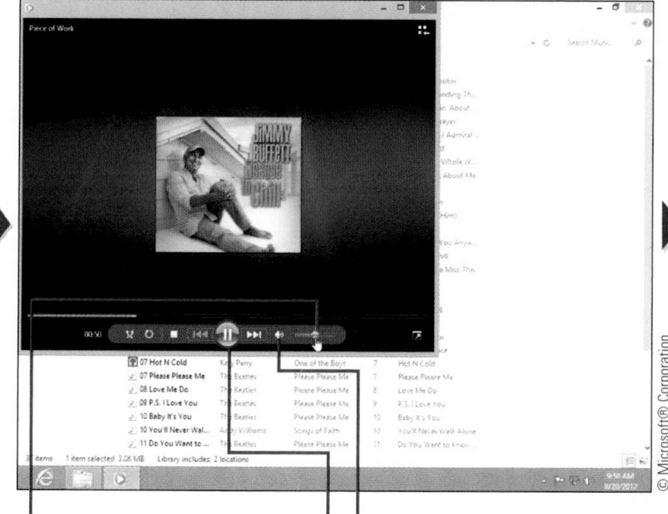

© Microsoft® Corporation

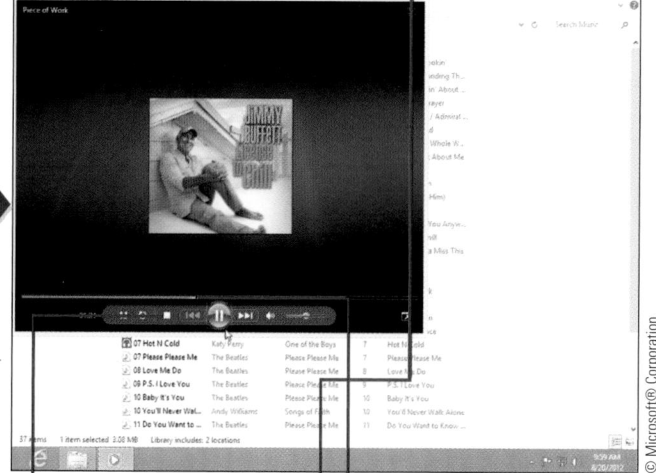

© Microsoft® Corporation

4 To adjust the volume, drag the ⊸ left or right to decrease or increase the volume.

Note: If the slider does not appear, increase the size of the window to display the slider. To resize a window, see ***Chapter 2****.*

5 To mute the sound, click 🔊. (🔊 changes to 🔇.)

■ You can click 🔇 to once again turn on the sound.

6 To pause the video or sound, click ⏸. ⏸ changes to ▶.

■ To stop the video or sound, click ■. (⏸ changes to ▶.)

■ You can click ▶ to once again play the video or sound.

■ This bar indicates the progress of the video or sound.

7 When you finish playing the video or sound, click ✕ to close the Windows Media Player window.

New to Windows 8 is the Music app. From the Music app, you can choose what music you want to hear and learn more about your favorite musicians.

You can play the music you have stored on your computer.

PLAY MUSIC WINDOWS 8 STYLE

1 From the Start screen, click **Music**.

■ Depending on your screen size and resolution, you may have to scroll to the right to locate Music.

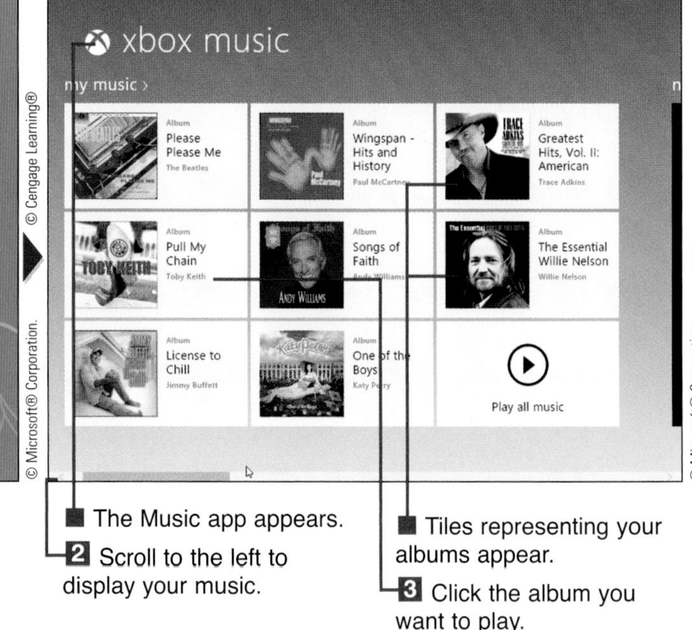

■ The Music app appears.

2 Scroll to the left to display your music.

■ Tiles representing your albums appear.

3 Click the album you want to play.

What do the headings in the Music app represent?

There are three headings in the Music app. My music represents the music you have stored on your computer or SkyDrive; Xbox music store is where you can purchase almost any music from any artist; and Most popular is similar to the Xbox music store. In the Most popular section, the choices include today's most popular artists.

Click any heading, and you can select your favorite genre. Many of the genres then display additional filtering of the genre.

From there you can select an album, preview the music, and, if desired, buy the album.

© Microsoft® Corporation

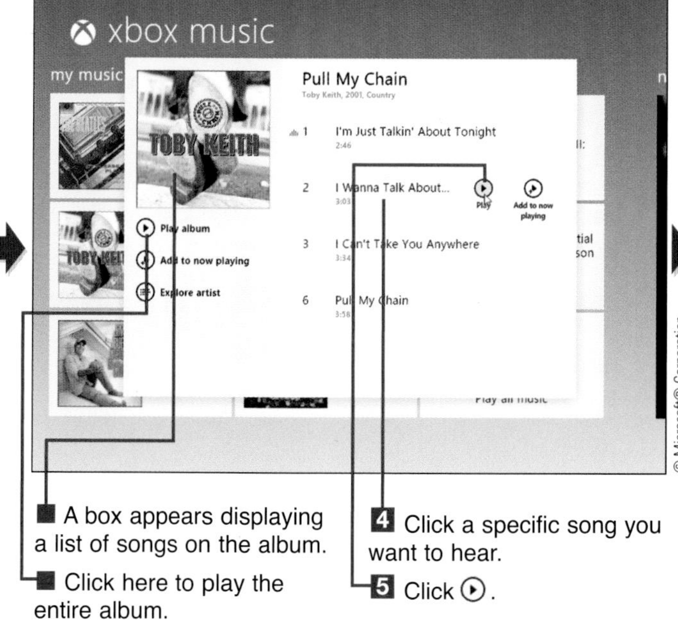

© Microsoft® Corporation

■ A box appears displaying a list of songs on the album.

■ Click here to play the entire album.

4 Click a specific song you want to hear.

5 Click ⊙.

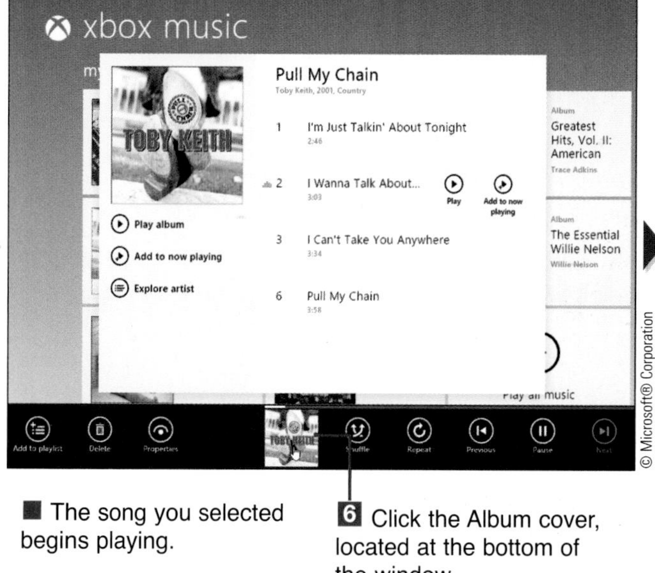

© Microsoft® Corporation

■ The song you selected begins playing.

6 Click the Album cover, located at the bottom of the window.

CONTINUED

With the Music app, you have an opportunity to purchase additional music by your favorite artists.

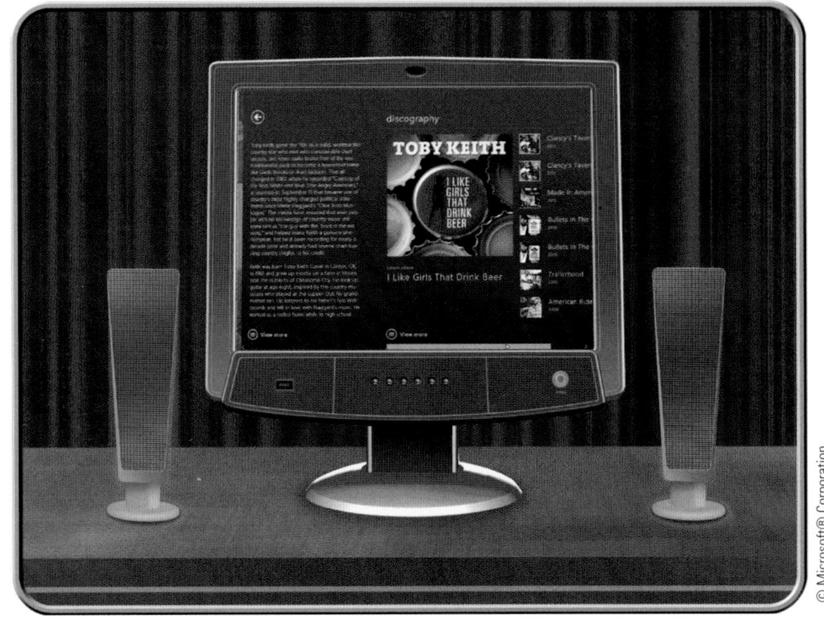

© Microsoft® Corporation

PLAY MUSIC WINDOWS 8 STYLE (CONTINUED)

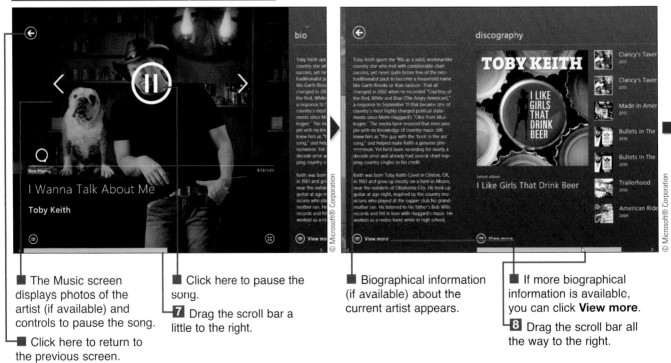

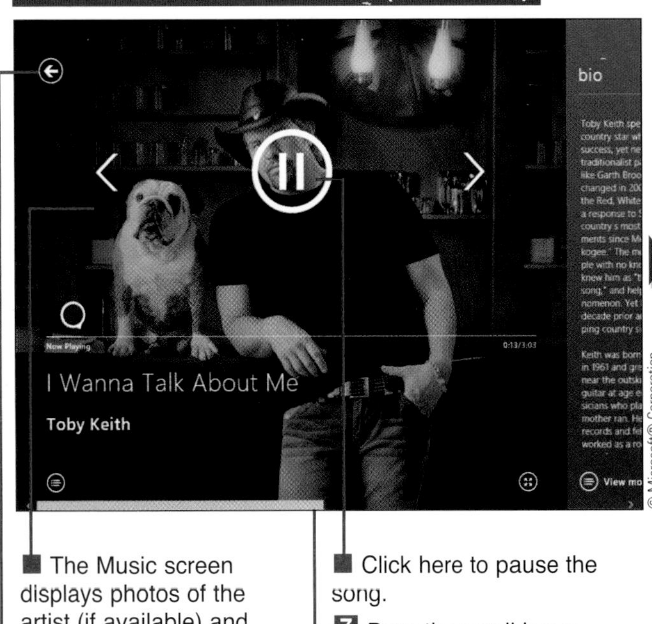

© Microsoft® Corporation

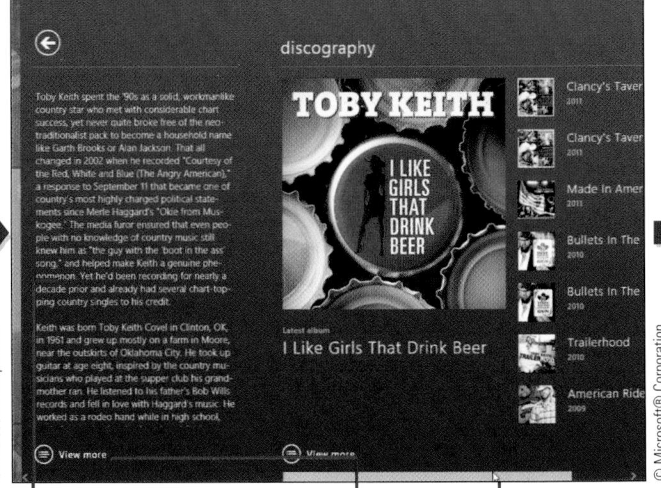

© Microsoft® Corporation

■ The Music screen displays photos of the artist (if available) and controls to pause the song.

■ Click here to return to the previous screen.

■ Click here to pause the song.

7 Drag the scroll bar a little to the right.

■ Biographical information (if available) about the current artist appears.

■ If more biographical information is available, you can click **View more**.

8 Drag the scroll bar all the way to the right.

How do I buy music from the Music app?

The Music app store uses a point system called Microsoft Points. You buy points though a secure Microsoft site by using a credit card. Microsoft tracks the points you have available, and then you can spend them as desired.

The first time you buy points, you are asked for your name, address, and phone number. You then must enter a credit card number for your purchase.

You buy points in lumps. The smallest amount is 400 points, which costs around $5.00, and the largest amount is 6,000 points, which costs around $75.00. A single song costs about 100 points, and a complete album costs around 800 points.

© Microsoft® Corporation

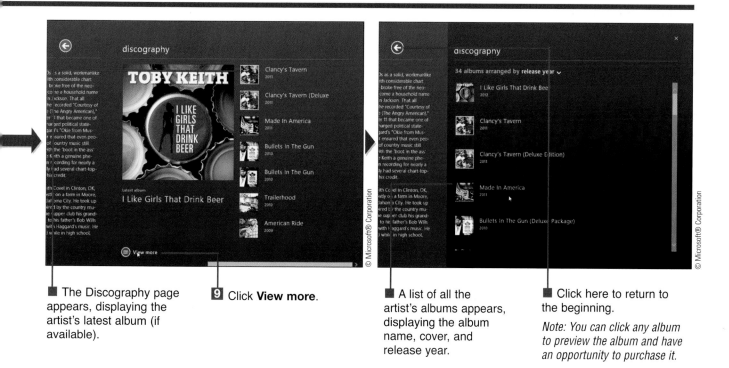

■ The Discography page appears, displaying the artist's latest album (if available).

9 Click **View more**.

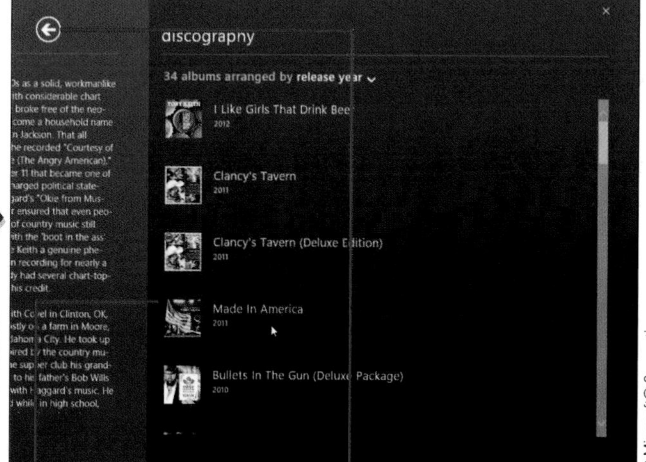

© Microsoft® Corporation

■ A list of all the artist's albums appears, displaying the album name, cover, and release year.

■ Click here to return to the beginning.

Note: You can click any album to preview the album and have an opportunity to purchase it.

PLAY A MUSIC CD

You can use your computer to play music CDs while you work.

If this is the first time Windows Media Player starts, the Welcome to Windows Media Player window appears, asking you to choose your setting for the player. I suggest you choose **Recommended settings** and click **Finish**.

PLAY A MUSIC CD

© Cengage Learning®

© Microsoft® Corporation.

© Cengage Learning®

© Microsoft® Corporation.

1 Insert your CD into your CD or DVD drive.

2 Click this box.

3 Click **Play audio CD**. You have to click this only the first time you use it. Windows remembers your selection the next time.

*Note: To adjust the volume, see the previous section **"Play a Video or Sound."***

How does Windows Media Player know the CD cover and the name of the songs on my music CD?

When you play a music CD, Windows Media Player attempts to obtain CD information from the Internet, including the CD cover and track names. If you are not connected to the Internet or information about the CD is unavailable, Windows Media Player displays a generic CD cover and the track number of each song instead. If Windows Media Player is able to obtain the CD information, it recognizes the CD and displays the appropriate information each time you insert the CD.

Can I play the songs on a music CD in random order?

Yes. If you want to play the songs on a music CD in random order, click [shuffle icon] at the bottom of the Windows Media Player window. To once again play the songs in numerical order, click [shuffle icon] again.

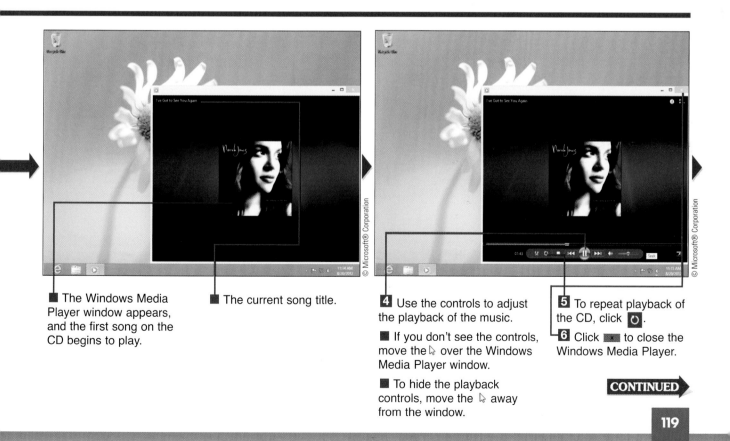

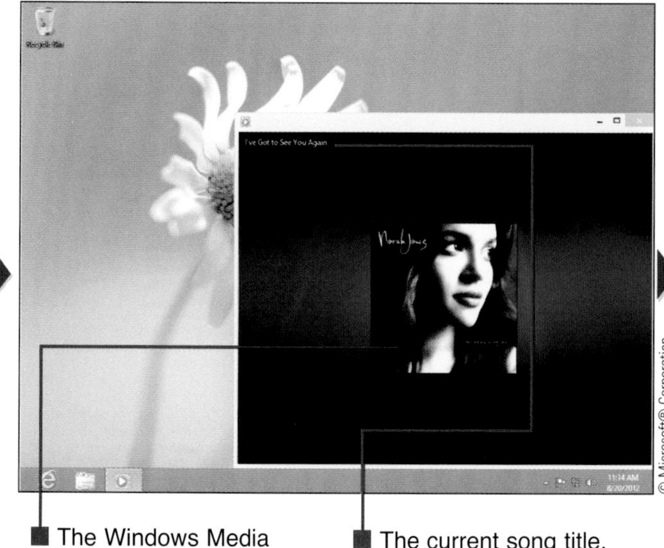

© Microsoft® Corporation

■ The Windows Media Player window appears, and the first song on the CD begins to play.

■ The current song title.

© Microsoft® Corporation

4 Use the controls to adjust the playback of the music.

■ If you don't see the controls, move the [pointer] over the Windows Media Player window.

■ To hide the playback controls, move the [pointer] away from the window.

5 To repeat playback of the CD, click [repeat icon].

6 Click [close icon] to close the Windows Media Player.

CONTINUED

If you want to listen to a specific song from the CD, you can choose it from the library.

PLAY A MUSIC CD (CONTINUED)

© Microsoft® Corporation

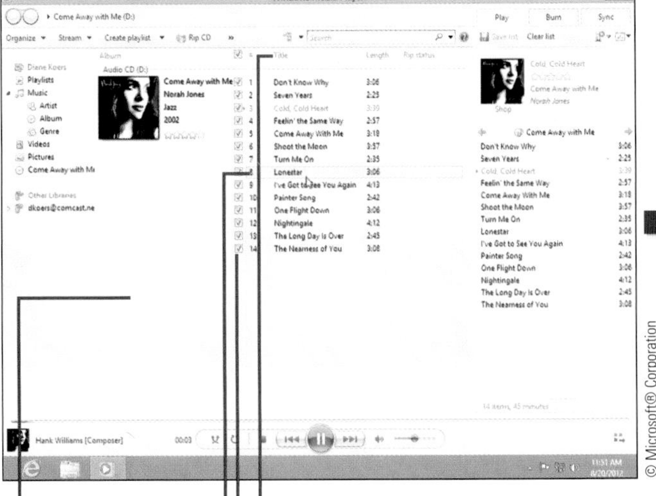

© Microsoft® Corporation

CHOOSE A SPECIFIC SONG FROM THE CD LIBRARY

1 From the Windows Media Player, click [library icon] to switch to the library.

■ If you don't see the controls, move the [pointer] over the Windows Media Player window.

■ The Windows Media Player details window opens.

Note: The currently playing song title appears in a slightly different color from the other song titles.

2 Click a column heading to change the way the song titles are sorted.

3 If you want to skip a particular song, click ✔ next to the song you don't want to play. (✔ changes to ☐.)

4 Double-click the song title you want to play.

What else can I do in the Windows Media Player details window?

You can choose from media other than what's on your CD. For example, you can choose music or videos stored in your Music or Video libraries, just as if you had accessed them from File Explorer. You can also view your pictures.

To select other media locations, click the appropriate library from the Navigation pane on the left side of the screen.

I have a lot of music stored on my computer. Is there a way to easily sort it?

Yes. Click Music from the Navigation pane, and then click whether you want the music sorted by Artist, Album, or Genre.

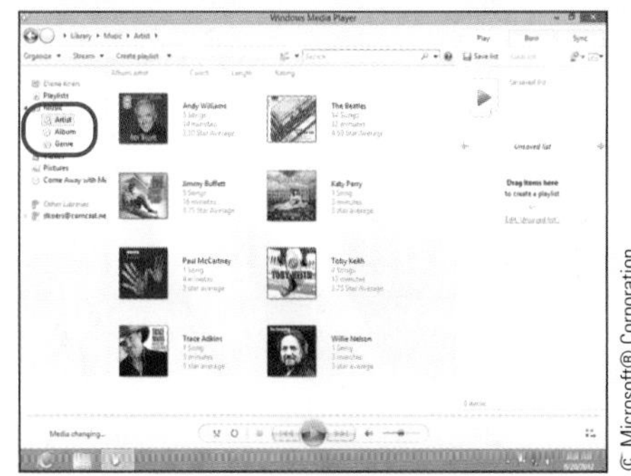

© Microsoft® Corporation

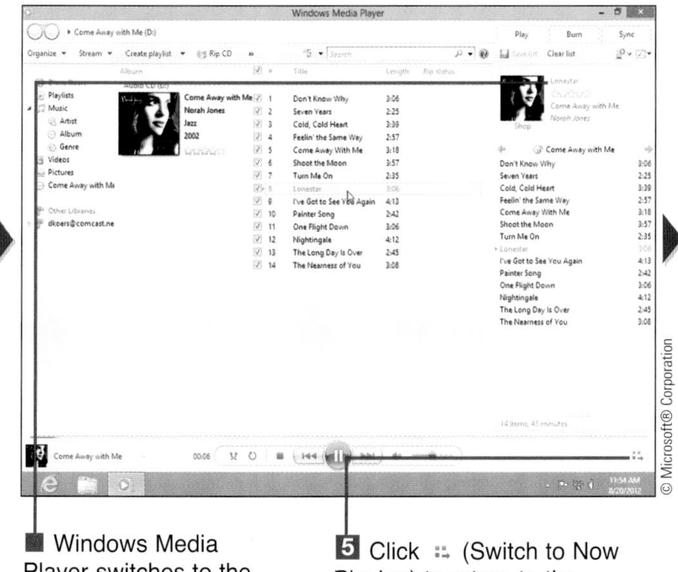

© Microsoft® Corporation

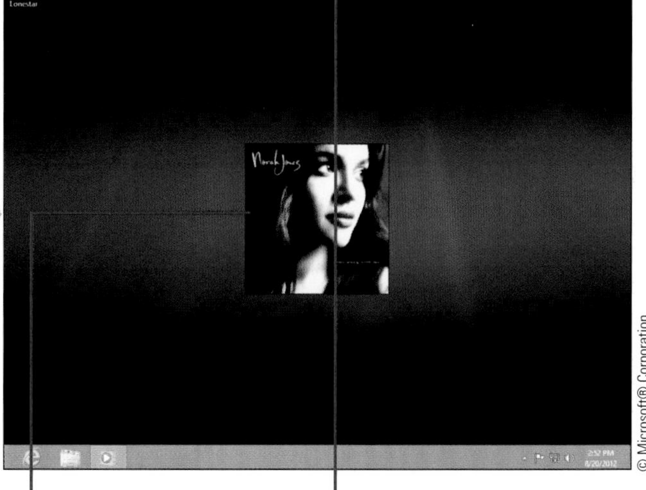

© Microsoft® Corporation

■ Windows Media Player switches to the selected song.

5 Click (Switch to Now Playing) to return to the standard Windows Media Player window.

■ Windows Media Player switches back to the Now Playing view.

6 When you are finished listening to your music, click to close the Windows Media Player.

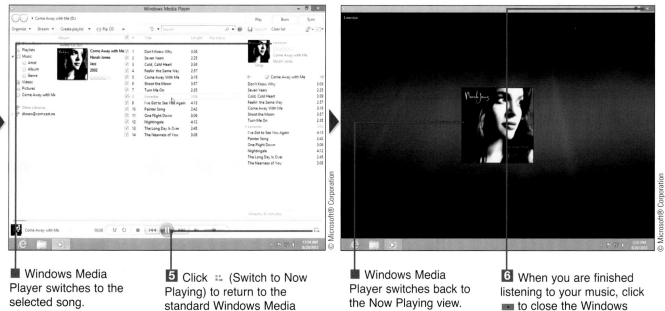

CREATE A PLAYLIST

You can create personalized lists, called *playlists*, of your favorite songs, videos, and pictures.

Playlists allow you to group items you would like to listen to or view regularly. For example, you can create a playlist that contains your favorite rock songs.

CREATE A PLAYLIST

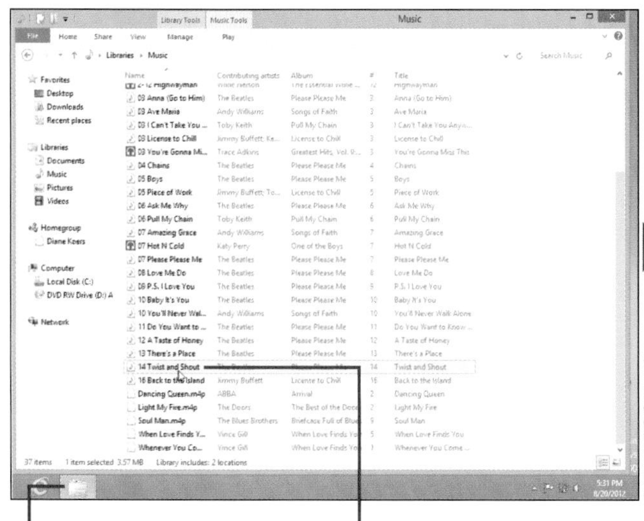

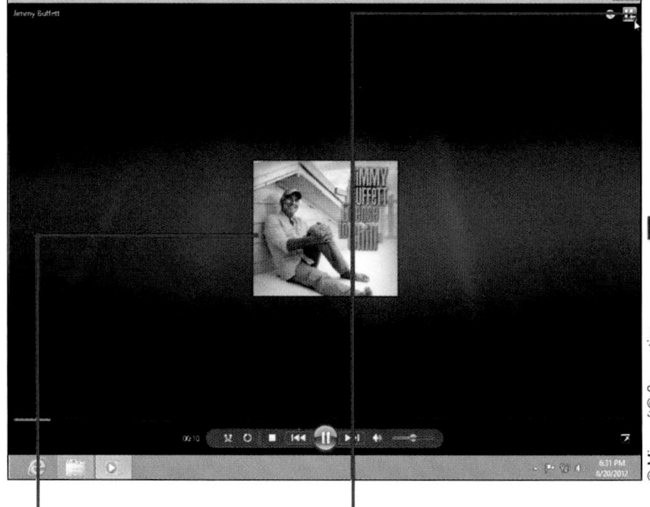

1 From the Windows desktop, click File Explorer and open the Music library.

2 Double-click any song to start the Windows Media Player.

■ The Windows Media Player window appears.

3 Click ▦ to switch to the library.

How do I change the order of items in a playlist?

From the Navigation pane, click the name of the playlist you want to change. In the List pane, drag an item up or down in the playlist.

How do I remove items from a playlist?

From the Navigation pane, click the name of the playlist you want to change. Click the item you want removed and then press Delete.

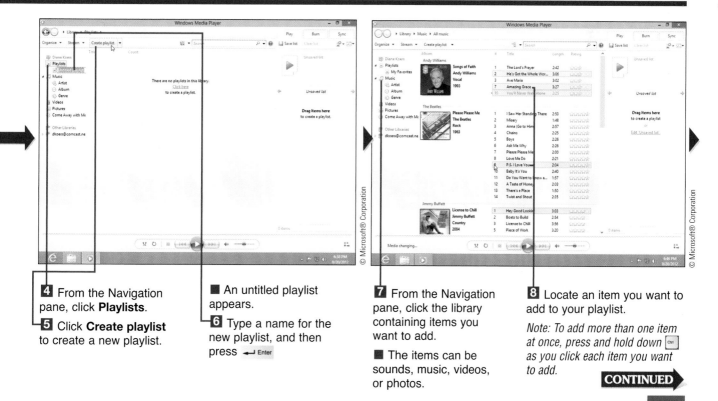

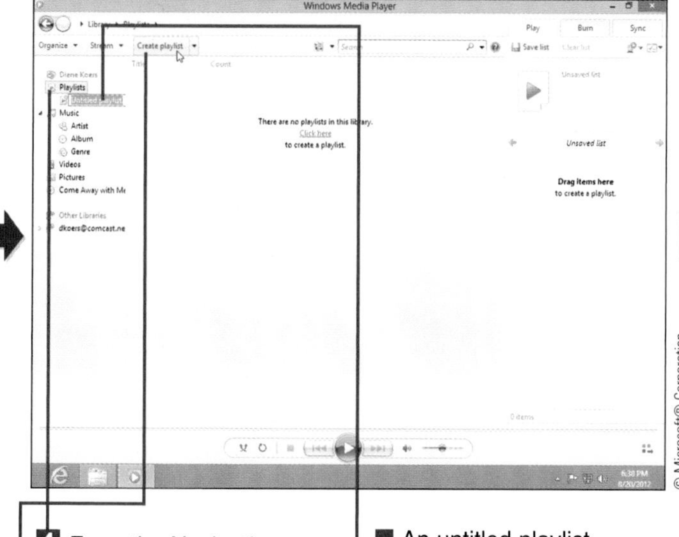

© Microsoft® Corporation

4 From the Navigation pane, click **Playlists**.

5 Click **Create playlist** to create a new playlist.

■ An untitled playlist appears.

6 Type a name for the new playlist, and then press Enter.

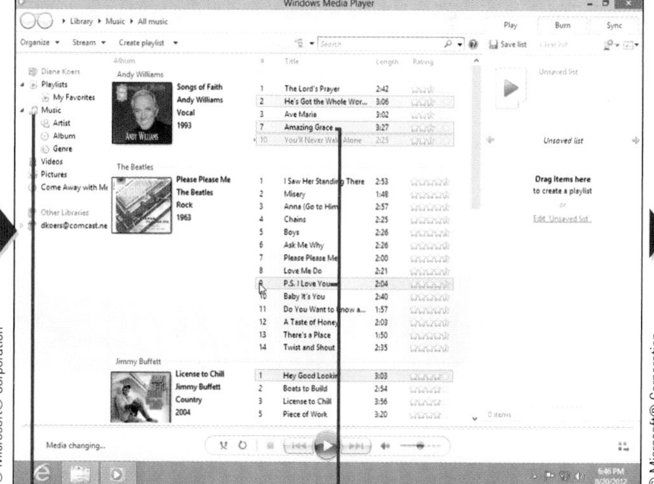

© Microsoft® Corporation

7 From the Navigation pane, click the library containing items you want to add.

■ The items can be sounds, music, videos, or photos.

8 Locate an item you want to add to your playlist.

Note: To add more than one item at once, press and hold down Ctrl as you click each item you want to add.

CONTINUED

Once you create your playlist, you can easily add your favorite music to the list.

CREATE A PLAYLIST (CONTINUED)

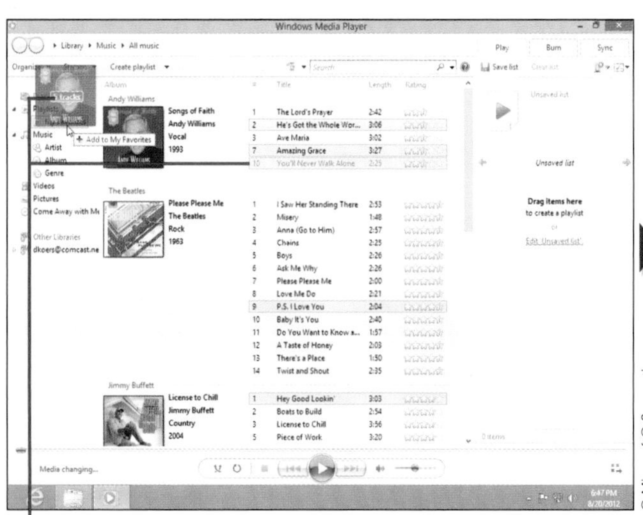

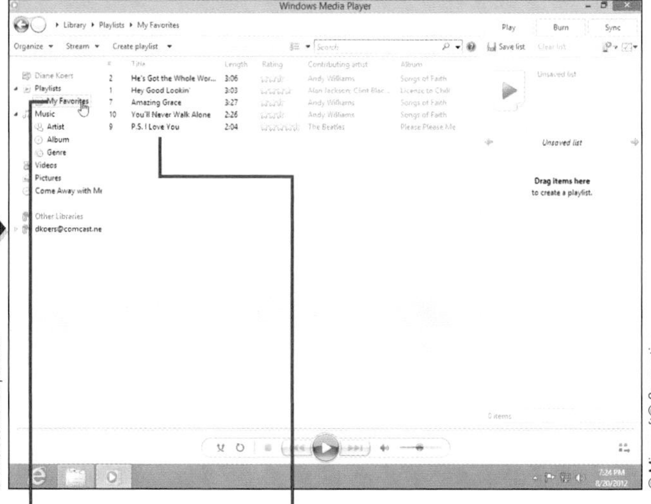

© Microsoft® Corporation

© Microsoft® Corporation

9 Position the ⇖ over any of the selected items, and then drag the items to the desired playlist in the Navigation pane.

10 When the items are over the playlist, release the mouse button.

11 Click the playlist.

■ The items appear in the playlist.

12 Repeat steps **7** through **10** for each item you want to add to the playlist.

Can I rename the playlist?

Yes. Right-click the playlist you want to rename, and choose **Rename**. Type the new name and press Enter.

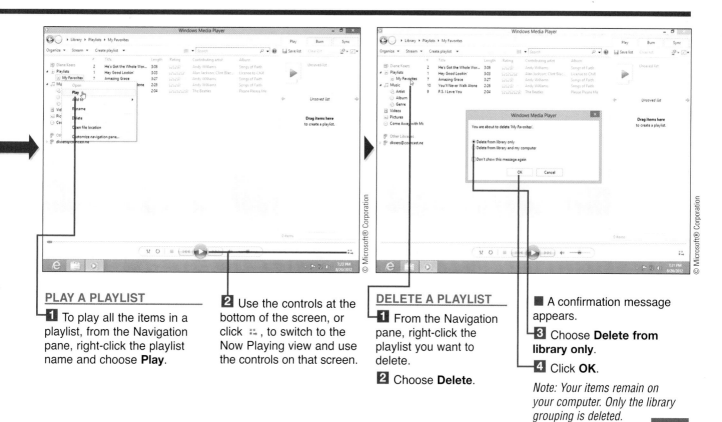

© Microsoft® Corporation

© Microsoft® Corporation

PLAY A PLAYLIST

1 To play all the items in a playlist, from the Navigation pane, right-click the playlist name and choose **Play**.

2 Use the controls at the bottom of the screen, or click ⠶, to switch to the Now Playing view and use the controls on that screen.

DELETE A PLAYLIST

1 From the Navigation pane, right-click the playlist you want to delete.

2 Choose **Delete**.

■ A confirmation message appears.

3 Choose **Delete from library only**.

4 Click **OK**.

Note: Your items remain on your computer. Only the library grouping is deleted.

COPY SONGS FROM A MUSIC CD

You can copy songs from a music CD onto your computer.

Copying songs from a music CD, also known as *ripping* music, allows you to play the songs at any time without having to insert the CD into your computer. Copying songs from a music CD also allows you to later copy the songs to a recordable CD or a portable device, such as an iPod or other music player.

COPY SONGS FROM A MUSIC CD

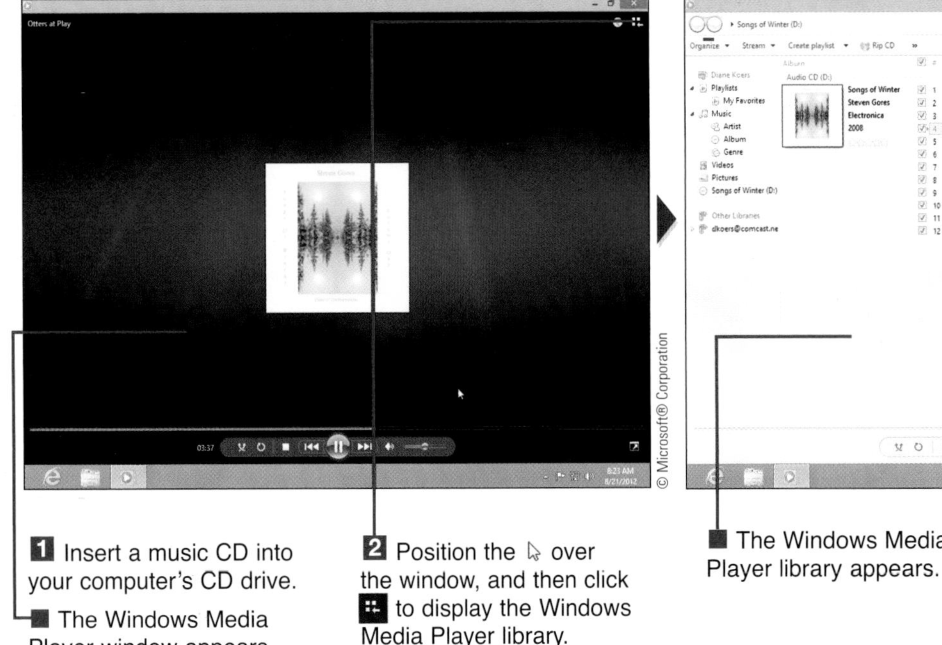

© Microsoft® Corporation

1 Insert a music CD into your computer's CD drive.

■ The Windows Media Player window appears, and the CD begins to play.

2 Position the pointer over the window, and then click the switch-to-library button to display the Windows Media Player library.

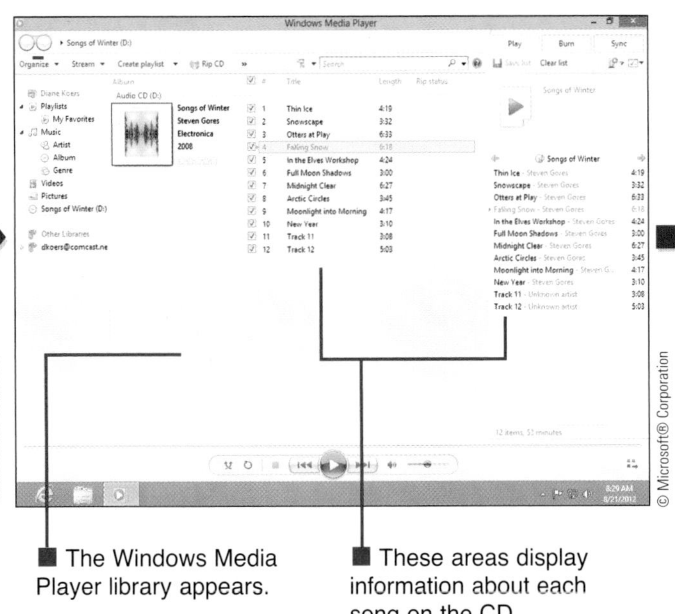

© Microsoft® Corporation

■ The Windows Media Player library appears.

■ These areas display information about each song on the CD.

How can I play a song I copied from a music CD?

Songs you copy from a music CD appear in the Music library on your computer. The Music library displays a folder for each artist whose songs you have copied to your computer. To view the Music library, see **"Play a Video or Sound"** earlier in this chapter. When you see a song you want to play in the Music library, double-click the song to play it.

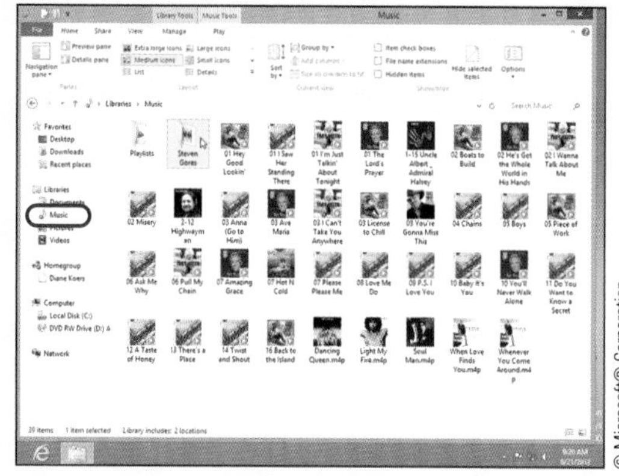

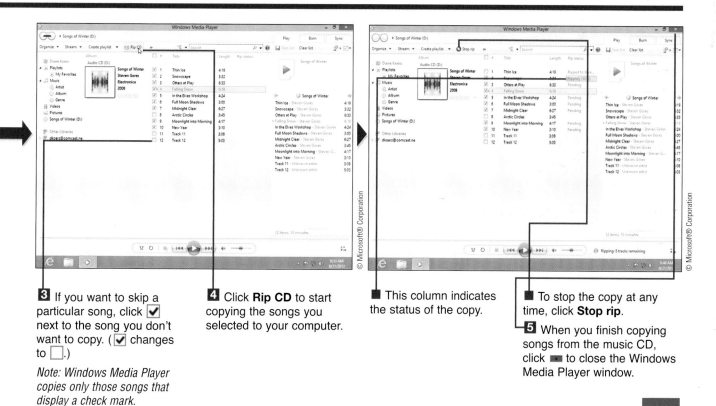

3 If you want to skip a particular song, click ☑ next to the song you don't want to copy. (☑ changes to ☐.)

Note: Windows Media Player copies only those songs that display a check mark.

4 Click **Rip CD** to start copying the songs you selected to your computer.

■ This column indicates the status of the copy.

■ To stop the copy at any time, click **Stop rip**.

5 When you finish copying songs from the music CD, click ▬ to close the Windows Media Player window.

COPY SONGS TO A CD

You can use Windows Media Player to copy songs on your computer to a CD.

Copying songs to a CD is known as *burning* a CD.

COPY SONGS TO A CD

1 Insert a blank CD into your computer's CD or DVD drive.

2 Click here.

3 Click **Burn an audio CD**. You only have to click this the first time you use it. Windows remembers your selection the next time.

Tip

Can I copy songs from multiple albums?

The song titles you choose do not have to be from a single album. You can select songs from different albums.

You can also change the order of the music by dragging a song title to the position you want it in the burn list.

Tip

How many songs can I fit on a CD?

A CD holds about 70 minutes of music. If you add more than 70 minutes, Windows Media Player creates a Disc 2 and moves some of the music to the second disc.

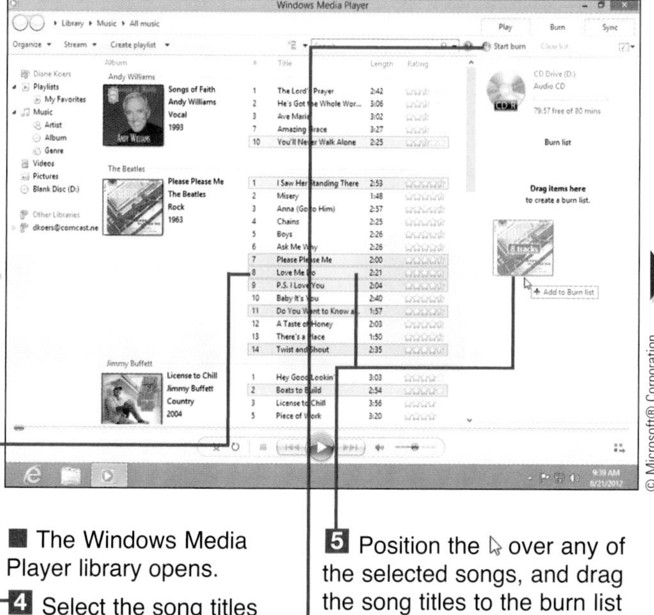

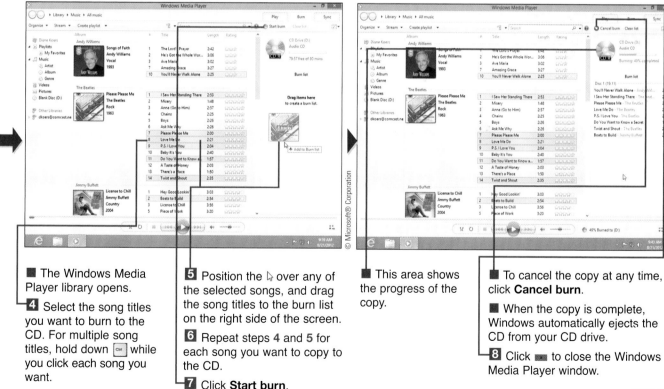

■ The Windows Media Player library opens.

4 Select the song titles you want to burn to the CD. For multiple song titles, hold down Ctrl while you click each song you want.

5 Position the ↖ over any of the selected songs, and drag the song titles to the burn list on the right side of the screen.

6 Repeat steps **4** and **5** for each song you want to copy to the CD.

7 Click **Start burn**.

■ This area shows the progress of the copy.

■ To cancel the copy at any time, click **Cancel burn**.

■ When the copy is complete, Windows automatically ejects the CD from your CD drive.

8 Click ✕ to close the Windows Media Player window.

DVD-WRITER
CD-ROM
MULTI-CARD
READER
-AUDIO-

CHAPTER 7

Customize Windows

CHANGE THE DESKTOP BACKGROUND

Many users will spend a great deal of their time on the desktop. You can change the picture used to decorate your desktop.

© Microsoft® Corporation. © Cengage Learning®

Windows comes with many desktop backgrounds that you can choose from. You can also use one of your own pictures as your desktop background.

You can change your desktop background by selecting a different theme. To select a different theme, see **"Change the Theme"** later in this chapter.

CHANGE THE DESKTOP BACKGROUND

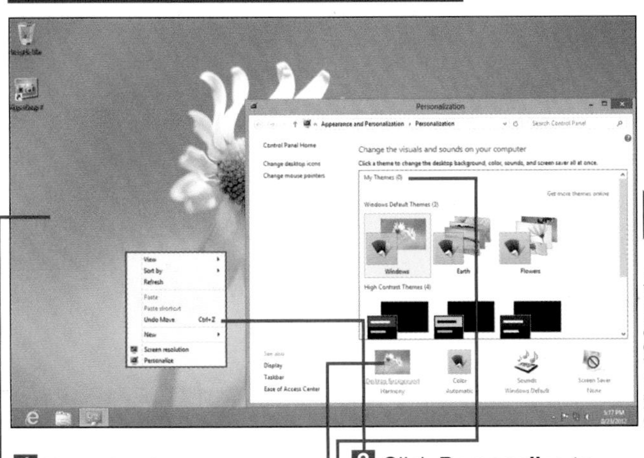

© Microsoft® Corporation

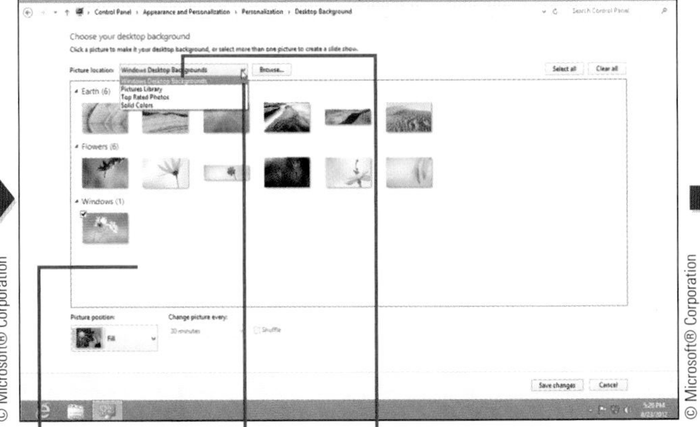

© Microsoft® Corporation

1 From the Start screen, click **Desktop**.

2 Right-click a blank area on your desktop. A menu appears.

3 Click **Personalize** to personalize your computer.

■ The Personalization window appears.

4 Click **Desktop Background** to personalize your desktop background.

■ The Desktop Background window appears.

5 Click this area to display a list of picture locations.

6 Click the location or type of picture you want.

Note: You can select from desktop backgrounds that come with Windows, pictures in your Pictures library, your top-rated photos, and solid colors.

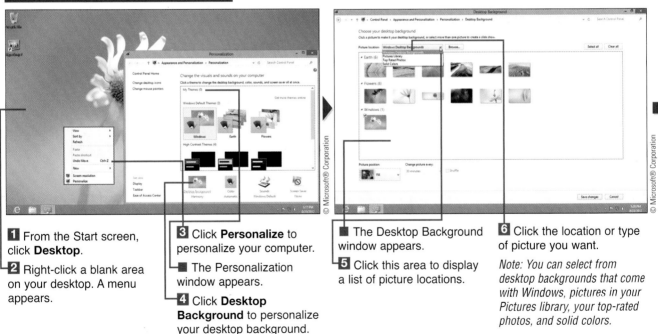

Can I have my background picture automatically change every so often?

Yes. By default, once you access this screen and choose a Picture location of Windows Desktop Backgrounds or Pictures Library, Windows assumes you want all the images selected and changes the desktop background every day, every hour, or after a time period you select.

If you don't want certain pictures included, you can deselect them by clicking the check box in the upper-left corner of the image you don't want. (✔ changes to ☐.) If you want to quickly deselect all the pictures, click **Clear all**. Then hold down Ctrl and click the images you want for a slide show.

To specify how often you want the desktop picture to change, click the area below **Change picture every** and select a time. Be sure to click **Save changes** when you are finished.

I cannot find the picture I want to use as my desktop background. What can I do?

If you cannot find the picture you want to use as your desktop background, click **Browse** in the Desktop Background window. In the dialog box that appears, locate and click the folder that contains the picture and then click **OK**. The pictures in the folder you selected appear in the Desktop Background window.

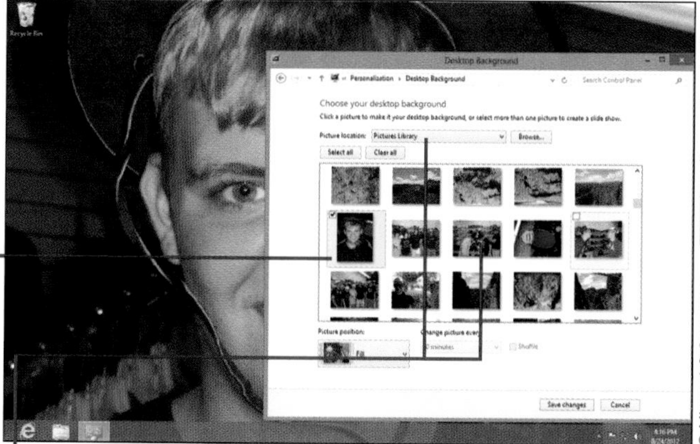

■ This area displays the pictures in the location you selected.

7 Click the picture you want to display on your desktop.

■ The picture you selected immediately appears on your desktop.

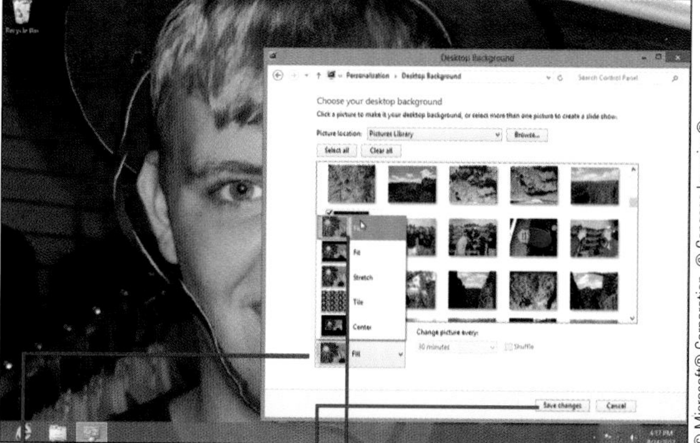

8 Click this area to select the way you want to position the picture on your desktop.

9 Click an option to crop the picture to fill the screen, resize the picture to fit the screen, stretch the picture to fill the screen, tile the picture to appear several times to fill the screen, or center the picture on the screen.

10 Click **Save changes** to save your changes.

MODIFY THE SCREEN SAVER

A *screen saver* is a picture or animation that appears on the screen when you do not use your computer for a period of time.

You can use a screen saver to hide your work while you are away from your desk. Windows is initially set up to not display a screen saver.

MODIFY THE SCREEN SAVER

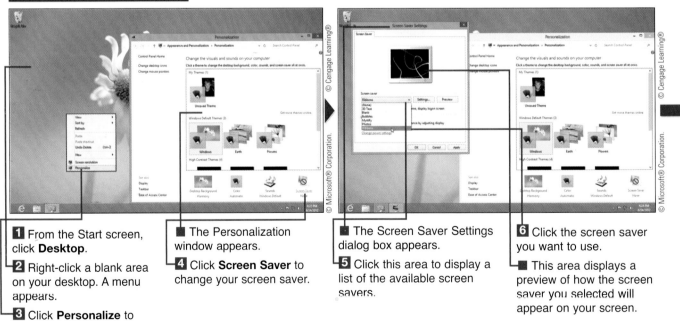

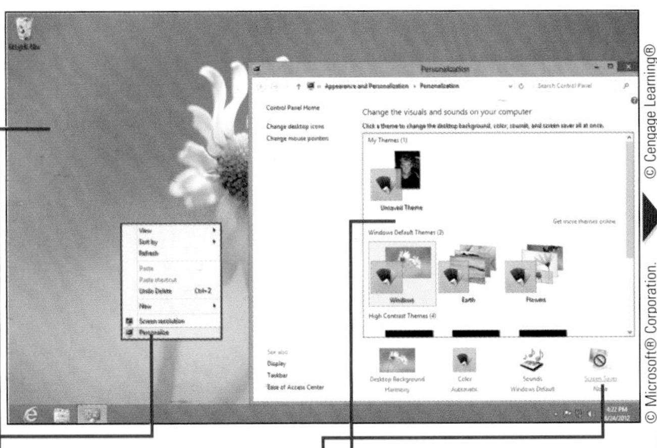

1 From the Start screen, click **Desktop**.

2 Right-click a blank area on your desktop. A menu appears.

3 Click **Personalize** to personalize your computer.

■ The Personalization window appears.

4 Click **Screen Saver** to change your screen saver.

■ The Screen Saver Settings dialog box appears.

5 Click this area to display a list of the available screen savers.

6 Click the screen saver you want to use.

■ This area displays a preview of how the screen saver you selected will appear on your screen.

What does the Photos screen saver do?

You can select the Photos screen saver to have the pictures in your Pictures library appear as your screen saver. Windows rotates through all the pictures in the library. For information on the Pictures library, see **Chapter 4**.

Can I customize my screen saver?

After you select the screen saver you want to use, you can click the Settings button to customize some screen savers. For example, if you select the 3D Text screen saver, you can customize the text that you want to appear on your screen, such as your company's name.

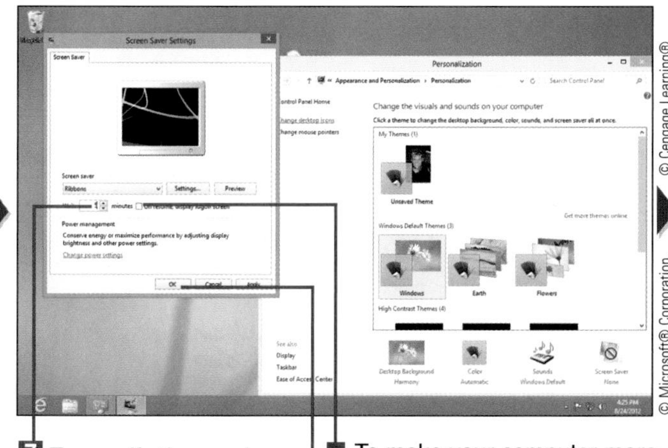

7 To specify the number of minutes your computer must be inactive before the screen saver appears, double-click this area. Then type the number of minutes.

■ To make your computer more secure, this option requires you to sign in to Windows each time you remove the screen saver. You can click this option to turn the option on (☑) or off (☐).

*Note: For information on signing in to Windows, see **Chapter 1**.*

8 Click **OK**.

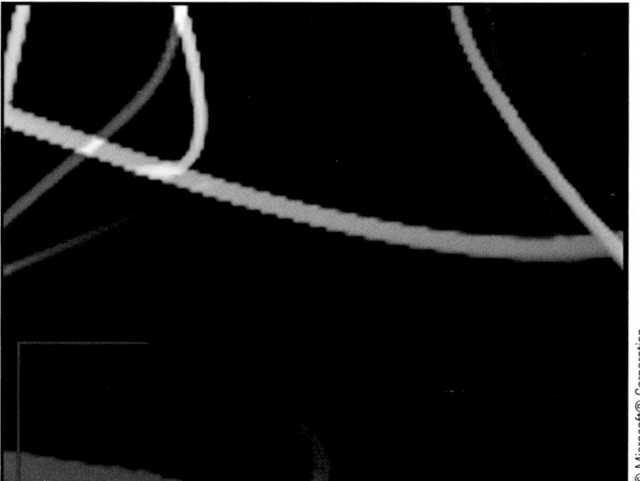

■ The screen saver appears when you do not use your computer for the number of minutes you specified.

■ You can move the mouse or press a key on the keyboard to remove the screen saver from your screen.

*Note: To stop a screen saver from appearing, perform steps **1** to **6**, selecting (**None**) in step **6**. Then perform step **8**.*

ALTER THE COLOR OF WINDOWS

You can add a personal touch to your computer by changing the color used to display windows on your screen. The color you select also changes the color of the taskbar and the Start menu.

You can also change the color used to display windows on your screen by selecting a different theme. To select a different theme, see **"Change the Theme"** later in this chapter.

ALTER THE COLOR OF WINDOWS

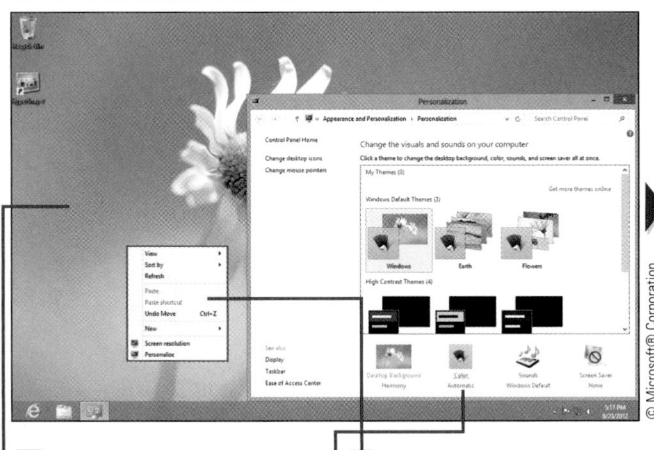

1 From the Start screen, click **Desktop**.

2 Right-click a blank area on your desktop. A menu appears.

3 Click **Personalize** to personalize your computer.

■ The Personalization window appears.

4 Click **Color** to change the color used to display windows on your screen.

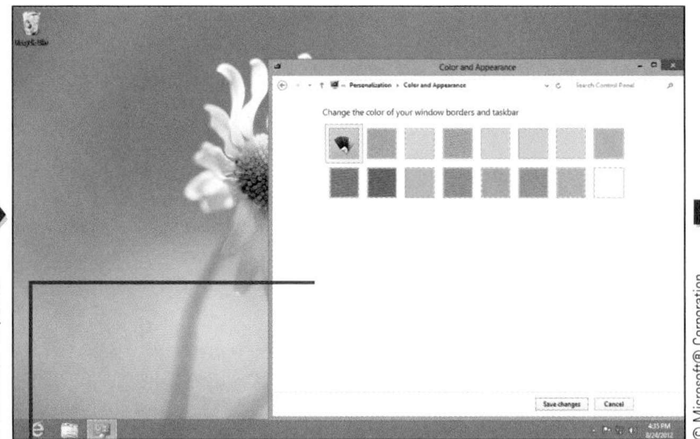

■ The Color and Appearance window appears.

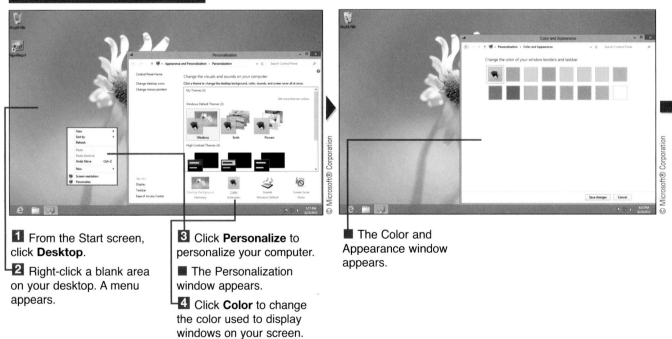

Tip

Can I create my own color?

Yes. If you do not see a color you like in the Color and Appearance window, click **Show color mixer** to create your own color. Drag the sliders that appear beside Hue (color), Saturation (intensity of color), and Brightness until the windows on your screen display the color you like.

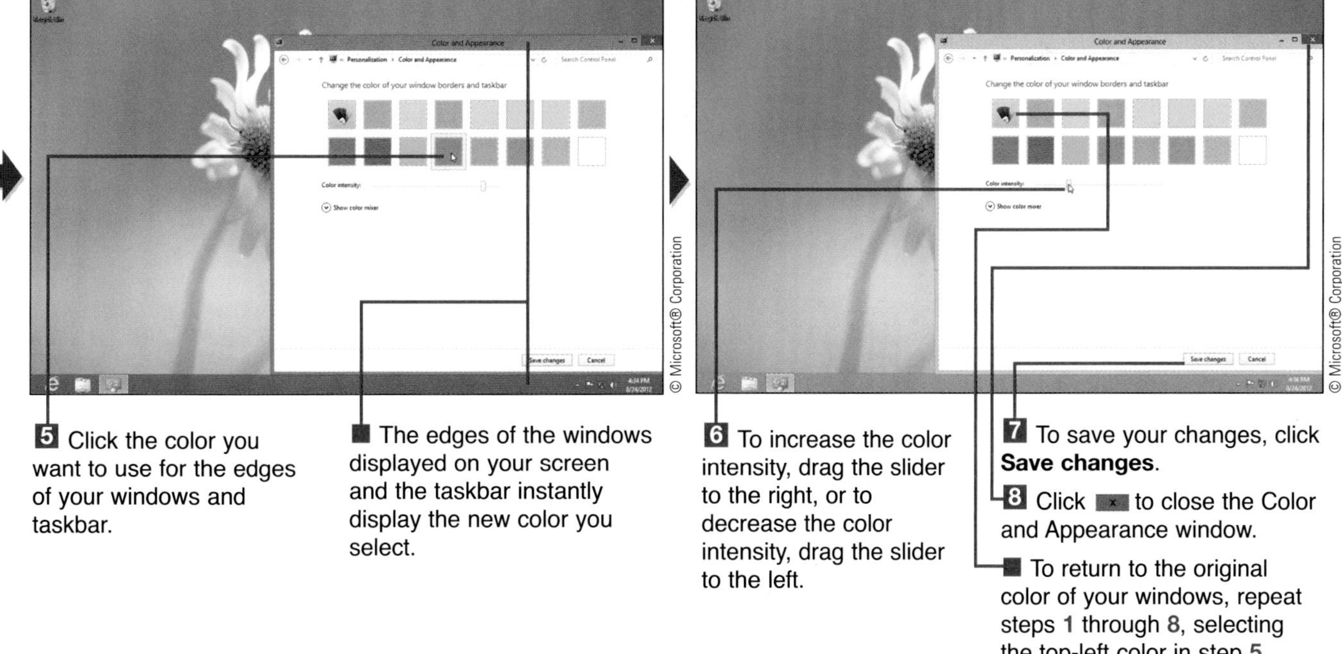

5 Click the color you want to use for the edges of your windows and taskbar.

■ The edges of the windows displayed on your screen and the taskbar instantly display the new color you select.

6 To increase the color intensity, drag the slider to the right, or to decrease the color intensity, drag the slider to the left.

7 To save your changes, click **Save changes**.

8 Click ✕ to close the Color and Appearance window.

■ To return to the original color of your windows, repeat steps 1 through 8, selecting the top-left color in step 5.

CHANGE THE THEME

You can change the theme to personalize the overall appearance of Windows.

Each theme contains several coordinated items, including a desktop background, a window color, sounds, and a screen saver. Some themes also include desktop icons and mouse pointers.

Windows comes with several themes that you can choose from.

CHANGE THE THEME

1 From the Start screen, click **Desktop**.

2 Right-click a blank area on your desktop. A menu appears.

3 Click **Personalize** to personalize your computer.

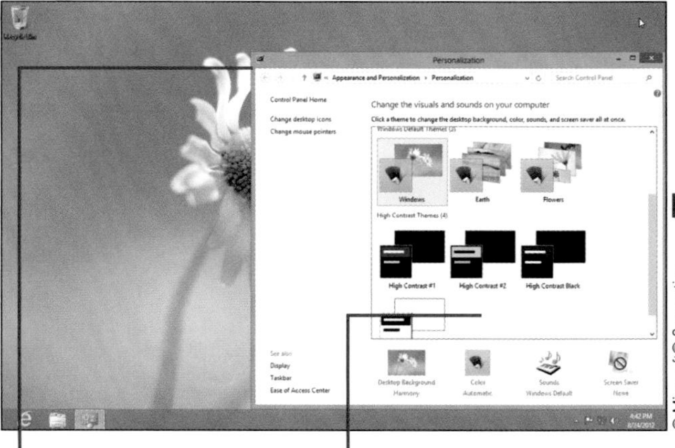

■ The Personalization window appears.

■ This area displays the available themes. You can use the scroll bar to browse through the available themes.

Note: If you have a visual impairment, the High Contrast themes can make the items on your screen easier to see.

Where can I get more themes?

You can get more themes on the Internet. To quickly find more themes online, click **Get more themes online** in the Personalization window. A web page appears, showing a list of the available themes that you can download and use on your computer. Most are free.

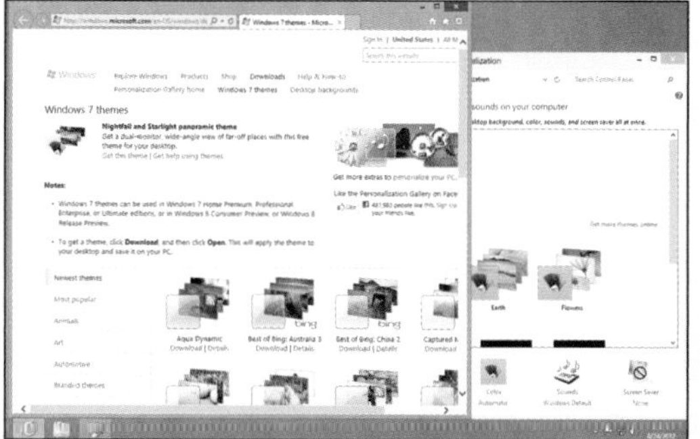

© Microsoft® Corporation

Can I customize a theme?

Yes. After you select a theme, you can change the parts of a theme individually by changing the desktop background, window color, sounds, or screen saver. You can change one or more of these elements until the theme looks the way you want. Your customized theme appears under My Themes in the Personalization window.

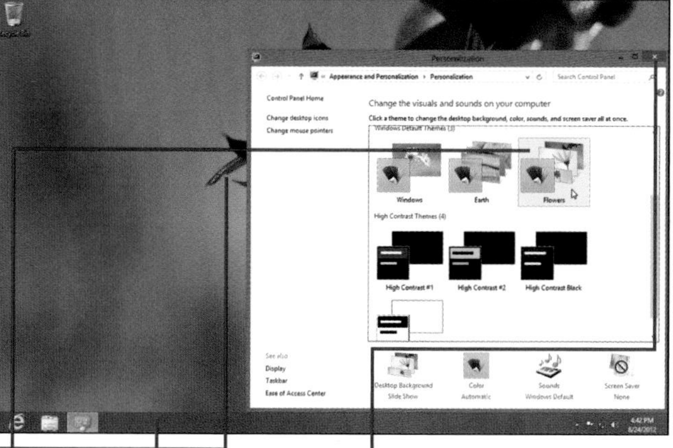

© Microsoft® Corporation

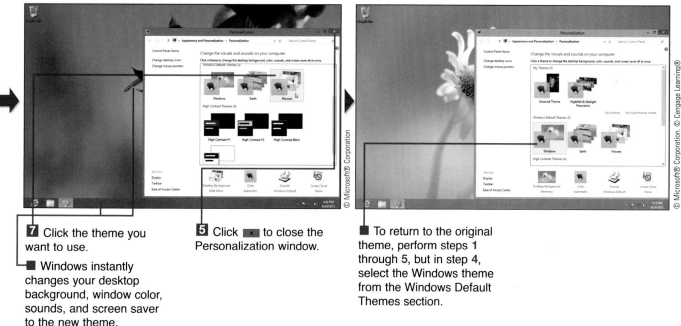

7 Click the theme you want to use.

■ Windows instantly changes your desktop background, window color, sounds, and screen saver to the new theme.

5 Click ✕ to close the Personalization window.

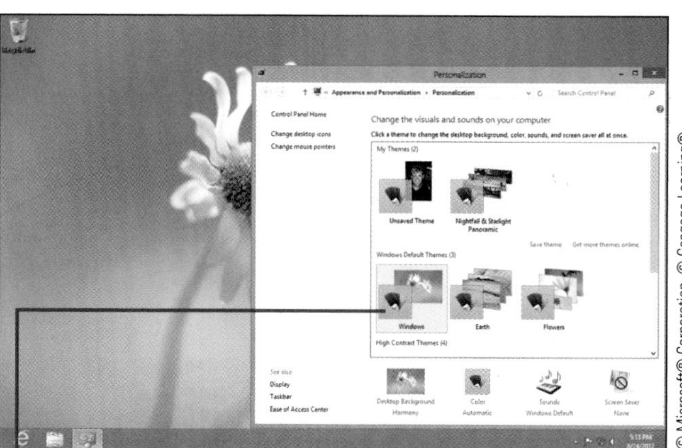

© Microsoft® Corporation. © Cengage Learning®

■ To return to the original theme, perform steps **1** through **5**, but in step **4**, select the Windows theme from the Windows Default Themes section.

ADJUST THE VOLUME

You can adjust the volume of sound on your computer.

© Microsoft® Corporation

Windows allows you to easily adjust the volume of your speakers. You can also adjust the volume of individual devices and programs on your computer without affecting the volume of other devices and programs.

ADJUST THE VOLUME

© Microsoft® Corporation

© Microsoft® Corporation

1 From the Start screen, click **Desktop**.

2 In the lower-right corner of the taskbar, click 🔊 to display the Volume control.

■ The Volume control appears.

3 Drag the slider up or down to increase or decrease the volume.

Note: As you drag the slider, the number beside the slider indicates the speaker volume strength as a percentage from 0 to 100.

4 To turn off the sound coming from your speakers, click 🔊. (🔊 changes to 🔇.)

Note: After you turn off the sound, 🔊 changes to 🔇.

■ To once again turn on the sound, click 🔇. (🔇 changes to 🔊.)

5 When you finish adjusting the speaker volume, click a blank area on your desktop to hide the Volume control.

What devices and programs can appear in the Volume Mixer dialog box?

The devices and programs that appear in the Volume Mixer dialog box depend on the devices that are connected to your computer and the programs you have open that produce sound. Here are some devices and programs you can see in the dialog box:

Speakers—Adjusts the volume of your speakers.

System Sounds—Adjusts the volume of sounds that play when certain events, such as the arrival of new email messages, occur on your computer.

Windows Media Player—Adjusts the sound volume playing in Windows Media Player. This appears only if you are actually using Windows Media Player.

Is there another way that I can adjust the speaker volume?

Yes. Many speakers have a volume control that you can use to adjust the volume. Your speakers may also have a power button that you can use to turn the sound on or off. Some keyboards, especially laptop computer keyboards, have keys that you can press to adjust the volume of the computer's speakers.

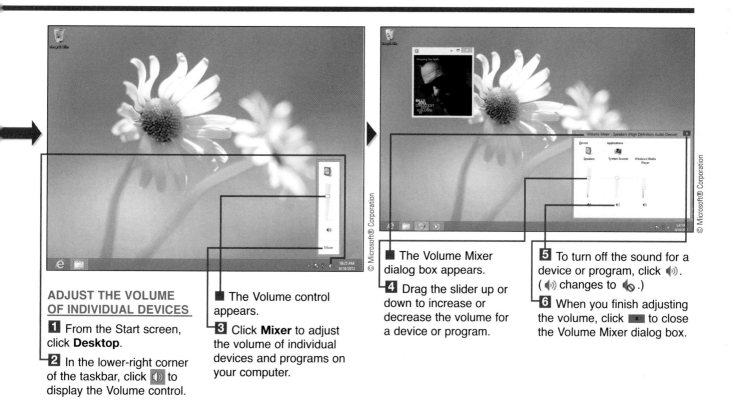

ADJUST THE VOLUME OF INDIVIDUAL DEVICES

1 From the Start screen, click **Desktop**.

2 In the lower-right corner of the taskbar, click to display the Volume control.

■ The Volume control appears.

3 Click **Mixer** to adjust the volume of individual devices and programs on your computer.

■ The Volume Mixer dialog box appears.

4 Drag the slider up or down to increase or decrease the volume for a device or program.

5 To turn off the sound for a device or program, click . (changes to .)

6 When you finish adjusting the volume, click to close the Volume Mixer dialog box.

MODIFY THE COMPUTER SOUNDS

You can change the sounds that your computer plays when certain events occur on your computer. For example, you can hear a short tune when you log on to Windows.

MODIFY THE COMPUTER SOUNDS

1 From the Start screen, click **Desktop**.

2 Right-click a blank area on your desktop. A menu appears.

3 Click **Personalize**.

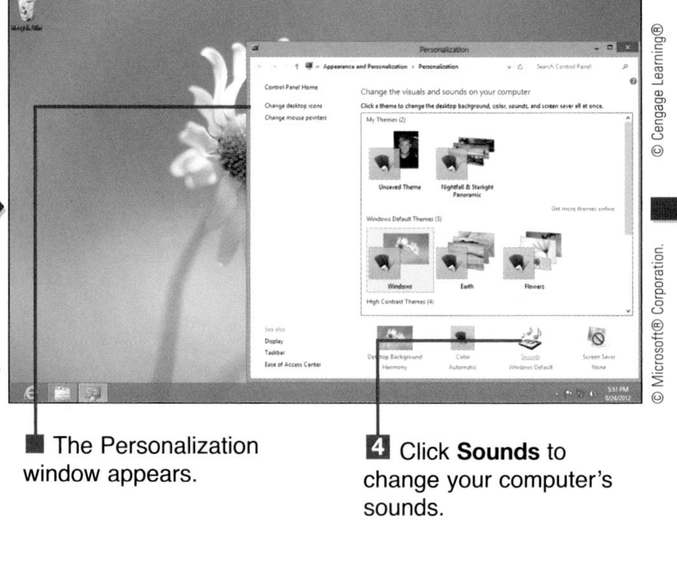

■ The Personalization window appears.

4 Click **Sounds** to change your computer's sounds.

What events can Windows play sounds for?

Windows can play sounds for more than 45 events on your computer. Here are some examples:

Close Program—A sound plays each time you close a program.

Device Connect—A sound plays each time you connect a device to your computer.

Empty Recycle Bin—A sound plays each time you empty your Recycle Bin.

Low Battery Alarm—A sound plays each time your laptop battery gets low.

Maximize—A sound plays each time you maximize a window.

New Mail Notification—A sound plays each time you receive a new email message.

Print Complete—A sound plays when the printing of a file is complete.

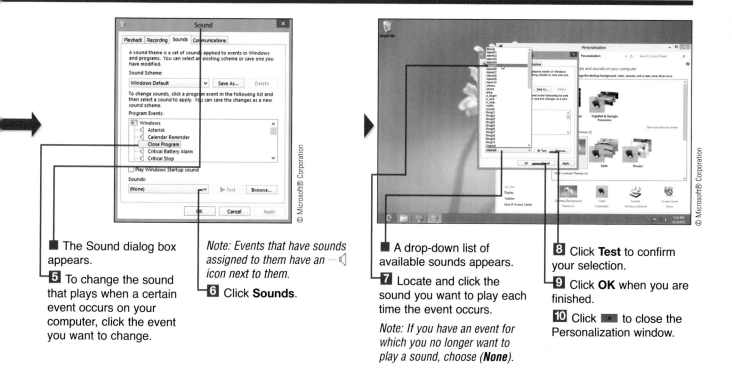

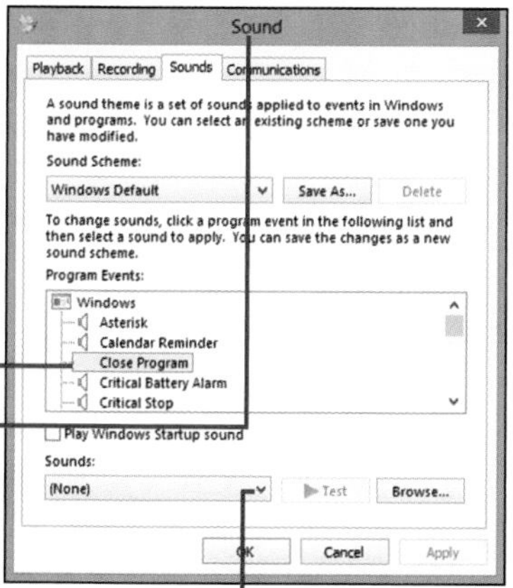

■ The Sound dialog box appears.

5 To change the sound that plays when a certain event occurs on your computer, click the event you want to change.

Note: Events that have sounds assigned to them have an icon next to them.

6 Click **Sounds**.

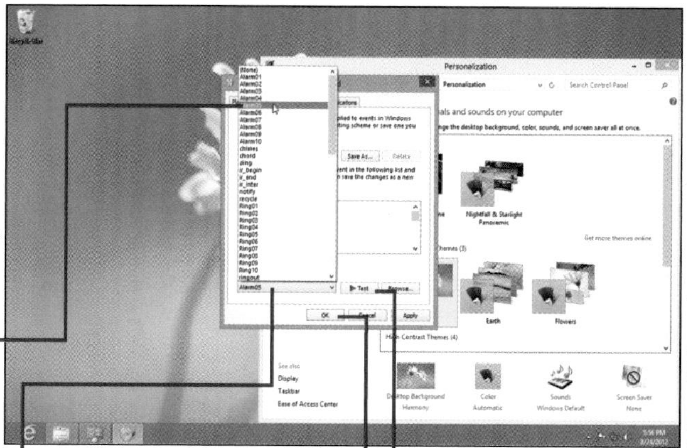

■ A drop-down list of available sounds appears.

7 Locate and click the sound you want to play each time the event occurs.

*Note: If you have an event for which you no longer want to play a sound, choose (**None**).*

8 Click **Test** to confirm your selection.

9 Click **OK** when you are finished.

10 Click ✕ to close the Personalization window.

VIEW AND CHANGE THE DATE AND TIME

You can view and change your computer's date and time settings. Windows uses the date and time to record when you create and update your files.

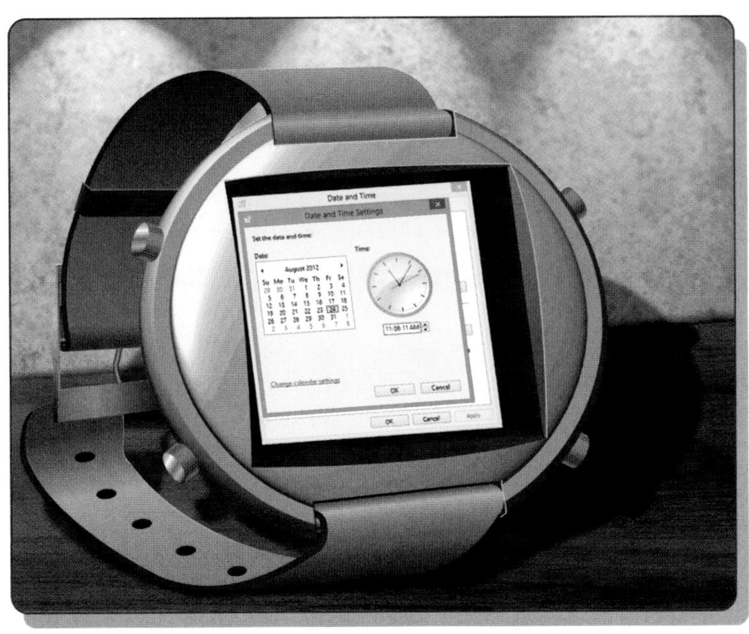

© Microsoft® Corporation

Your computer has a built-in clock that keeps track of the date and time even when you turn off your computer.

To ensure that your computer's clock is accurate, Windows automatically synchronizes your computer's clock with a time server on the Internet about once a week. Your computer must be connected to the Internet for the synchronization to occur.

VIEW AND CHANGE THE DATE AND TIME

© Microsoft® Corporation

1 From the Start screen, click **Desktop**.

■ This area displays the time and date.

2 To view a calendar and the current time, click the time or date.

© Microsoft® Corporation

■ A calendar appears, displaying the days in the current month. The current day appears in blue and displays a border.

3 To browse through the months in the calendar, click ◀ or ▶ to display the previous or next month.

4 When you finish viewing the calendar, click a blank area on your screen to close the window.

Why won't my computer let me change the date and time?

If you do not have an administrator account, you need to type an administrator password and then click **Yes** to be able to change the date and time.

How do I change the time zone?

To change the time zone, click **Change time zone** in the Date and Time dialog box. In the dialog box that appears, select a time zone from the list of available time zones, and then click **OK** to save your change. You may want to change the time zone when traveling or after you move to a new city.

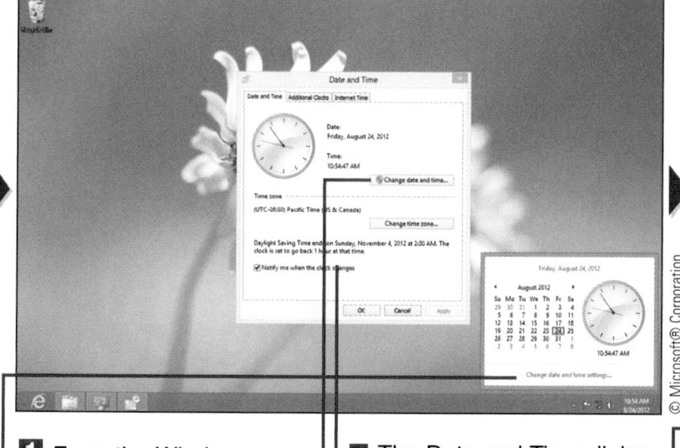

© Microsoft® Corporation

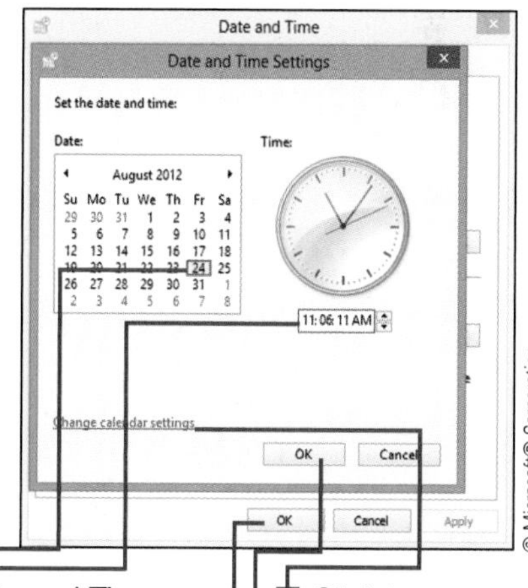

© Microsoft® Corporation

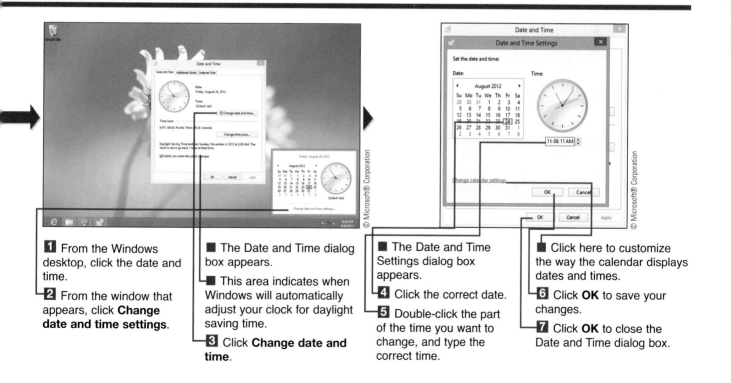

1 From the Windows desktop, click the date and time.

2 From the window that appears, click **Change date and time settings**.

■ The Date and Time dialog box appears.

■ This area indicates when Windows will automatically adjust your clock for daylight saving time.

3 Click **Change date and time**.

■ The Date and Time Settings dialog box appears.

4 Click the correct date.

5 Double-click the part of the time you want to change, and type the correct time.

■ Click here to customize the way the calendar displays dates and times.

6 Click **OK** to save your changes.

7 Click **OK** to close the Date and Time dialog box.

CUSTOMIZE THE MODERN UI

The Windows 8 Modern UI interface is easily customizable.

© Microsoft® Corporation

You can select different pictures for the Lock screen, Start screen, and even your Account picture.

CUSTOMIZE THE MODERN UI

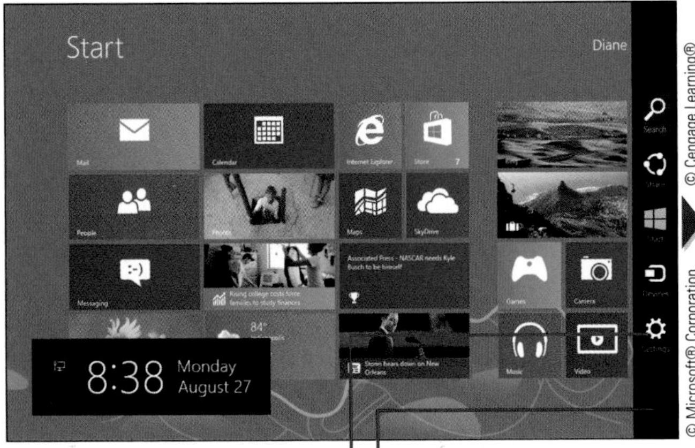

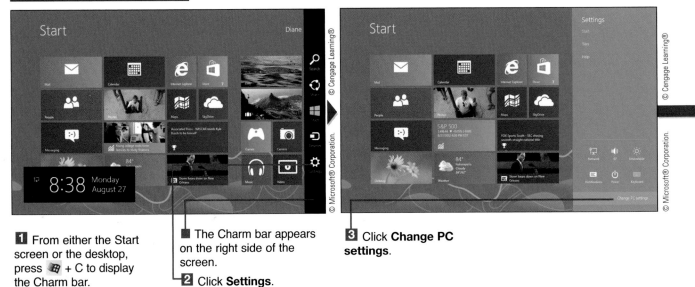

© Microsoft® Corporation. © Cengage Learning®

© Microsoft® Corporation. © Cengage Learning®

1 From either the Start screen or the desktop, press ⊞ + C to display the Charm bar.

■ The Charm bar appears on the right side of the screen.

2 Click **Settings**.

3 Click **Change PC settings**.

What if I want a picture different from the ones offered?

Click the **Browse** button. The Pictures app displays your pictures. Locate the one you want to use, and click **Choose picture**.

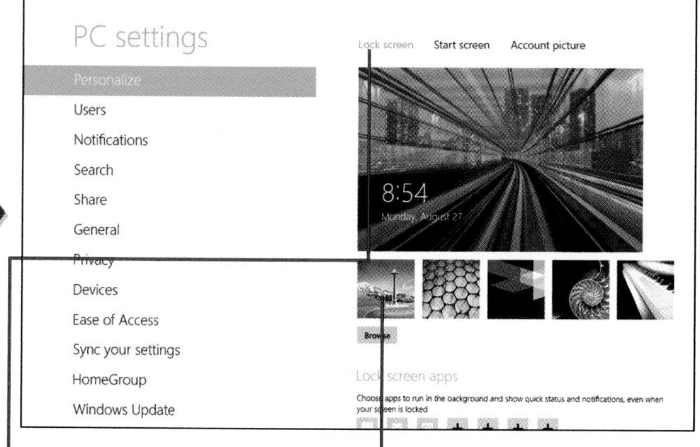

© Microsoft® Corporation

© Microsoft® Corporation

CHANGE THE LOCK SCREEN

■ The PC settings screen appears.

4 Click **Lock screen**. It's probably already selected, but clicking it again just assures you are choosing the right option.

5 Click a picture you want to use for your lock screen.

6 Press ⊞ to return to the Start screen or the desktop.

■ When the Lock screen appears, you see the image you selected. (See **Chapter 1** for more information about the Lock screen.)

CONTINUED

When Windows 8 was installed, it prompted for a color to use on the Start screen.

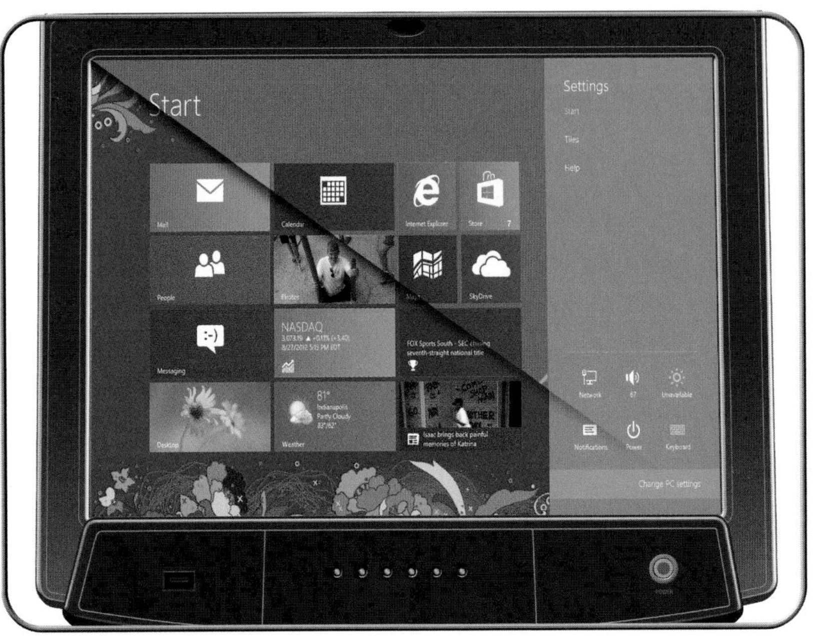

You can change that color any time you want.

CUSTOMIZE THE MODERN UI (CONTINUED)

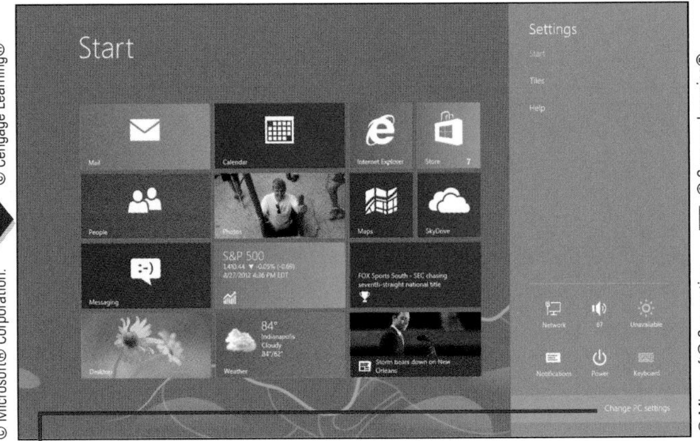

CHANGE THE START SCREEN

1 From either the Start screen or the desktop, press ⊞ + C to display the Charm bar.

■ The Charm bar appears on the right side of the screen.

2 Click **Settings**.

3 Click **Change PC settings**.

Can I use my own picture as a background on the Start screen?

No. There is no provision for using your own picture here.

Additionally, due to the busy collection of Modern UI apps on the Start screen, using anything other than the simplest of designs would be very distracting.

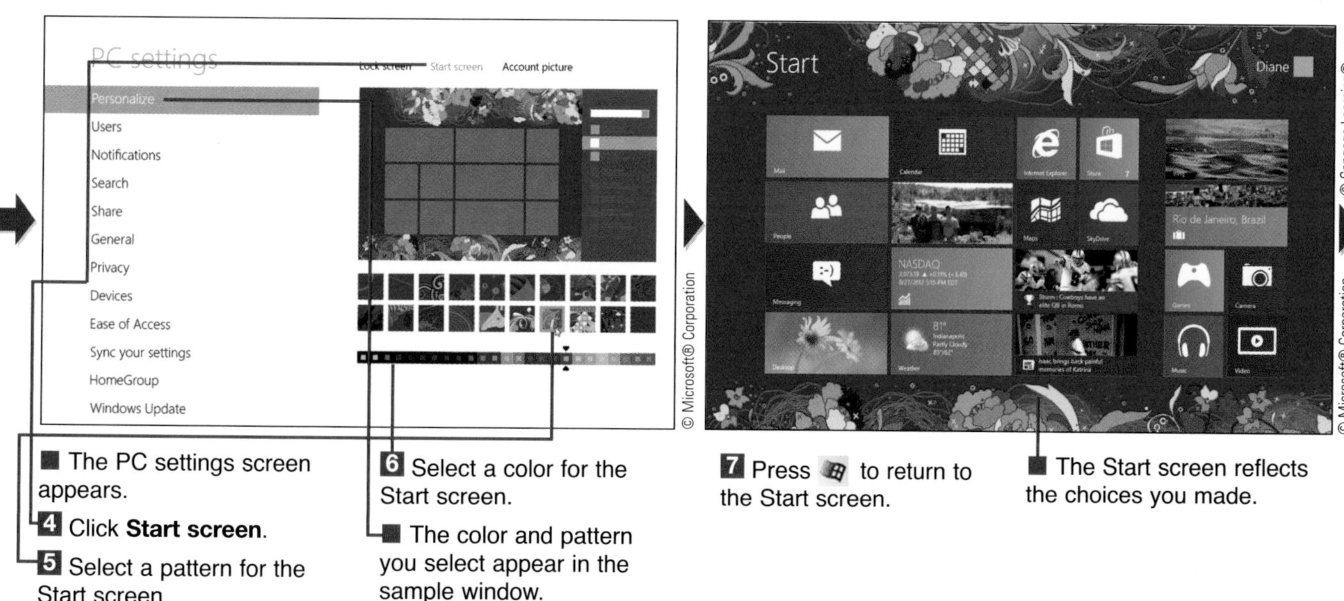

■ The PC settings screen appears.

4 Click **Start screen**.

5 Select a pattern for the Start screen.

6 Select a color for the Start screen.

■ The color and pattern you select appear in the sample window.

7 Press [Windows key] to return to the Start screen.

■ The Start screen reflects the choices you made.

CONTINUED

The Account picture is the one that appears next to your name on the Start screen, in the upper-right corner.

Your Account picture can be any image you choose. It can be you, your dog, your spouse, your grandkids, or even your favorite vacation spot.

CUSTOMIZE THE MODERN UI (CONTINUED)

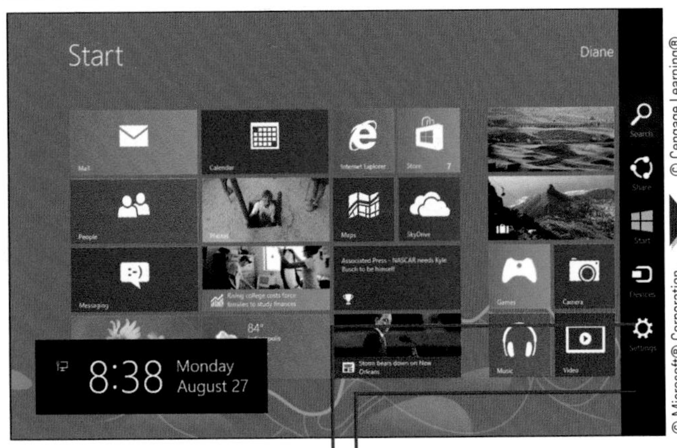

CHANGE THE START SCREEN

1 From either the Start screen or the desktop, press ⊞ + c to display the Charm bar.

■ The Charm bar appears on the right side of the screen.

2 Click **Settings**.

3 Click **Change PC settings**.

What if the picture I want is stored on a flash drive and not in my Pictures library?

From the Pictures screen, click **Go up**, and then click **Go up** again. Next, click **Computer**. Locate and double-click your flash drive letter.

From there, you can click the image you want to use and then click **Choose image**.

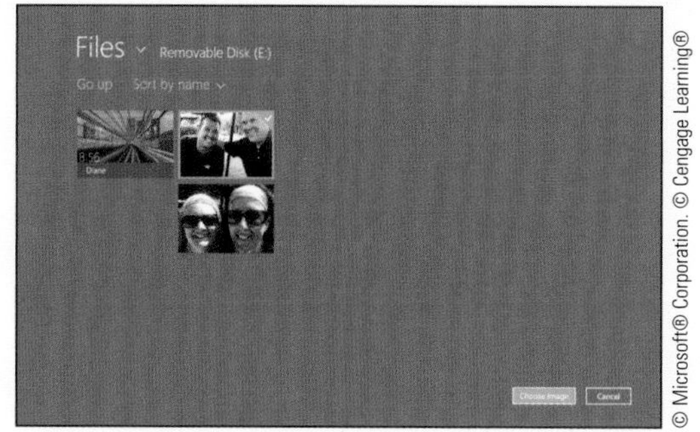

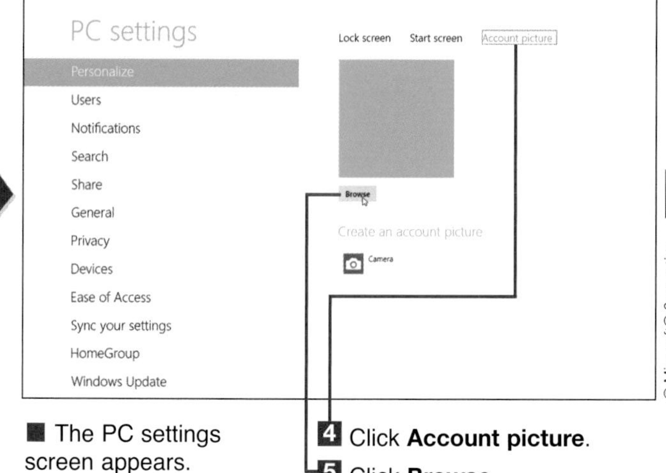

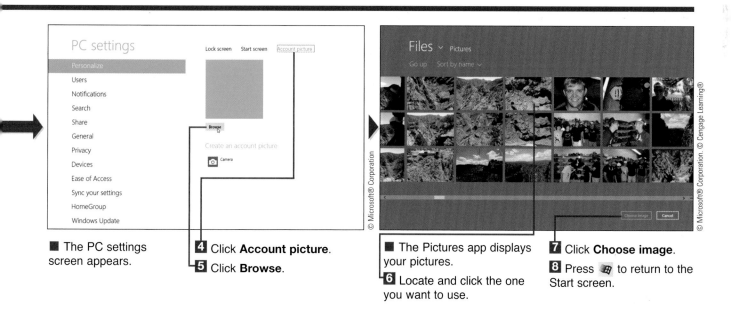

■ The PC settings screen appears.

4 Click **Account picture**.

5 Click **Browse**.

■ The Pictures app displays your pictures.

6 Locate and click the one you want to use.

7 Click **Choose image**.

8 Press the Windows key to return to the Start screen.

USER ACCOUNTS
TOM
ALEX
SIMON
SUSAN
DVD-WRITER
CD-ROM
MULTI-CARD READER
AUDIO

CHAPTER 8

Share Your Computer

CREATE A USER ACCOUNT

If you share your computer with other people, you should create a personalized user account for each person.

Windows keeps your personal files separate from the personal files created by other users. For example, your Documents, Pictures, and Music libraries display the files you have created. Internet Explorer also keeps your lists of recently visited web pages and favorite web pages separate from the lists of other users.

CREATE A USER ACCOUNT

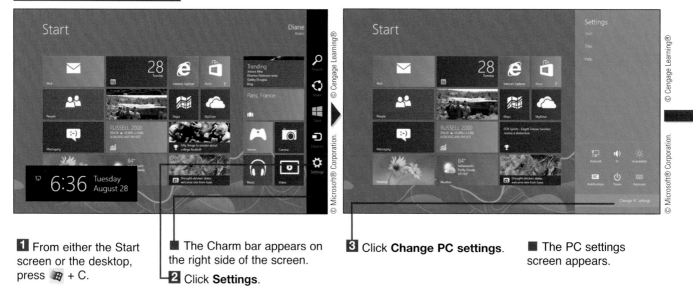

© Microsoft® Corporation. © Cengage Learning®

© Microsoft® Corporation. © Cengage Learning®

1 From either the Start screen or the desktop, press ⊞ + C.

■ The Charm bar appears on the right side of the screen.

2 Click **Settings**.

3 Click **Change PC settings**.

■ The PC settings screen appears.

Should each user have a unique Microsoft account?

It's a good idea for each user to have a separate Microsoft account. The Microsoft account also tracks the user's system preferences, and with separate accounts, each user can have his own set of preferences and other settings. A user can sign in with a local account instead of a Microsoft account, but then he won't be able to access many of the new Modern UI apps that appear in Windows 8.

Is a password required?

No. You don't need a password if you are creating the user with a Local account.

A password is recommended but not required. If you don't have a password, anyone can log on as you and have access to your personal files.

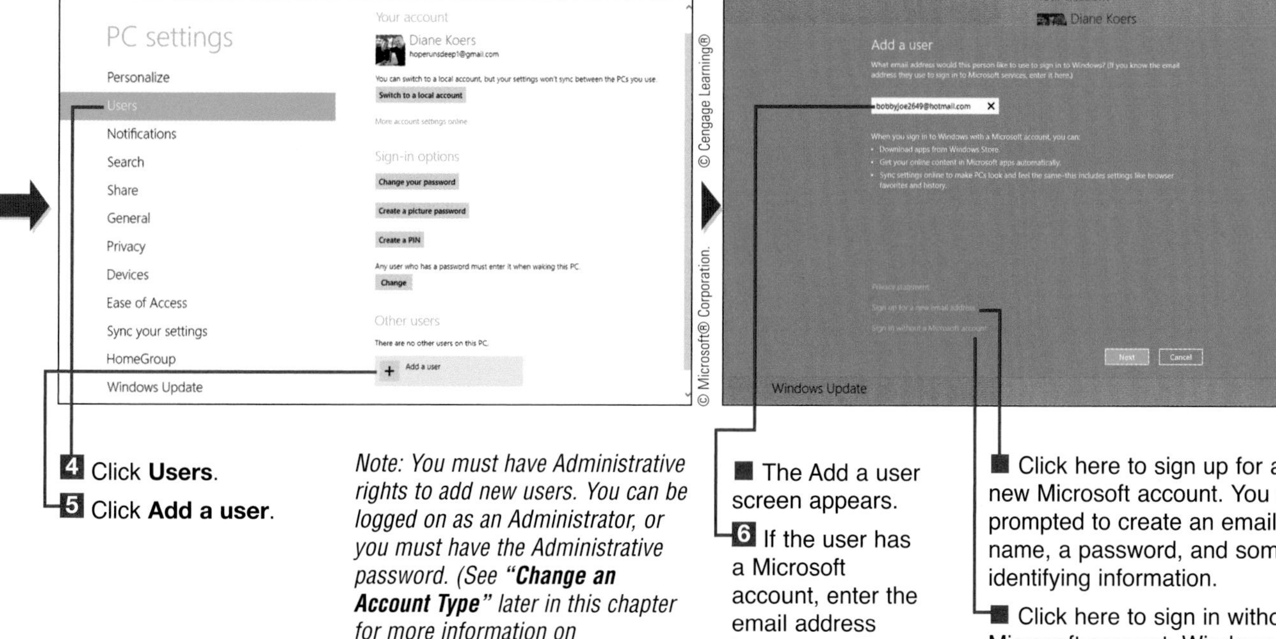

4 Click **Users**.

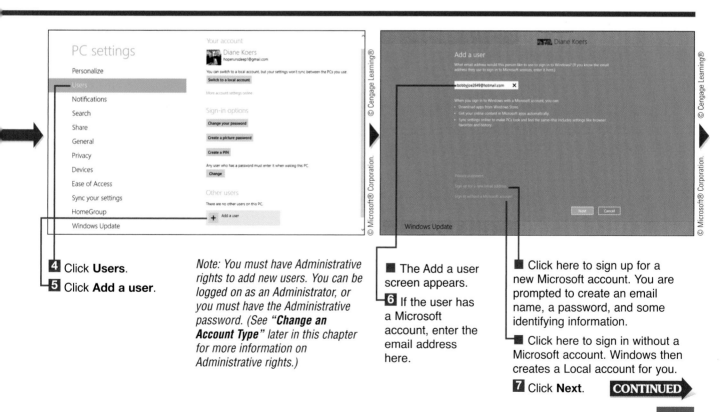

5 Click **Add a user**.

*Note: You must have Administrative rights to add new users. You can be logged on as an Administrator, or you must have the Administrative password. (See **"Change an Account Type"** later in this chapter for more information on Administrative rights.)*

■ The Add a user screen appears.

6 If the user has a Microsoft account, enter the email address here.

■ Click here to sign up for a new Microsoft account. You are prompted to create an email name, a password, and some identifying information.

■ Click here to sign in without a Microsoft account. Windows then creates a Local account for you.

7 Click **Next**.

CONTINUED

When creating separate user accounts, Windows creates separate folders to store each user's documents, pictures, music, and videos.

Each user can also have his own personalization options.

CREATE A USER ACCOUNT (CONTINUED)

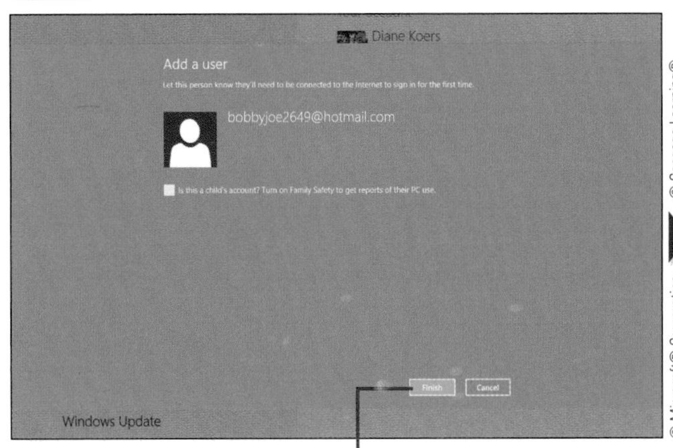

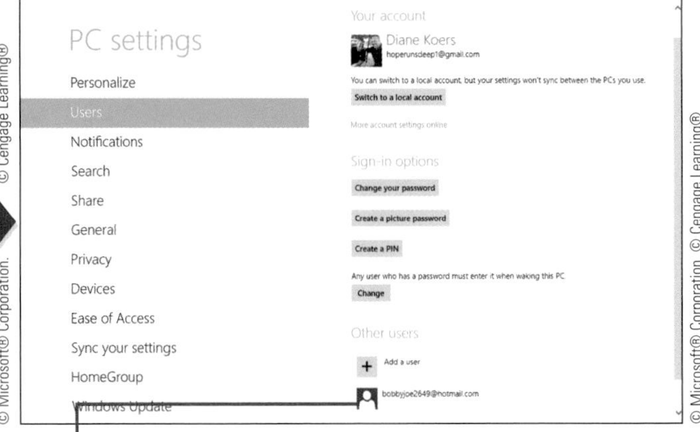

■ A confirmation screen appears.

8 Click **Finish**.

■ The new user appears here.

Note: You can create as many new users as you need.

■ After the new user signs in to Windows 8, he can personalize the user account by changing the desktop background, window color, screen saver, and more. See **Chapter 7** for several ways to personalize a user account.

9 Press the Windows key to return to the Start screen.

CHANGE AN ACCOUNT TYPE

The first user created in Windows 8 is an Administrator. Each subsequent user is created as a Standard account.

You can change a Standard account to an Administrative account, and you can change an Administrative account to a Standard account.

You must, however, koop at loact ono Administrative account.

CHANGE AN ACCOUNT TYPE

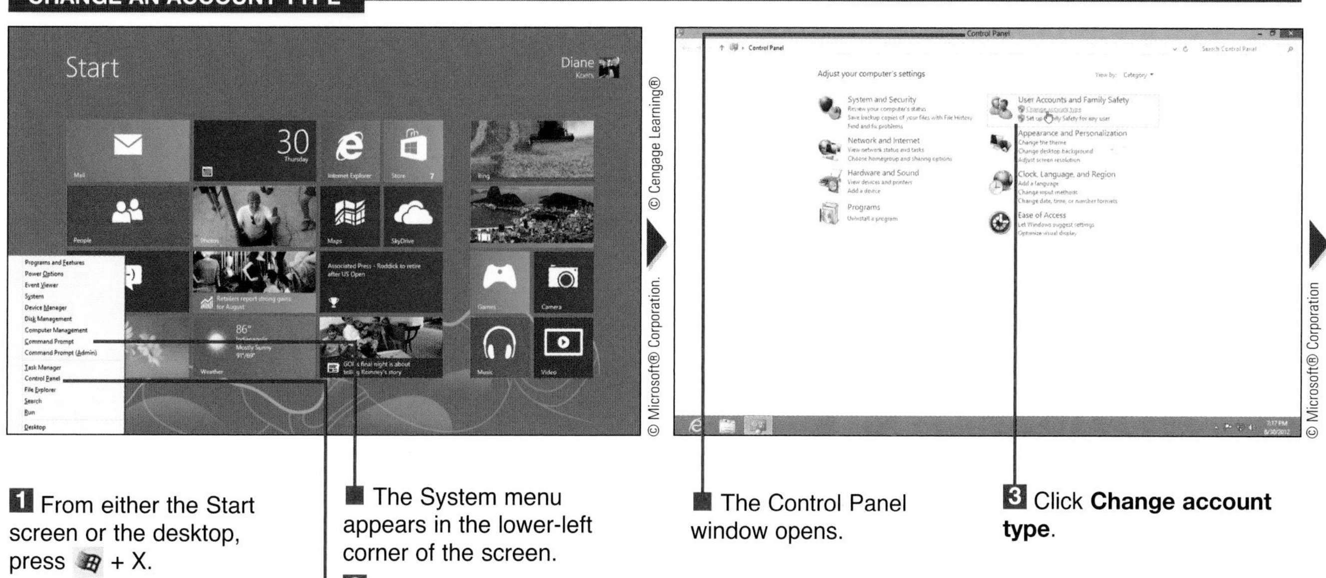

1 From either the Start screen or the desktop, press (Windows key) + X.

■ The System menu appears in the lower-left corner of the screen.

2 Click **Control Panel**.

■ The Control Panel window opens.

3 Click **Change account type**.

CONTINUED

If you are using a Standard account type, you may be prompted for an Administrative password.

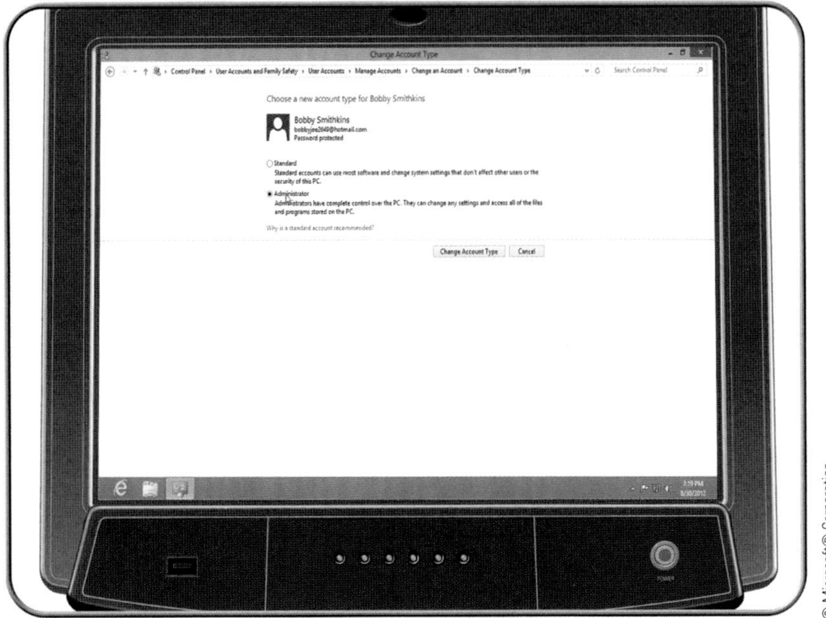

CHANGE AN ACCOUNT TYPE (CONTINUED)

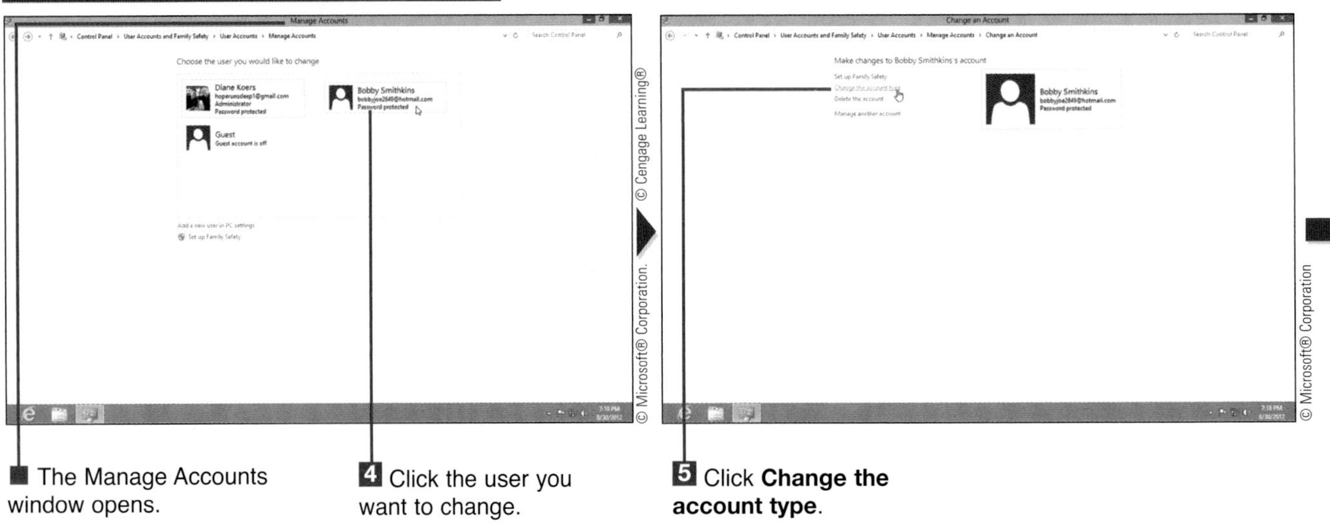

■ The Manage Accounts window opens.

4 Click the user you want to change.

5 Click **Change the account type**.

What is the difference between an Administrator and a Standard user account?

As a Standard user, you can perform almost any task on the computer. However, you cannot perform tasks that affect other users or the security of the computer without first entering an Administrator password.

As an Administrator, you can perform any task on the computer.

Why does Windows sometimes prompt me for an Administrative password?

You must have Administrative rights to add, modify, or delete users. If you are logged on as a Standard user, Windows prompts you for the Administrator password.

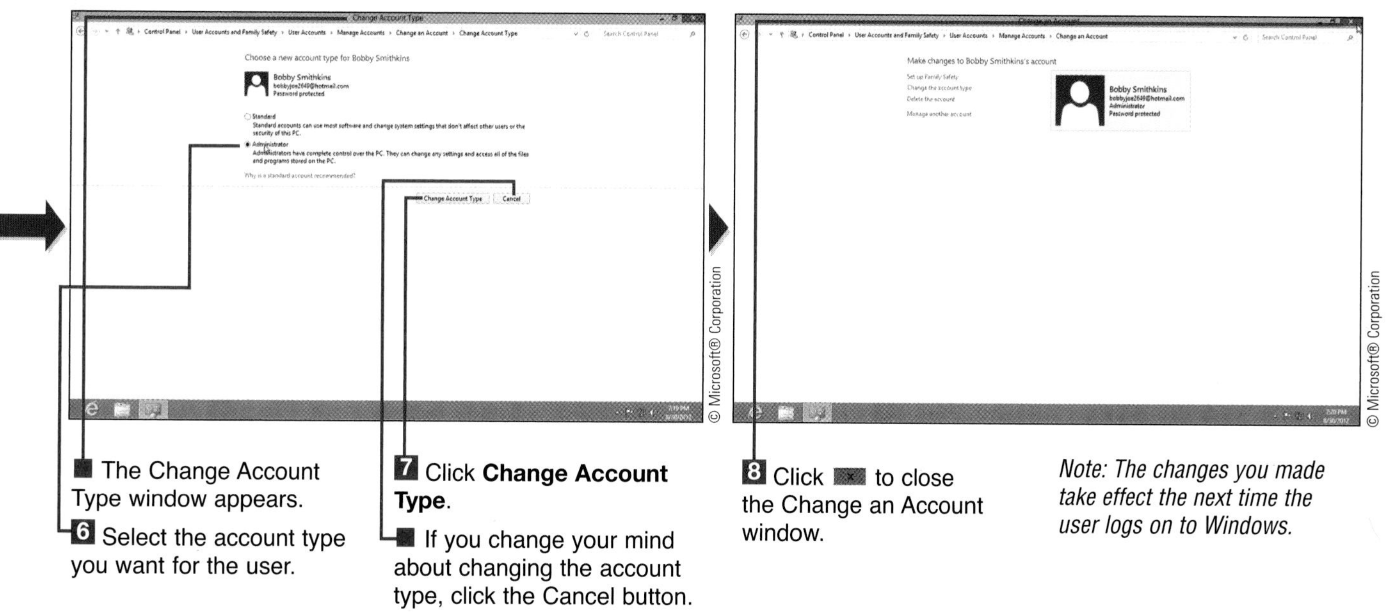

© Microsoft® Corporation

© Microsoft® Corporation

■ The Change Account Type window appears.

6 Select the account type you want for the user.

7 Click **Change Account Type**.

■ If you change your mind about changing the account type, click the Cancel button.

8 Click ✕ to close the Change an Account window.

Note: The changes you made take effect the next time the user logs on to Windows.

DELETE A USER ACCOUNT

If a person no longer uses your computer, you can choose to delete the person's user account from your computer.

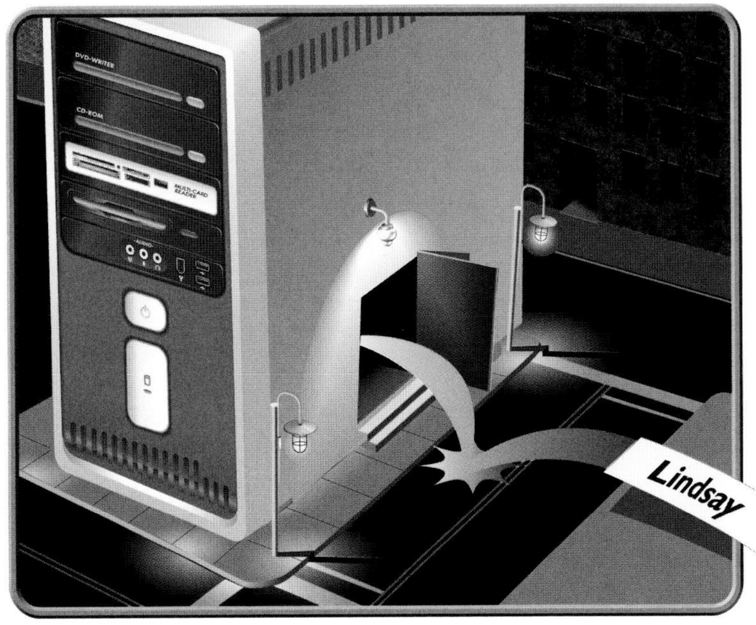

When you delete a user account, Windows permanently removes the account from your computer.

DELETE A USER ACCOUNT

© Cengage Learning®

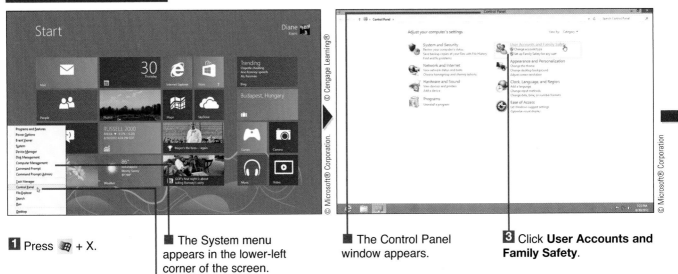

© Microsoft® Corporation.

1 Press + X.

■ The System menu appears in the lower-left corner of the screen.

2 Click **Control Panel**.

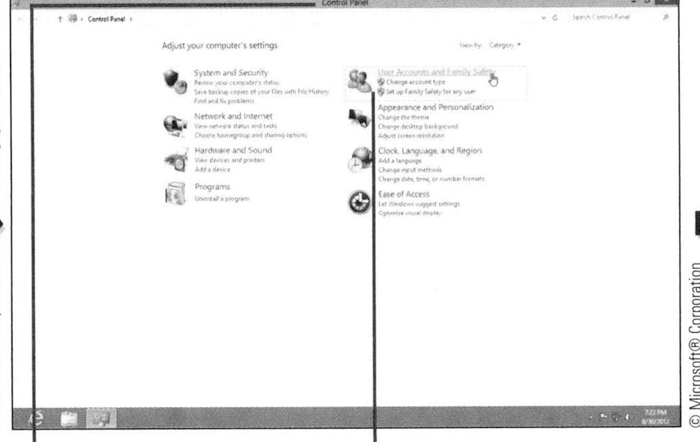

© Microsoft® Corporation

■ The Control Panel window appears.

3 Click **User Accounts and Family Safety**.

When I delete a user account, which personal files can Windows save?

When you delete a user account, Windows can save the user's personal files that are displayed on the desktop and the files in the My Documents, My Music, My Pictures, and My Videos folders. Windows can also save the user's list of favorite web pages. The files are saved on your desktop in a new folder that has the same name as the deleted account. Windows does not save the user's email messages or computer settings.

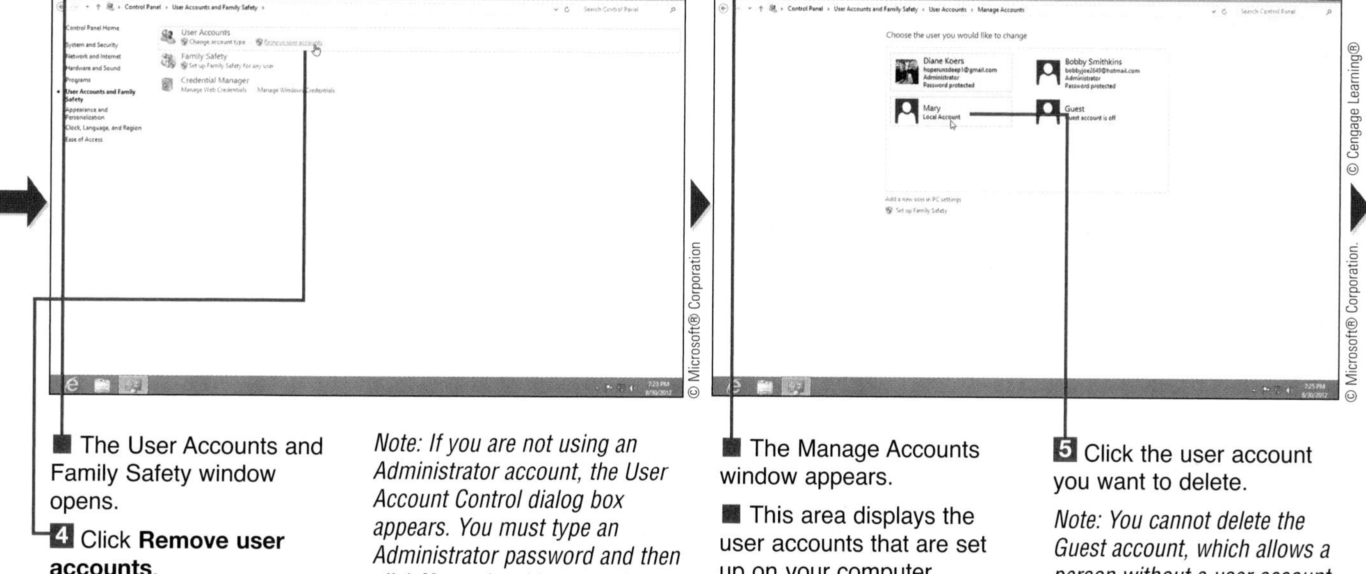

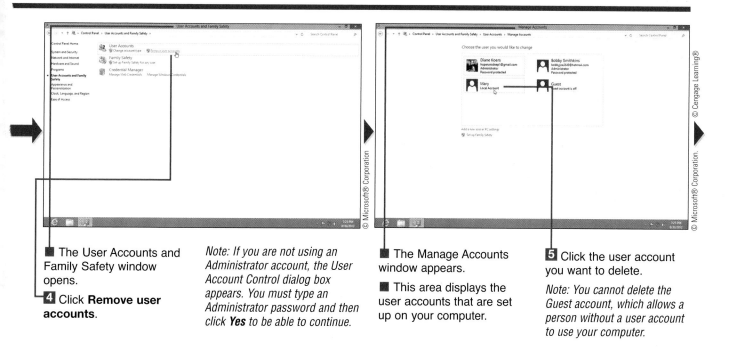

■ The User Accounts and Family Safety window opens.

4 Click **Remove user accounts**.

*Note: If you are not using an Administrator account, the User Account Control dialog box appears. You must type an Administrator password and then click **Yes** to be able to continue.*

■ The Manage Accounts window appears.

■ This area displays the user accounts that are set up on your computer.

5 Click the user account you want to delete.

Note: You cannot delete the Guest account, which allows a person without a user account to use your computer.

CONTINUED

When you delete a user, Windows gives you the option of retaining or deleting the user's personal files.

DELETE A USER ACCOUNT (CONTINUED)

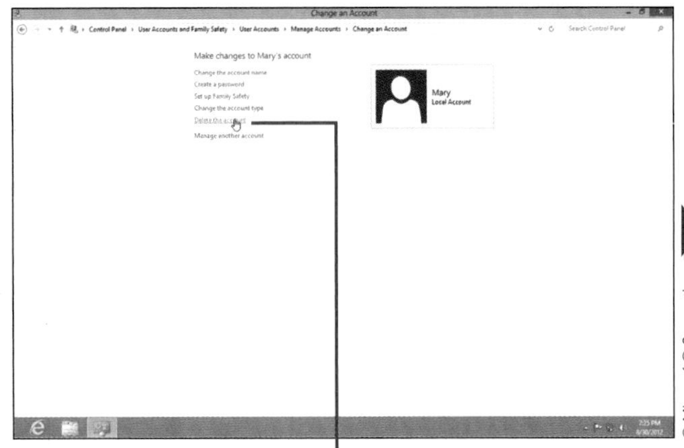

■ A list of tasks appears, allowing you to make changes to the account.

6 Click **Delete the account**.

■ Windows asks if you want to keep the user's personal files.

7 Click an option to specify if you want to delete or keep the user's personal files.

Can I delete an Administrator account?

Yes. You can delete Administrator accounts.

However, Windows does not allow you to delete the last Administrator account on your computer.

This ensures that one Administrator account always exists on the computer.

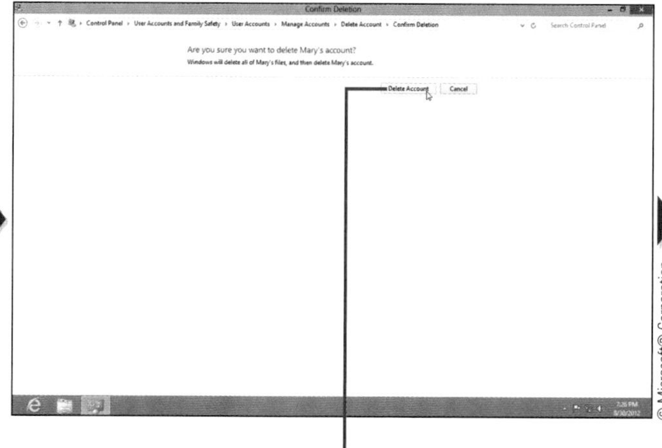

© Microsoft® Corporation

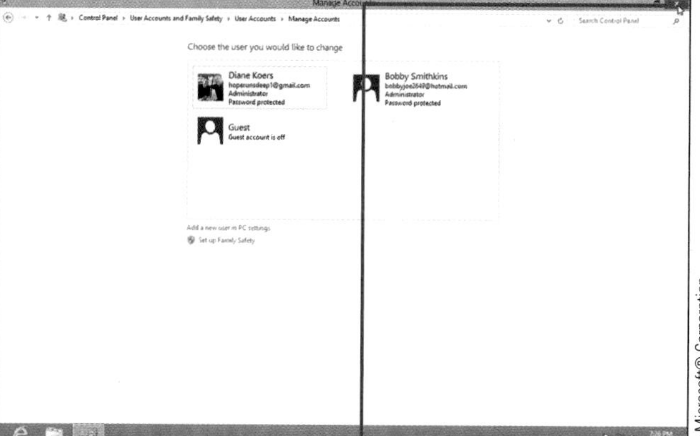

© Microsoft® Corporation

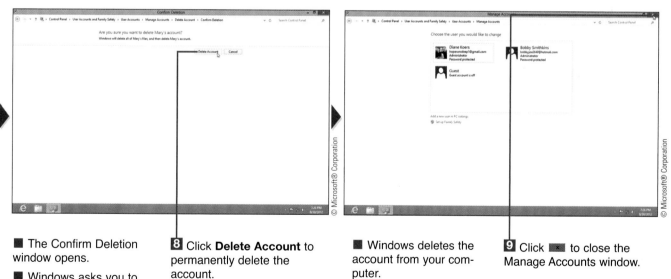

■ The Confirm Deletion window opens.

■ Windows asks you to confirm that you want to delete the account.

8 Click **Delete Account** to permanently delete the account.

■ Windows deletes the account from your computer.

9 Click ✕ to close the Manage Accounts window.

SWITCH USERS

If another person wants to use your computer, you can allow the person to switch to his user account. Windows keeps your files and programs open while the other person logs on to Windows and uses the computer.

When you switch between users, you can quickly return to your files and programs after the other person finishes using the computer.

SWITCH USERS

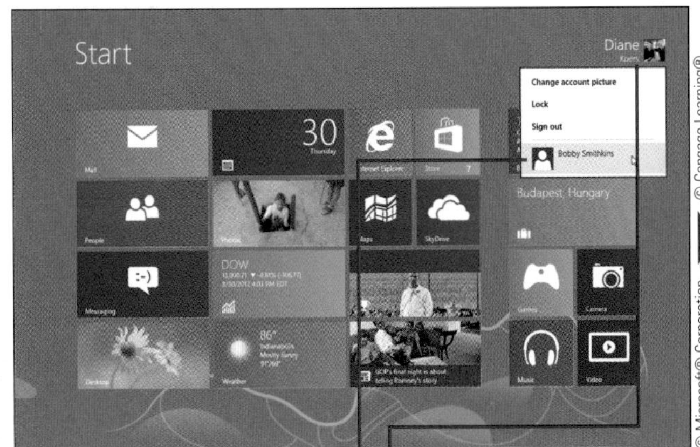

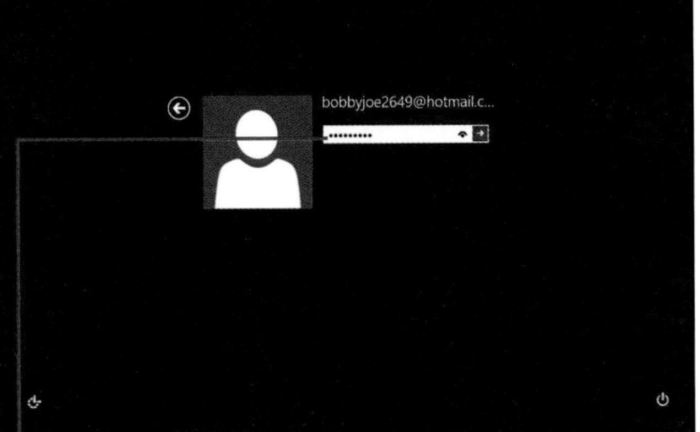

■ Before switching users, you should save any files you have open.

Note: If another person turns off the computer, any unsaved changes you have made to your files are lost.

1 From the Start screen, click the current username.

■ A list of options appears.

2 Click the user to whom you want to switch.

■ The Welcome screen appears, allowing the second user to log on to Windows to use the computer. To log on to Windows, see **Chapter 1**.

Note: If the second user does not have a password, you do not see the Welcome screen.

■ Windows keeps your user account *logged on*, which means that your files and programs remain open on the computer.

SIGN OUT A USER

When you finish using your computer, you can sign out of your user account to allow another person to use the computer.

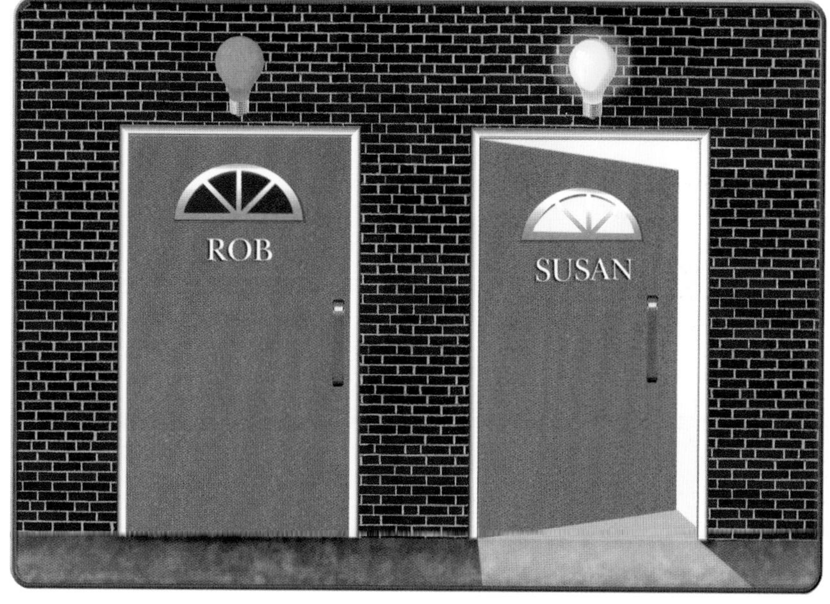

When you sign out of Windows, your user account is temporarily closed, but your computer remains on.

SIGN OUT A USER

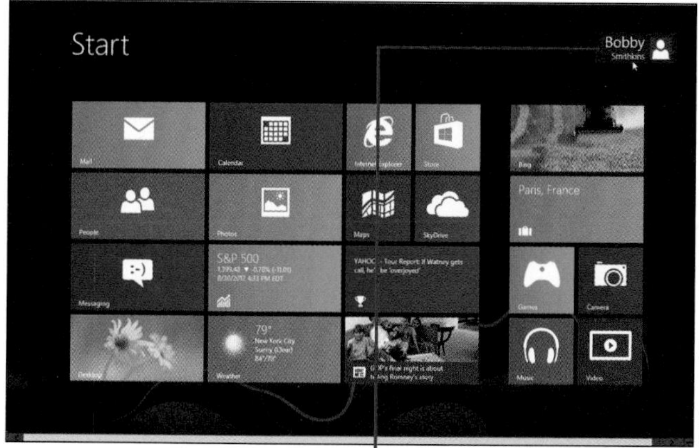

■ Before signing out, you should close your open files and programs.

1 From the Start screen, click the current username.

■ A list of options appears.

2 Click **Sign out** to log off Windows.

■ The Lock screen appears, allowing another person to sign in to Windows to use the computer. To sign in to Windows, see **Chapter 1**.

■ If another person turns off the computer, the person does not need to worry about losing any of your information because your user account is signed out.

SWITCH ACCOUNTS

If you are signed in with a local account, you might want to switch to a Microsoft account so you can access more of the Modern UI apps.

© Microsoft® Corporation

Or, perhaps you are already signed in to your Microsoft account and you want to switch to a local account.

You can easily switch between account types.

SWITCH ACCOUNTS

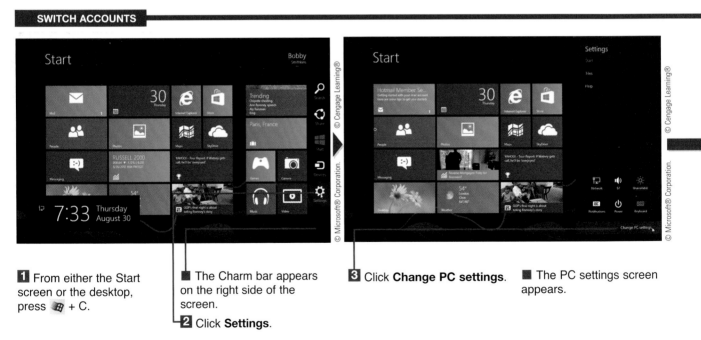

© Cengage Learning®

© Microsoft® Corporation.

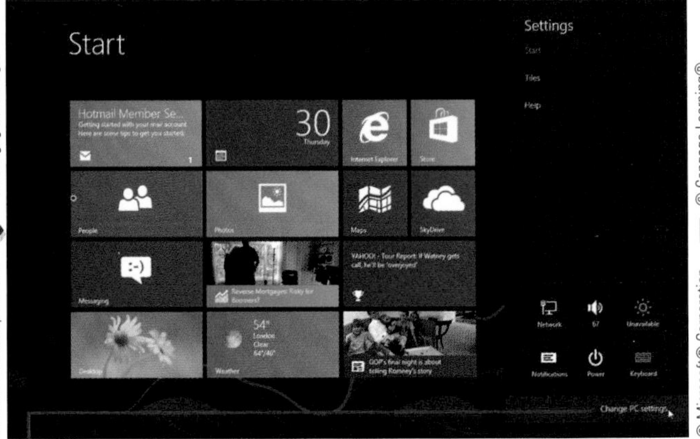

© Cengage Learning®

© Microsoft® Corporation.

1 From either the Start screen or the desktop, press ⊞ + C.

■ The Charm bar appears on the right side of the screen.

2 Click **Settings**.

3 Click **Change PC settings**.

■ The PC settings screen appears.

What are some tips for a good password?

A really good password:

- Contains at least eight characters.
- Contains uppercase letters (A, B, C), lowercase letters (a, b, c), numbers (0, 1, 2, 3), and symbols found on the keyboard (!, @, #, $, %), or spaces.
- Does not contain your real name, company name, or username.
- Does not contain a complete word.
- Is easy to remember, such as:

  Msb=8/Apr 94 means "My son's birthday is April 8, 1994"

  iL2e CwDp! Means "I like to eat chips with dip!"

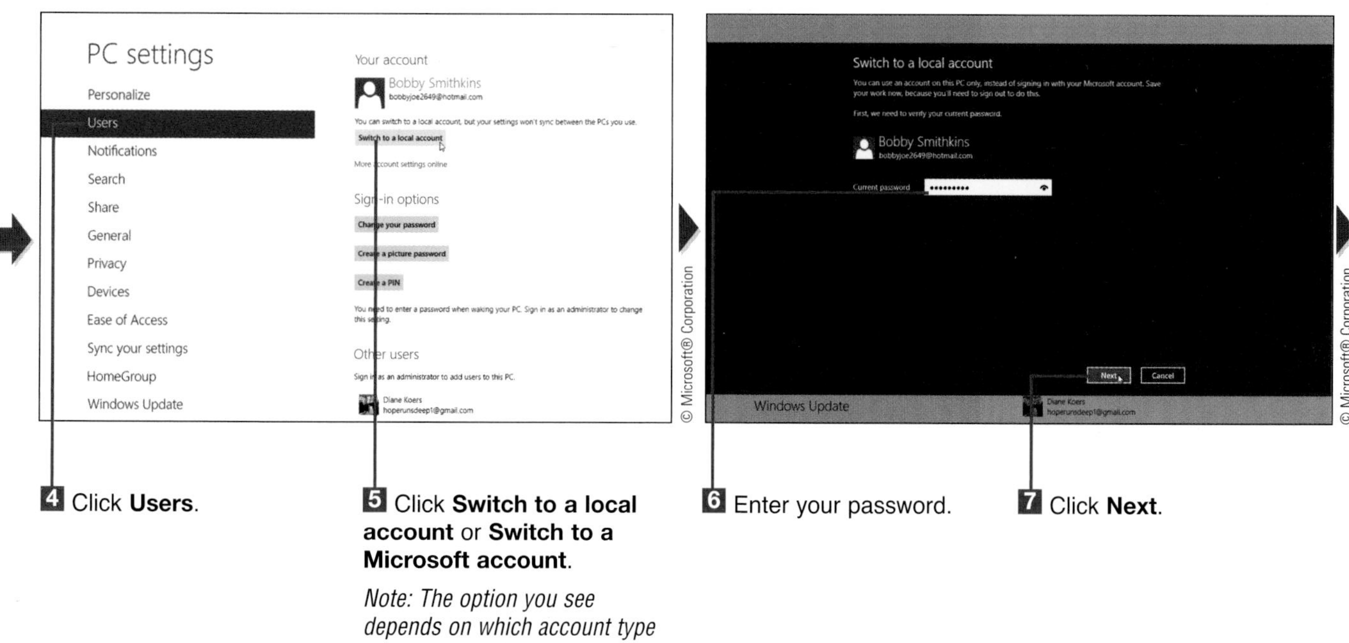

4 Click **Users**.

5 Click **Switch to a local account** or **Switch to a Microsoft account**.

Note: The option you see depends on which account type you are currently using.

6 Enter your password.

7 Click **Next**.

CONTINUED

When you switch accounts, you may be prompted for an email address, password, password hint, or even a security question.

SWITCH ACCOUNTS (CONTINUED)

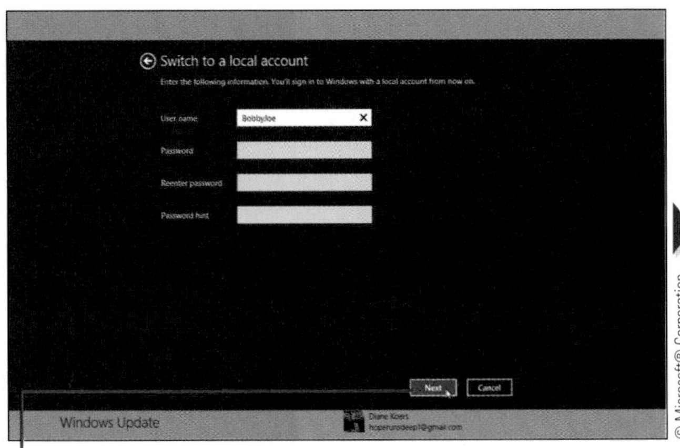

© Microsoft® Corporation

© Microsoft® Corporation

8 Follow the onscreen prompts and click **Next**.

9 Click **Sign out and Finish**.

■ The Lock screen appears.

10 Click anywhere in the Lock screen.

Besides being able to access many of the Modern UI apps, what's an advantage of using a Microsoft account versus a local account?

If you sign in with a Microsoft account, you have an option available called Sync your settings. This option saves your preferences, favorites, and other information with your Microsoft ID. That way, if something happens to your computer and you need to reload Windows 8, your preferences restore as well.

Sync your settings is located on the PC settings screen. (Press + C, click **Settings**, and then click **Change PC settings**.) From this screen, you can choose which settings you want to sync.

11 Click the account you want to use.

12 If the account has a password, enter the password for the account and press Enter.

■ The Start screen appears.

SHARE FILES WITH OTHER USERS

You can share files with other users set up on your computer by adding files to one of the Public folders. Every user on your computer can access the files stored in the Public folders.

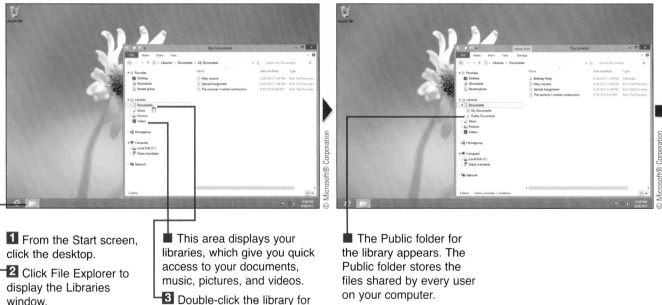

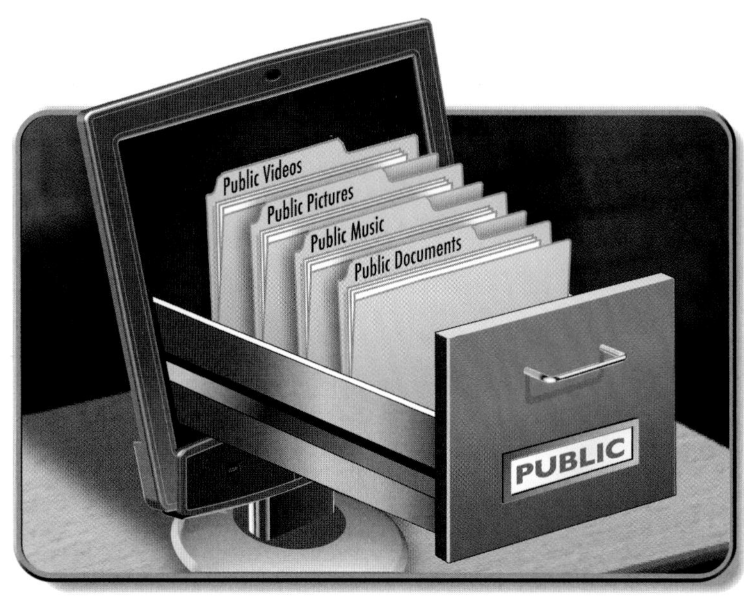

You will find a Public folder in each of your libraries. Windows offers a Public Documents, Public Music, Public Pictures, and Public Videos folder.

SHARE FILES WITH OTHER USERS

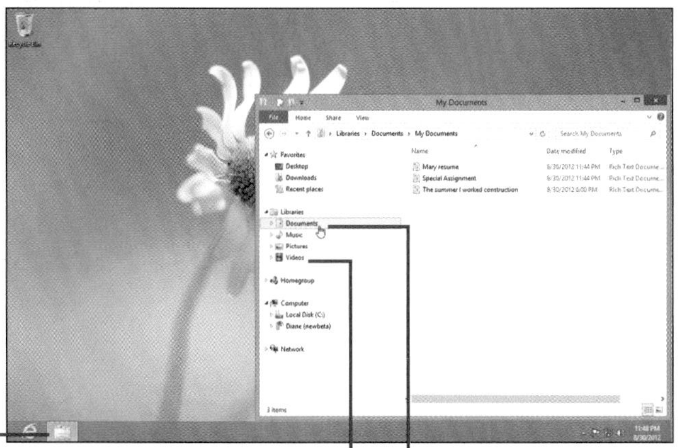

© Microsoft® Corporation

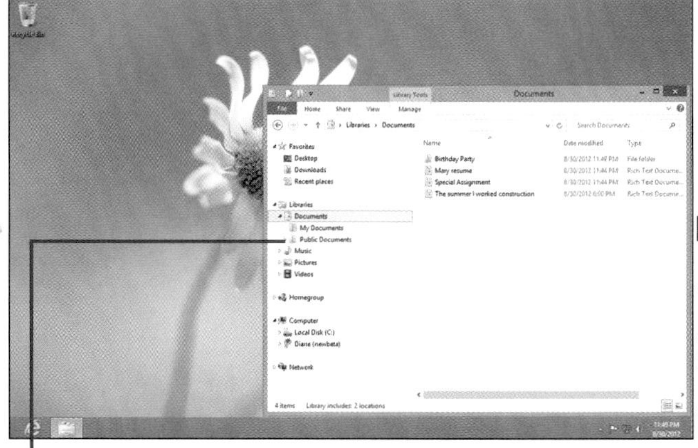

© Microsoft® Corporation

1 From the Start screen, click the desktop.

2 Click File Explorer to display the Libraries window.

■ The Libraries window appears.

■ This area displays your libraries, which give you quick access to your documents, music, pictures, and videos.

3 Double-click the library for the type of file you want to share.

■ The Public folder for the library appears. The Public folder stores the files shared by every user on your computer.

How can I see the files shared by other users on my computer?

In each library, you can see the files shared by other users on your computer as well as your own personal files. Each library displays the contents of two folders. For example, the Documents library displays the contents of the My Documents folder, which contains your personal files, and the Public Documents folder, which contains the files shared by every user on your computer.

How do I no longer share a file on my computer?

If you no longer want to share a file with other users on your computer, you need to move the file out of the Public folder. To do so, repeat steps **4** to **6** here, except drag the file to the My Documents, My Music, My Pictures, or My Videos folder. Only you can see the files in these folders.

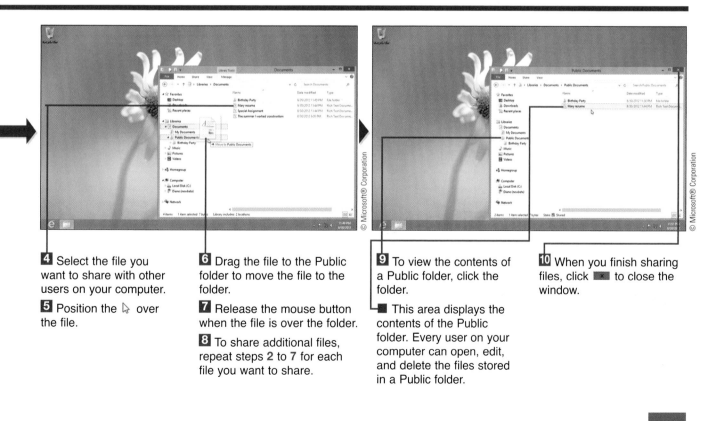

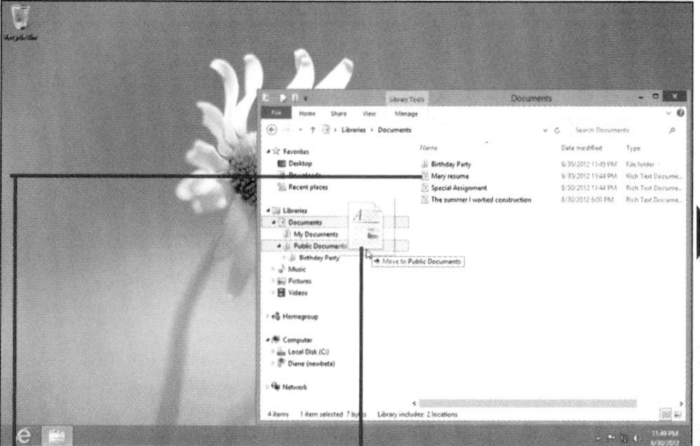

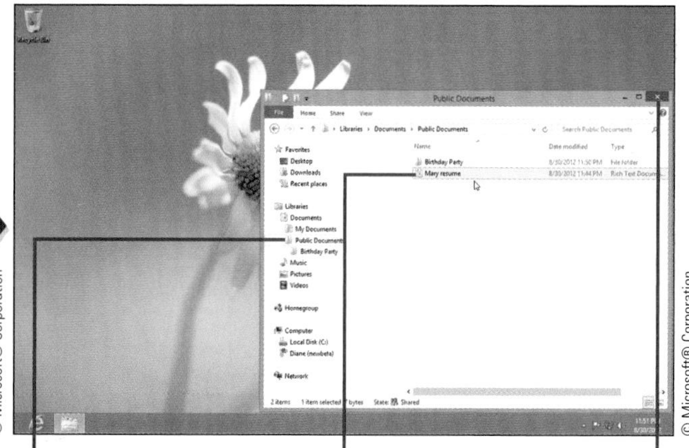

4 Select the file you want to share with other users on your computer.

5 Position the pointer over the file.

6 Drag the file to the Public folder to move the file to the folder.

7 Release the mouse button when the file is over the folder.

8 To share additional files, repeat steps **2** to **7** for each file you want to share.

9 To view the contents of a Public folder, click the folder.

■ This area displays the contents of the Public folder. Every user on your computer can open, edit, and delete the files stored in a Public folder.

10 When you finish sharing files, click ✕ to close the window.

SET UP FAMILY SAFETY CONTROLS

You can set up family safety controls to help control how and when users use your computer.

Before setting up family safety controls, make sure your Administrator accounts are password protected to prevent other users from bypassing or turning off family safety controls.

Primarily designed for parents, you can set up time limits to control when your children can use the computer. You can also control which games your children can play and the programs they can use.

SET UP FAMILY SAFETY CONTROLS

© Cengage Learning®

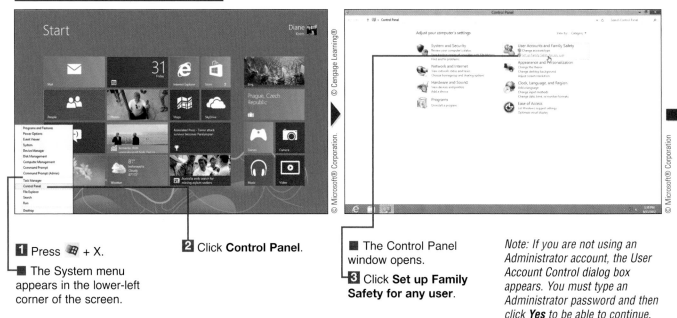

© Microsoft® Corporation.

© Microsoft® Corporation

1 Press ⊞ + X.

■ The System menu appears in the lower-left corner of the screen.

2 Click **Control Panel**.

■ The Control Panel window opens.

3 Click **Set up Family Safety for any user**.

*Note: If you are not using an Administrator account, the User Account Control dialog box appears. You must type an Administrator password and then click **Yes** to be able to continue.*

What is web filtering?

Web filtering allows you to limit the websites the user can visit. You can restrict a website by its content type and by its rating. However, you should know that not all websites are rated.

For example, you can create a specific list of allowable websites, or you can allow only those that are designed for children.

Additionally, you can block the user from downloading any files, which can help protect your computer from viruses and malware.

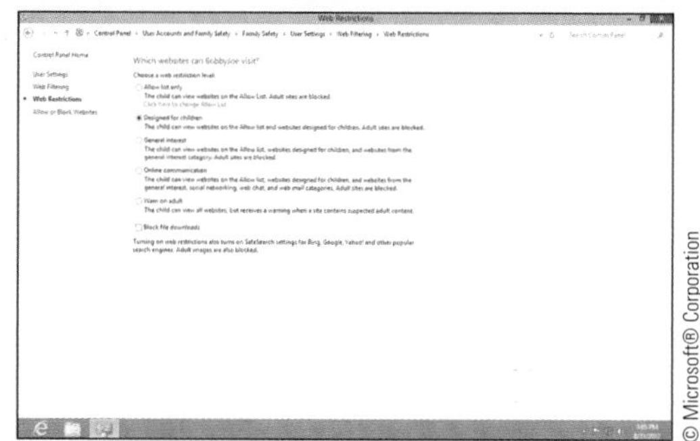

© Microsoft® Corporation

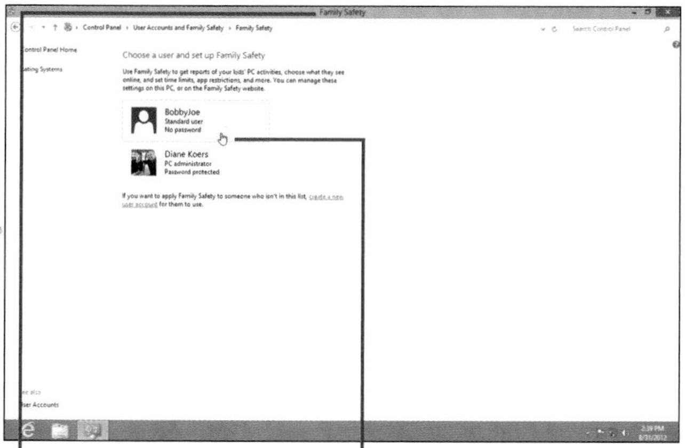

© Microsoft® Corporation. © Cengage Learning®

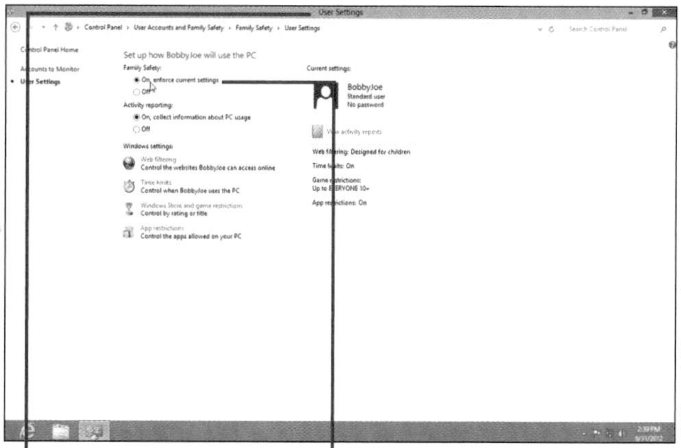

© Microsoft® Corporation

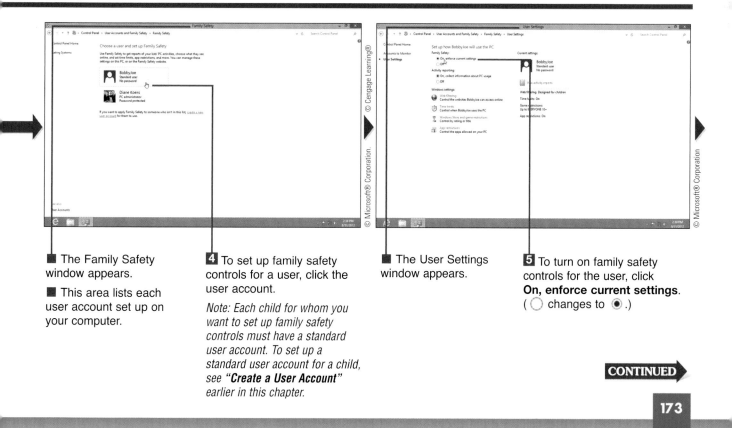

■ The Family Safety window appears.

■ This area lists each user account set up on your computer.

4 To set up family safety controls for a user, click the user account.

Note: Each child for whom you want to set up family safety controls must have a standard user account. To set up a standard user account for a child, see ***"Create a User Account"*** *earlier in this chapter.*

■ The User Settings window appears.

5 To turn on family safety controls for the user, click **On, enforce current settings**. (◯ changes to ◉.)

CONTINUED

SET UP FAMILY SAFETY CONTROLS (CONTINUED)

You can set up time limits to control how long the user can use the computer.

For example, you might only want your child to be on the computer a maximum of one hour per day during the week.

SET UP FAMILY SAFETY CONTROLS (CONTINUED)

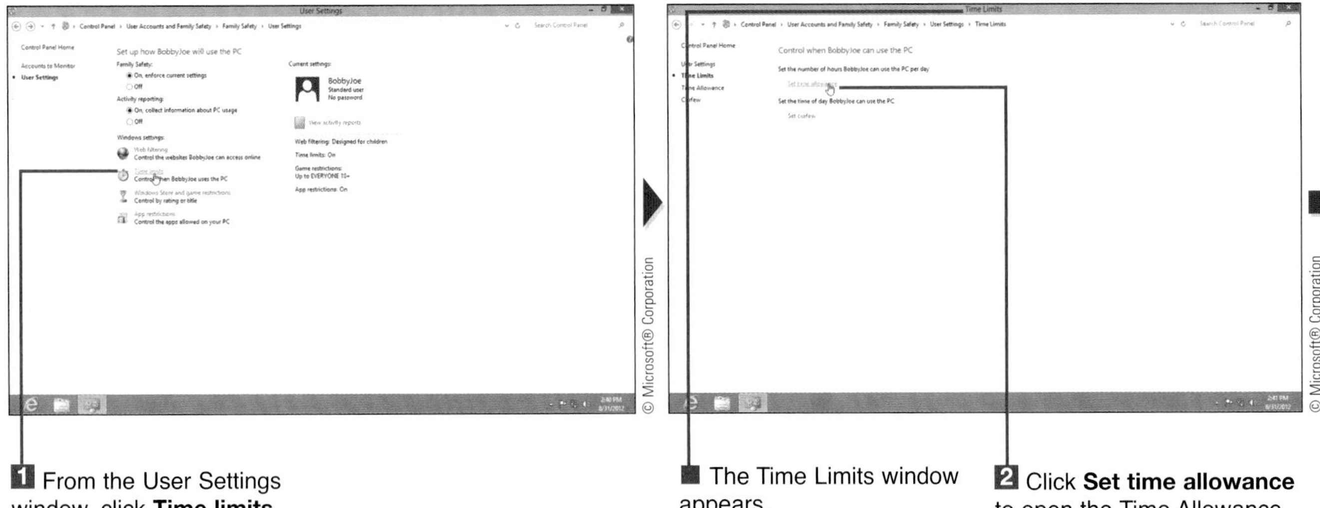

1 From the User Settings window, click **Time limits**.

■ The Time Limits window appears.

2 Click **Set time allowance** to open the Time Allowance window.

What else can I do to help protect my children when they use the computer?

Although the Family Safety Controls feature included with Windows can help manage how your children use the computer, it should not replace family safety supervision. Constant adult supervision is the best way to protect your children. Here are some tips:

- Keep the family computer in a high-traffic area in your house, such as the kitchen or family room, so you can monitor all activity.
- Maintain an ongoing conversation with your children about their computer activities.
- Tell your children not to provide their photo or personal information—such as their name, address, phone number, or school name—to anyone they meet on the Internet.
- Tell your children not to meet in person with anyone they have met on the Internet.

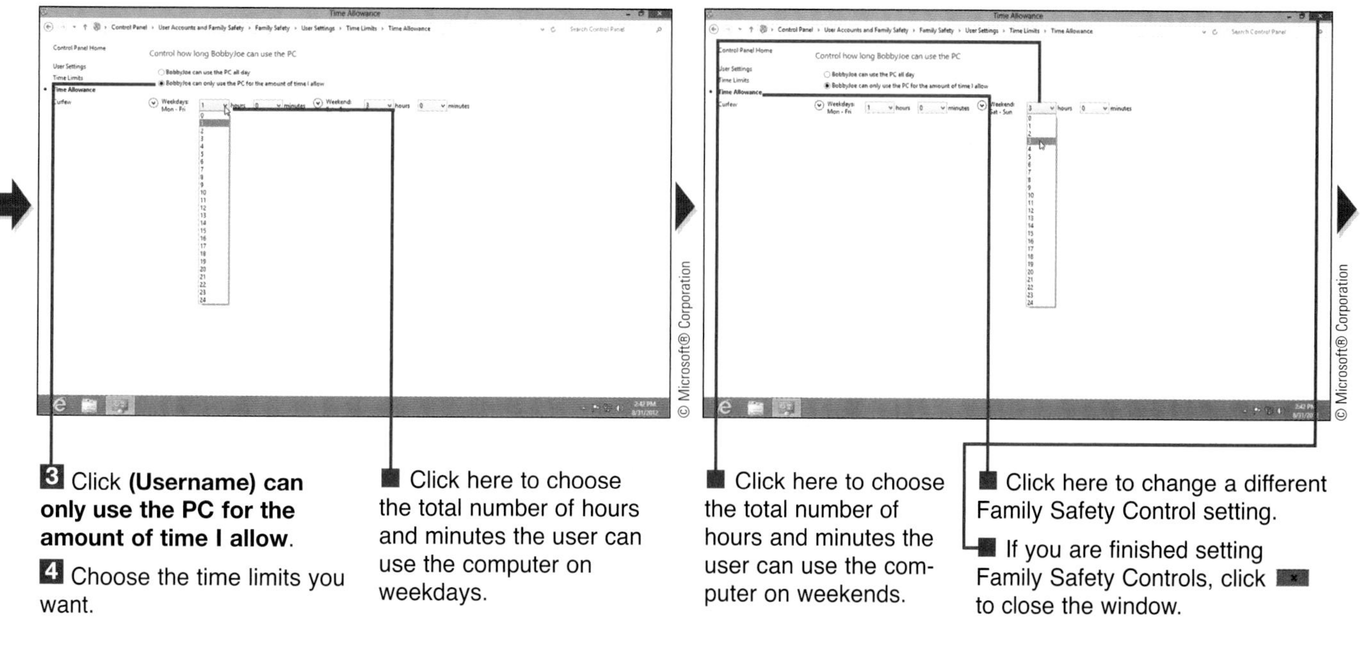

3 Click **(Username) can only use the PC for the amount of time I allow**.

4 Choose the time limits you want.

■ Click here to choose the total number of hours and minutes the user can use the computer on weekdays.

■ Click here to choose the total number of hours and minutes the user can use the computer on weekends.

■ Click here to change a different Family Safety Control setting.

■ If you are finished setting Family Safety Controls, click ☒ to close the window.

CONTINUED

The curfew option allows you to determine what hours of the day the user is allowed to access the computer.

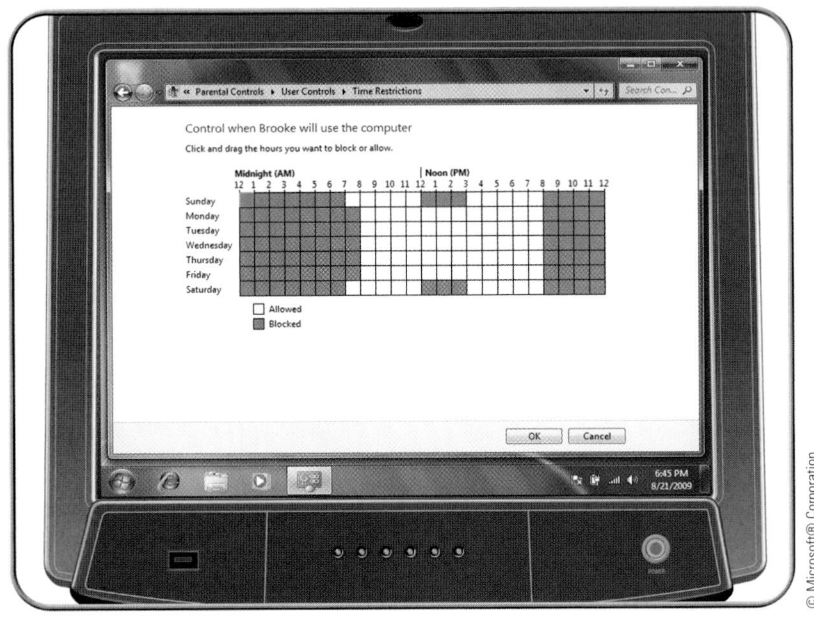

For example, if you don't want your child to use the computer after school and before you get home from work, you might block the hours of 3 p.m. to 6 p.m.

SET UP FAMILY SAFETY CONTROLS (CONTINUED)

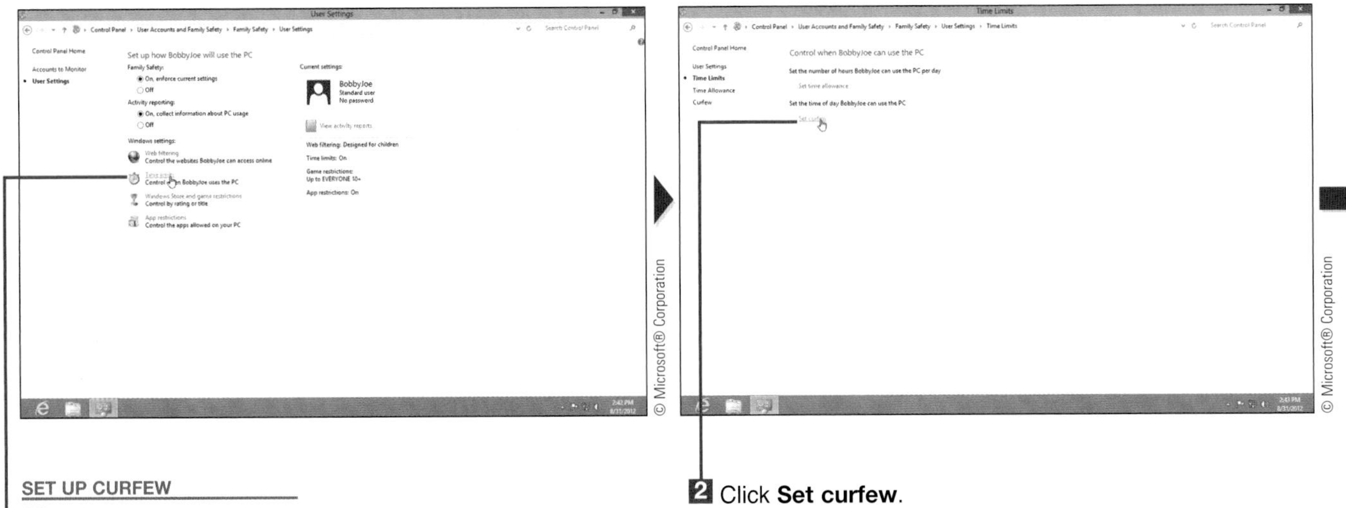

SET UP CURFEW

1 From the User Settings window, click **Time limits**.

2 Click **Set curfew**.

Tip

Can I block my children from playing a game that is not age appropriate?

Yes. From the User Settings window, click **Windows Store and game restrictions**.

Click the option **The user can only use the games and Windows Store apps I allow**; then click **Set game and Windows Store ratings**.

In the window that appears, click a game rating that is appropriate for your child. At the top of the window, click an option to allow or block games with no rating. Your child can now play only the games with the rating you selected.

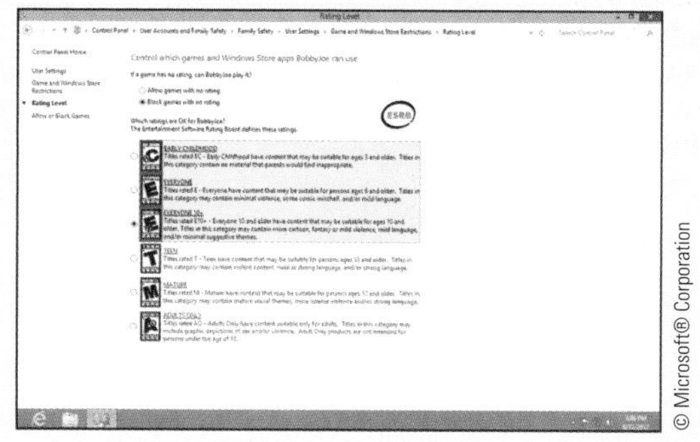

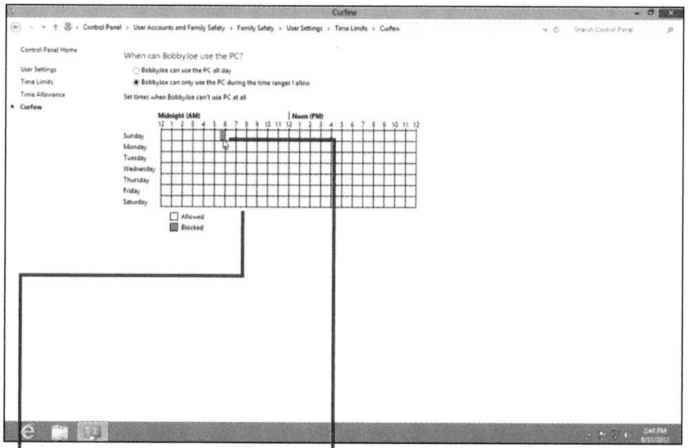

- This area shows a schedule with a for every hour of each day.

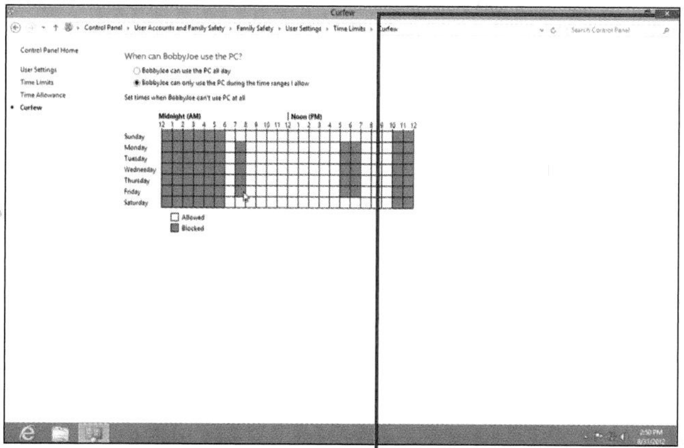

3 To stop the user from using the computer at specific times, click each half-hour you want to block the child from using the computer. (changes to .)

- To block more than one half-hour at once, drag the over the hours.

Note: To unblock a time you accidentally selected, click the time box again.

- If you are finished setting Family Safety Controls, click to close the window.

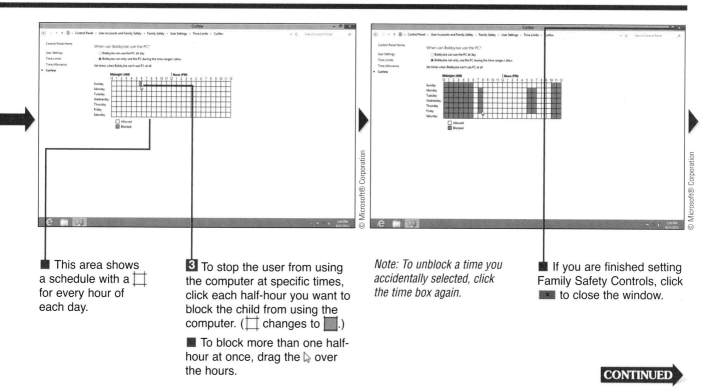

CONTINUED

You can choose to block a user from opening specific programs.

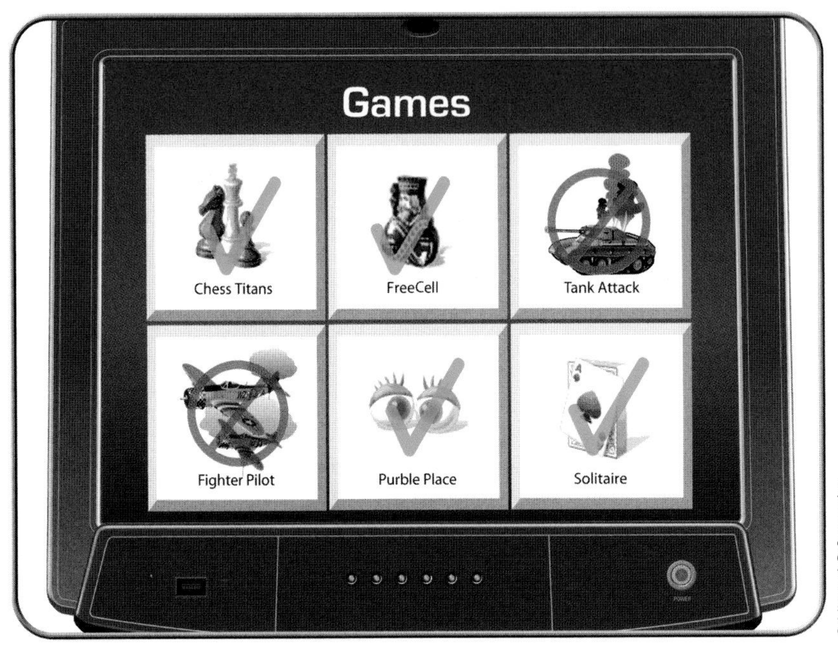

© Microsoft® Corporation

For example, you can prevent someone from opening a program that you use to keep track of your finances.

SET UP FAMILY SAFETY CONTROLS (CONTINUED)

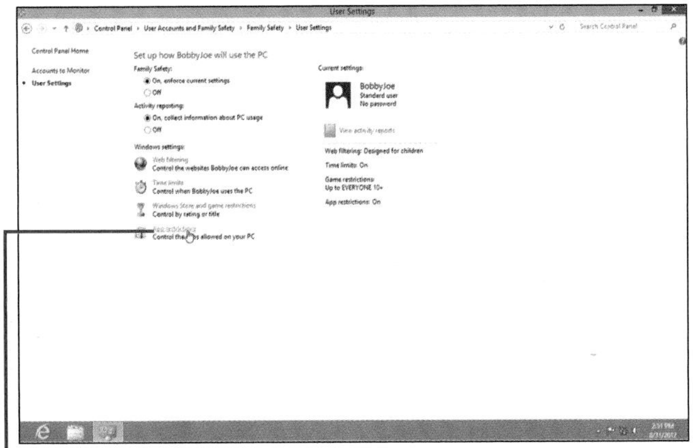

© Microsoft® Corporation

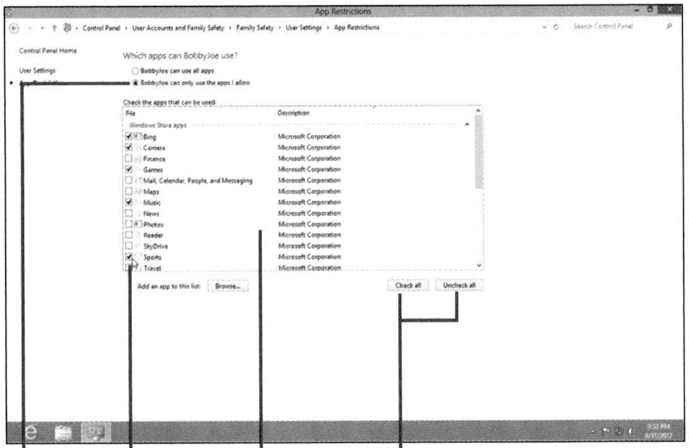

© Microsoft® Corporation

BLOCK SPECIFIC PROGRAMS

1 From the User Settings window, choose **App restrictions**.

■ The App Restrictions window appears.

2 Click **(Username) can only use the apps I allow**. (◯ changes to ◉.)

■ This area lists the apps and programs on your computer.

3 Click ☐ beside each program you want your child to be able to use. (☐ changes to ☑.)

■ To quickly select or deselect all programs in the list, click **Check all** or **Uncheck all**.

■ If you are finished setting Family Safety Controls, click ☒ to close the window.

How can I help keep my children safer online?

Visit the Microsoft Safety & Security Center at www.microsoft.com/security/family-safety/childsafety-internet.aspx.

It contains a plethora of information from Microsoft about Internet safety for your children. You can also see tips for keeping your child safe using social media such as Facebook, Twitter, and Instagram.

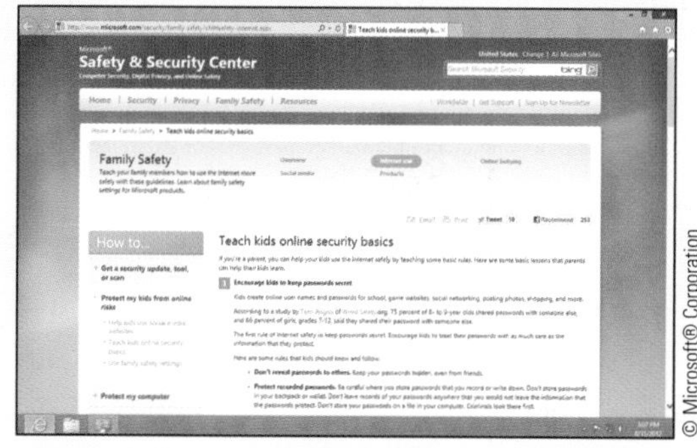

© Microsoft® Corporation

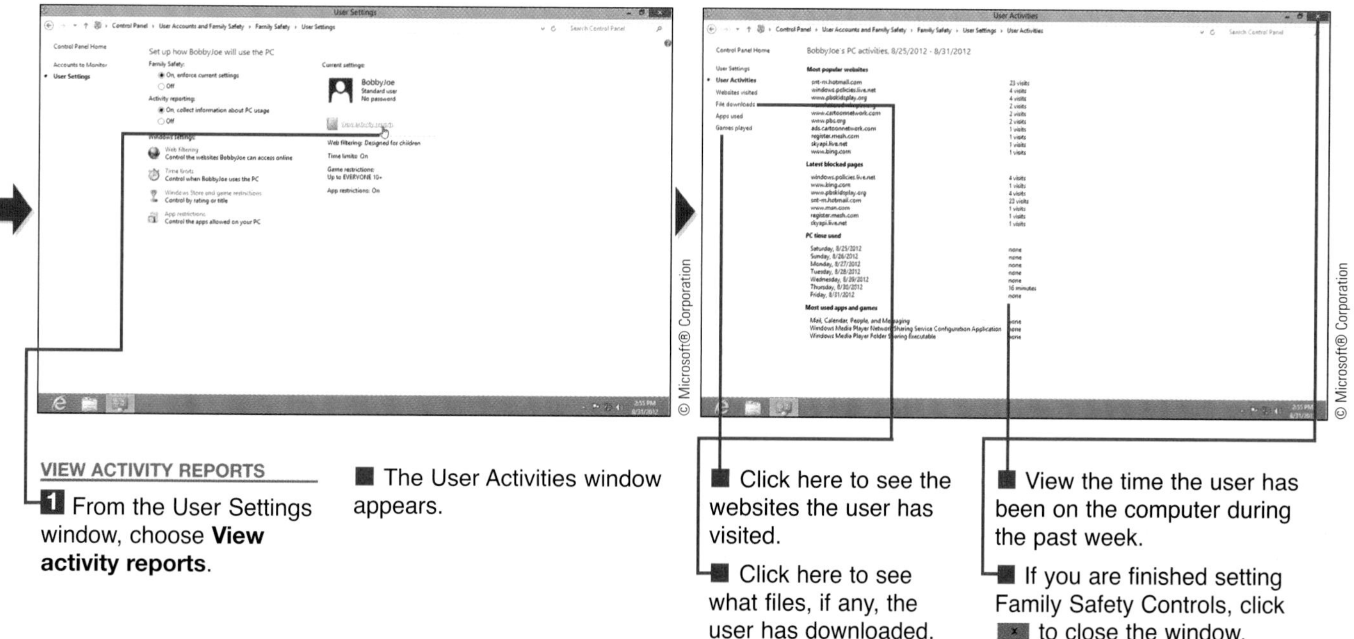

© Microsoft® Corporation

© Microsoft® Corporation

VIEW ACTIVITY REPORTS

1 From the User Settings window, choose **View activity reports**.

■ The User Activities window appears.

■ Click here to see the websites the user has visited.

■ Click here to see what files, if any, the user has downloaded.

■ View the time the user has been on the computer during the past week.

■ If you are finished setting Family Safety Controls, click ✕ to close the window.

maran
illustrated
Keep
Welcome to the maranGraphics Web site. We are extremely excited to announce
of our new series, Maran Illustrated™.
Sincerely,
Home
Lifestyle Books
Computer Books
Sneak Previews
About Us
Contact Us
Order Books
Keep Me Updated
Lifestyle Books
Guitar
Yoga
Piano
NEW BOOKS
Internet | Protected Mode: On
Smithsonian
VISIT
MEMBERS
SCIENCE
EDUCATION
MEET OUR ANIMALS
CLOUDED LEOPARD CUBS
ZOO NEWS
US FOREST SERVICE
Welcome
6767

CHAPTER 9

Browse the Web

START INTERNET EXPLORER

You can start Internet Explorer to browse through the information on the web. You need a connection to the Internet to browse the information there.

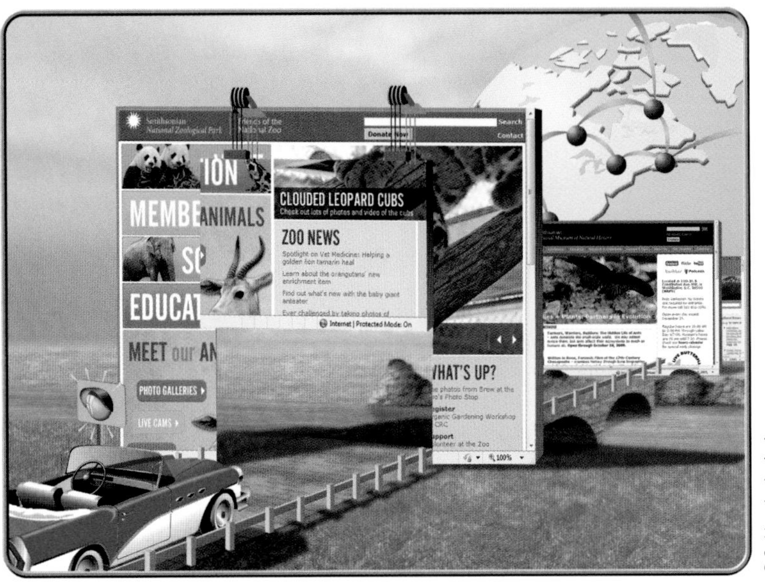

© Smithsonian Institution

Windows 8 comes with two flavors of Internet Explorer. You access one through the Start screen and the other from the desktop. The Internet Explorer from the desktop provides more flexibility when surfing through websites.

START INTERNET EXPLORER

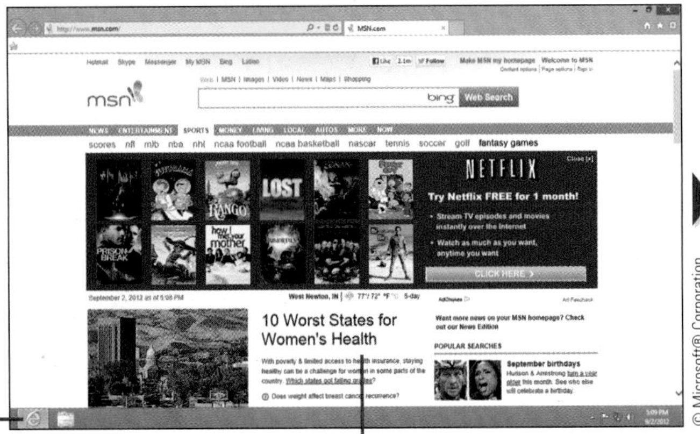

© Microsoft® Corporation

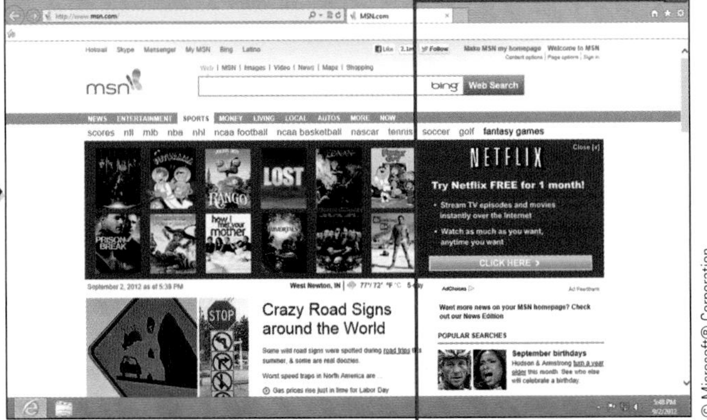

© Microsoft® Corporation

1 From the Start menu, click **Desktop**.

2 Click Internet Explorer.

Note: The first time you start Internet Explorer, the Welcome to Internet Explorer dialog box appears, allowing you to choose your settings.

■ The Internet Explorer window appears, displaying your home page.

Note: Your home page is the web page that appears each time you start Internet Explorer. To change your home page, see ***"Change Your Home Page"*** *later in this chapter.*

3 When you finish browsing the web, click ■ to close Internet Explorer.

DISPLAY A WEB PAGE

You can display any web page on the Internet that you have heard or read about.

© Cengage Learning®

Every web page has a unique address. You need to know the address of a web page you want to view.

Internet Explorer blocks *pop-up windows*, which are small windows that often display advertisements and usually appear as soon as you visit a website.

Internet Explorer also blocks content that might not be safe. For example, a website may try to collect information about you, download harmful files, or install software without your consent.

DISPLAY A WEB PAGE

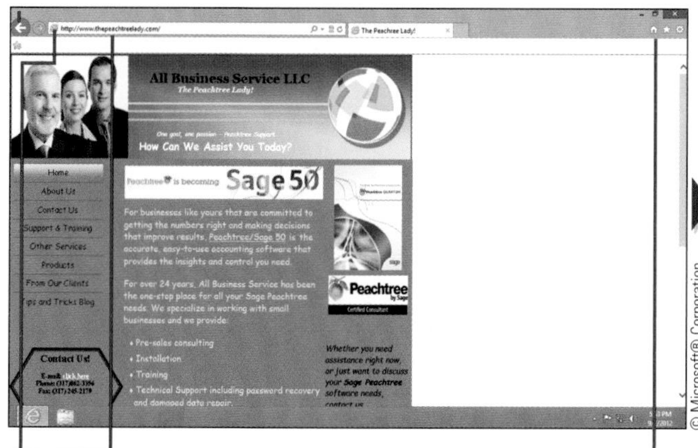

© Microsoft® Corporation

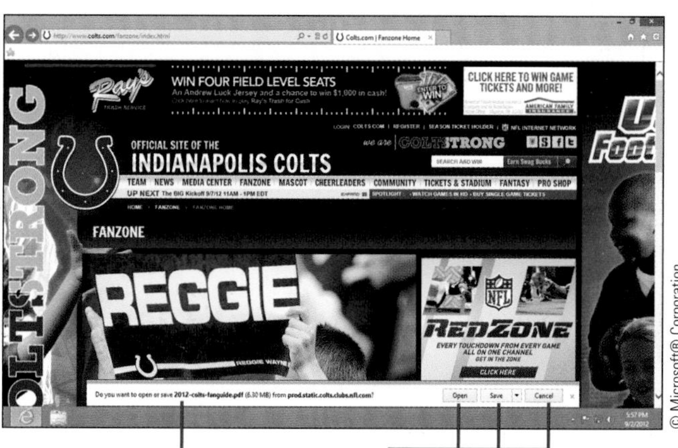

© Microsoft® Corporation

1 Click this area to highlight the current web page address. This area is known as the *address bar*.

2 Type the address of the web page you want to display, and then press Enter.

Note: As you type, a list of matching web pages that you have recently viewed may appear. If you want to display a web page on the list, click the web address in the list.

■ The web page appears on your screen.

3 Press the Home button to quickly return to your home page.

VIEW BLOCKED CONTENT

■ The Information bar appears when Internet Explorer blocks a pop-up window or blocks content that might not be safe.

1 If you want to view, download, or install the blocked content, click the option that allows you to access the content.

WORK WITH WEB PAGES

There are many ways that you can work with web pages in Internet Explorer. For example, when viewing a web page, you can select a link to display related information.

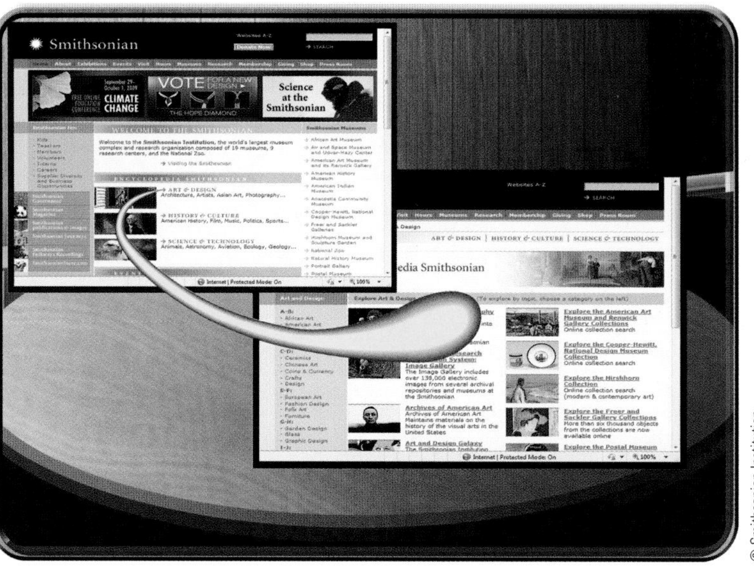

© Smithsonian Institution

A link connects text or an image found on one web page to another web page. When you click the text or image, the linked web page appears.

When working with web pages, you can also move backward and forward through web pages you have viewed and stop the transfer of a web page to your computer. You can also refresh a web page to transfer a fresh copy of the web page to your computer.

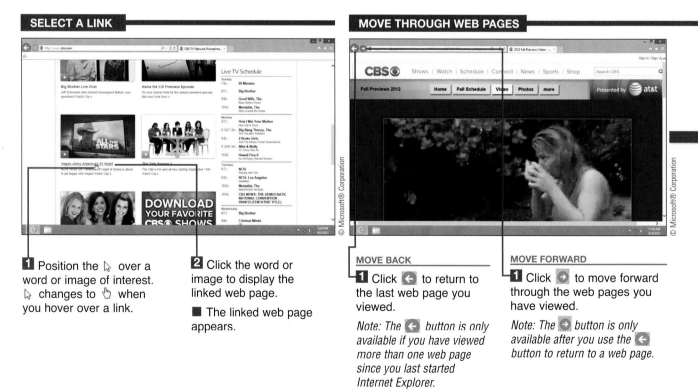

SELECT A LINK

© Microsoft® Corporation

1 Position the ⇖ over a word or image of interest.

⇖ changes to ☝ when you hover over a link.

2 Click the word or image to display the linked web page.

■ The linked web page appears.

MOVE THROUGH WEB PAGES

© Microsoft® Corporation

MOVE BACK

1 Click ← to return to the last web page you viewed.

Note: The ← button is only available if you have viewed more than one web page since you last started Internet Explorer.

MOVE FORWARD

1 Click → to move forward through the web pages you have viewed.

Note: The → button is only available after you use the ← button to return to a web page.

Can I make a web page larger?

Yes. If you have trouble reading small text on a web page, you can enlarge a web page. At the top right of the Internet Explorer window, click Tools and click **Zoom** from the resulting menu. Click the zoom percentage you want to use.

Additionally, if your mouse has a scroll wheel, you can hold down the Ctrl key and scroll the mouse wheel forward to zoom in on the web page, or hold down the Ctrl key and scroll the mouse wheel backward to zoom out on the web page.

Finally, some web pages include controls on the page that allow you to make the print larger or smaller.

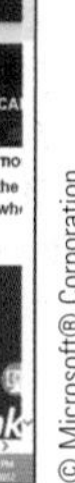

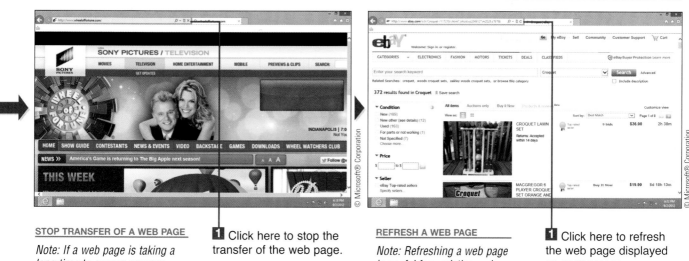

STOP TRANSFER OF A WEB PAGE

Note: If a web page is taking a long time to appear on your screen or contains information that does not interest you, you can stop its transfer.

1 Click here to stop the transfer of the web page.

REFRESH A WEB PAGE

Note: Refreshing a web page is useful for updating web pages that contain regularly changing information, such as news or images from a live camera.

1 Click here to refresh the web page displayed on your screen.

When browsing the web, you can use tabs to view and work with more than one web page at a time within the Internet Explorer window.

© MyMoney.gov

WORK WITH TABS

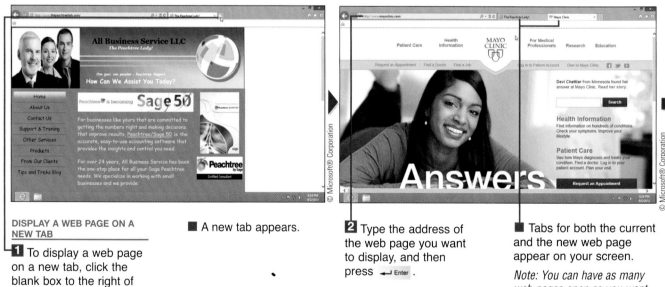

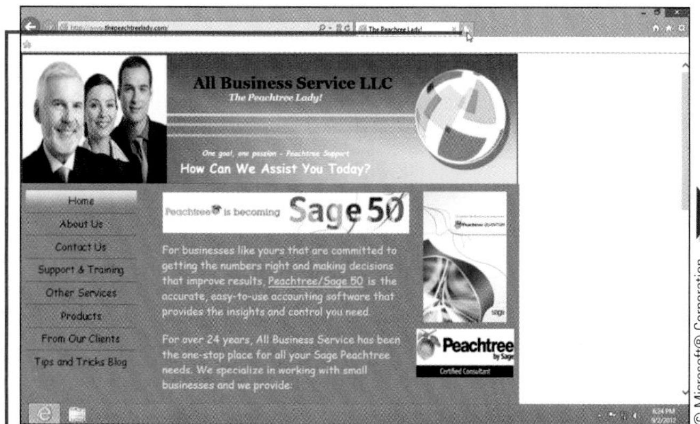
© Microsoft® Corporation

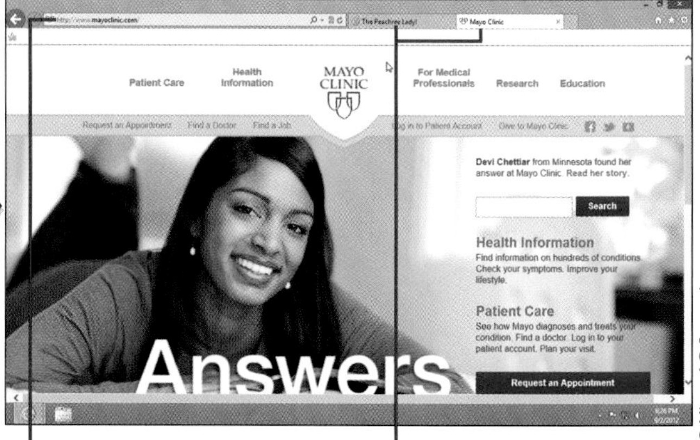
© Microsoft® Corporation

DISPLAY A WEB PAGE ON A NEW TAB

1 To display a web page on a new tab, click the blank box to the right of the tabs.

■ A new tab appears.

2 Type the address of the web page you want to display, and then press Enter.

■ Tabs for both the current and the new web page appear on your screen.

Note: You can have as many web pages open as you want.

What happens if I have several tabs open when I close Internet Explorer?

If you have several tabs open when you click ✕ to close Internet Explorer, a dialog box appears asking if you want to close all the tabs or just the current tab. To close all the tabs and close Internet Explorer, click **Close all tabs**. To close only the currently displayed tab and leave Internet Explorer open, click **Close current tab**.

Can I click a link on a page and have the link open in a new tab?

Yes. To open a link on a web page on a new tab, press and hold down the Ctrl key as you click the link on the web page. Windows groups the original and linked web pages by displaying their tabs in the same color.

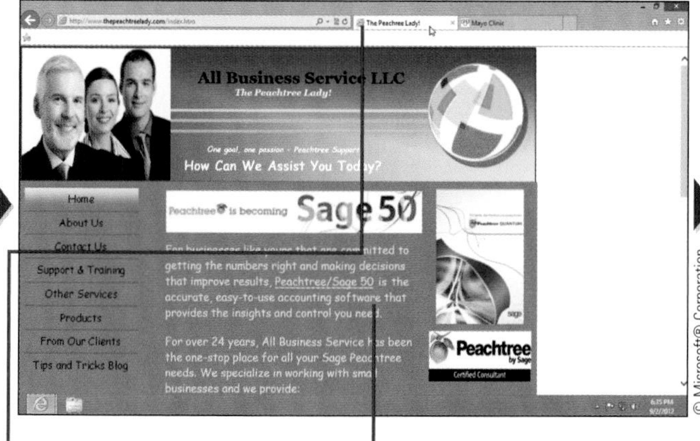

© Microsoft® Corporation

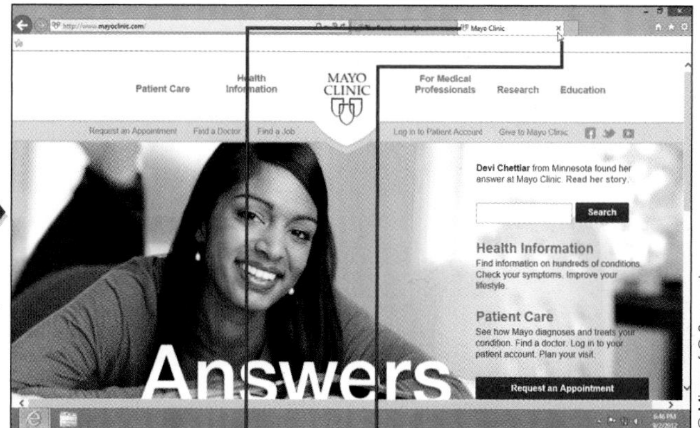

© Microsoft® Corporation

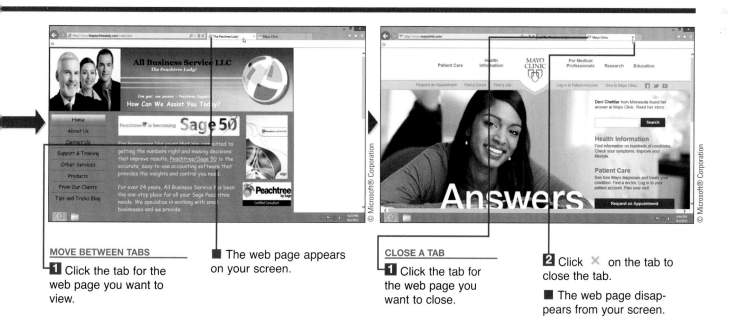

MOVE BETWEEN TABS

1 Click the tab for the web page you want to view.

■ The web page appears on your screen.

CLOSE A TAB

1 Click the tab for the web page you want to close.

2 Click ✕ on the tab to close the tab.

■ The web page disappears from your screen.

PRINT A WEB PAGE

You can produce a paper copy of a web page displayed on your screen. Before printing a web page, you can preview how the web page will look when printed.

PREVIEW A WEB PAGE BEFORE PRINTING

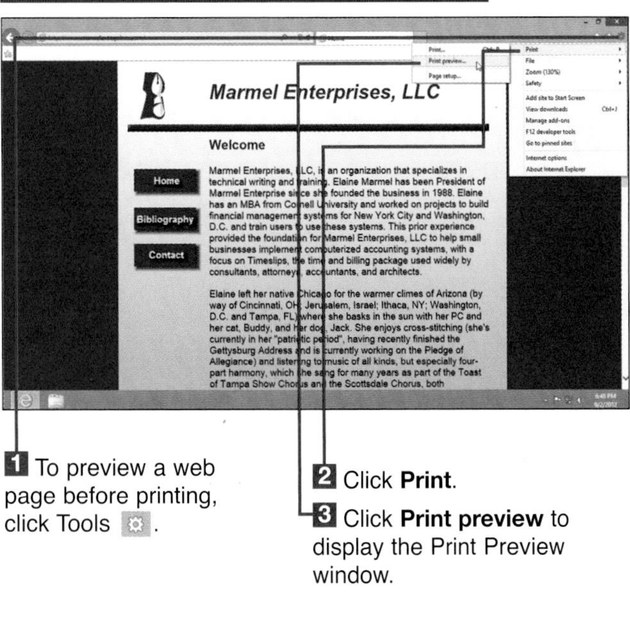

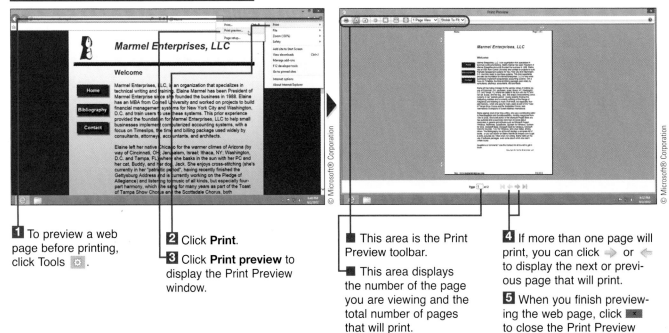

1 To preview a web page before printing, click Tools .

2 Click **Print**.

3 Click **Print preview** to display the Print Preview window.

■ This area is the Print Preview toolbar.

■ This area displays the number of the page you are viewing and the total number of pages that will print.

4 If more than one page will print, you can click or to display the next or previous page that will print.

5 When you finish previewing the web page, click to close the Print Preview window.

Why does the text on a web page appear so small when it prints?

When you print a web page, Internet Explorer shrinks the content of the web page to fit across a piece of paper. This prevents the right side of a web page from being cut off, but it may make the text smaller and more difficult to read. To print the content of a web page at a larger size, you can click [A] in the toolbar at the top of the Print Preview window to change to the landscape orientation. Doing so prints the content of a web page across the longer side of your paper.

Note: If you want to return to the portrait orientation, click [A] in the Print Preview window.

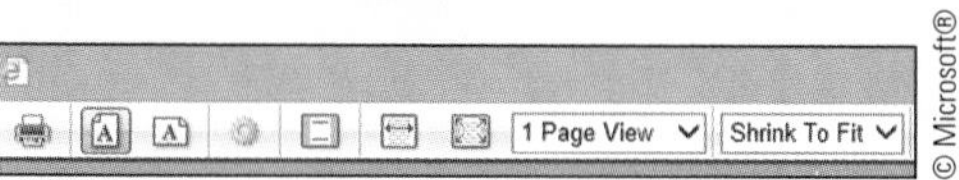

Can I print only specific pages of a web page?

Yes. After previewing how a web page will print, you may want to print only specific pages. The Print dialog box displays options you can select for printing the web page. Double-click the number beside Pages and then type the pages you want to print, such as 1 or 2–4.

PRINT A WEB PAGE

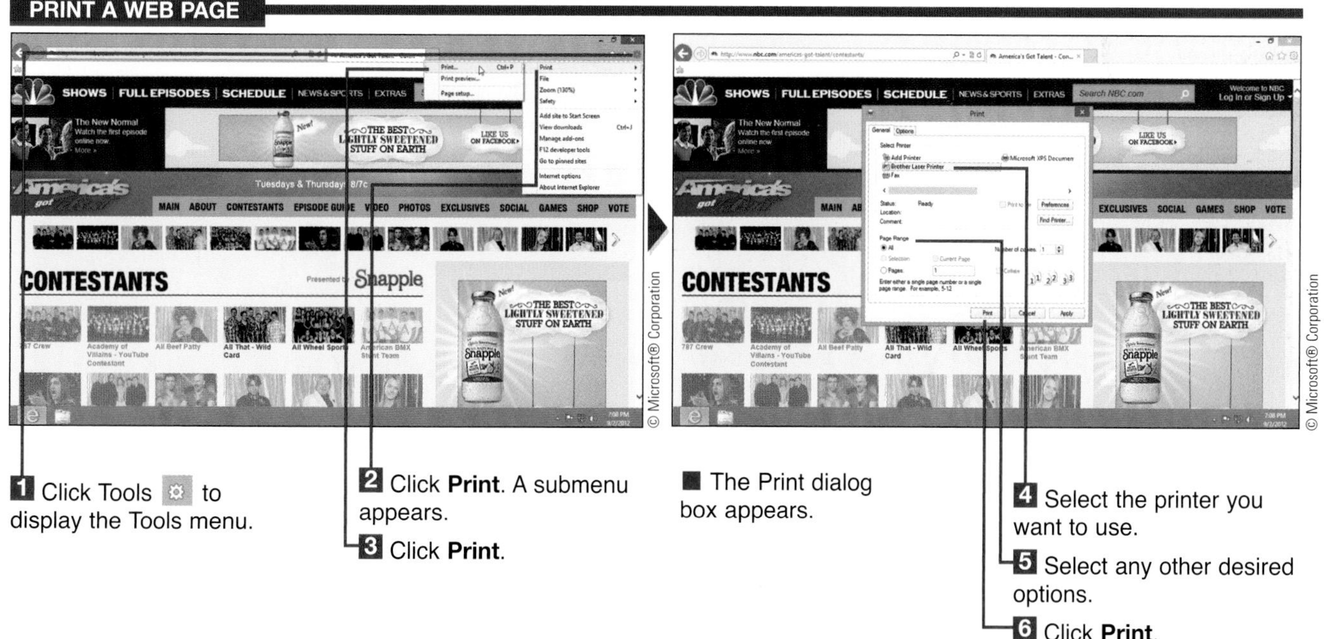

1 Click Tools ⚙ to display the Tools menu.

2 Click **Print**. A submenu appears.

3 Click **Print**.

■ The Print dialog box appears.

4 Select the printer you want to use.

5 Select any other desired options.

6 Click **Print**.

SEARCH THE WEB

You can search for web pages that discuss topics of interest to you.

© Smithsonian Institution. © US Forest Service
© maranGraphics, Inc.

Websites that allow you to search for information on the web are known as *search providers*.

Many websites also have their own search boxes, which allow you to search for specific information within their website.

SEARCH THE WEB

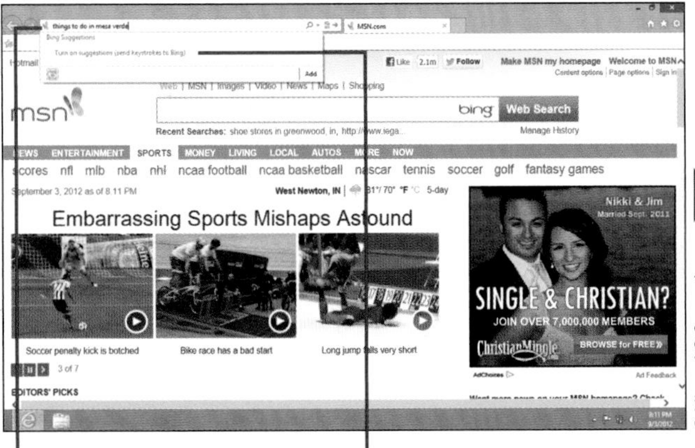

© Microsoft® Corporation

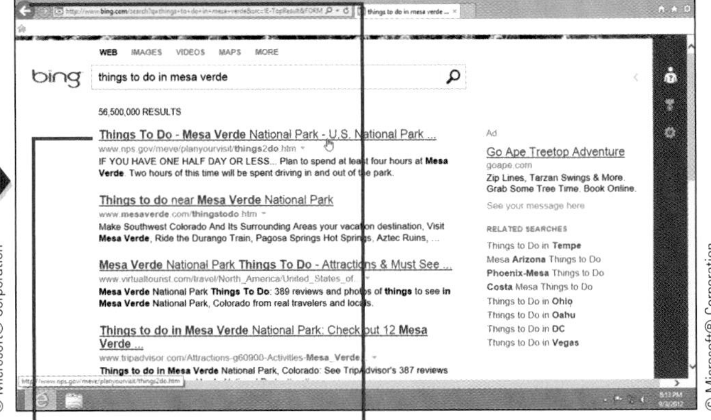

© Microsoft® Corporation

1 Click in the address bar. If there is text in the address bar, drag the ↖ across it to highlight it.

2 Type the word or phrase for which you want to search. Press Enter to start the search.

■ As you type, a list of search suggestions may appear, along with a list of matching web pages that you have recently viewed. If you want to use a search suggestion to perform the search or display a web page on the list, click the item.

■ A list of matching web pages appears.

3 To display a web page of interest, click the title of the web page.

■ The web page you selected appears.

■ You can click ← to return to the list of web pages and select another page.

What are search providers, and how do they work?

A *search provider* is a complex software program that searches for sites based on the words that you designate as search terms. They include incredibly detailed processes and methodologies, and they are updated all the time.

Search providers have three main functions. The first is to *crawl* around through the millions of web pages on the Internet, looking for the information in the web pages. Next, the search provider sorts and stores, or *indexes*, the information it finds and stores it in its database for the time someone needs that information. Finally, when you search for something, the search providers look through (*search*) their own databases of information to find what it is that you are looking for.

Most search providers are general in the information they search for, but others are more specialized, focusing on specific topics such as images, jobs, blogs, and so forth.

ADD A SEARCH PROVIDER

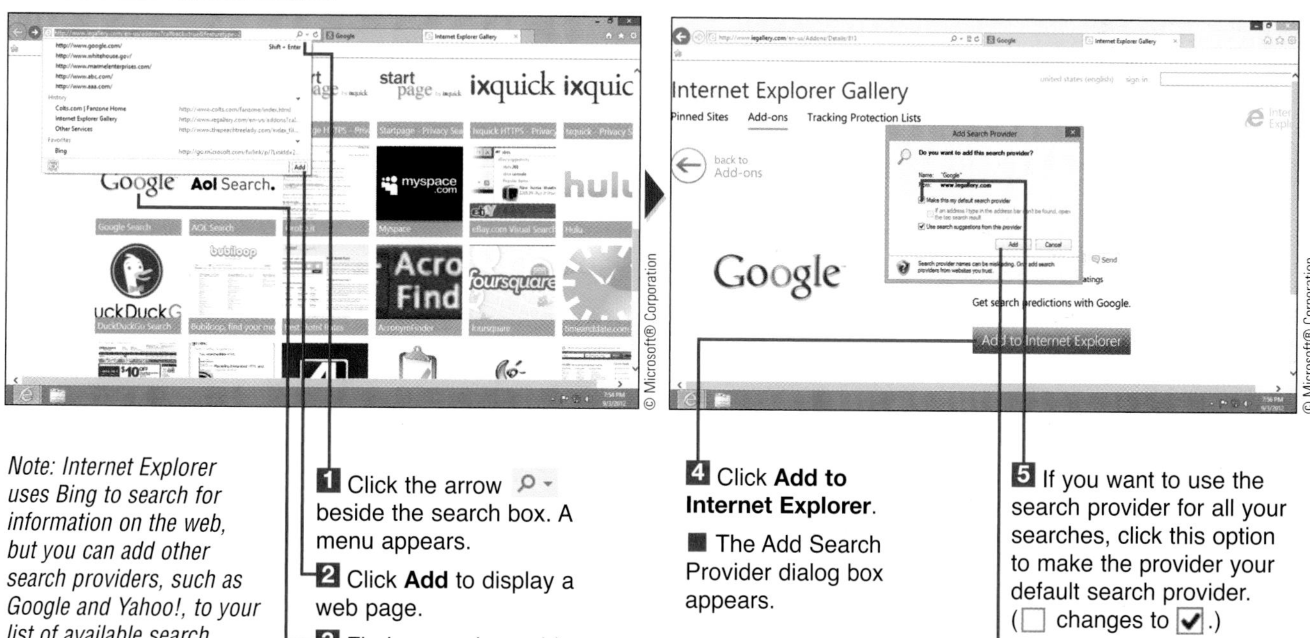

© Microsoft® Corporation

© Microsoft® Corporation

Note: Internet Explorer uses Bing to search for information on the web, but you can add other search providers, such as Google and Yahoo!, to your list of available search providers.

1 Click the arrow (search arrow) beside the search box. A menu appears.

2 Click **Add** to display a web page.

3 Find a search provider you want to add, and click the provider icon.

4 Click **Add to Internet Explorer**.

■ The Add Search Provider dialog box appears.

5 If you want to use the search provider for all your searches, click this option to make the provider your default search provider. (☐ changes to ☑.)

6 Click **Add** to add the search provider.

CHANGE YOUR HOME PAGE

When you start Internet Explorer, the first page that appears is called your *home page*. Windows 8 automatically goes to www.msn.com, but you can change your home page if you want something else to come up instead.

Internet Explorer allows you to have more than one home page. If you set up multiple home pages, also known as *home page tabs*, each page appears on its own tab when you start Internet Explorer.

CHANGE YOUR HOME PAGE

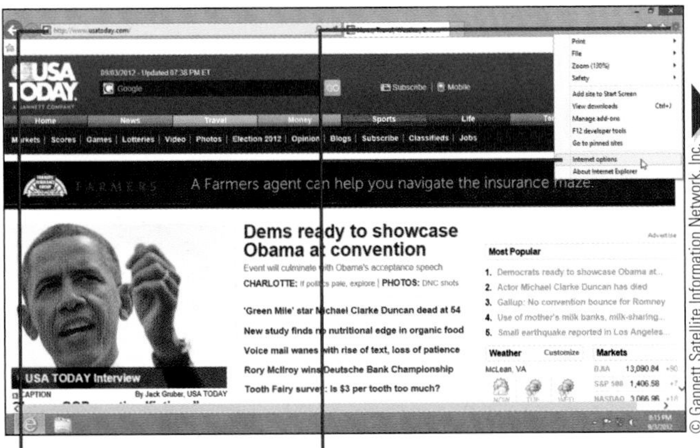

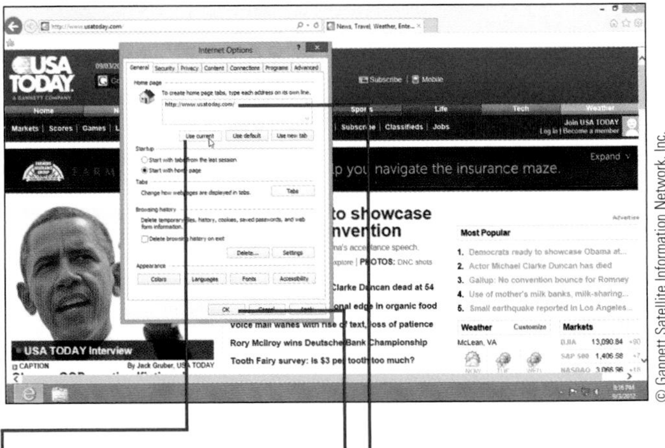

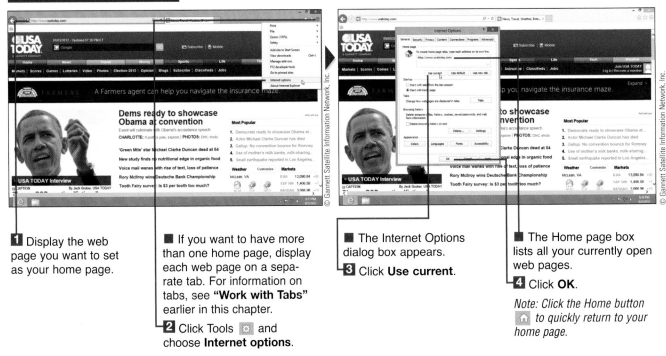

1 Display the web page you want to set as your home page.

■ If you want to have more than one home page, display each web page on a separate tab. For information on tabs, see **"Work with Tabs"** earlier in this chapter.

2 Click Tools and choose **Internet options**.

■ The Internet Options dialog box appears.

3 Click **Use current**.

■ The Home page box lists all your currently open web pages.

4 Click **OK**.

Note: Click the Home button to quickly return to your home page.

Which web page should I set as a home page?

You can set any page on the web as a home page. A web page you choose should be a page you want to frequently visit. You may want to choose a web page that provides a good starting point for exploring the web, such as www.google.com, or a page that provides information relevant to your personal interests or work.

REMOVE A HOME PAGE

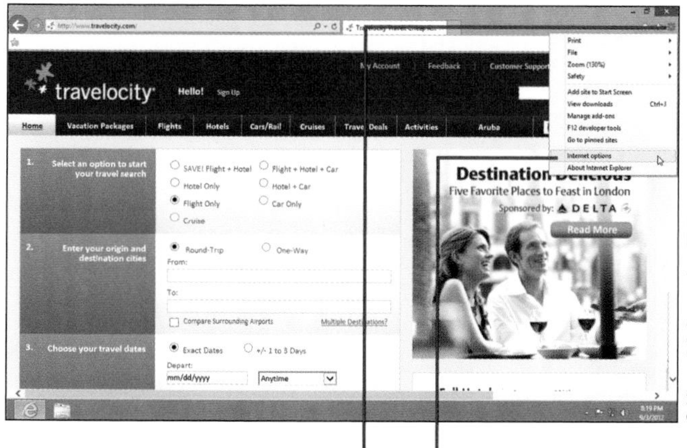

© Microsoft® Corporation

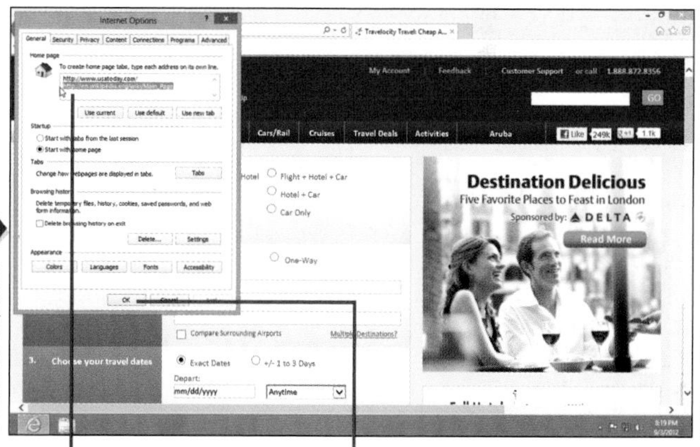

© Microsoft® Corporation

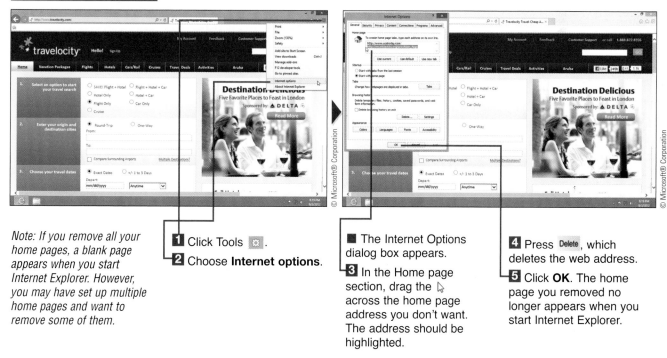

Note: If you remove all your home pages, a blank page appears when you start Internet Explorer. However, you may have set up multiple home pages and want to remove some of them.

1 Click Tools ⚙.

2 Choose **Internet options**.

■ The Internet Options dialog box appears.

3 In the Home page section, drag the ⇖ across the home page address you don't want. The address should be highlighted.

4 Press Delete, which deletes the web address.

5 Click **OK**. The home page you removed no longer appears when you start Internet Explorer.

DISPLAY HISTORY OF VIEWED WEB PAGES

Internet Explorer uses the history list to keep track of the web pages you have recently viewed. You can display the history list at any time to redisplay a web page.

By default, the history list keeps track of the web pages you have viewed over the past 20 days.

DISPLAY HISTORY OF VIEWED WEB PAGES

1 Click Favorites (☆) to display the Favorites Center.

2 Click the History tab to display your history list.

■ This area displays a list of the web pages you have recently viewed, organized by week and day. Each week and day displays the (▦) symbol.

3 Click the week or day you viewed the web page that you want to view again.

■ The websites you viewed during the week or that day appear.

4 Click the website of interest.

■ The web pages you viewed at the website appear.

5 Click the web page you want to view.

■ The web page appears.

Can I change the way my list of recently viewed web pages is organized?

Yes. Internet Explorer initially organizes your list of recently viewed web pages by date. To change the way your history list is organized, click the arrow next to the View by option. On the menu that appears, click the way you want to organize your history list. You can view your history list by date, website, most visited, or the order visited today.

Can I display my list of recently viewed web pages all the time?

Yes. If you want your list of recently viewed web pages to appear all the time, you can pin the Favorites Center to the page. When you click [icon] at the left edge of the Favorites pane, the list moves to the left side of your screen. When you select a web page in your history list, the list no longer disappears. At any time, you can click [icon] above your history list to remove the list from your screen.

DELETE WEB PAGE HISTORY

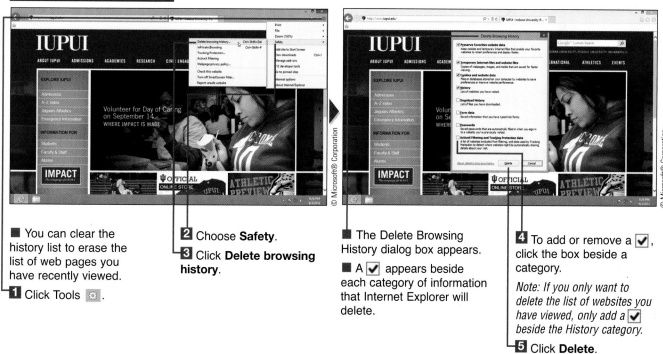

© Microsoft® Corporation

■ You can clear the history list to erase the list of web pages you have recently viewed.

1 Click Tools [icon].

2 Choose **Safety**.

3 Click **Delete browsing history**.

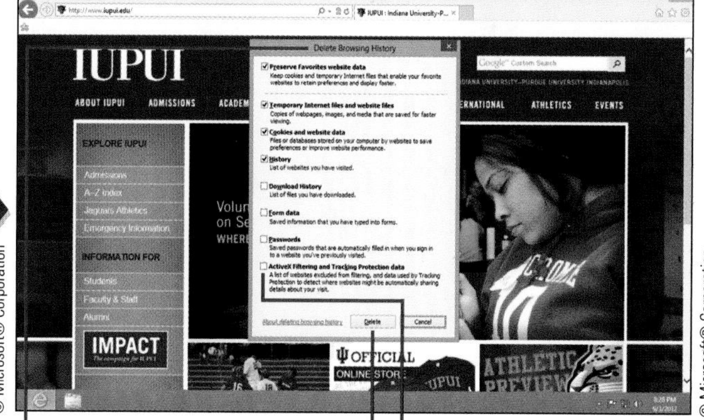

© Microsoft® Corporation

■ The Delete Browsing History dialog box appears.

■ A [✓] appears beside each category of information that Internet Explorer will delete.

4 To add or remove a [✓], click the box beside a category.

Note: If you only want to delete the list of websites you have viewed, only add a [✓] beside the History category.

5 Click **Delete**.

ADD A WEB PAGE TO FAVORITES

You can keep a list of your favorite web pages so you can quickly return to them at any time.

© Smithsonian Institution

Selecting web pages from your list of favorites saves you from having to remember and constantly retype the same web page addresses over and over again.

ADD A WEB PAGE TO FAVORITES

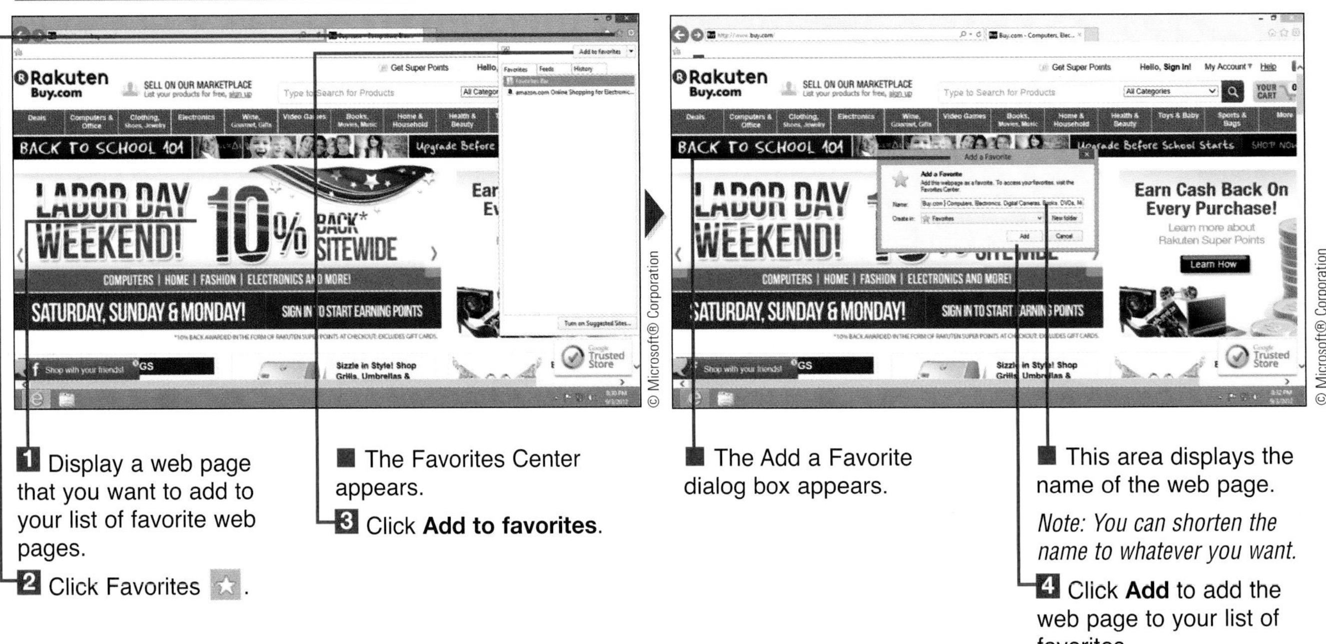

© Microsoft® Corporation

1 Display a web page that you want to add to your list of favorite web pages.

2 Click Favorites.

■ The Favorites Center appears.

3 Click **Add to favorites**.

■ The Add a Favorite dialog box appears.

■ This area displays the name of the web page.

Note: You can shorten the name to whatever you want.

4 Click **Add** to add the web page to your list of favorites.

Can I organize my favorites?

Yes. Through the Organize Favorites dialog box, you can create new folders and move favorites into those folders. You can also rename favorites and delete favorites.

To access the Organize Favorites dialog box, click Favorites ☆, and then click ▾ next to the Add to Favorites button. From the menu that appears, click **Organize Favorites** to display the Organize Favorites dialog box.

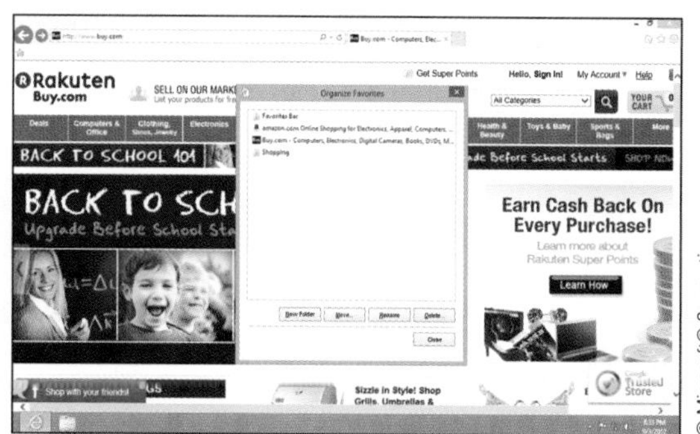

© Microsoft® Corporation

If you want a new folder, click the New Folder button and type a name for the new folder. Press Enter.

If you want to move a favorite into a folder, select the favorite you want to move into the new folder, and click the **Move** button. Choose the folder you want to move the Favorite into, and click **OK**.

When you are finished with the Organize Favorites dialog box, click ✕.

VIEW A FAVORITE WEB PAGE

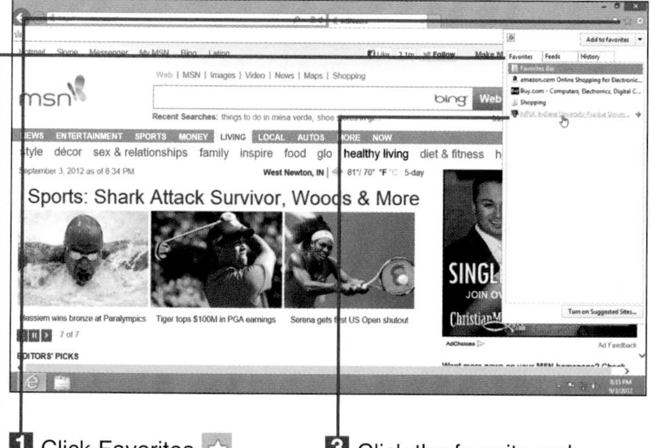

© Microsoft® Corporation

© Microsoft® Corporation

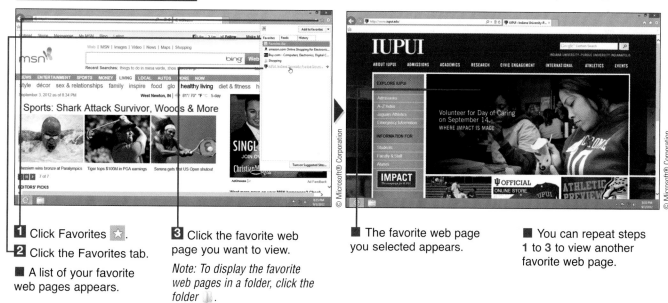

1 Click Favorites ☆.

2 Click the Favorites tab.

■ A list of your favorite web pages appears.

3 Click the favorite web page you want to view.

Note: To display the favorite web pages in a folder, click the folder.

■ The favorite web page you selected appears.

■ You can repeat steps **1** to **3** to view another favorite web page.

USE THE FAVORITES BAR

You can add your favorite web pages to the Favorites bar so you can instantly return to the web pages. The Favorites bar provides quick access to the web pages you most often visit.

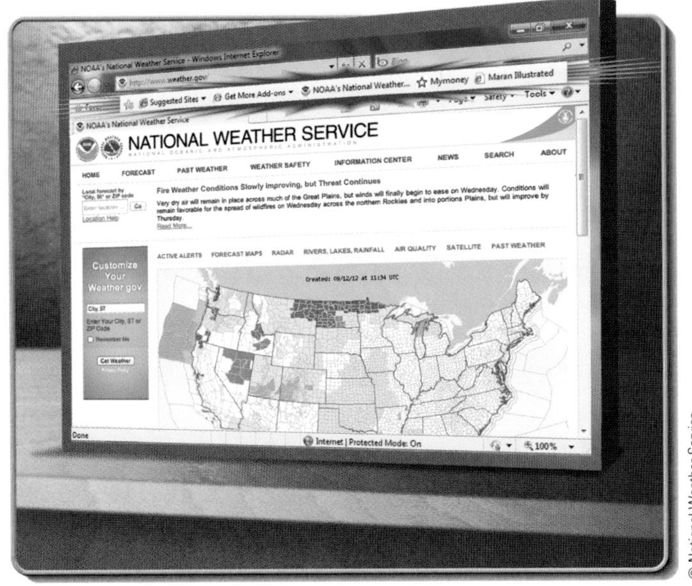

© National Weather Service

USE THE FAVORITES BAR

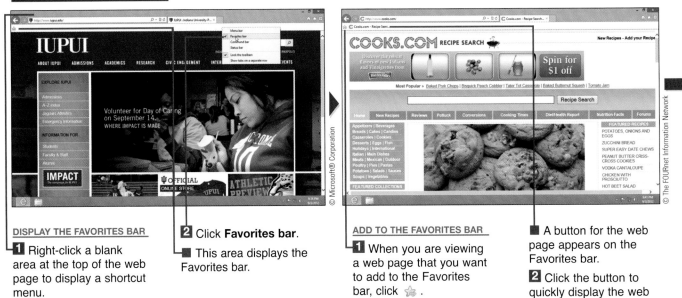

© Microsoft® Corporation

DISPLAY THE FAVORITES BAR

1 Right-click a blank area at the top of the web page to display a shortcut menu.

2 Click **Favorites bar**.

■ This area displays the Favorites bar.

© The FOURnet Information Network

ADD TO THE FAVORITES BAR

1 When you are viewing a web page that you want to add to the Favorites bar, click ☆.

■ A button for the web page appears on the Favorites bar.

2 Click the button to quickly display the web page.

Tip: How many favorites can I add to the Favorites bar?

The number of favorites you can add is unlimited; however, if you have more of them than can fit on the Favorites bar, a scroll bar appears.

You can fit more shortcuts on the Favorites bar if you display only the icon for the site. Right-click a favorite on the toolbar. From the shortcut menu that appears, choose **Customize title widths**, and then choose **Icons only**.

How do I remove a web page from the Favorites bar?

If you no longer want the button for a web page to appear on the Favorites bar, right-click the button and then click **Delete** on the menu that appears. In the confirmation dialog box that appears, click **Yes**.

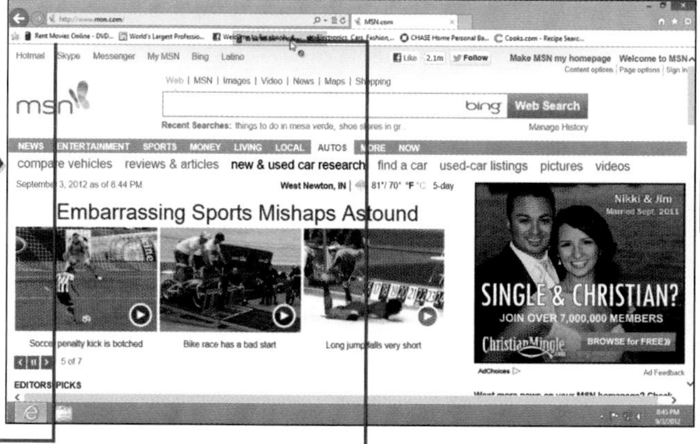

© Microsoft® Corporation

© Microsoft® Corporation

REARRANGE WEB PAGES

1 To rearrange web pages on the Favorites bar, position the ⇖ over the button for the web page that you want to move.

2 Drag the button for the web page to where you want the button to appear on the Favorites bar.

■ A black line indicates where the button for the web page will appear.

■ The button for the web page appears in the new location on the Favorites bar.

PIN A SITE TO THE START SCREEN

If you have a website that you visit frequently, you can pin it to the Start screen.

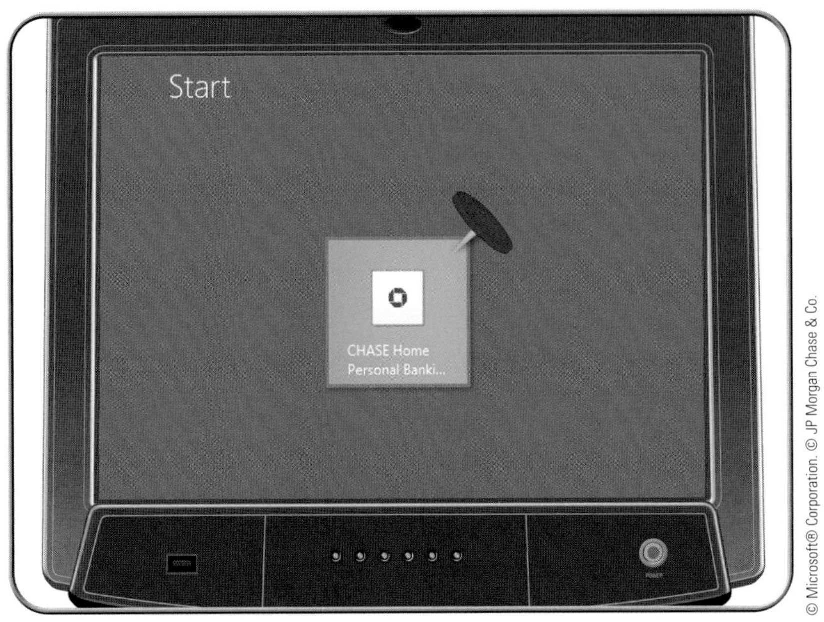

© Microsoft® Corporation. © JP Morgan Chase & Co.

Then you are only a single mouse click away from the web page.

PIN A SITE TO THE START SCREEN

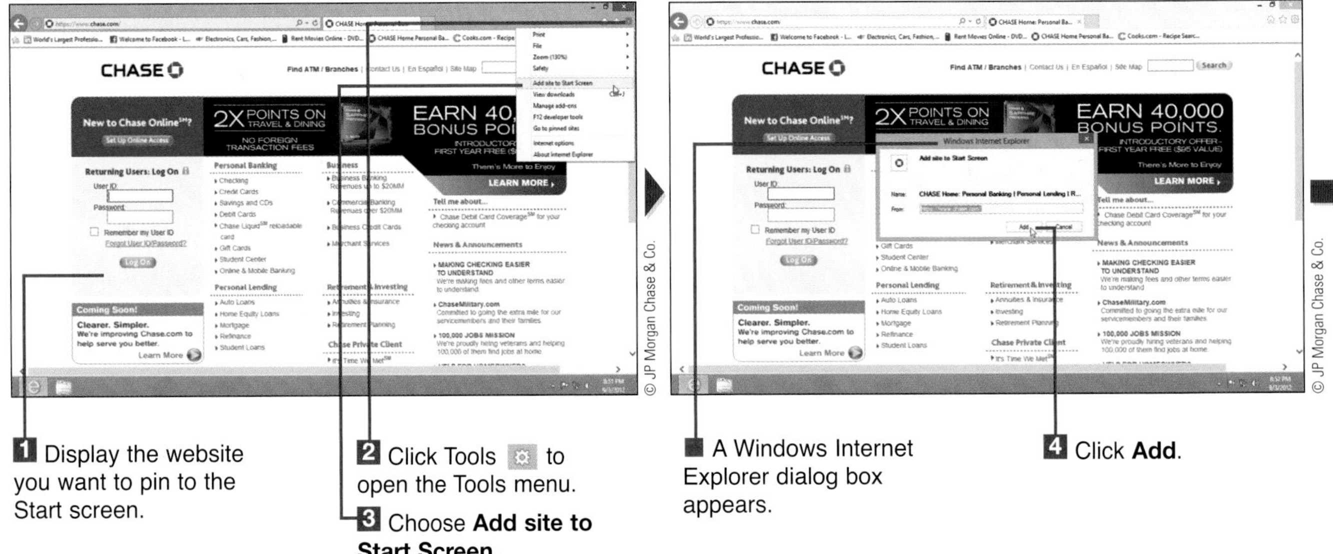

© JP Morgan Chase & Co.

© JP Morgan Chase & Co.

1 Display the website you want to pin to the Start screen.

2 Click Tools to open the Tools menu.

3 Choose **Add site to Start Screen**.

■ A Windows Internet Explorer dialog box appears.

4 Click **Add**.

Can I change the name that appears on the Start screen?

Yes. After you add it to the Start screen, right-click the tile and choose **Open Folder Location** from the App bar. In the File Explorer window that appears, right-click the entry and choose **Rename**. Then type the new name and press Enter. Click ✕ to close the File Explorer window.

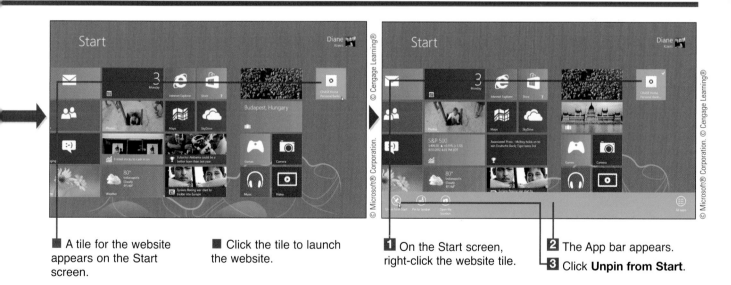

© Microsoft® Corporation. © Cengage Learning®

© Microsoft® Corporation. © Cengage Learning®

■ A tile for the website appears on the Start screen.

■ Click the tile to launch the website.

1 On the Start screen, right-click the website tile.

2 The App bar appears.

3 Click **Unpin from Start**.

BROWSE THE WEB PRIVATELY

You can browse the web without leaving any trace of your web activity in Internet Explorer.

For example, you may want to browse the web privately when shopping for a surprise gift on a family computer or checking email at an Internet café.

When browsing the web privately, other people who use your computer will not see the websites you visit, the searches you perform, and the usernames and passwords you enter.

Browsing the web privately does not prevent another person on your network, such as a network administrator, from viewing the websites you visit.

BROWSE THE WEB PRIVATELY

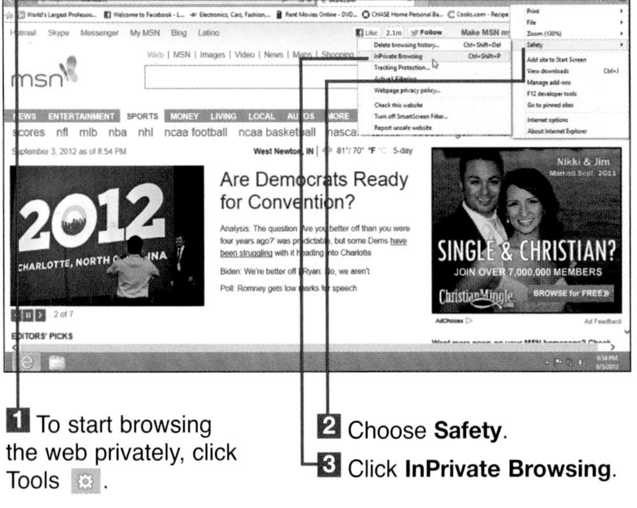

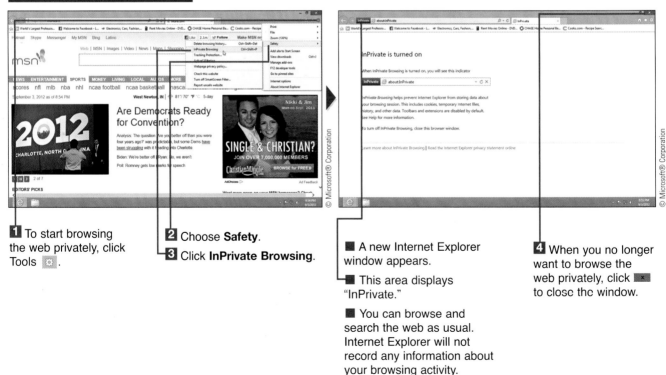

1 To start browsing the web privately, click Tools ⚙.

2 Choose **Safety**.

3 Click **InPrivate Browsing**.

■ A new Internet Explorer window appears.

■ This area displays "InPrivate."

■ You can browse and search the web as usual. Internet Explorer will not record any information about your browsing activity.

4 When you no longer want to browse the web privately, click ✕ to close the window.

USE ACCELERATORS

With Accelerators, you can select a word or phrase on a web page and then choose from a variety of online services to instantly learn more about the text.

© maranGraphics, Inc.

For example, you can select a word or phrase on a web page and then instantly show a map, search the web, translate the text, and more.

USE ACCELERATORS

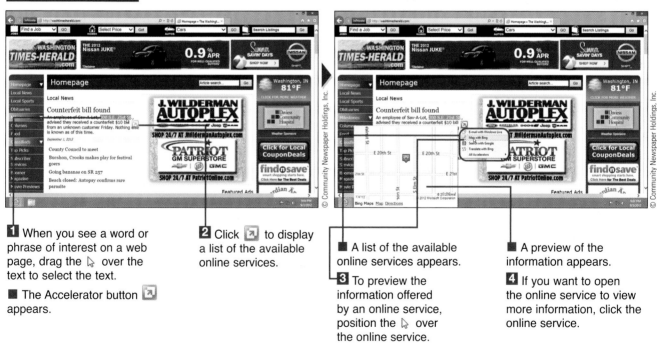

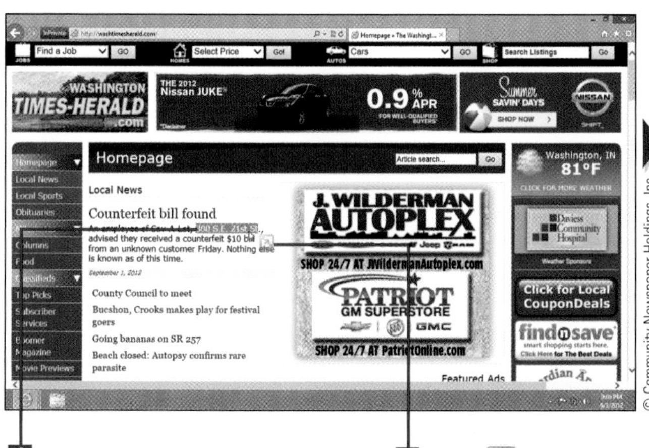
© Community Newspaper Holdings, Inc.

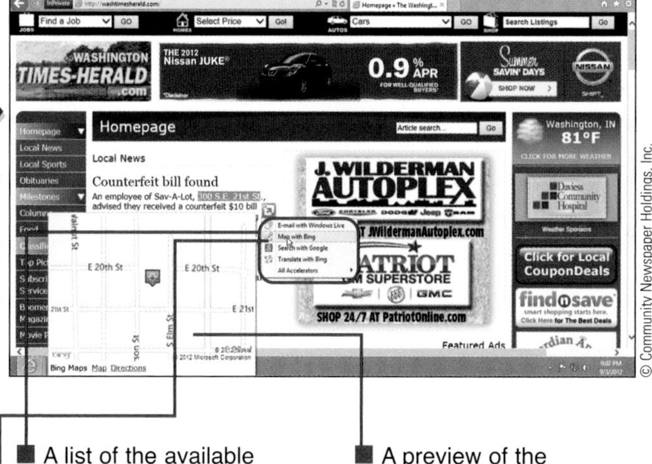
© Community Newspaper Holdings, Inc.

1 When you see a word or phrase of interest on a web page, drag the ⇖ over the text to select the text.

■ The Accelerator button appears.

2 Click to display a list of the available online services.

■ A list of the available online services appears.

3 To preview the information offered by an online service, position the ⇖ over the online service.

■ A preview of the information appears.

4 If you want to open the online service to view more information, click the online service.

Exchange Email

START MAIL

You can start the Mail app to open and read the contents of your email messages.

The first time you start Mail, a dialog box appears if you have not yet set up an email account. Follow the instructions in the dialog box to add an email account.

If you need assistance setting up your email, contact your Internet service provider, or if you are in a corporate environment, contact your network administrator.

START WINDOWS MAIL

1 From the Start screen, click Mail.

■ The Windows Mail window appears.

READ MESSAGES

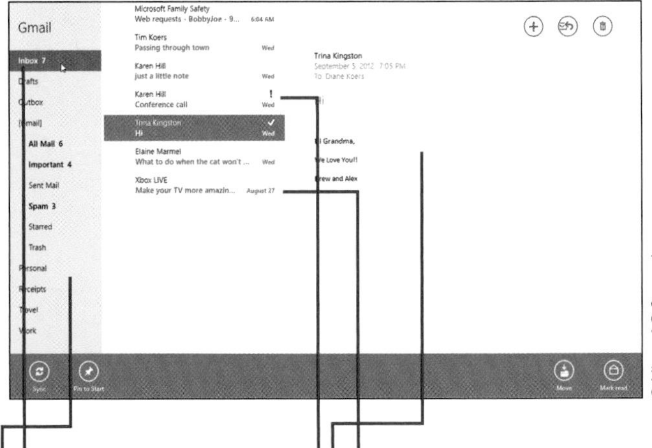

1 Click **Inbox** to display your email messages.

■ This area contains the mail folders.

■ This area shows a list of the message senders and subjects.

■ This area displays the selected message content.

■ Messages marked with ! are flagged as high priority.

What folders are used to store my messages?

The exact choices you see will vary depending on the type of email you use. Here are the typical mail folders:

Inbox—Stores messages sent to you.

Drafts—Stores messages you have not yet sent.

Important—Stores messages marked with a high priority.

Sent mail—Stores copies of messages you have sent.

Spam—Stores junk messages sent to you.

Trash—Stores messages you have deleted.

Additional folders may appear where you can separate and store your personal messages from work messages and such.

DISPLAY A WEB PAGE

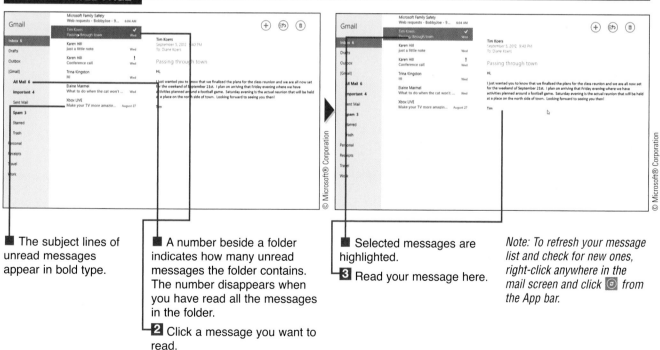

■ The subject lines of unread messages appear in bold type.

■ A number beside a folder indicates how many unread messages the folder contains. The number disappears when you have read all the messages in the folder.

2 Click a message you want to read.

■ Selected messages are highlighted.

3 Read your message here.

Note: To refresh your message list and check for new ones, right-click anywhere in the mail screen and click from the App bar.

You can print an email message. For example, if someone emails you directions to her house, you might want to print a copy of the email to take with you.

A staff meeting will be held in Conference Room A at 4:10 p.m. on each of the following days:
June 17th
July 7th
August 23rd
September 15th
All staff members must attend these meetings!
David Walker
President

You can mark a message as unread to remind you to review the message again later.

PRINT A MESSAGE

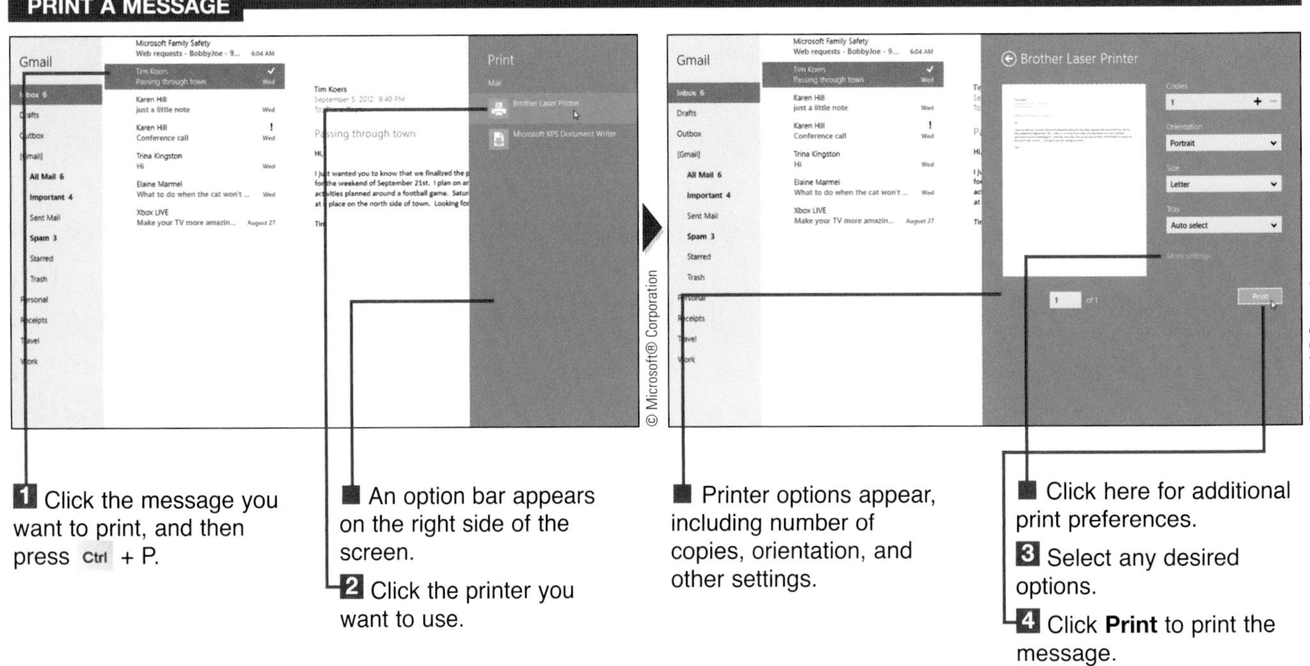

1 Click the message you want to print, and then press Ctrl + P.

■ An option bar appears on the right side of the screen.

2 Click the printer you want to use.

■ Printer options appear, including number of copies, orientation, and other settings.

■ Click here for additional print preferences.

3 Select any desired options.

4 Click **Print** to print the message.

What are some of the additional print settings?

The actual choices vary depending on the printer you selected. Most often, you can set print layout choices such as orientation, collation, and number of pages to print on each sheet of paper.

You can also set the paper size and type and choose which printer paper tray the paper should come from.

MARK A MESSAGE AS UNREAD

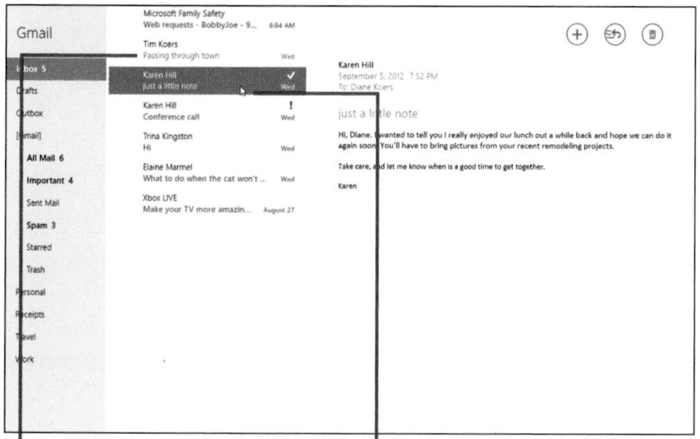

© Microsoft® Corporation

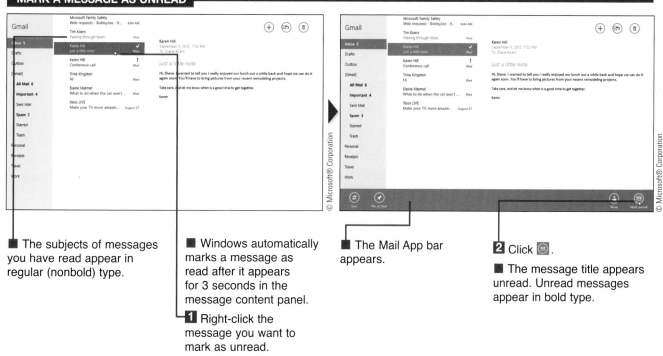

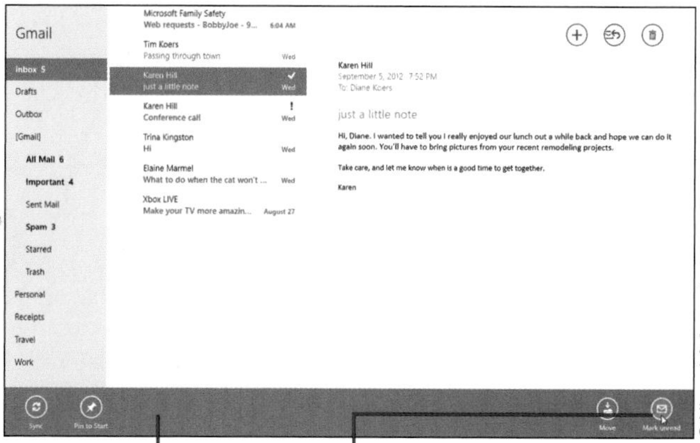

■ The subjects of messages you have read appear in regular (nonbold) type.

■ Windows automatically marks a message as read after it appears for 3 seconds in the message content panel.

1 Right-click the message you want to mark as unread.

© Microsoft® Corporation

■ The Mail App bar appears.

2 Click .

■ The message title appears unread. Unread messages appear in bold type.

VIEW BLOCKED CONTENT

Windows Mail examines messages you receive to determine if they are junk mail. Messages that appear to be junk mail are automatically moved to a special Spam email folder.

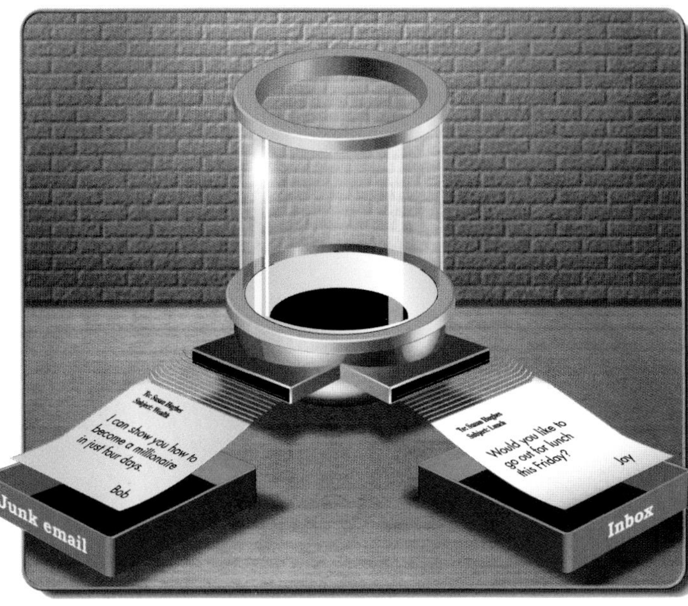

All links, images, or attachments in a message in the Spam folder are unavailable.

For example, a *phishing* message is a message that may appear to be from a real company but will send you to a fake website or scam you into providing personal information.

Sometimes regular messages are moved to the Spam folder even though they are legitimate and from a reliable source. In that case, you will want to view the message. You need to move the message before you can view it.

VIEW BLOCKED CONTENT

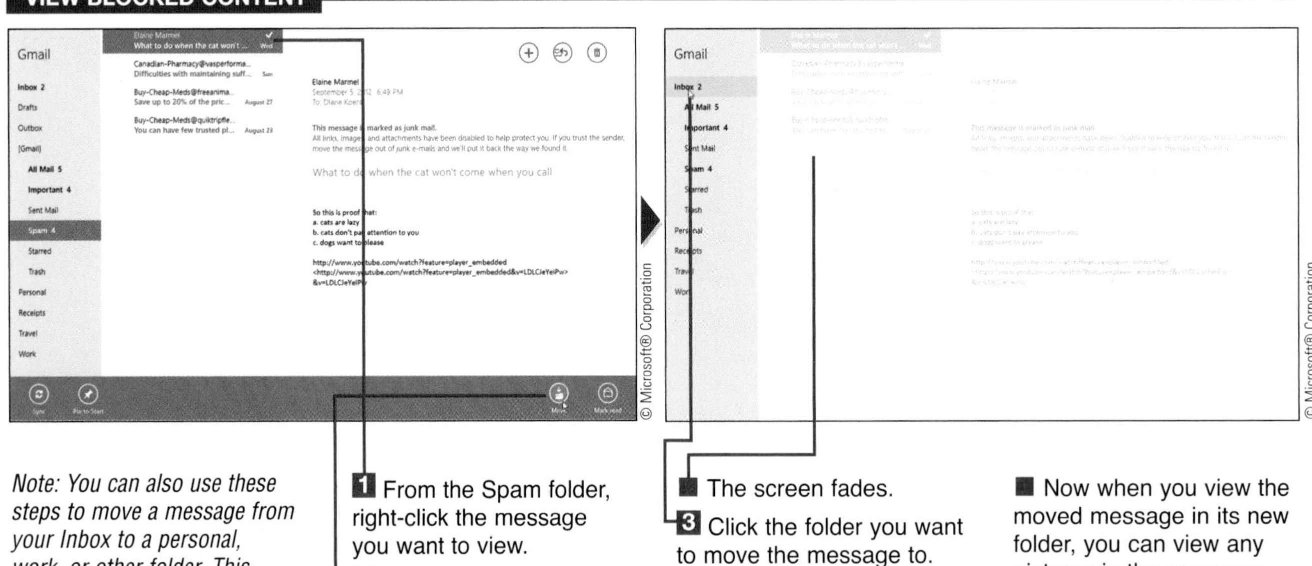

© Microsoft® Corporation

© Microsoft® Corporation

Note: You can also use these steps to move a message from your Inbox to a personal, work, or other folder. This keeps your Inbox from getting too cluttered.

1. From the Spam folder, right-click the message you want to view.
2. From the App bar, click .

■ The screen fades.

3. Click the folder you want to move the message to.

■ The message moves from the Spam folder into the folder you selected.

■ Now when you view the moved message in its new folder, you can view any pictures in the message, and the links become enabled. You can now read the message in its entirety.

DELETE A MESSAGE

You can delete a message you no longer need. Deleting messages prevents your folders from becoming cluttered.

You may want to delete messages after you have read and replied to or forwarded them.

DELETE A MESSAGE

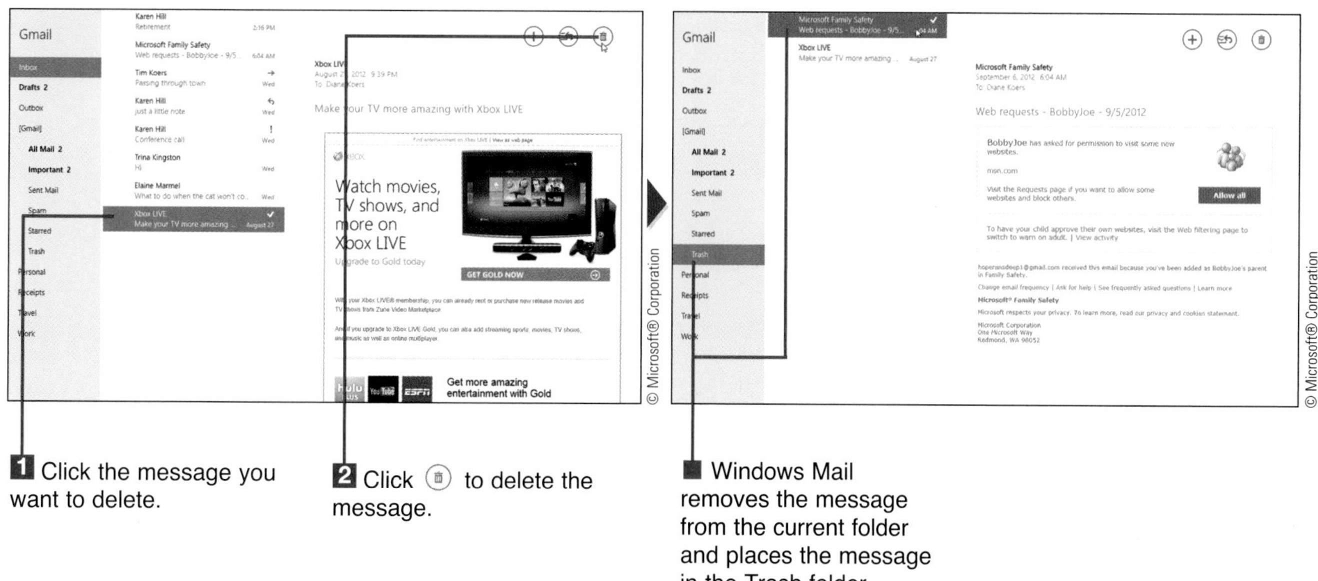

1 Click the message you want to delete.

2 Click (delete icon) to delete the message.

■ Windows Mail removes the message from the current folder and places the message in the Trash folder.

REPLY TO A MESSAGE

You can reply to a message to answer a question, express an opinion, or supply additional information.

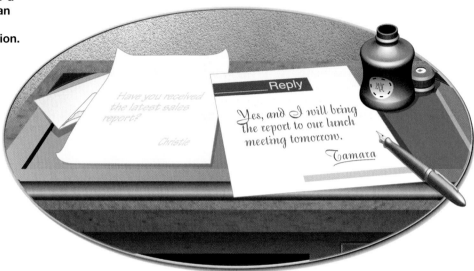

REPLY TO A MESSAGE

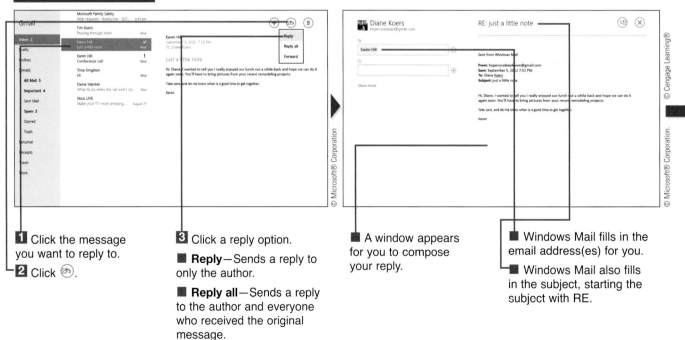

1 Click the message you want to reply to.

2 Click ⮌.

3 Click a reply option.

■ **Reply**—Sends a reply to only the author.

■ **Reply all**—Sends a reply to the author and everyone who received the original message.

■ A window appears for you to compose your reply.

■ Windows Mail fills in the email address(es) for you.

■ Windows Mail also fills in the subject, starting the subject with RE.

If I choose Reply all, how do I know who the message is going to?

When you see the reply message, Windows Mail displays all addresses on the left and in the body of the message. The only exception is if the original message was sent with a Bcc (blind carbon copy); in that case, you will not see any addresses.

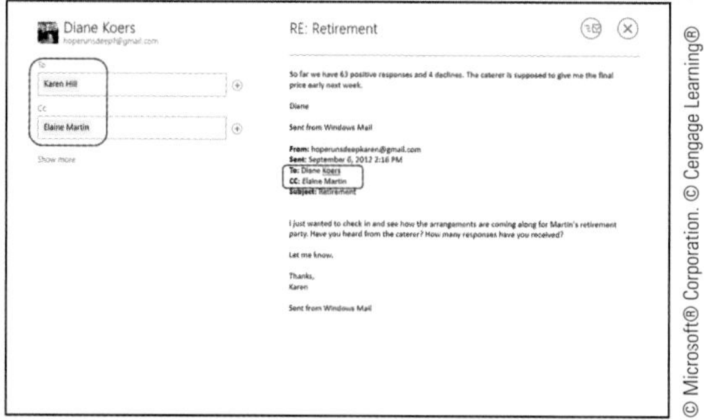

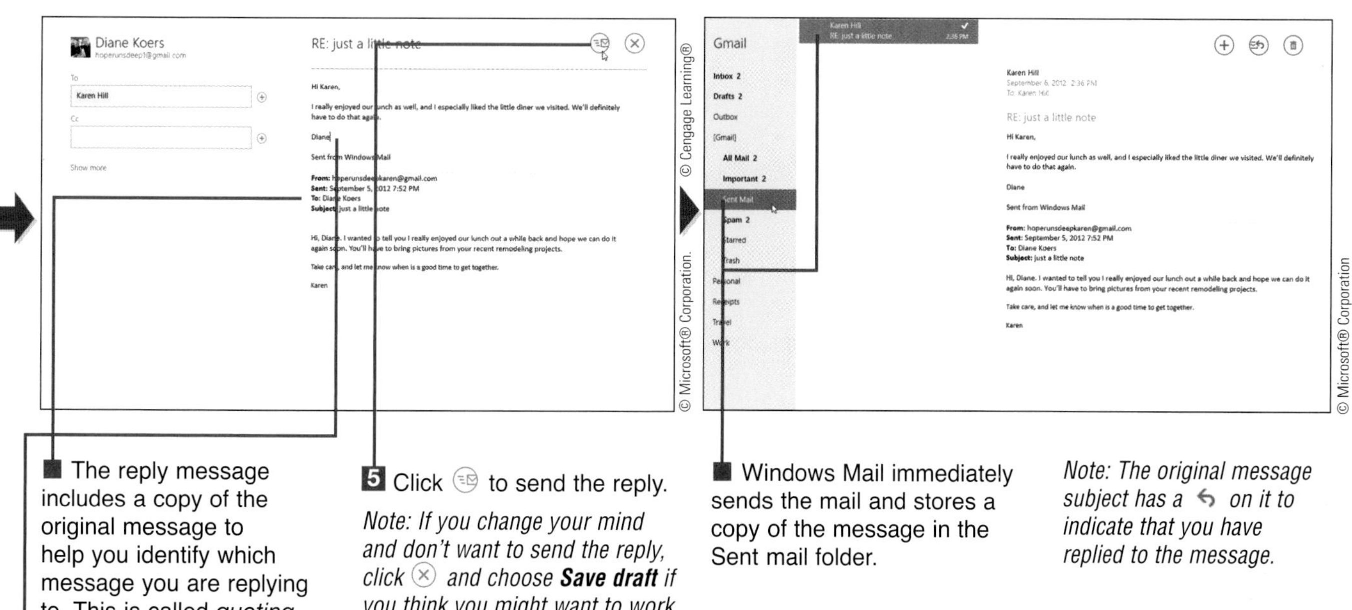

■ The reply message includes a copy of the original message to help you identify which message you are replying to. This is called *quoting*.

4 Click this area and then type your reply.

5 Click ✉ to send the reply.

Note: If you change your mind and don't want to send the reply, click ⊗ and choose ***Save draft*** *if you think you might want to work on the reply later, or choose* ***Delete draft*** *if you don't want to keep the reply you started.*

■ Windows Mail immediately sends the mail and stores a copy of the message in the Sent mail folder.

Note: The original message subject has a ↩ on it to indicate that you have replied to the message.

FORWARD A MESSAGE

After reading a message, you can add comments and then forward the message to a friend, family member, or colleague.

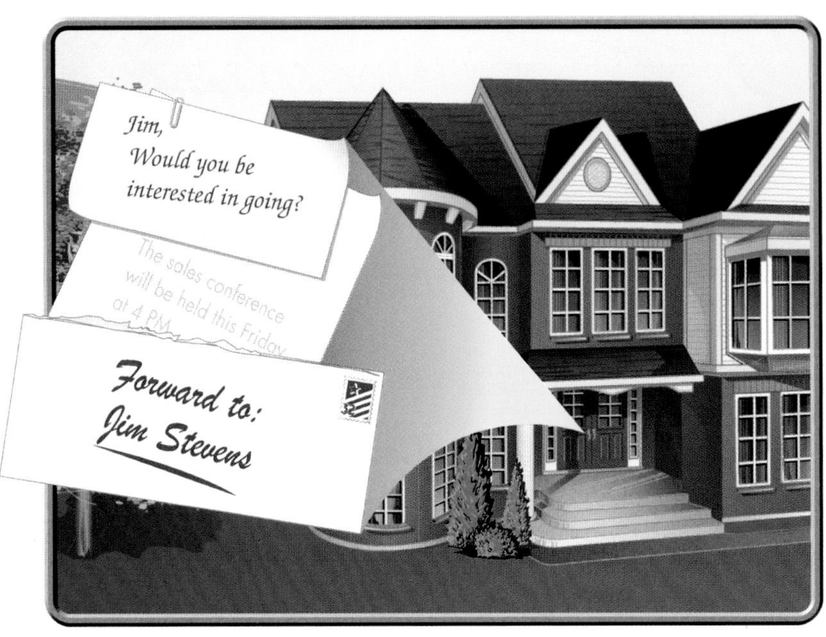

Forwarding a message is useful when you know another person would be interested in a message.

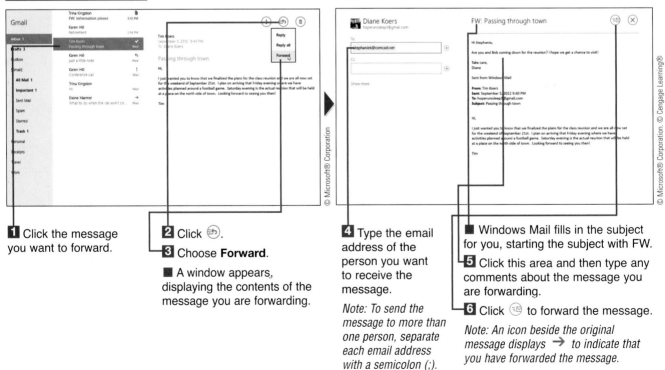

FORWARD A MESSAGE

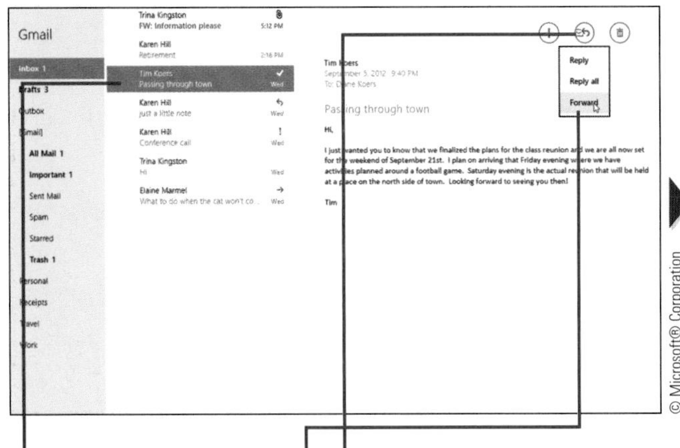

1 Click the message you want to forward.

2 Click .

3 Choose **Forward**.

■ A window appears, displaying the contents of the message you are forwarding.

4 Type the email address of the person you want to receive the message.

Note: To send the message to more than one person, separate each email address with a semicolon (;).

■ Windows Mail fills in the subject for you, starting the subject with FW.

5 Click this area and then type any comments about the message you are forwarding.

6 Click to forward the message.

Note: An icon beside the original message displays → to indicate that you have forwarded the message.

CREATE AND SEND A MESSAGE

You can quickly and easily send an email message to a friend, family member, or colleague.

Sending a message written in CAPITAL LETTERS is annoying and difficult to read. It's a process known as *shouting*. Always use upper- and lowercase letters when typing messages.

CREATE AND SEND A MESSAGE

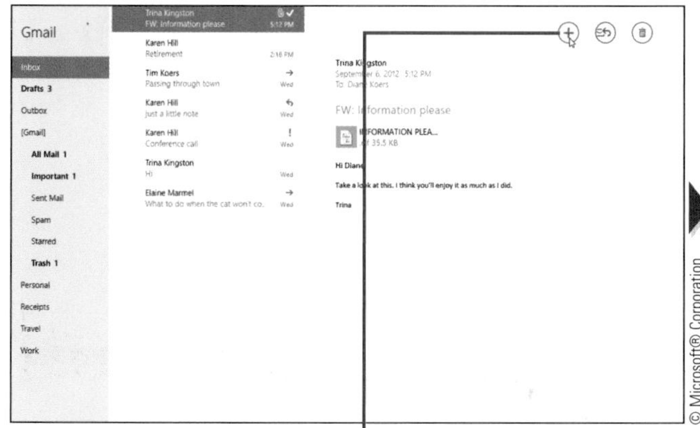

© Microsoft® Corporation

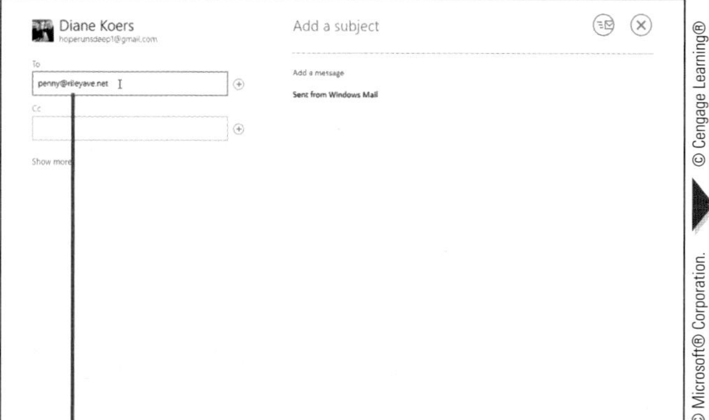

© Cengage Learning®

© Microsoft® Corporation.

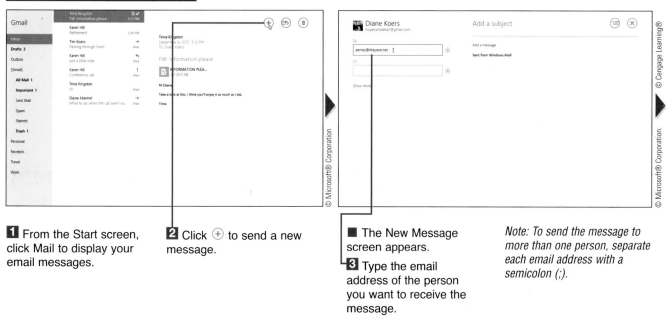

1 From the Start screen, click Mail to display your email messages.

2 Click ⊕ to send a new message.

■ The New Message screen appears.

3 Type the email address of the person you want to receive the message.

Note: To send the message to more than one person, separate each email address with a semicolon (;).

CREATE AND SEND A MESSAGE (CONTINUED)

When sending a message, you can send a carbon copy (Cc) of a message or a blind carbon copy (Bcc) of a message.

Carbon copy sends a copy of a message to a person who is not directly involved but would be interested in the message.

Blind carbon copy sends a copy of a message to a person without anyone else knowing that the person received the message.

CREATE AND SEND A MESSAGE (CONTINUED)

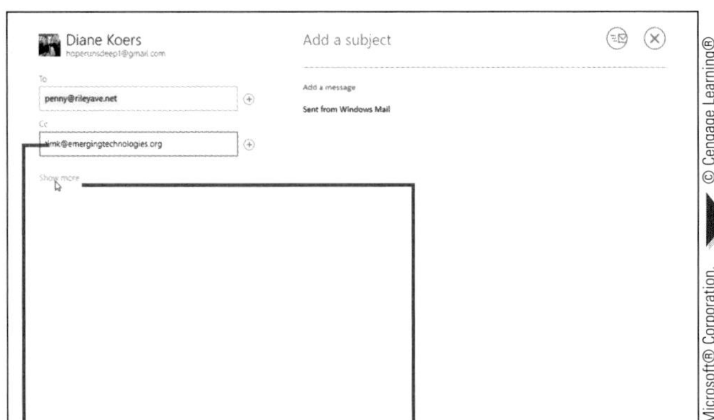

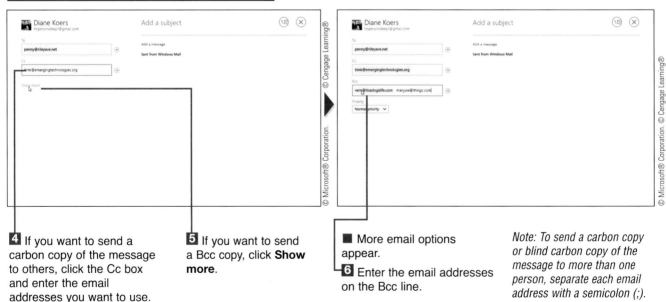

4 If you want to send a carbon copy of the message to others, click the Cc box and enter the email addresses you want to use.

5 If you want to send a Bcc copy, click **Show more**.

■ More email options appear.

6 Enter the email addresses on the Bcc line.

Note: To send a carbon copy or blind carbon copy of the message to more than one person, separate each email address with a semicolon (;).

What does Priority do?

You can flag messages with a High priority, Normal priority, or Low priority to give the recipient a heads-up to the message's importance.

Windows Mail takes messages flagged with a High priority and copies them to the Important folder, thereby encouraging the recipient to read them first.

USER SIGNOUT

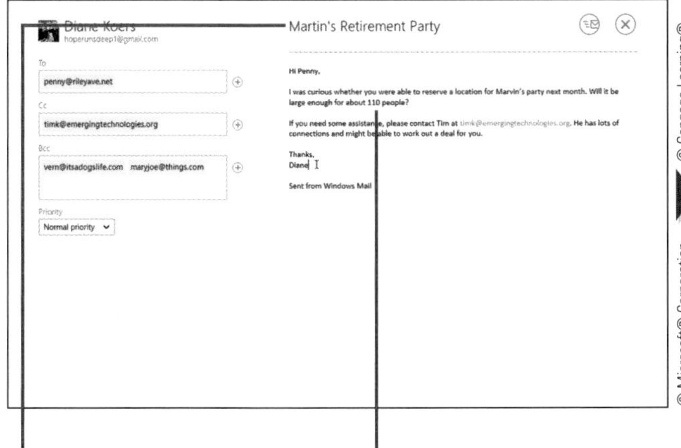

© Microsoft® Corporation. © Cengage Learning®

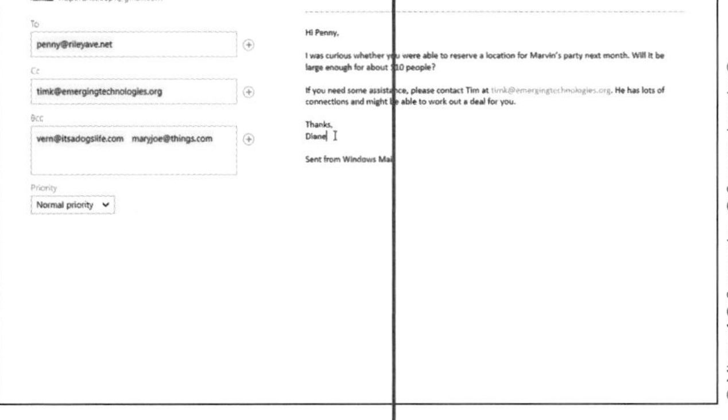

© Microsoft® Corporation. © Cengage Learning®

7 Click this area and then type the subject of the message.

8 Click this area and then type the message.

Note: If you type an email or web address in the message body, Windows Mail automatically formats it as a hyperlink and displays the text in a different color.

9 Click (send icon) when you are ready to send the message.

■ Windows Mail sends the message and stores a copy of it in the Sent items folder.

FORMAT A MESSAGE

You can dress up your message—whether a new message, a reply message, or a forwarded message—by changing the font, font size, or even the text color.

Additionally, you can add emphasis by making the text bold, italic, or underlined.

Some messages look good with bulleted or numbered lists.

FORMAT A MESSAGE

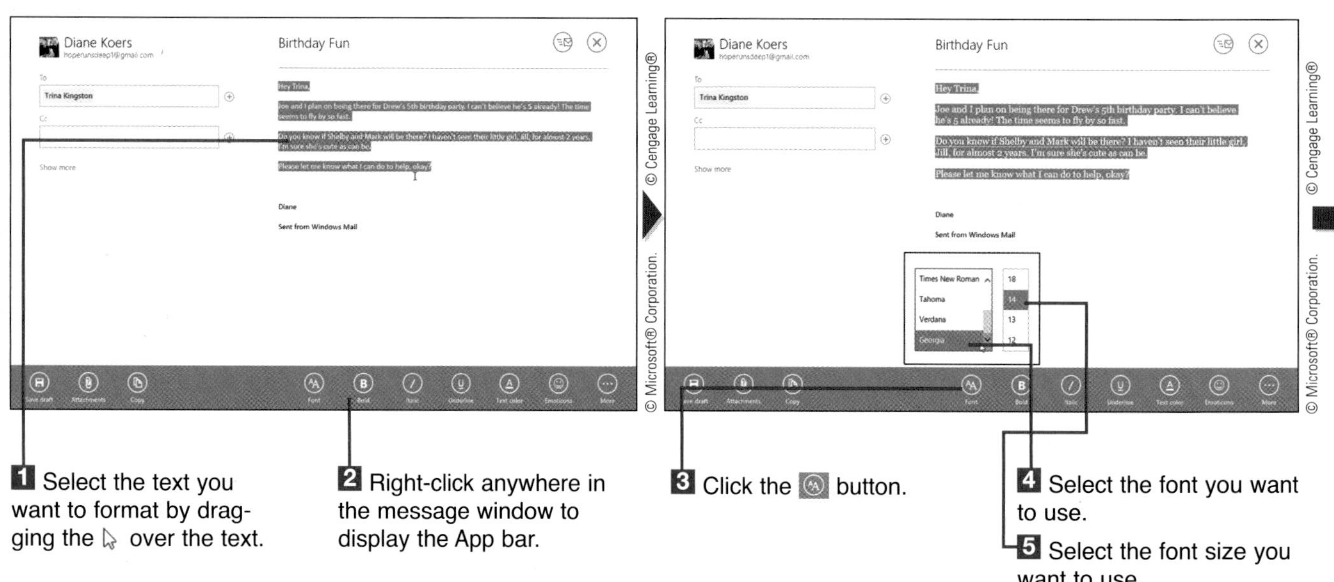

1 Select the text you want to format by dragging the ⇖ over the text.

2 Right-click anywhere in the message window to display the App bar.

3 Click the (Font) button.

4 Select the font you want to use.

5 Select the font size you want to use.

What are emoticons?

Emoticons are those cute little smiley faces and other iconic characters that you can add to your email messages. Windows Mail provides over 600 different emoticons and divides them into 7 different groups, including smileys, food, travel, and others.

You add an emoticon by clicking in the message where you want the emoticon, right-clicking the mouse, choosing ☺ from the App bar, and clicking the emoticon you want.

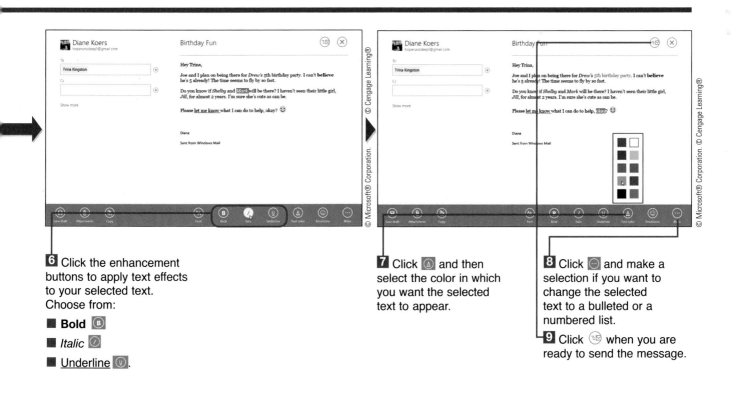

6 Click the enhancement buttons to apply text effects to your selected text. Choose from:

- **Bold** (B)
- *Italic* (/)
- <u>Underline</u> (U).

7 Click (A) and then select the color in which you want the selected text to appear.

8 Click (…) and make a selection if you want to change the selected text to a bulleted or a numbered list.

9 Click (send) when you are ready to send the message.

ADD ATTACHMENTS TO A MESSAGE

You can also send documents, spreadsheets, videos, and other types of files.

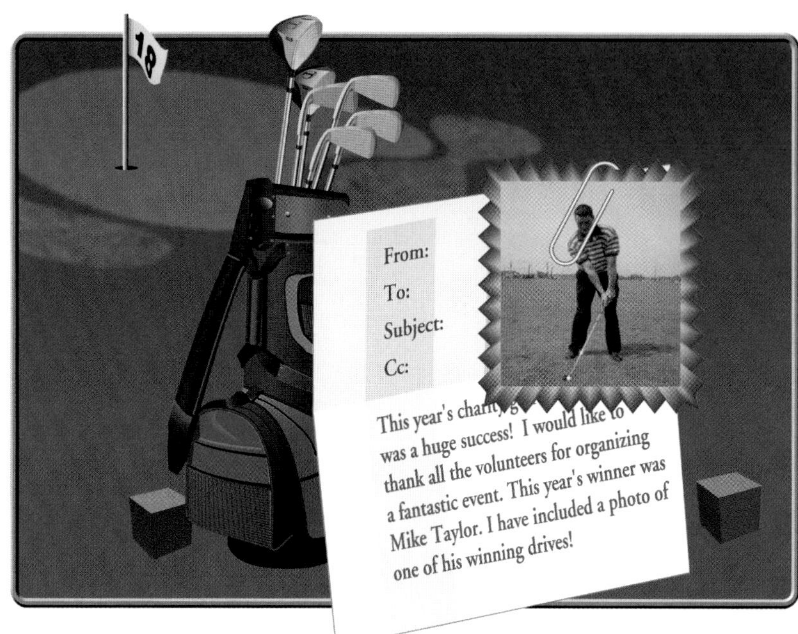

ADD ATTACHMENTS TO A MESSAGE

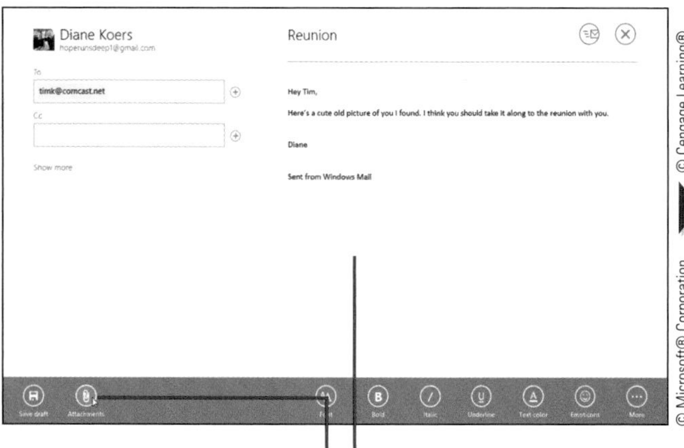

© Microsoft® Corporation. © Cengage Learning®

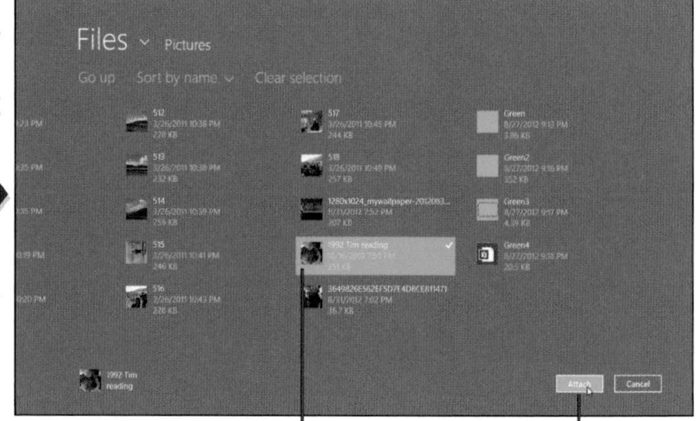

© Microsoft® Corporation. © Cengage Learning®

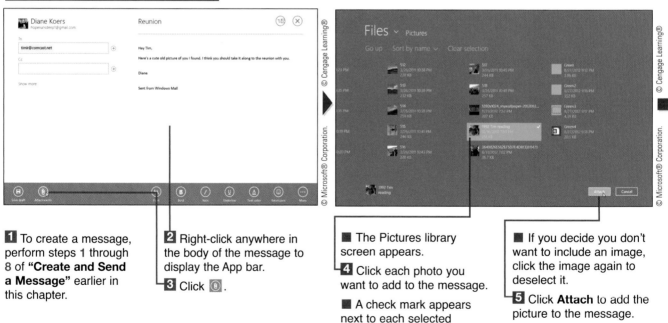

1 To create a message, perform steps 1 through 8 of **"Create and Send a Message"** earlier in this chapter.

2 Right-click anywhere in the body of the message to display the App bar.

3 Click ⓘ.

■ The Pictures library screen appears.

4 Click each photo you want to add to the message.

■ A check mark appears next to each selected image.

■ If you decide you don't want to include an image, click the image again to deselect it.

5 Click **Attach** to add the picture to the message.

The pictures are so small I can't tell which picture I want. Is there a way to view them larger?

Pause your mouse over any image, and a larger preview of the image appears.

You also see additional information about the image, such as type, size, date, and folder location.

How do I send a message with a file other than a picture?

When the Files screen appears, click **Go up**. Locate and click the library containing the file you want. Click the file you want to send, and then choose **Attach**.

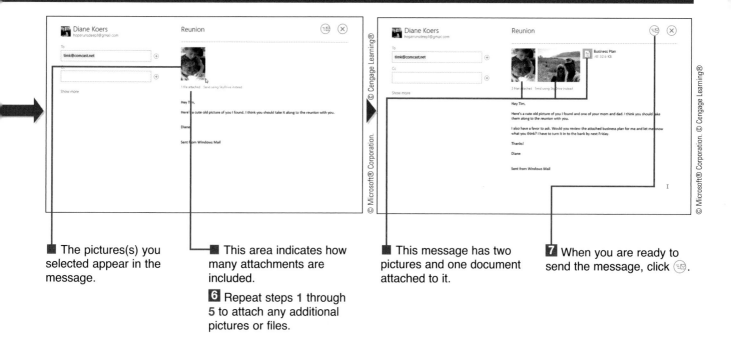

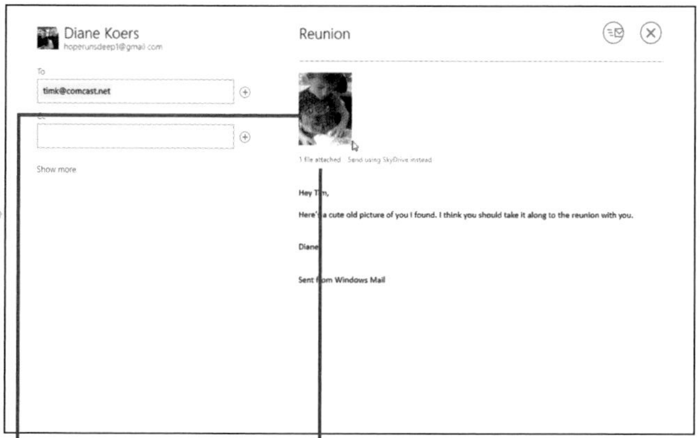

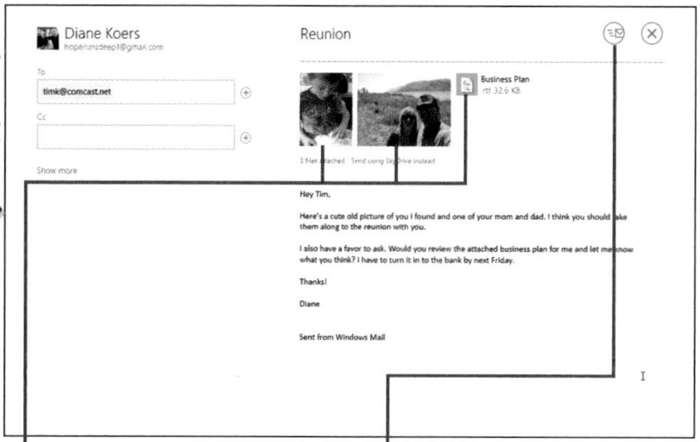

■ The pictures(s) you selected appear in the message.

■ This area indicates how many attachments are included.

6 Repeat steps **1** through **5** to attach any additional pictures or files.

■ This message has two pictures and one document attached to it.

7 When you are ready to send the message, click the Send icon.

OPEN AN ATTACHED FILE

You can open a file attached to a message you receive, but you must have a program associated with the file to open it.

For example, if someone sends you a PowerPoint presentation and you don't have PowerPoint on your computer, you will not be able to open the file.

OPEN AN ATTACHED FILE

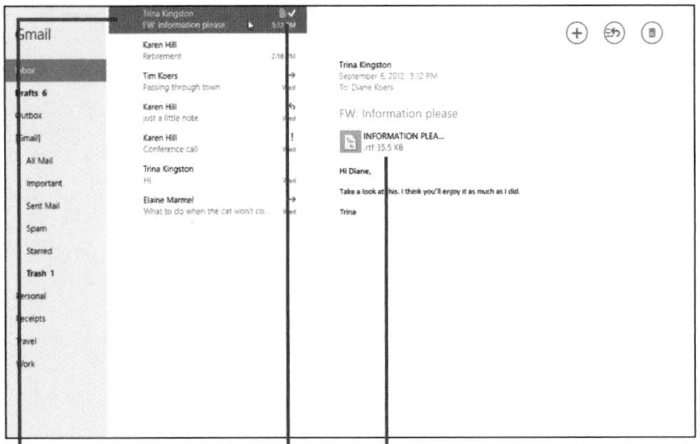

© Microsoft® Corporation

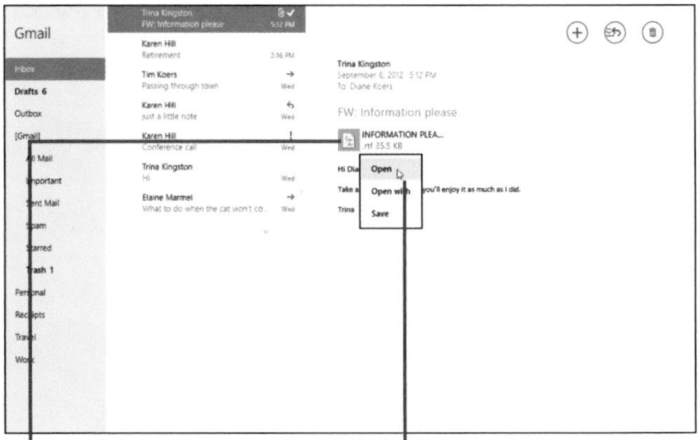

1 Click a message with an attached file.

■ A message with an attached file displays a paper clip icon (📎).

■ This area displays the contents of the message and an icon for the attachment.

Note: If an attached file is a picture, the picture often appears in the contents of the message.

© Microsoft® Corporation

2 Click the file attachment to display a menu.

3 Click **Open** to open and view the file.

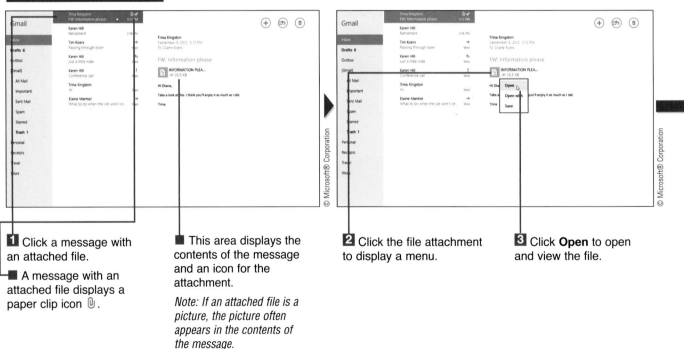

Is there a danger in opening files from others?

Yes. Before opening an attached file, make sure the file comes from a person you trust. Some files contain a virus, which can damage the information on your computer. You can use an antivirus program to help protect your computer from viruses.

Can I save an attachment independent from the email message it came with?

Yes. In step 3, choose **Save** instead of Open. The library screen appears. If necessary, click **Go Up** until you locate the library where you want to save the file.

Click the **Save** button that appears in the library window.

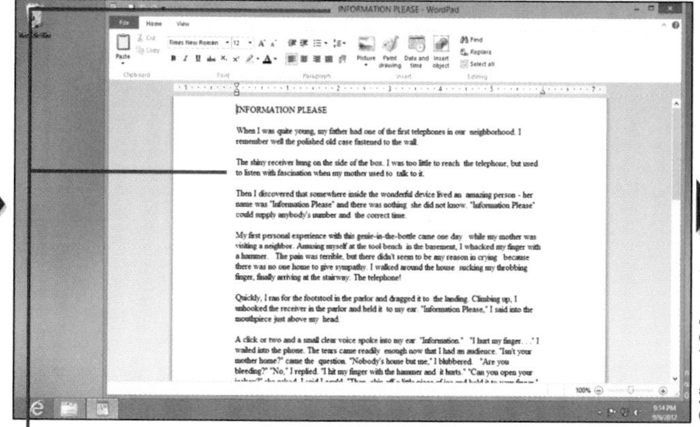

■ The file opens in the program that created it.

Note: If you want to make any changes to the document, you must first save the file to a location on your computer.

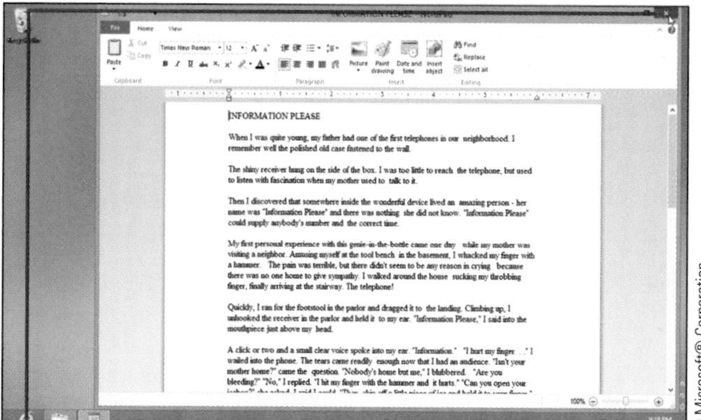

4 When you are finished reviewing the attachment, click ×.

ADD A CONTACT

You can add contacts to store and then easily use email addresses and other information about friends, family members, and clients, including phone numbers, addresses, and birthdays.

Windows 8 stores contact information in the People app.

ADD A CONTACT

© Microsoft® Corporation. © Cengage Learning®

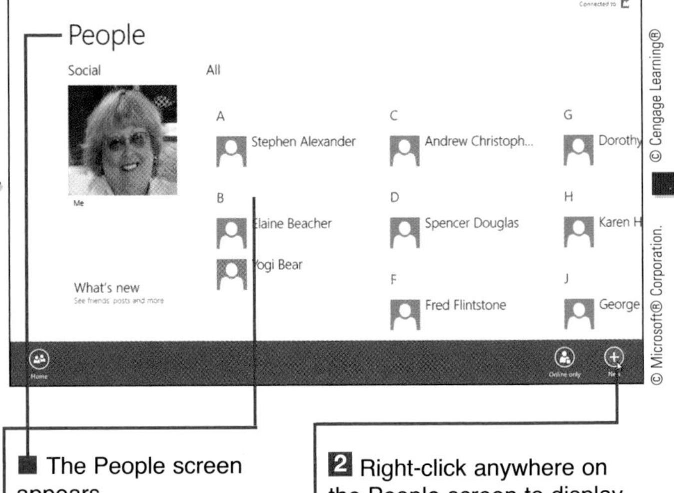

© Microsoft® Corporation. © Cengage Learning®

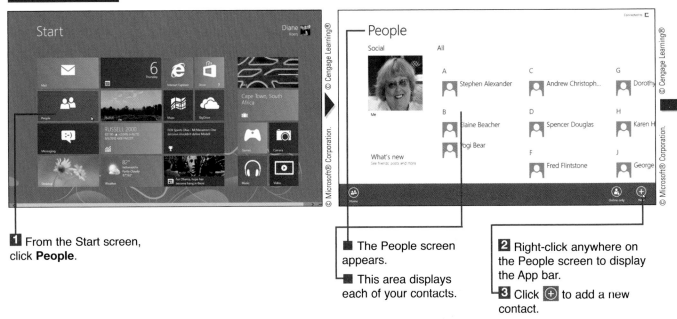

1 From the Start screen, click **People**.

■ The People screen appears.

■ This area displays each of your contacts.

2 Right-click anywhere on the People screen to display the App bar.

3 Click ⊕ to add a new contact.

How do I change the information for a contact?

To change the information for a contact, click the contact you want to change. From the contact information screen, right-click and choose [edit icon]. Make any desired changes, and then click [save icon].

How do I delete a contact?

To delete a contact, click the contact you want to delete. From the contact information screen, right-click and choose [delete icon]. A confirmation message appears. Click the **Delete** button.

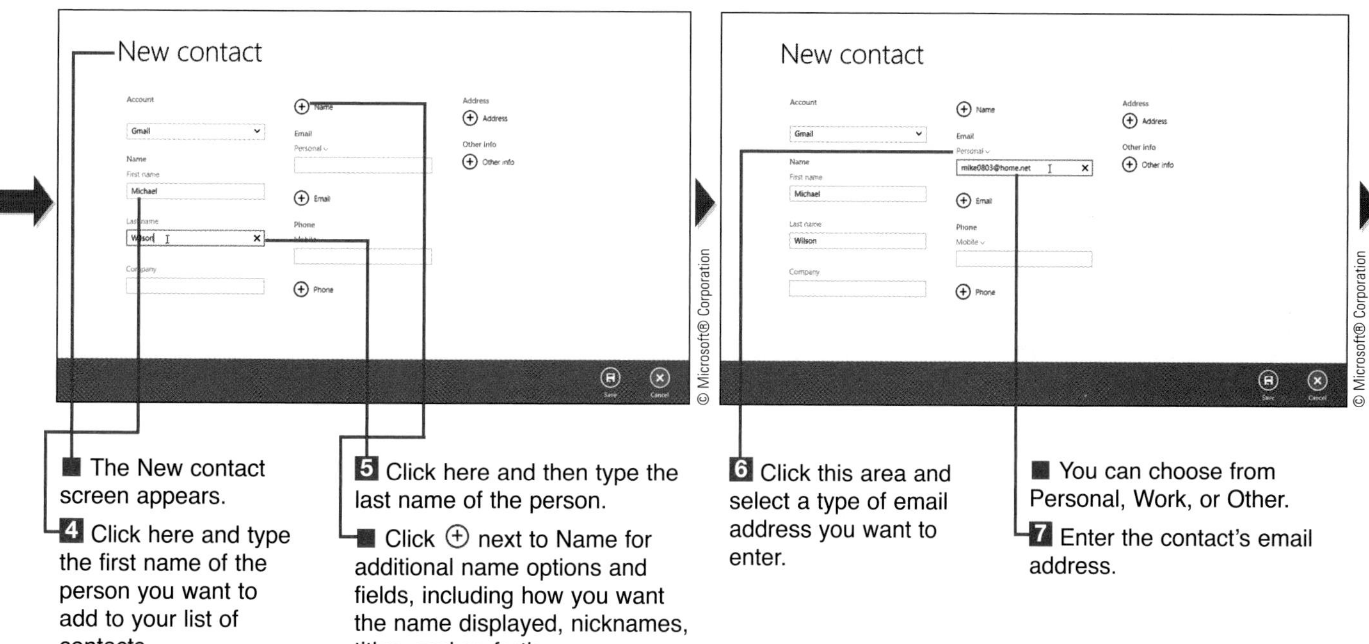

■ The New contact screen appears.

4 Click here and type the first name of the person you want to add to your list of contacts.

5 Click here and then type the last name of the person.

■ Click ⊕ next to Name for additional name options and fields, including how you want the name displayed, nicknames, titles, and so forth.

6 Click this area and select a type of email address you want to enter.

■ You can choose from Personal, Work, or Other.

7 Enter the contact's email address.

CONTINUED

ADD A CONTACT (CONTINUED)

When you send an email message, you can select a contact to have Windows Mail quickly fill in the email address of the person for you.

ADD A CONTACT (CONTINUED)

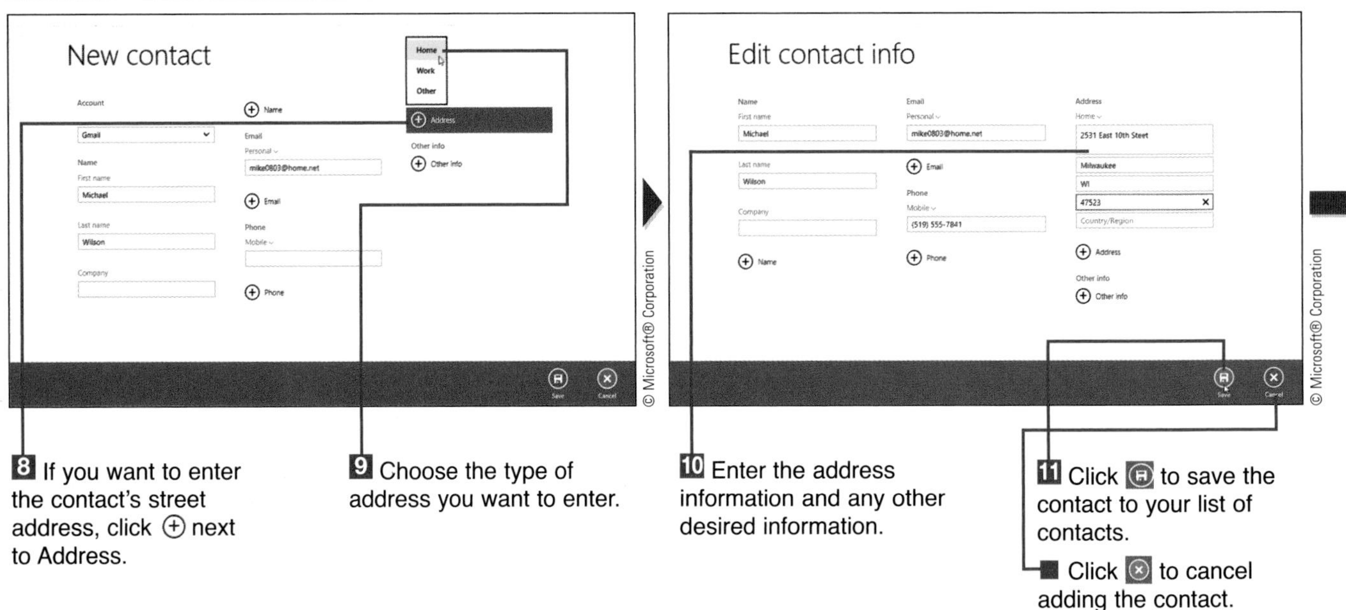

8 If you want to enter the contact's street address, click ⊕ next to Address.

9 Choose the type of address you want to enter.

10 Enter the address information and any other desired information.

11 Click (save icon) to save the contact to your list of contacts.

■ Click (cancel icon) to cancel adding the contact.

Can I store more than one email address, telephone number, and street address for a contact?

Yes. You can store up to three different email addresses, eight different phone numbers, and three different street addresses.

As you choose the different options, the contact screen expands to add the additional fields.

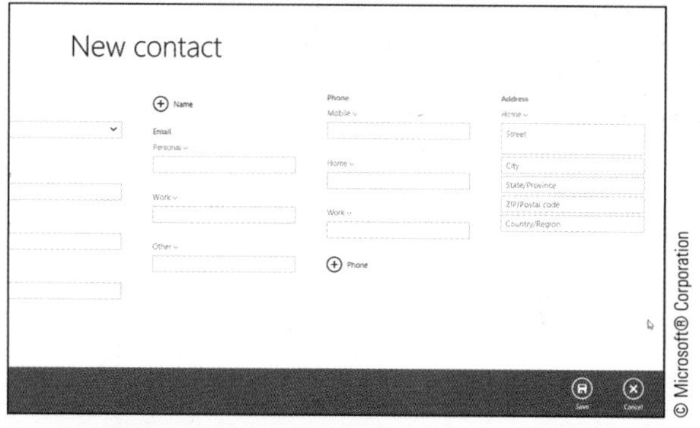

© Microsoft® Corporation

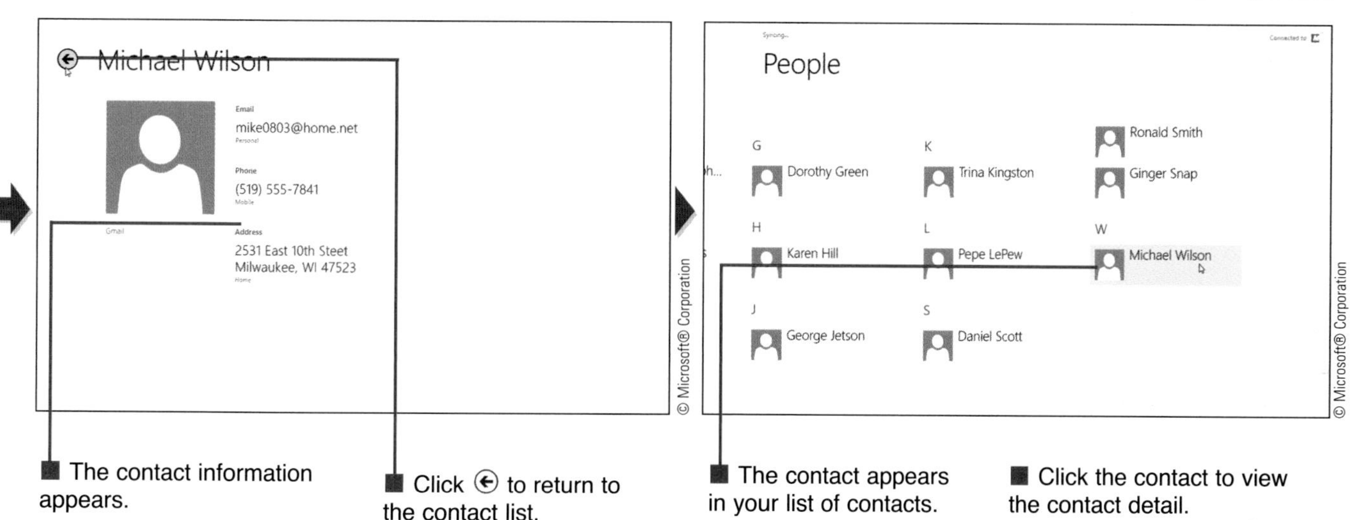

© Microsoft® Corporation

© Microsoft® Corporation

■ The contact appears in your list of contacts.

■ Click the contact to view the contact detail.

■ The contact information appears.

■ Click ⊕ to return to the contact list.

SEND A MESSAGE TO A CONTACT

When sending a message, you can select the name of the person you want to receive the message from your list of contacts.

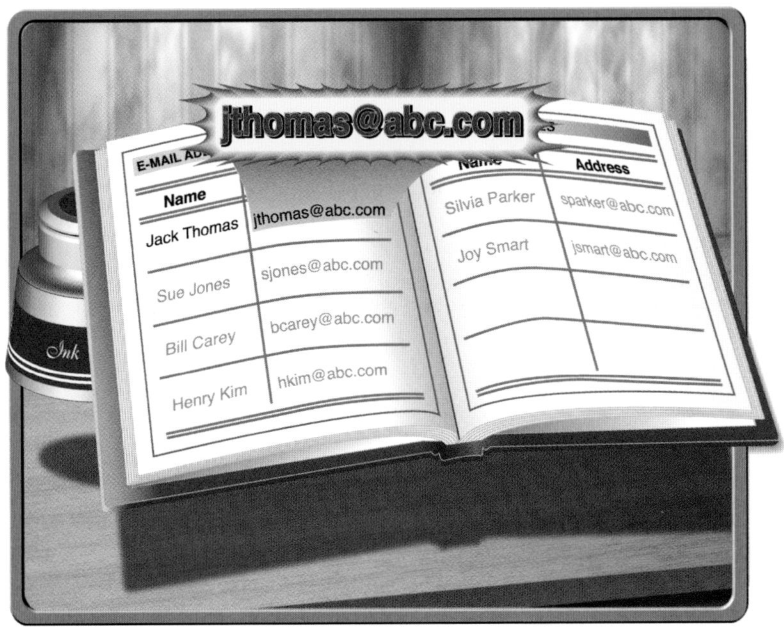

jthomas@abc.com
E-MAIL AD
Name
Jack Thomas
jthomas@abc.com
Sue Jones
sjones@abc.com
Bill Carey
bcarey@abc.com
Henry Kim
hkim@abc.com
Address
Silvia Parker
sparker@abc.com
Joy Smart
jsmart@abc.com
Ink

Selecting names from your list of contacts saves you from having to remember the email addresses of people to whom you often send messages.

SEND A MESSAGE TO A CONTACT

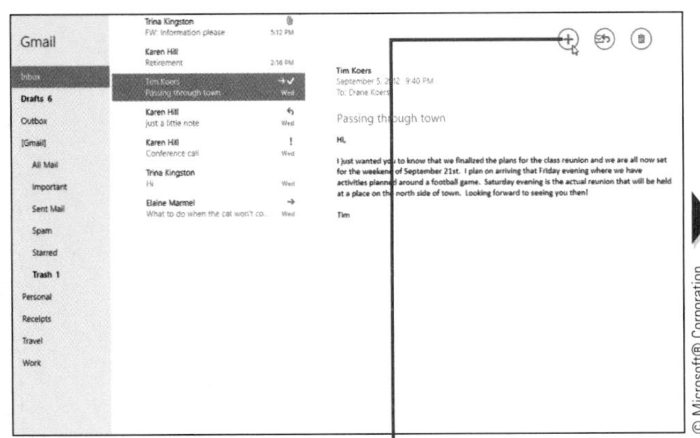

© Microsoft® Corporation

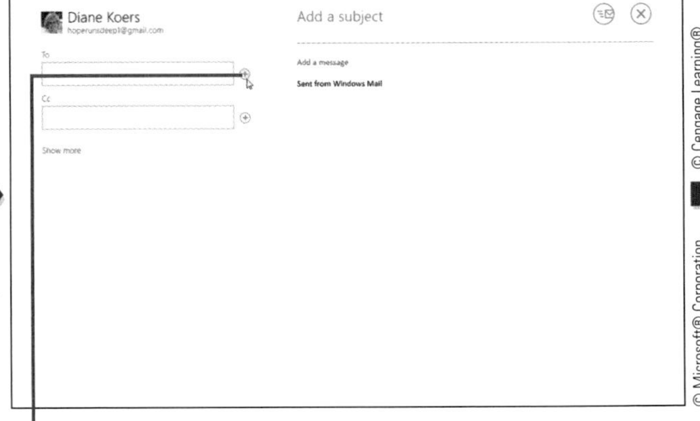

© Cengage Learning®

© Microsoft® Corporation.

1 From the Start screen, click Mail to display your email messages.

2 Click ⊕ to send a new message.

■ The New Message window appears.

3 Click ⊕ next to the To box.

Is there a faster way to select a name from my list of contacts?

Yes. When sending a message, you can quickly select a name from your list of contacts by typing the first few letters of a person's name or email address in the To, Cc, or Bcc area. As you type, a list of matching contacts appears. Click the name of the person you want to receive the message.

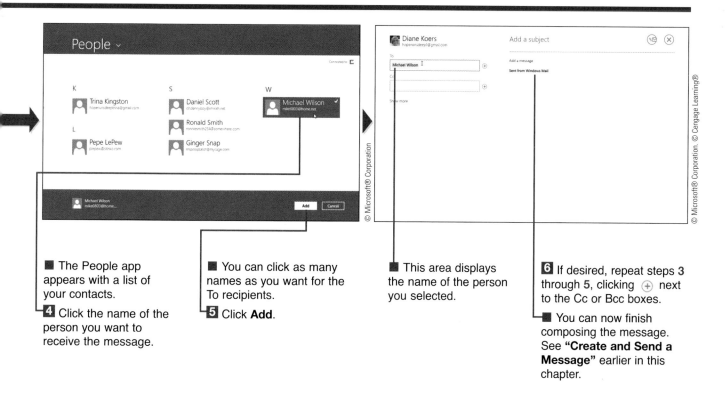

■ The People app appears with a list of your contacts.

4 Click the name of the person you want to receive the message.

■ You can click as many names as you want for the To recipients.

5 Click **Add**.

■ This area displays the name of the person you selected.

6 If desired, repeat steps **3** through **5**, clicking ⊕ next to the Cc or Bcc boxes.

■ You can now finish composing the message. See **"Create and Send a Message"** earlier in this chapter.

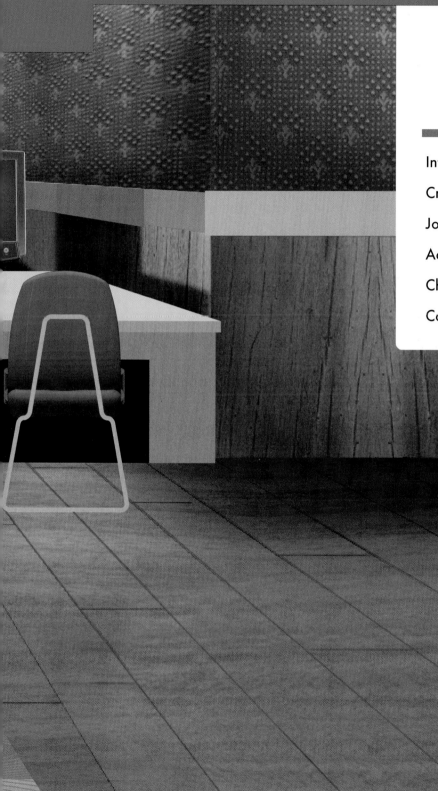

CHAPTER 11

Work on a Network

INTRODUCTION TO NETWORKS

If you have more than one computer at home or at a small office, you can set up a network so the computers can exchange information as well as share a printer and an Internet connection.

WIRED NETWORKS

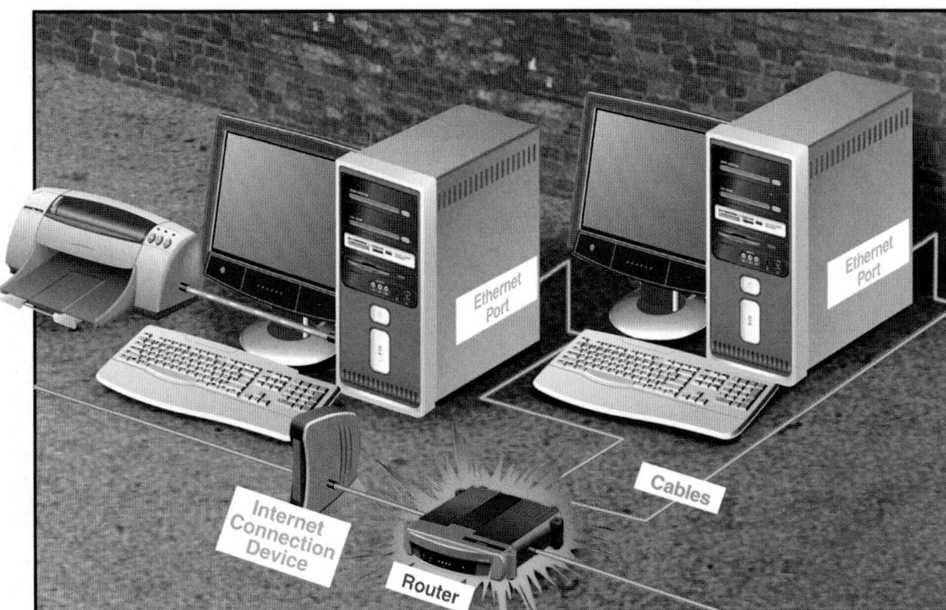

A *wired* network uses wires, or cables, to send information between computers.

Advantages of Wired Networks

✓ Fast, reliable transfer of data between computers on the network.

✓ Secure. To connect to a wired network, a computer must physically connect to the network using a cable.

✓ Ideal when computers on a network are close to each other.

EQUIPMENT NEEDED

Ethernet Port

Each computer on the network requires an Ethernet port. An *Ethernet port* allows each computer to connect to the network so the computers can communicate. Most computers come with an Ethernet port.

Router

A *router* is a device that provides a central location where all the cables on the network meet. A router also allows the computers on the network to share one Internet connection.

Internet Connection Device

An *Internet connection device*, such as a cable modem or Digital Subscriber Line (DSL) modem, allows you to connect to the Internet. The Internet connection device connects to the router using a cable.

Cables

Ethernet *cables* physically connect each computer to the network.

WIRELESS NETWORKS

A *wireless* network uses radio signals instead of cables to send information between computers.

Advantages of Wireless Networks

✓ No cables to connect.

✓ Useful when computers are located where cables are not practical or economical.

✓ Ideal for allowing laptop computers to access a network from many locations in a home or office.

Note: Some devices can interfere with a wireless network, such as a cordless phone, a microwave oven, or another wireless device.

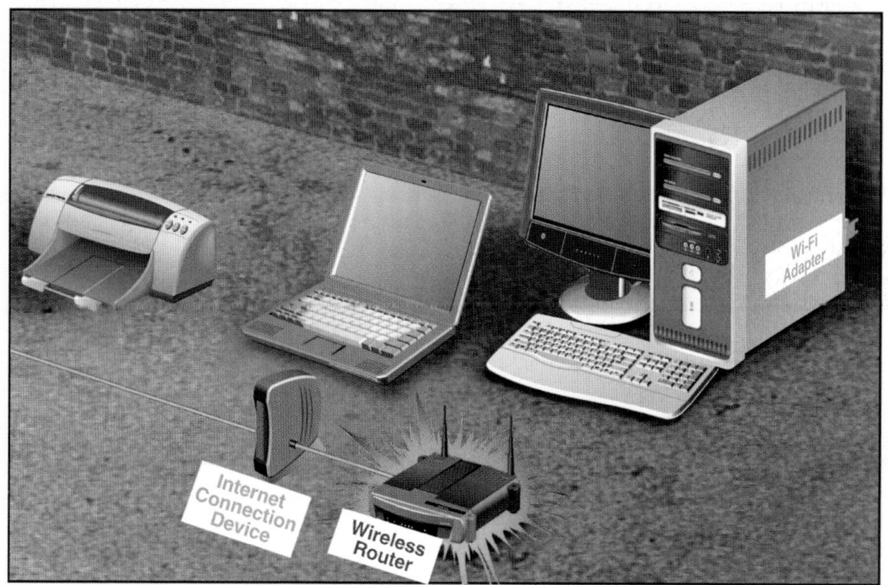

EQUIPMENT NEEDED

Wi-Fi Networking Hardware

Each computer on a wireless network requires *Wi-Fi* capability. This allows each computer on the wireless network to communicate. Most laptop computers come with built-in Wi-Fi capability. You can add Wi-Fi capability to a computer by plugging a small Wi-Fi adapter into a computer's USB port.

Wireless Router

A *wireless router* is a device that provides a central location where all the cables on the network meet and transmits and receives data between computers on a network using radio signals. A wireless router also allows all the computers on a network to share one Internet connection.

Internet Connection Device

An *Internet connection device*, such as a cable modem or DSL modem, allows you to connect to the Internet. The Internet connection device connects to the wireless router using a cable.

CREATE A HOMEGROUP

You can create a homegroup so the computers on your home network can share files and printers.

© Petrenko Andriy/Shutterstock.com

When you install Windows, you will be able to create a homegroup if one does not already exist on your home network.

CREATE A HOMEGROUP

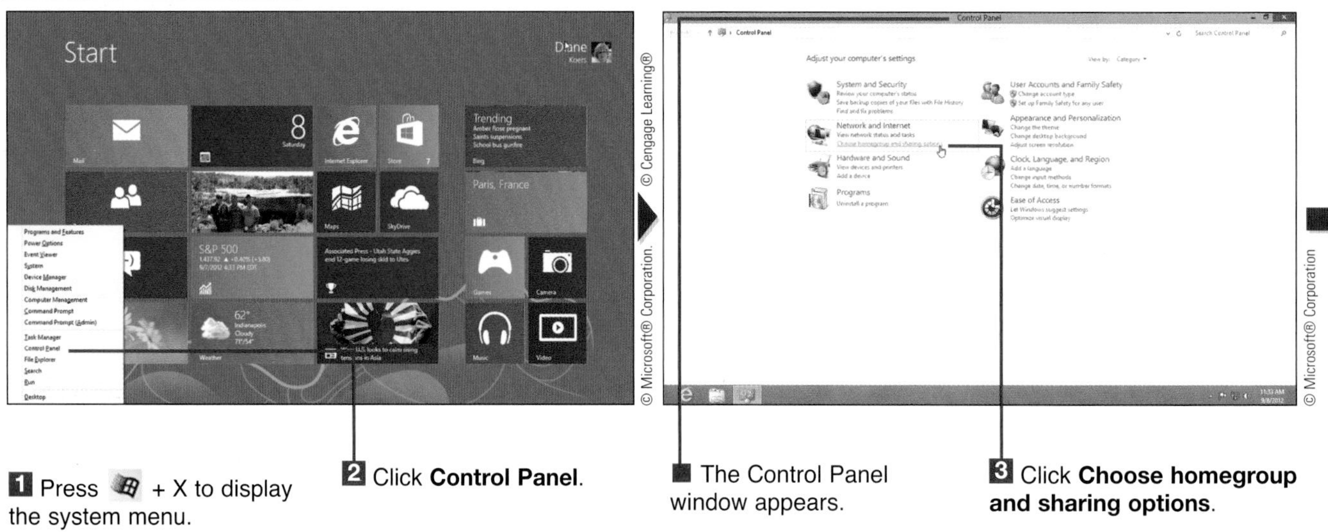

© Microsoft® Corporation. © Cengage Learning®

© Microsoft® Corporation

1 Press [Windows key] + X to display the system menu.

2 Click **Control Panel**.

■ The Control Panel window appears.

3 Click **Choose homegroup and sharing options**.

When I connect my computer to a network, why does Windows ask me to select a location?

The first time you connect a computer to a network, a window appears, asking you to select a location for the network. Windows allows you to set up to three types of networks: Home, Work, and Public. You can create a homegroup only if your network is set up as a Home network.

Can I later change the types of files I selected to share?

Yes. After you create a homegroup, you can change the types of files you selected to share on your computer. To do so, press ⊞ + C and click **Settings** from the Charm bar. Then click **Change PC settings**.

From the PC settings screen, click **HomeGroup** and then click ▮▭ or ▭▮ beside the library you want to change permissions for.

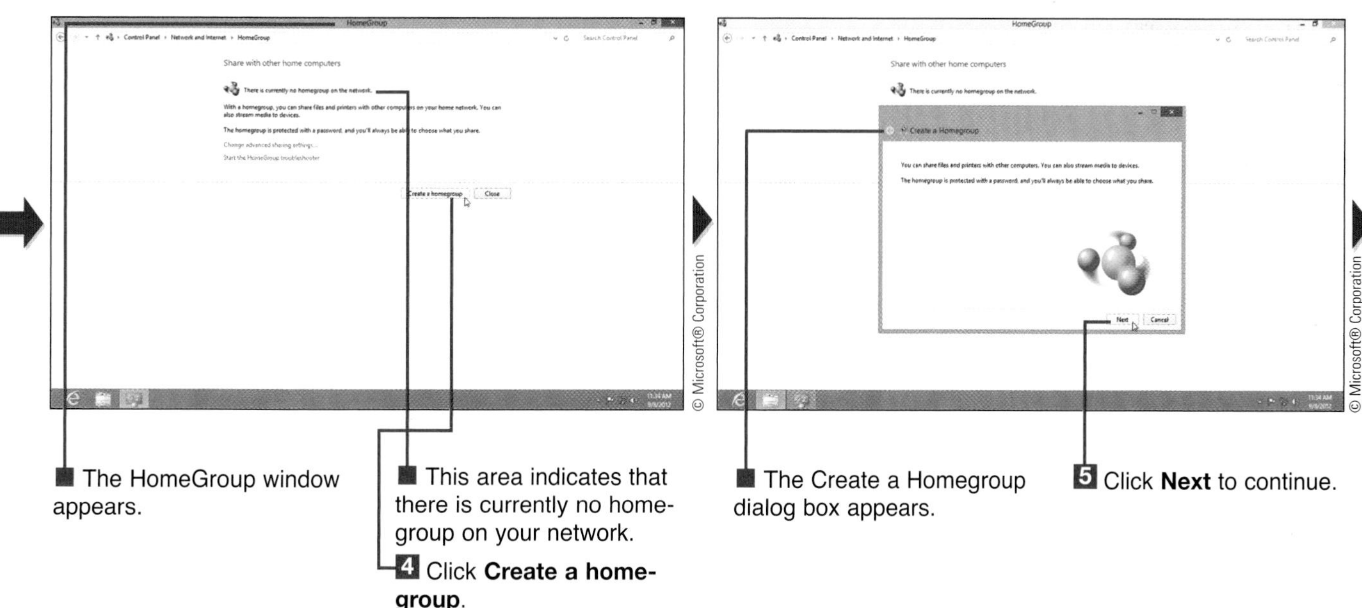

■ The HomeGroup window appears.

■ This area indicates that there is currently no homegroup on your network.

4 Click **Create a homegroup**.

■ The Create a Homegroup dialog box appears.

5 Click **Next** to continue.

CONTINUED

CREATE A HOMEGROUP (CONTINUED)

When creating a homegroup, Windows generates a password that you will use to add other computers on your network to the homegroup.

A homegroup password prevents unauthorized people from accessing your homegroup.

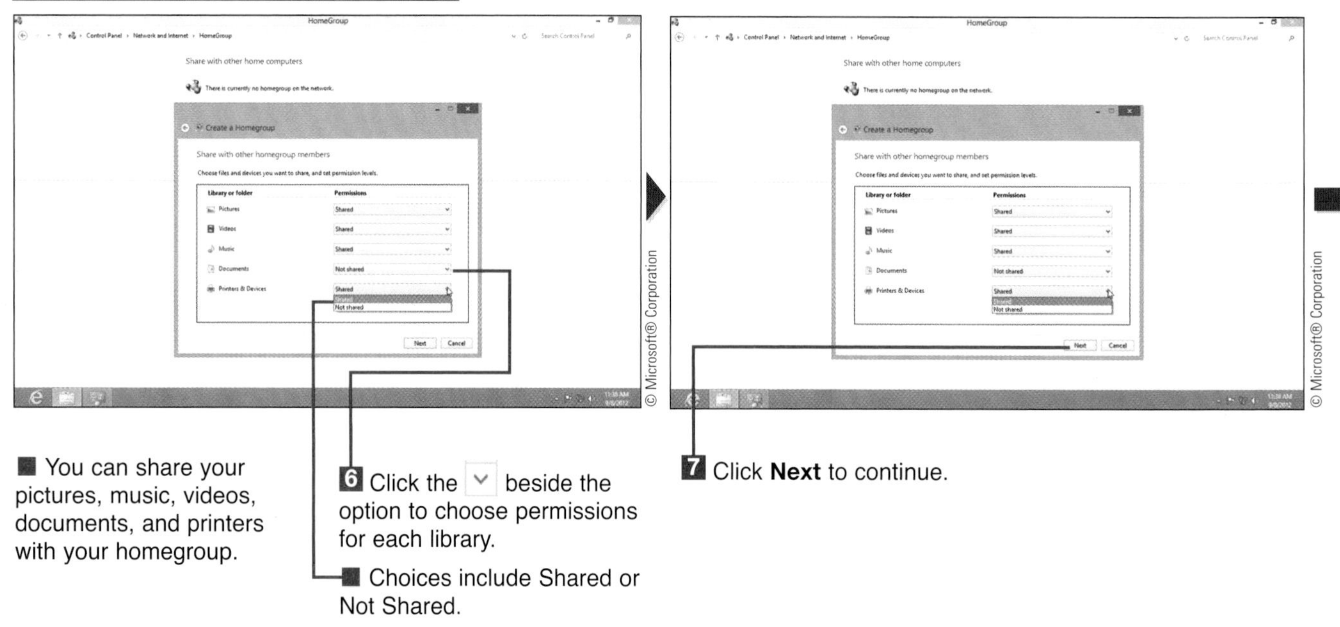

■ You can share your pictures, music, videos, documents, and printers with your homegroup.

6 Click the ⌄ beside the option to choose permissions for each library.

■ Choices include Shared or Not Shared.

7 Click **Next** to continue.

When I connect to a network, Windows asks me what type of location I am connecting to. Which one should I choose?

Home network—Choose Home network when connecting to a network set up in your home or when you know and trust the people on your network.

Work network—Choose Work network when connecting to small office or other workplace networks.

Public network—Choose Public network when connecting to networks in public places, such as coffee shops and airports, or if your computer connects directly to the Internet without using a router.

Can I create a homegroup on a work or public network?

No. Computers connected to a Work network or Public network cannot belong to a homegroup. You can only belong to a homegroup if your computer's network location is set to Home network.

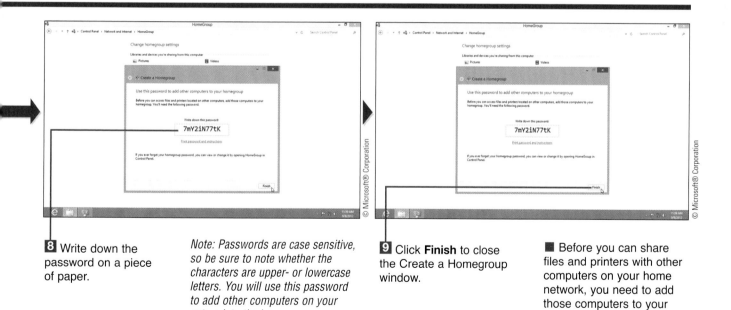

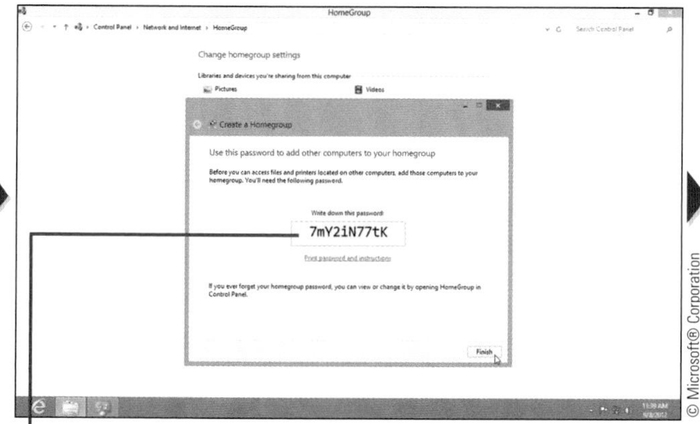

© Microsoft® Corporation

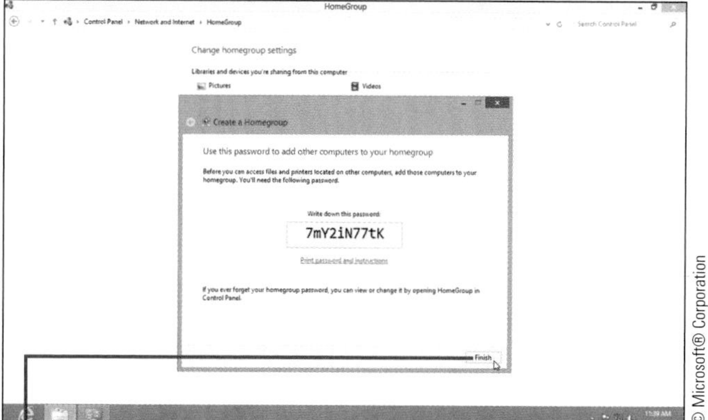

© Microsoft® Corporation

8 Write down the password on a piece of paper.

Note: Passwords are case sensitive, so be sure to note whether the characters are upper- or lowercase letters. You will use this password to add other computers on your network to the homegroup.

9 Click **Finish** to close the Create a Homegroup window.

■ Before you can share files and printers with other computers on your home network, you need to add those computers to your homegroup.

JOIN A HOMEGROUP

After you create a homegroup, you can add other computers on your home network to it. Computers that belong to the same homegroup can share files and printers.

You need to perform the following steps on each computer that you want to join to your homegroup.

JOIN A HOMEGROUP

© Microsoft® Corporation

© Microsoft® Corporation

1 From the other computer that you want to join to the homegroup, press ⊞ + C to display the Charm bar.

2 Click **Settings**.

3 Click **Change PC settings**.

What if I don't know the homegroup password?

If you don't know the password, from a computer that belongs to the homegroup, perform steps **1** to **3** of this section, click the **HomeGroup** category, and scroll down to the Membership section where you will see the homegroup password.

Do all the computers in my homegroup need to have Windows 8?

Not necessarily. Computers on your home network must be running either Windows 7 or Windows 8 to belong to a homegroup. Computers running an operating system earlier than Windows 7 cannot connect to homegroups.

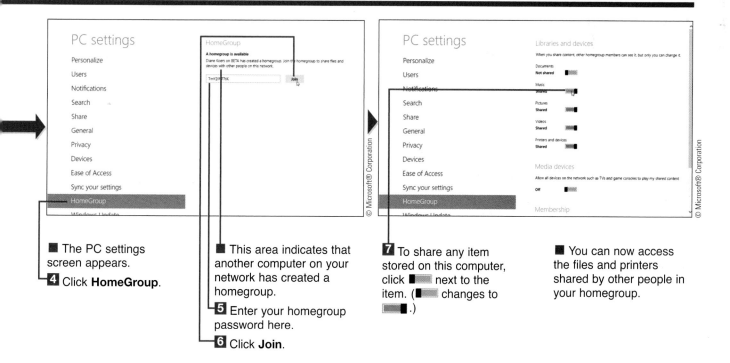

■ The PC settings screen appears.

4 Click **HomeGroup**.

■ This area indicates that another computer on your network has created a homegroup.

5 Enter your homegroup password here.

6 Click **Join**.

7 To share any item stored on this computer, click next to the item. (changes to .)

■ You can now access the files and printers shared by other people in your homegroup.

ACCESS FILES ACROSS A HOMEGROUP

You can share your pictures, music, videos, documents, and printers with other people in your homegroup.

You can only access the files shared on other computers in your homegroup. To add a computer to your home-group, see **"Join a Homegroup"** earlier in this chapter.

ACCESS FILES ACROSS A HOMEGROUP

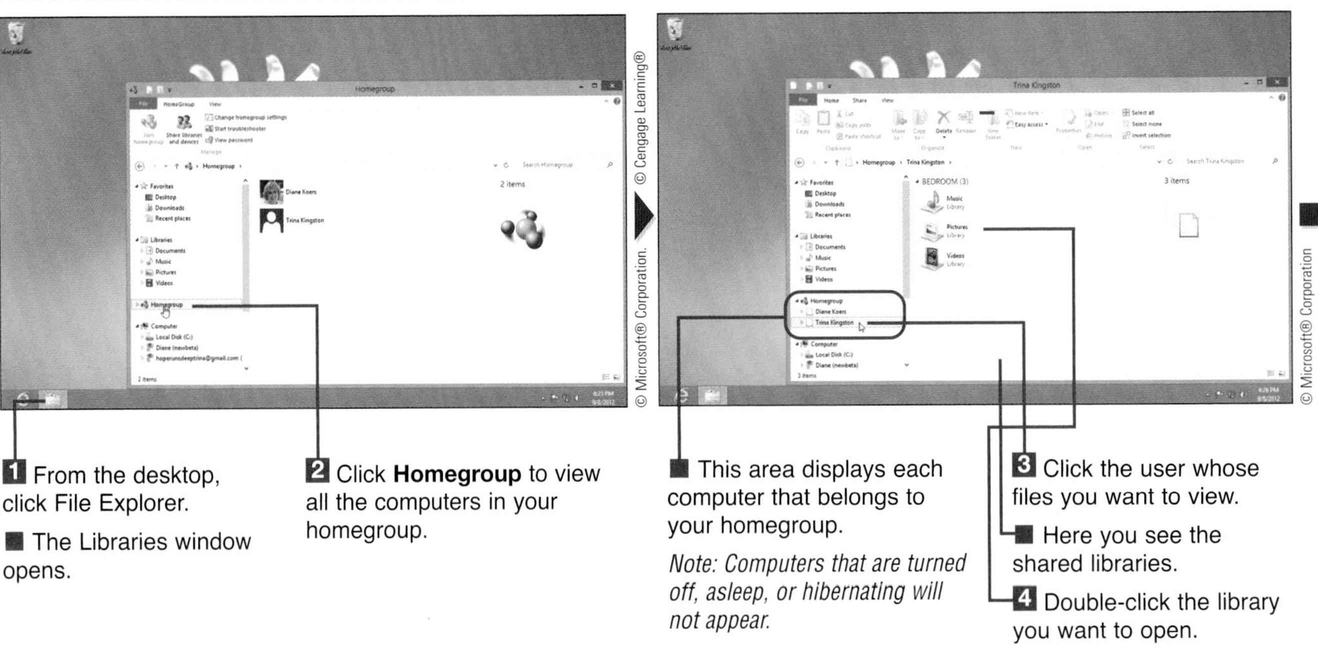

1 From the desktop, click File Explorer.

■ The Libraries window opens.

2 Click **Homegroup** to view all the computers in your homegroup.

■ This area displays each computer that belongs to your homegroup.

Note: Computers that are turned off, asleep, or hibernating will not appear.

3 Click the user whose files you want to view.

■ Here you see the shared libraries.

4 Double-click the library you want to open.

Why can't I see the other user's documents?

If the other user did not choose to share the Documents library, a Documents library doesn't appear in the homegroup.

To see the Documents library, the other user, from his computer, must set the option to share the Documents library.

How do I access a printer on my network?

If another person has shared a printer on your network, you can use the printer to print files as if the printer was directly connected to your computer. Before you can use another person's printer, make sure his computer and printer are turned on.

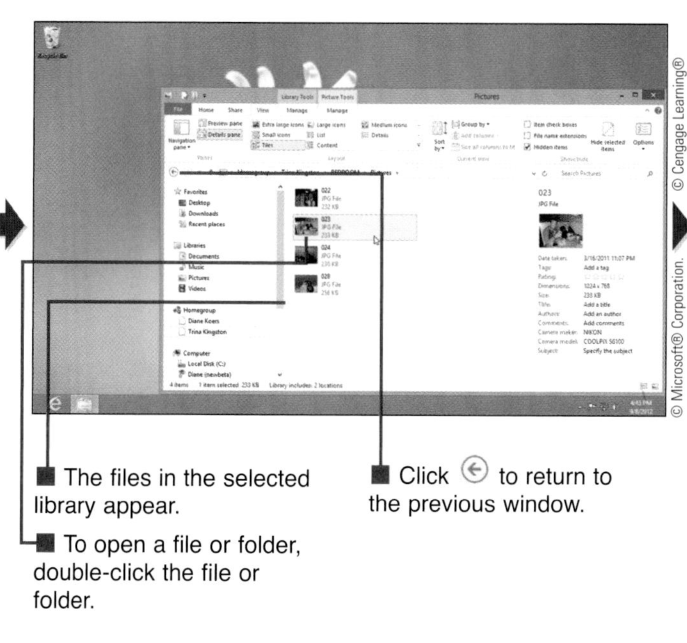

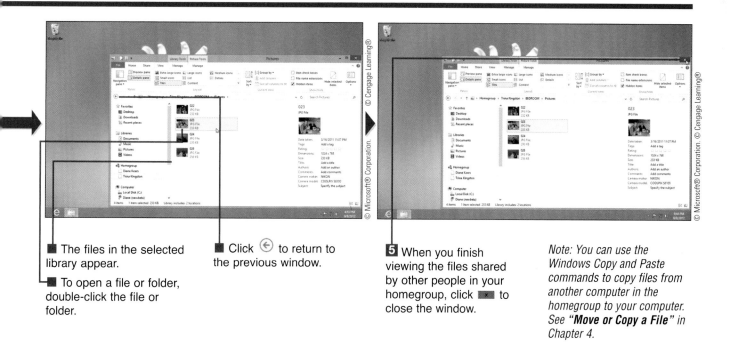

■ The files in the selected library appear.

■ To open a file or folder, double-click the file or folder.

■ Click ⓔ to return to the previous window.

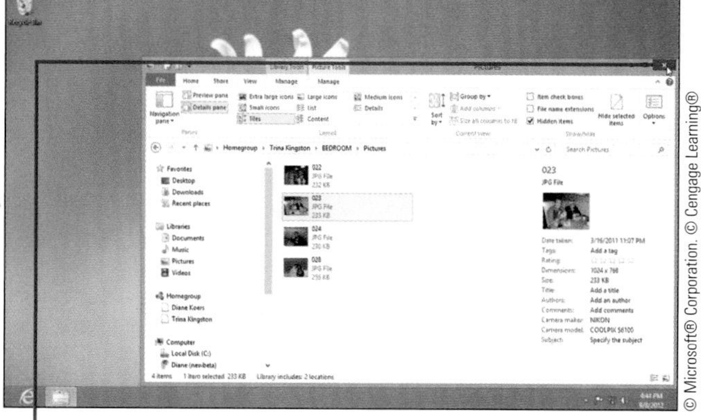

5 When you finish viewing the files shared by other people in your homegroup, click ✕ to close the window.

*Note: You can use the Windows Copy and Paste commands to copy files from another computer in the homegroup to your computer. See **"Move or Copy a File"** in Chapter 4.*

CHANGE HOW FILES ARE SHARED

After you create or join a homegroup, you can change how files on your computer are shared with other people in your homegroup.

By default, other people in your homegroup cannot make changes to files you have shared on your computer.

You can change what other people in your homegroup can do with your shared files as well as block people from accessing certain files that you want to keep private.

CHANGE HOW FILES ARE SHARED

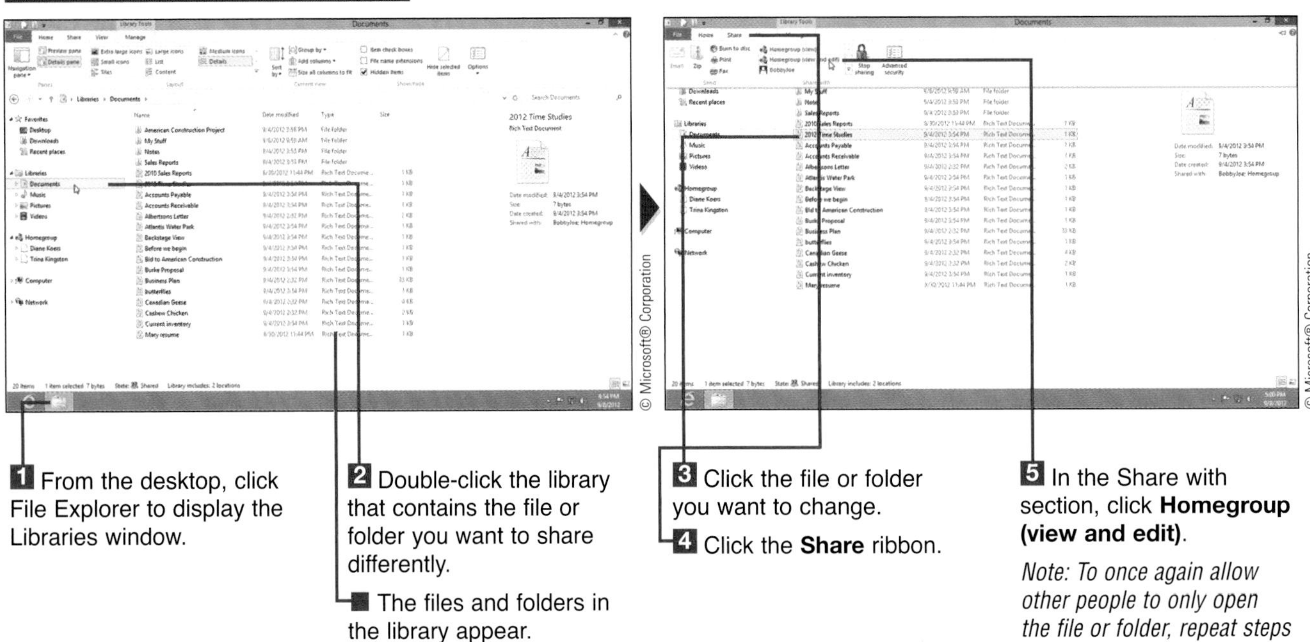

© Microsoft® Corporation

© Microsoft® Corporation

1 From the desktop, click File Explorer to display the Libraries window.

2 Double-click the library that contains the file or folder you want to share differently.

■ The files and folders in the library appear.

3 Click the file or folder you want to change.

4 Click the **Share** ribbon.

5 In the Share with section, click **Homegroup (view and edit)**.

*Note: To once again allow other people to only open the file or folder, repeat steps **1** to **5**, selecting **Homegroup (view)** in step **5**.*

What sharing options are available?

Stop sharing—Click this button to stop sharing the selected file or folder. Only you have access to the file.

Specific—Share the file with specific people you choose in your network or your homegroup.

Homegroup (view)—Share the file with your entire homegroup. Homegroup members can open but not edit or delete the file.

Homegroup (view and edit)—Share the file with your entire homegroup. Homegroup members can open, edit, and delete the file.

How can I share a file that is not in a library?

When you create or join a homegroup, you select the libraries you want to share with other people in your home-group, such as the Documents, Music, Pictures, and Videos libraries. If you want to share a file that is not in a library, such as a file on your desktop, you can right-click the file and then click **Share with** on the menu that appears. Then click the sharing option you want.

STOP SHARING A FILE

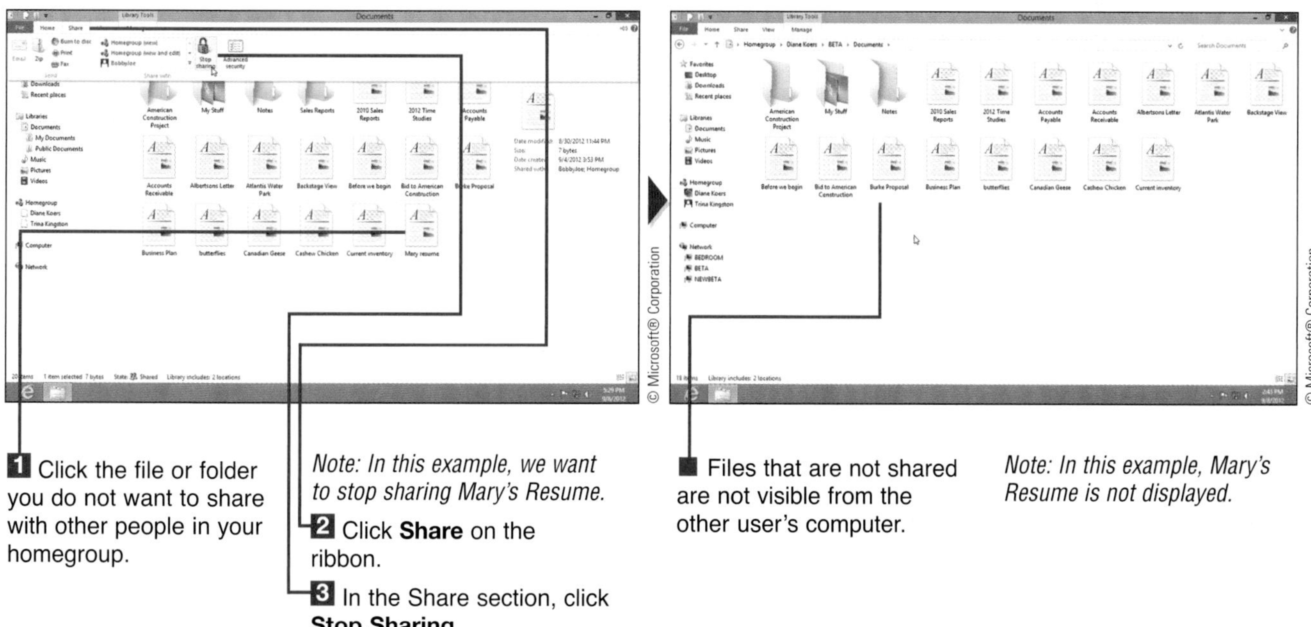

1 Click the file or folder you do not want to share with other people in your homegroup.

Note: In this example, we want to stop sharing Mary's Resume.

2 Click **Share** on the ribbon.

3 In the Share section, click **Stop Sharing**.

■ Files that are not shared are not visible from the other user's computer.

Note: In this example, Mary's Resume is not displayed.

CONNECT TO A WIRELESS NETWORK

You can easily connect to a wireless network at home or at the office to access the information and printers available on the network.

If a wireless network is connected to the Internet, connecting to the network also allows you to access the Internet.

CONNECT TO A WIRELESS NETWORK

© Microsoft® Corporation

© Microsoft® Corporation

1 From the desktop, click ▪ to view the wireless networks that are available to you.

■ A box appears, displaying the available wireless networks.

■ The green bars beside each wireless network indicate the signal strength of each network.

2 Click the wireless network to which you want to connect.

3 Click **Connect** to connect to the wireless network.

Note: You may be prompted to enter a network security key. A network security key, sometimes called a WEP *key or a* passphrase, *prevents unauthorized people from accessing a wireless network. If you do not know the security key for the network, ask the person who set up the network.*

Can I connect to a wireless network when I am away from home or the office?

Many public places, such as coffee shops, hotels, and airports, allow you to connect to the Internet through wireless networks set up on their premises. These locations are called *Wi-Fi hotspots*, or *wireless hotspots*, and provide a convenient way of accessing the Internet while you are away from home or the office.

Should I only connect to secure wireless networks?

Whenever possible, you should only connect to secure wireless networks. If you connect to a wireless network that is not secure, information sent over the network is visible to other people, including the websites you visit, the files you work with, and the passwords you enter.

© Microsoft® Corporation

■ You are now connected and can access information on the wireless network.

4 Click an empty area on your desktop to close the window.

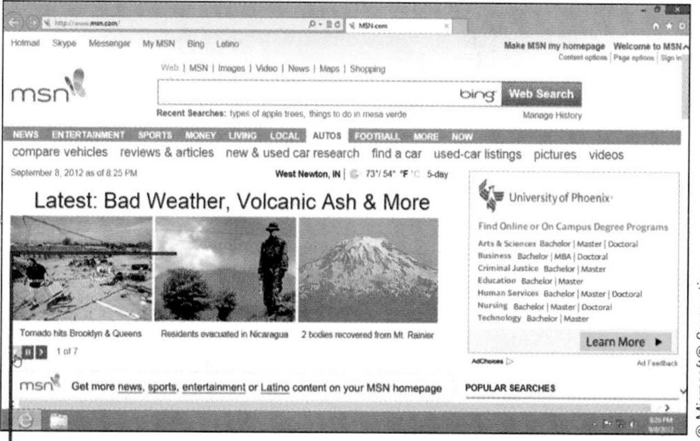

© Microsoft® Corporation

■ If the network is connected to the Internet, you can also access the Internet.

■ If you want to disconnect from a wireless network, repeat steps **1** through **3** but click **Disconnect** in step **3**.

DVD-WRITER
CD-ROM
MULTI-CARD READER
-AUDIO-

CHAPTER 12

Optimize Computer Performance

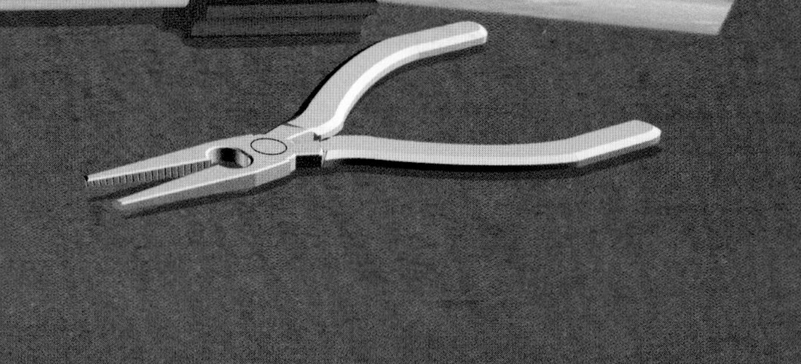

REMOVE A PROGRAM

You can remove a program you no longer use from your computer. Removing a program will free up space on your computer's hard drive.

Removing a program is different from removing a Modern UI app. See **"Uninstall Modern UI Apps"** in Chapter 1.

REMOVE A PROGRAM

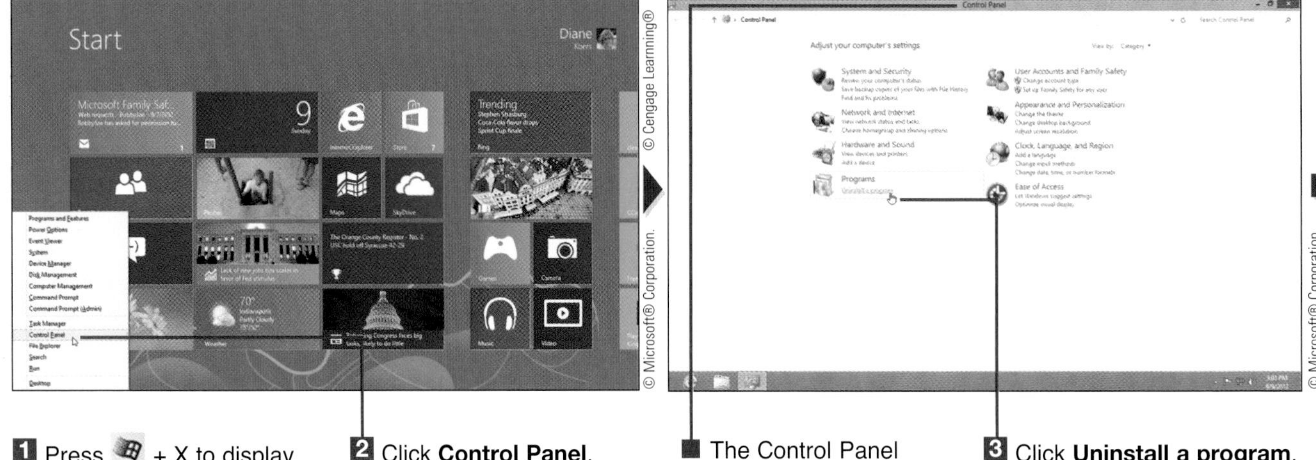

1 Press ⊞ + X to display the System menu.

2 Click **Control Panel**.

■ The Control Panel window appears.

3 Click **Uninstall a program**.

Why doesn't the program I want to remove appear in the Programs and Features window?

If the program you want to remove does not appear, the program may not have been designed for this version of Windows. Check the documentation supplied with the program to determine how to remove the program from your computer.

What should I do after I remove a program?

When you finish removing a program, you should restart your computer. Restarting your computer often deletes any remaining files that the program used. To restart your computer, see **"Restart Your Computer"** in Chapter 2.

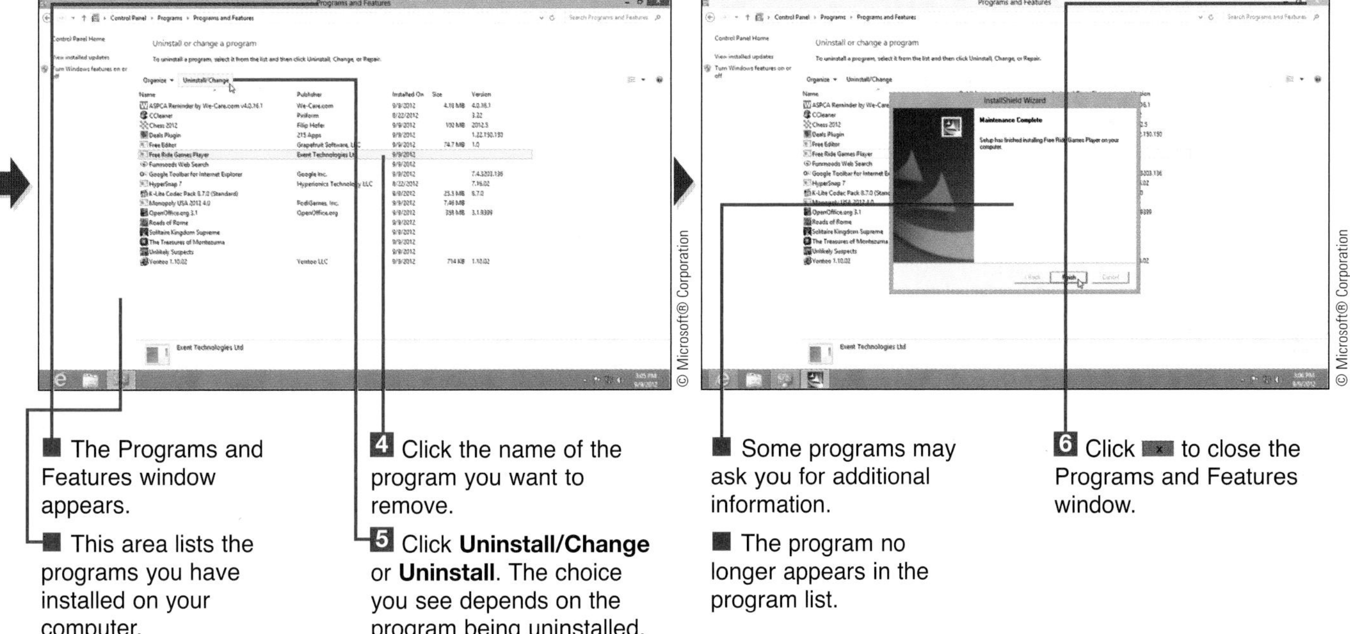

© Microsoft® Corporation

■ The Programs and Features window appears.

■ This area lists the programs you have installed on your computer.

4 Click the name of the program you want to remove.

5 Click **Uninstall/Change** or **Uninstall**. The choice you see depends on the program being uninstalled.

© Microsoft® Corporation

■ Some programs may ask you for additional information.

■ The program no longer appears in the program list.

6 Click ■ to close the Programs and Features window.

DELETE FILES USING DISK CLEANUP

You can use Disk Cleanup to remove unnecessary files from your computer to free up disk space and help your computer run faster.

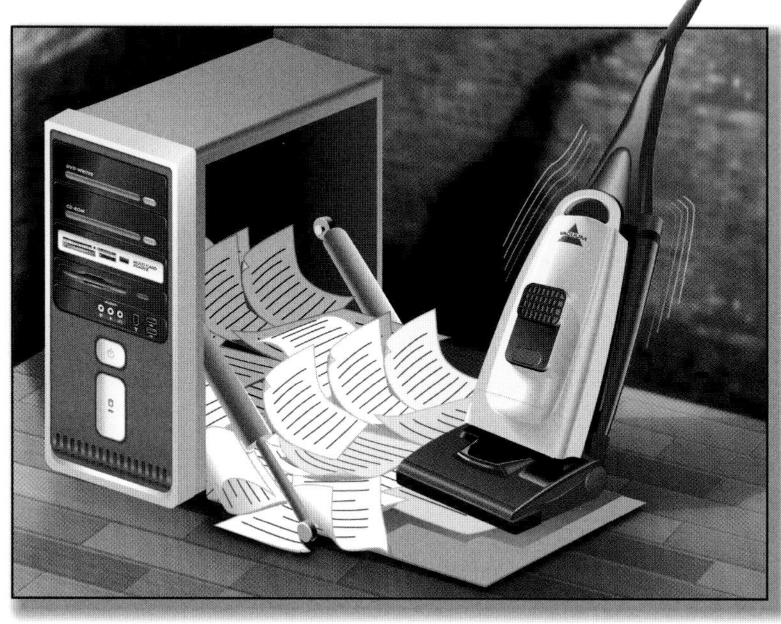

When you perform the next steps, Disk Cleanup removes only unnecessary files from your user account.

DELETE FILES USING DISK CLEANUP

1. Press ⊞ + X to display the System menu.
2. Click **Control Panel**.
3. Click **System and Security**.

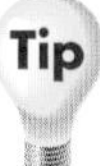

Are there other ways I can remove unnecessary files from my computer?

Yes. Programs you no longer use and files you no longer need take up valuable disk space on your computer. You can remove unnecessary programs and files to free up disk space. For more information, see **"Remove a Program"** earlier in this chapter and **"Delete a File"** in Chapter 4 to delete files.

Can I see which files Disk Cleanup will remove?

Yes. Before Disk Cleanup removes unnecessary files from your computer, you can see which files will be removed. In the Disk Cleanup dialog box, select a file type of interest and then click the View Files button. A window appears, displaying the files that Disk Cleanup will remove. The View Files button is not available for some file types.

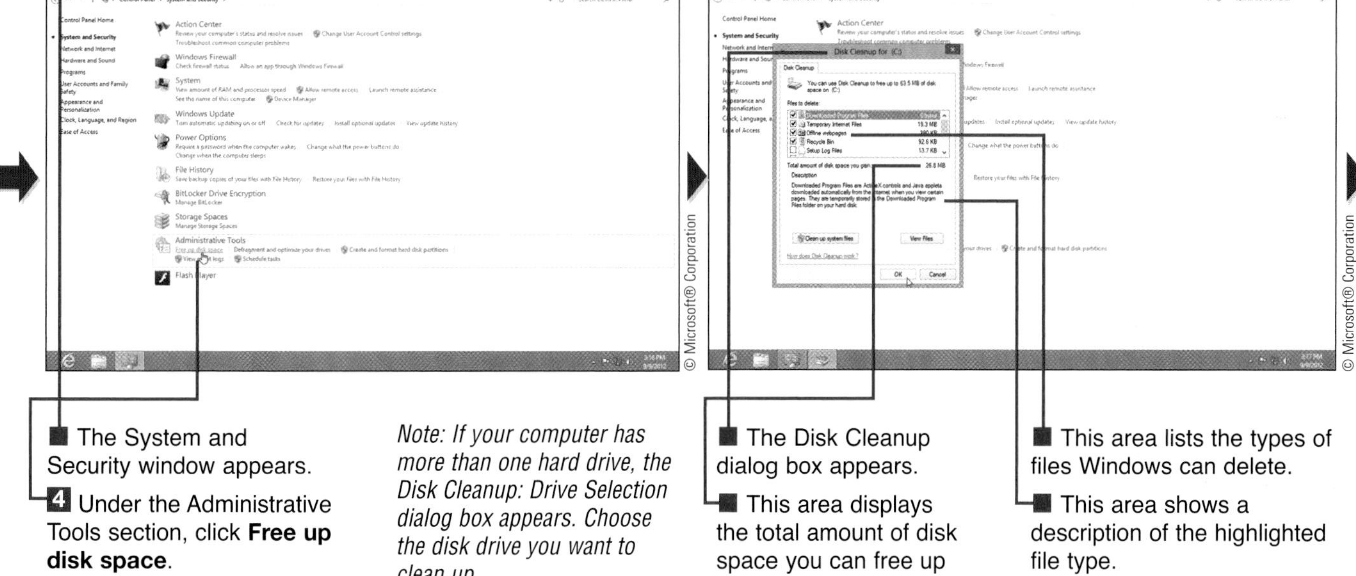

■ The System and Security window appears.

4 Under the Administrative Tools section, click **Free up disk space**.

Note: If your computer has more than one hard drive, the Disk Cleanup: Drive Selection dialog box appears. Choose the disk drive you want to clean up.

■ The Disk Cleanup dialog box appears.

■ This area displays the total amount of disk space you can free up based on the types of files you select.

■ This area lists the types of files Windows can delete.

■ This area shows a description of the highlighted file type.

CONTINUED

DELETE FILES USING DISK CLEANUP (CONTINUED)

Using the Disk Cleanup tool to remove unnecessary files from your computer removes only the files from *your* user account. Other users should also run Disk Cleanup.

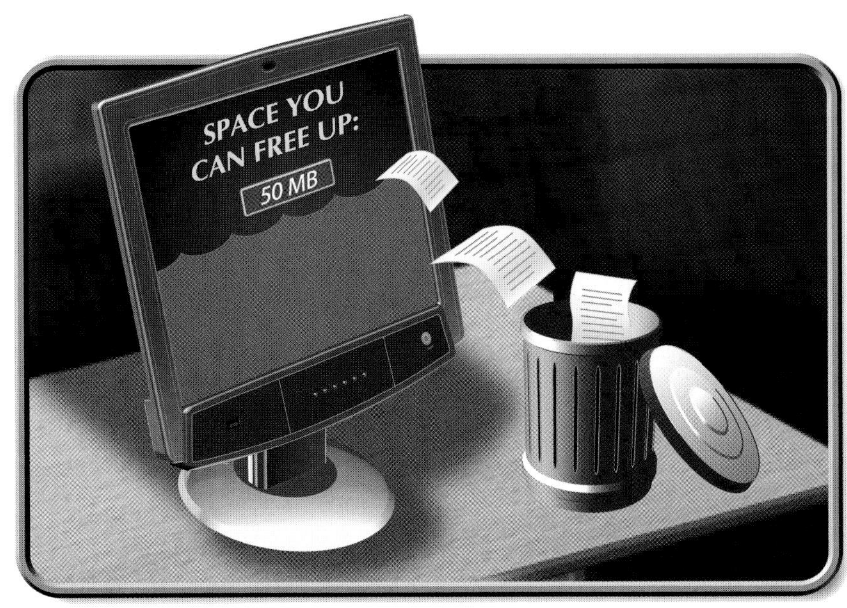

To keep your computer running optimally, you should run the Disk Cleanup tool at least once a month.

DELETE FILES USING DISK CLEANUP (CONTINUED)

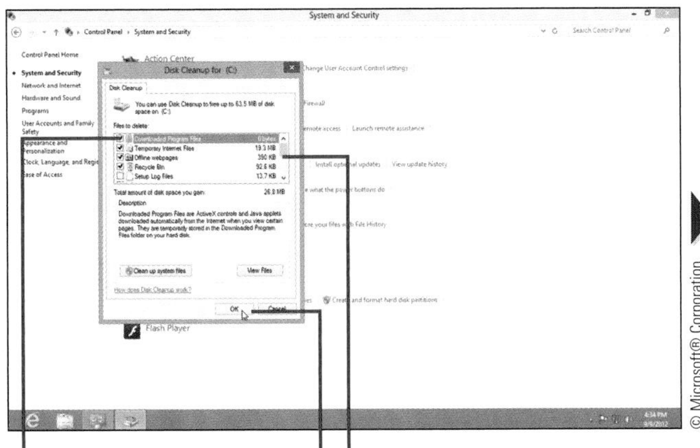

© Microsoft® Corporation

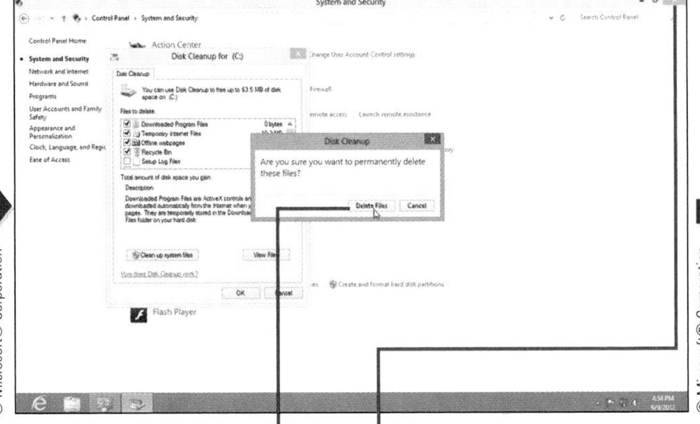

© Microsoft® Corporation

5 Windows deletes the files for each file type that displays a ☑. Click the ☐ beside a file type to add or remove a check mark.

■ This area displays the total disk space Windows will free up by deleting the types of files you selected.

6 When you finish selecting the types of files you want to delete, click **OK** to delete the files.

■ A dialog box appears, confirming that you want to delete the files.

7 Click **Delete Files** to permanently delete the files.

■ Windows removes the unnecessary files from your computer.

8 When finished, click ✕ to close the System and Security window.

OPTIMIZE YOUR HARD DRIVE

To keep your computer running at the speed it's designed for, after you delete programs and files, you should perform the maintenance option called *optimizing* your hard drive.

© Microsoft® Corporation

You must be an Administrative user or have access to an Administrative user password to optimize your drive.

OPTIMIZE YOUR HARD DRIVE

© Microsoft® Corporation. © Cengage Learning®

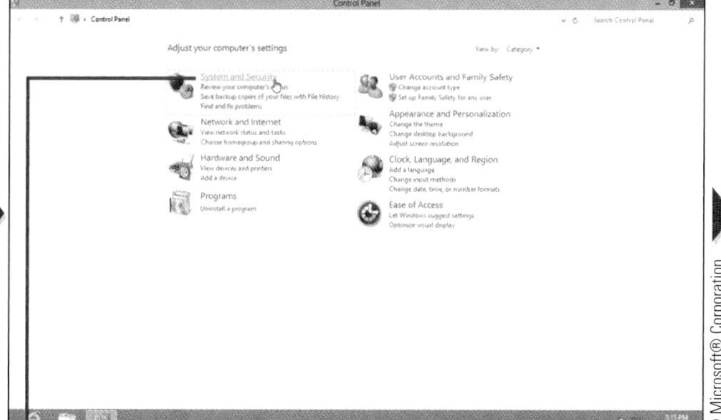

© Microsoft® Corporation

1 Press ⊞ + X to display the System menu.

2 Click **Control Panel**.

3 Click **System and Security**.

CONTINUED

Windows 8 automatically optimizes your hard drive every week, but it's a good idea to occasionally optimize it manually.

OPTIMIZE YOUR HARD DRIVE (CONTINUED)

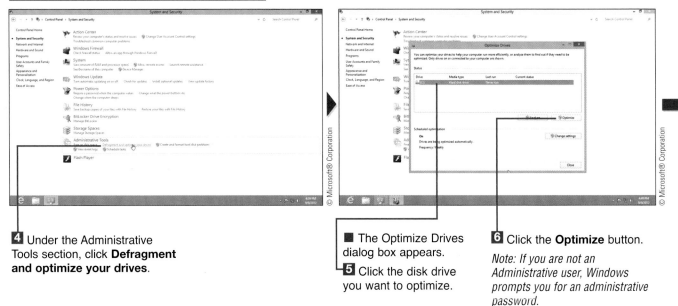

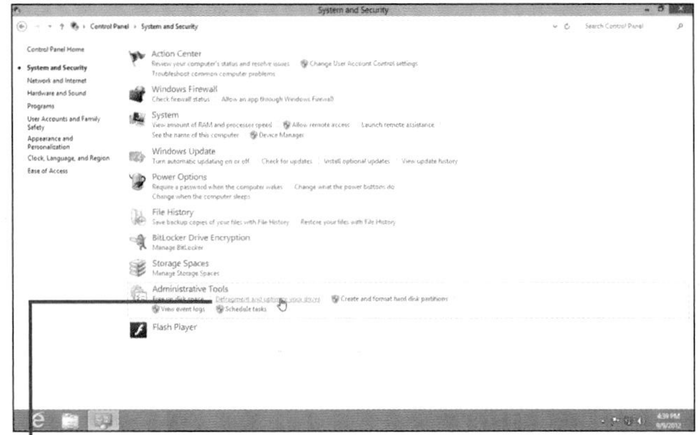

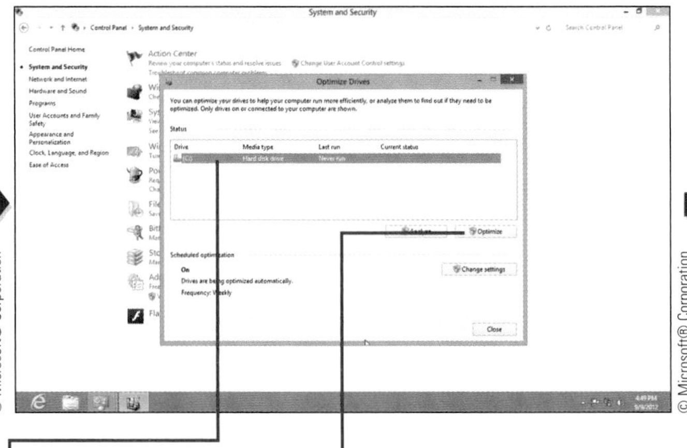

4 Under the Administrative Tools section, click **Defragment and optimize your drives**.

■ The Optimize Drives dialog box appears.

5 Click the disk drive you want to optimize.

6 Click the **Optimize** button.

Note: If you are not an Administrative user, Windows prompts you for an administrative password.

What is optimizing?

When you save a file, Windows looks for an empty space on the hard disk to write the data. If the first empty space it encounters isn't large enough to store the entire file, Windows divides the file among several smaller spaces. When a file is stored in more than one space, it is said to be *fragmented*.

The next time you open the file, Windows must locate each of the fragmented pieces, and that takes more time than it would if the file were stored all together in one space.

Optimizing combines the file pieces that are broken apart into one single piece and stores it in a single space, thereby making it faster for Windows to locate and open.

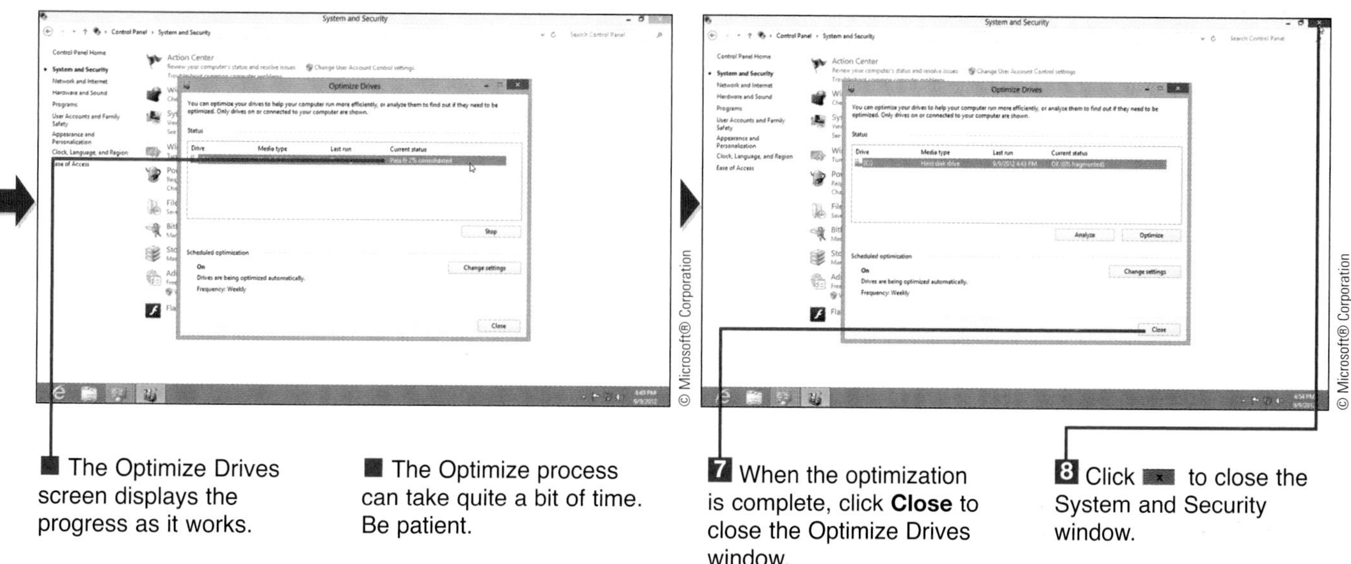

■ The Optimize Drives screen displays the progress as it works.

■ The Optimize process can take quite a bit of time. Be patient.

7 When the optimization is complete, click **Close** to close the Optimize Drives window.

8 Click ▪ to close the System and Security window.

CLOSE A MISBEHAVING PROGRAM

You can close a program that is no longer responding without having to shut down Windows.

When a program is not responding, you can wait a few minutes to see if Windows can fix the problem. If you choose not to wait and close the program yourself, you will lose any information you did not save in the program.

CLOSE A MISBEHAVING PROGRAM

1 Press ⊞ + X to display the System menu.

2 Click **Task Manager**.

- The Windows Task Manager window appears.
- This area lists the programs that are currently running. The phrase "Not Responding" appears beside the name of a misbehaving program.

How will I know if a program is not responding?

One or more of the following usually happens when a program crashes:

- The program won't let you do anything or it won't respond to options you choose.
- You may see a message on the program title bar (if it's a program you run under the desktop) that says, "Not responding."
- An informational message may pop up on the screen saying that the application is not functioning.
- The screen may fade to an almost white color.

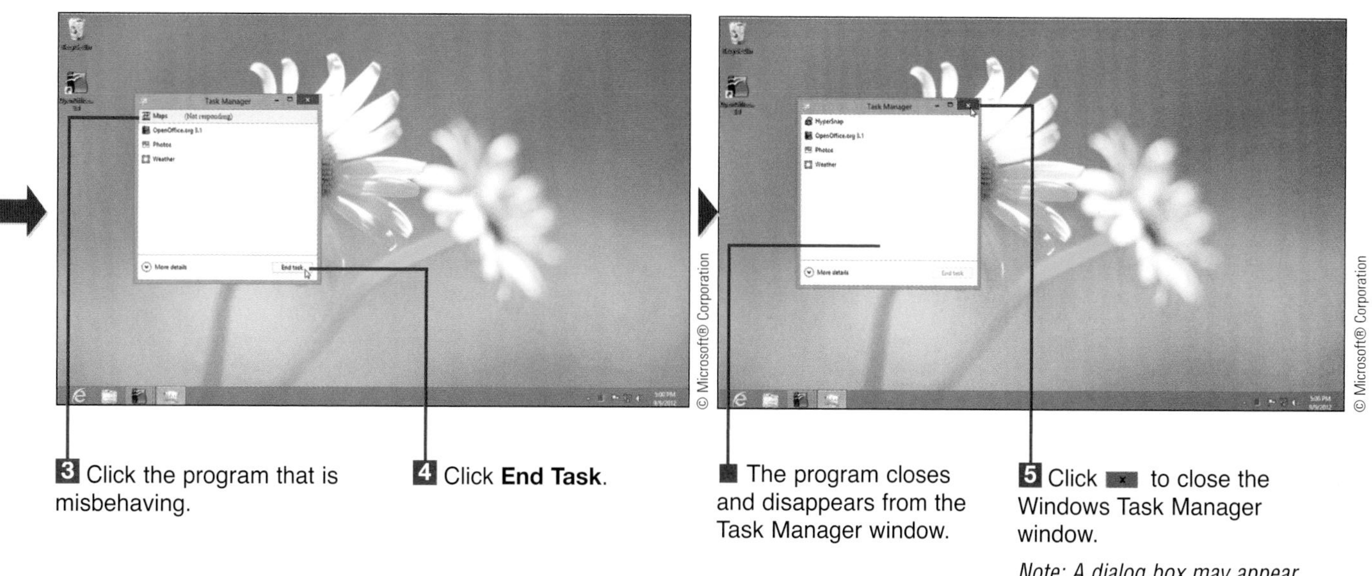

© Microsoft® Corporation

© Microsoft® Corporation

3 Click the program that is misbehaving.

4 Click **End Task**.

■ The program closes and disappears from the Task Manager window.

5 Click ✕ to close the Windows Task Manager window.

*Note: A dialog box may appear, asking if you want to send more information about the problem to Microsoft to help find a solution. Click **Send information** or **Cancel**.*

INDEX

C

F

G–H

I

J–K

L

M

N

O

P–Q

T

X–Z

maran illustrated BARTENDING

MARAN ILLUSTRATED™ Bartending is the perfect book for those who want to impress their guests with cocktails that are both eye-catching and delicious. This indispensable guide explains everything you need to know about bartending in the most simple and easy-to-follow terms. **Maran Illustrated™ Bartending** has recipes, step-by-step instructions and over 400 full-color photographs of all the hottest martinis, shooters, blended drinks and warmers. This guide also includes a section on wine, beer and alcohol-free cocktails as well as information on all of the tools, liquor and other supplies you will need to start creating drinks right away!

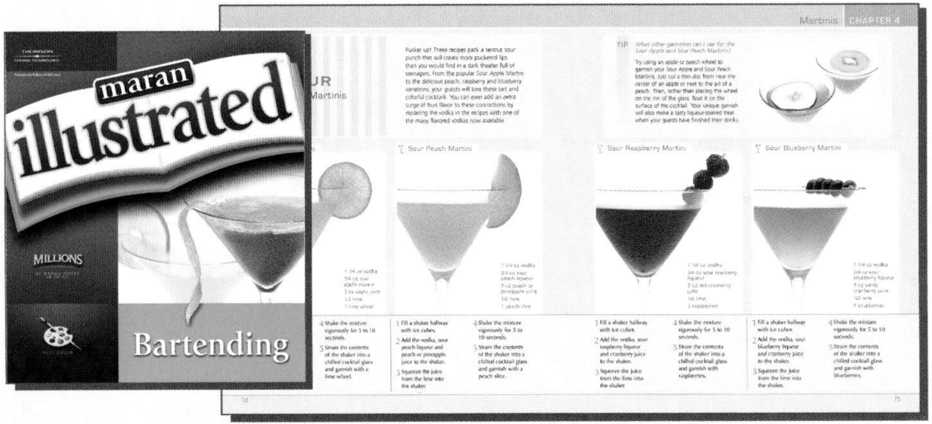

ISBN: 1-59200-944-1
Price: $19.99 US; $26.95 CDN
Page count: 256

maran illustrated PIANO

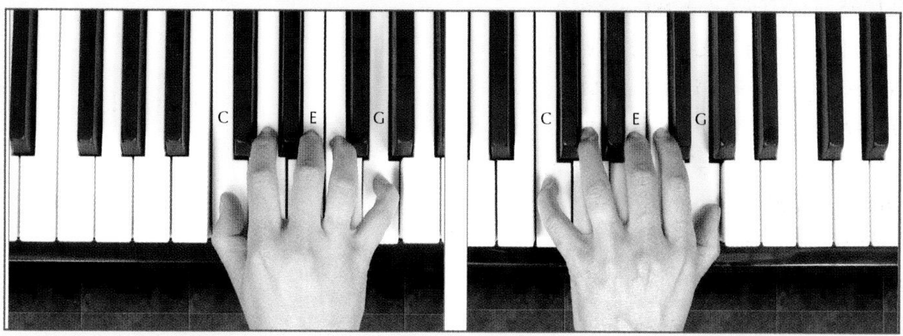

MARAN ILLUSTRATED™ Piano is an information-packed resource for people who want to learn to play the piano, as well as current musicians looking to hone their skills. Combining full-color photographs and easy-to-follow instructions, this guide covers everything from the basics of piano playing to more advanced techniques. Not only does **MARAN ILLUSTRATED™ Piano** show you how to read music, play scales and chords and improvise while playing with other musicians, it also provides you with helpful information for purchasing and caring for your piano.

ISBN: 1-59200-864-X
Price: $24.99 US; $33.95 CDN
Page count: 304

maran illustrated EFFORTLESS ALGEBRA

MARAN ILLUSTRATED™ Effortless Algebra is an indispensable resource packed with crucial concepts and step-by-step instructions that make learning algebra simple. This guide is perfect for those who wish to gain a thorough understanding of algebra's concepts, from the most basic calculations to more complex operations.

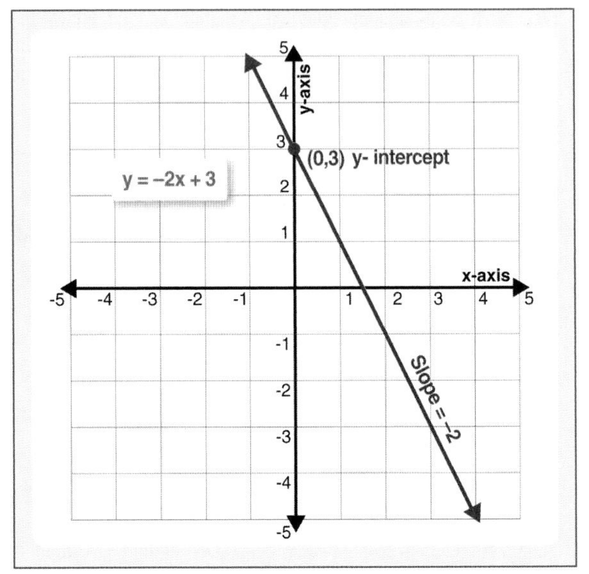

Clear instructions thoroughly explain every topic and each concept is accompanied by helpful illustrations. This book provides all of the information you will need to fully grasp algebra. **MARAN ILLUSTRATED™ Effortless Algebra** also provides an abundance of practice examples and tests to put your knowledge into practice.

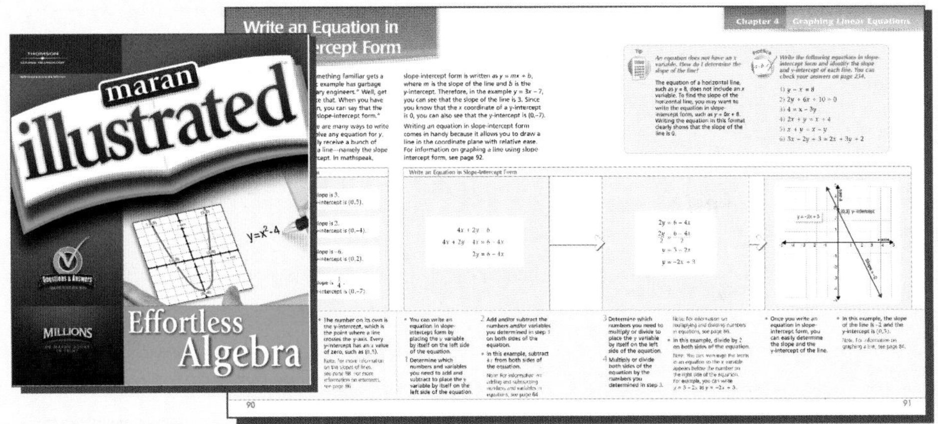

ISBN: 1-59200-942-5
Price: $24.99 US; $33.95 CDN
Page count: 304

maran illustrated DOG TRAINING

MARAN ILLUSTRATED™ Dog Training is an excellent guide for both current dog owners and people considering making a dog part of their family. Using clear, step-by-step instructions accompanied by over 400 full-color photographs, **MARAN ILLUSTRATED™ Dog Training** is perfect for any visual learner who prefers seeing what to do rather than reading lengthy explanations.

Beginning with insights into popular dog breeds and puppy development, this book emphasizes positive training methods to guide you through socializing, housetraining and teaching your dog many commands. You will also learn how to work with problem behaviors, such as destructive chewing.

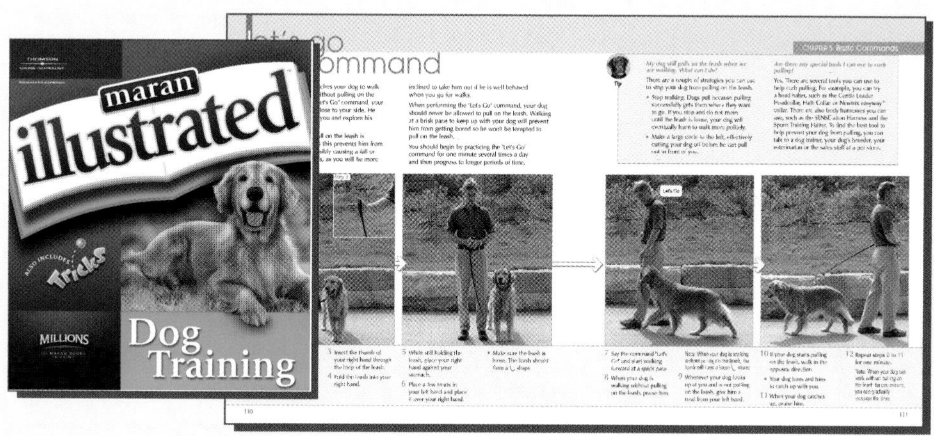

ISBN: 1-59200-858-5
Price: $19.99 US; $26.95 CDN
Page count: 256

maran illustrated | WINE

MARAN ILLUSTRATED™ Wine is an indispensable guide for your journey into the world of wine. The information-packed resource is ideal for people who are just beginning to explore wine as well as for wine enthusiasts who want to expand their knowledge.

This full-color guide, containing hundreds of photographs, walks you step by step through tasting and serving wine, reading a wine label and creating a wine collection. You will also find in-depth information about the wines of the world. **MARAN ILLUSTRATED™ Wine** will also introduce you to sparkling wines and Champagne as well as fortified and sweet wines. You will learn the basics of how wine is made, how to pair the right wine with your meal and much more.

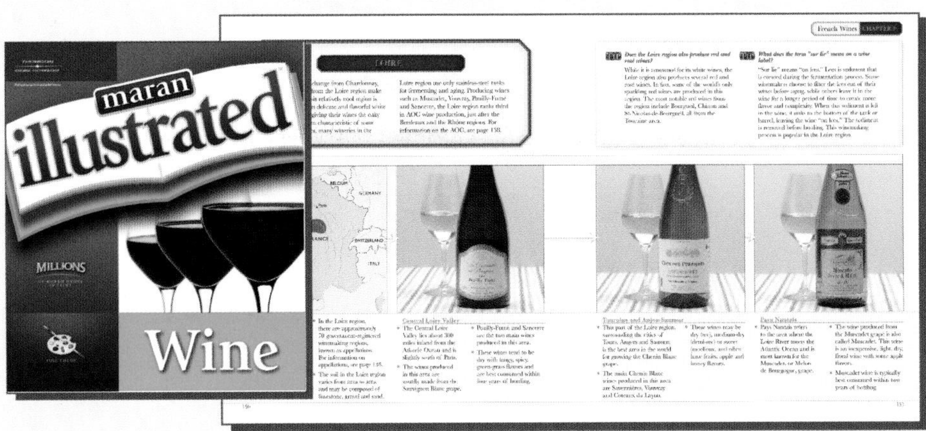

ISBN: 1-59863-318-X
Price: $24.99 US; $33.95 CDN
Page count: 288